W9-BUV-151

INTRODUCTION TO LANDSCAPING:

Design, Construction, and Maintenance

Second Edition

INTRODUCTION TO

Design, Construction,

Ronald J. Biondo

Landscape Designer and
FCAE Field Advisor in Agricultural Education
Countryside, Illinois

Charles B. Schroeder

Landscaper and
Head, Horticulture Department
Danville Area Community College
Danville, Illinois

LANDSCAPING

and Maintenance

AgriScience and Technology Series

Jasper S. Lee, Ph.D.
Series Editor

Interstate Publishers, Inc.

Danville, Illinois

INTRODUCTION TO LANDSCAPING
Design, Construction, and Maintenance

Second Edition

Photographs on the cover depict the major areas in landscaping.

Cover photo credits:

Illinois Landscape Contractors Association (photo of residence)
Knoblauch Studios (paver installation photo)

Title page photo credit:

Husqvarna Forest and Garden Company

Library of Congress Catalog No. 99-71469

ISBN 0-8134-3171-9

3 4 5 6 7 8 9 10   04 03 02 01

Order from

Interstate Publishers, Inc.

510 North Vermilion Street
P.O. Box 50
Danville, IL 61834-0050

Phone: (800) 843-4774
Fax. (217) 446-9706

Email: info-ipp@IPPINC.com
World Wide Web: http://www.IPPINC.com

Preface—Second Edition

Landscaping is one of the fastest growing segments of the horticulture industry! The design of new landscapes, the building of landscapes, and the maintenance of existing landscapes are in high demand. People appreciate well-planned landscapes. Well-planned landscapes are attractive and easily enjoyed. They are also functional, allowing many leisure time uses.

Introduction to Landscaping: Design, Construction, and Maintenance offers a practical approach to establishing and maintaining residential landscapes. It is intended to introduce the various aspects of the landscape industry to students of horticulture and agriculture. The authors have carefully written this book from a horticultural perspective. Plant selection and care are the foundation of this book. This book has been organized in three distinct parts—landscape design, landscape construction, and landscape maintenance.

The steps to developing a complete and functional landscape plan for the residential setting are identified and explained in an easy to understand writing style. Principles of art, defined in the text, are emphasized in the design portion of the book. The student is guided through the process of designing landscape projects from establishing customer needs to preparing and costing out the plan.

Tools and products used in landscape construction are explained in part two of this book. Procedures for preparing planting beds, installing plant materials, and constructing hardscape features such as fences, decks, and patios are discussed in detail.

Part three of this book focuses on the maintenance of landscapes. The latest findings from scientific research on plant care direct the writings on landscape maintenance. Major topics covered include establishing and maintaining turfgrass; fertilizing, watering, and mulching plants; pruning woody plants; and controlling plant pests.

This book is the result of the combined talents of Interstate's two most successful horticulture authors. The authors have applied their experiences in both the landscape industry and the horticulture classroom. The Second Edition expands information on water gardens, irrigation, and perennial gardens. New information has been included on selecting trees, turfgrass establishment, pesticide safety, and integrated pest management.

Acknowledgments

The authors of *Introduction to Landscaping: Design, Construction, and Maintenance* are grateful to many individuals for their assistance with this book. Some are acknowledged here. Others are recognized within the text.

Special acknowledgment is due to those who reviewed the manuscript. They include:

- Julian Smith, Horticulture Teacher, Bear Creek, North Carolina
- Ken Godfrey, Agriculture Department Chair, Riverside, California
- Gail Komoto, Agriculture Teacher, Vancouver, Washington
- Norman Hammond, State FFA advisor, North Scituate, Rhode Island
- Doug Prevette, Horticulture Teacher, Olin, North Carolina
- Susan Kelly, Program Specialist, Orlando, Florida

Other individuals receiving special acknowledgment for assistance with photographs follow: Robert Hursthouse, R.S. Hursthouse & Associates, Inc.; John Mitten, Church Landscape; Lorin Reicks, LANDCADD Division of Eagle Point Software; Patricia Cassady, Illinois Landscape Contractors Association; Greg Stack, University of Illinois Cooperative Extension Service; Kathy Freeland, Midwest Groundcovers; Harold Hoover, City of Elmhurst Forestry Department; Joe Karr, Joe Karr and Associates; Frank Mariani, Mariani Landscape; David Van Zelst, Van Zelst, Inc.; Dave Peters, Pavestone Company.

Special thanks goes to Robert Hursthouse, R.S. Hursthouse & Associates, Inc., and John Mitten, Church Landscape, for extensive interviews concerning the operations of businesses in the landscape industry.

Also, acknowledgment goes to Ester V. Biondo, Naperville, Illinois, and Cheryl Schroeder and Mark J. Schroeder, Danville, Illinois, for proofreading sections of the manuscript.

Finally, the authors are most appreciative of the staff at Interstate Publishers, Inc. for their commitment to quality learning tools in agricultural education. Interstate Publishers, Inc. President Vernie Thomas is specially acknowledge. Interstate Publishers, Inc. personnel deserving of acknowledgment for their involvement with the production of this book are Kim Romine, design and typesetting, Mary E. Carter, computer generated graphics; Mary Jane Weller, editing; and Dan Pentony, research and market development.

vi

Contents

PART ONE—Landscape Design

PART TWO—Landscape Construction

PART THREE—Landscape Maintenance

APPENDIXES

1

Landscape Design, Construction, and Maintenance

Have you ever mowed the lawn? Have you ever planted flowers in the yard? Have you tended a vegetable garden? If you have done these activities you have touched upon the landscape industry. Many people enjoy these gardening activities. In fact, national polls show gardening to be the most popular outdoor leisure activity in the United States.

Some people like landscape activities so much they find a career in the landscaping industry. The industry involving the design, construction, and maintenance of landscapes shows rapid growth. More people take interest in beautiful landscape settings than ever before. As a result, job opportunities are abundant.

1-1. More people take interest in beautiful landscape settings than ever before. (Courtesy, Church Landscape)

OBJECTIVES

1. Identify the purposes of landscape design

2. Describe the scope of landscape construction

3. Recognize the need for landscape maintenance

4. Identify careers found in the landscape industry

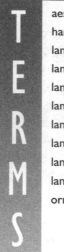

aesthetic value

hardscape

landscape architect

landscape construction

landscape contractor

landscape design

landscape designer

landscape maintenance

landscape supervisor

landscaping

ornamental horticulture

LANDSCAPING

Landscaping is a part of the ornamental horticulture industry. The *ornamental horticulture* industry uses plants and other materials for deco-

1-2. Landscaping surrounds us in the United States. (a.) schools and universities, (b.) churches, (c.) corporate offices, (d.) golf courses , (e.) cemeteries, (f.) government buildings, (g.) parks, (h.) residential housing.

rative purposes. In addition to landscaping, ornamental horticulture claims the areas of floral design, greenhouse management, and nursery management. *Landscaping* focuses on the beautification of outdoor terrain and, to some extent, interior settings. The practice of landscaping combines the principles of art with the science of growing plants. In the United States, nearly all developed areas are landscaped to some extent.

When we speak of landscaping, we are referring to efforts to improve the appearance of land. We usually think of the plants in the landscape. Landscaping involves the planting of ornamental trees, shrubs, vines, ground covers (including grasses), perennial flowers, annual flowers, and bulbs. Landscaping involves physical features or *hardscape*. Hardscape includes fences, terraces, retaining walls, patios, walks, drives, irrigation systems, and pools. Landscaping also results in the sculpting of the soil and natural lay of the land.

1-3. Hardscape involves installation of physical elements to the landscape. (Courtesy, Church Landscape)

Achieving an attractive landscape requires planning, proper construction techniques, and continued maintenance. It is not an easy task. Landscape professionals are challenged with every job. Landscaping is actually a practical application of problem solving. The challenge is for the landscape professional to determine the best method to beautify a piece of land.

Professional landscapers must consider many factors during the work on a landscape job. Some factors that influence landscapes are the terrain; the climate; the homes, buildings, and other physical structures; the intended use of the property; and the client's wants. The challenge for the

1-4. Landscaping involves problem solving. (Courtesy, Church Landscape)

landscaper is to allow for all the factors while developing a landscape that is both attractive and functional. The challenge with the landscape process is often quite complex.

1-5. This company has a landscape division along with a nursery and garden center.

The rewards for those in the landscape industry can be great. A 1995 Gallup poll found that in 1994 approximately 40.4 billion dollars were spent in the United States on landscape and gardening products. During that same period, 17.6 million households spent 13.4 billion dollars on professional landscape and lawn services. The 1994 totals show a 900 million-dollar increase over 1993 figures. Also, 35 percent of the landscape contractors recorded more than 500,000 dollars in gross receipts. Clearly, people value attractive landscaping, and there are productive career opportunities in the landscape industry.

This book will focus primarily on the design of residential landscapes and the three major segments of landscaping. The first segment, landscape design, deals with the planning of a landscape project. Once a design is prepared, work can begin on the second segment, installation or construction of the project. The third aspect involves the maintenance of the landscape so it will continue to be attractive over a long period.

LANDSCAPE BENEFITS

What are the benefits from well-landscaped residential properties? The obvious benefit is enjoyment given to the homeowner. Attractive or aesthetic views are pleasing. The beauty of a landscape is sometimes referred to as *aesthetic value.* Plants in the landscape convey warmth, protection, and comfort. Landscapes designed with function in mind also lend themselves well to many activities. You might enjoy using the landscape for volleyball, entertainment at a cookout, or for growing fresh vegetables.

The time and money put into establishing a nice landscape pay dividends when selling a house. A study by Weyerhaeuser Nursery Products Division estimated that landscaping can add as much as 15 percent to the resale value of a home. The landscape provides the first impression prospective buyers have of a home. Attractive landscapes draw buyers out of their cars and into the house. According to realtors and appraisers, a beautifully landscaped house sells faster and for more money than its neighbors.

1-6. Landscaping can add as much as 15 percent to the value of a home.

Landscape plants are good for the environment. The photosynthetic process in a leaf uses carbon dioxide and releases oxygen. Studies have shown that a 2,500 square foot area of turf releases enough oxygen for a family of four. Plants and soil organisms also scrub the air of pollutants, such as ammonia, benzene, toluene, trichloroethylene, and xylene.

Landscape trees play a major role in cooling the air. Shaded areas are naturally cooler than those in the direct sun. Well-placed trees cut cooling costs up to 20 percent. Carefully located landscape plantings also cut winter heating costs.

Well-landscaped properties reduce noise pollution. Noise from busy streets, railroad activity, and other sources is absorbed or deflected by landscape materials. The same barriers help to screen unwanted views and provide privacy.

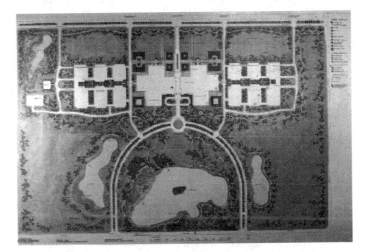

I-7. Landscape design is one segment of landscaping. (Courtesy, Joe Karr & Associates)

LANDSCAPE DESIGN

A well-thought-out plan simplifies problems confronted by landscapers. A good analogy to a landscape plan is the use of a road map on a cross-country trip. On such a trip, you would refer to a map as you traveled on roads you had not traveled on before. The road map gives you direction and removes guess work from your travel decisions. Landscape planning removes guesswork, too. Carefully planned projects are more likely to be attractive and functional than those with poor planning.

Landscape design is the practice of creating a plan to make the best use of available space in the most attractive way. Consideration is given to the relationships between the land, buildings, plants, and people. Pro-

1-8. Landscape design is the practice of creating a plan to make the best use of available space in the most attractive way. (Courtesy, R.S. Hursthouse & Associates, Inc.)

fessional designers have two main purposes in mind when designing landscape plans for a home or a building.

1. Show off the home or building to its best advantage.
2. Create both an attractive and useful setting for the inhabitants.

QUALIFIED DESIGN PROFESSIONALS

People trained in the area of landscape design fall into one of two categories. The two professional titles are landscape architect and landscape designer. It is sometimes confusing to determine the difference between landscape architects and landscape designers. In general, landscape architects tend to work on large scale projects, whereas, most landscape designers develop plans for residential landscapes.

Landscape Architect

Landscape architects are trained in engineering, graphic arts, and architectural technology. They are skilled in designing functional plans based on the interrelationship of people and their surroundings. They use their creative talents to design projects ranging from small gardens to entire cities. The vast majority of their work involves large-scale projects, such as parks, golf courses, community planning, and large corporate complexes. Some landscape architects find employment designing plans for residential homes.

1-9. Landscape architects are skilled with large-scale projects.

Most states require landscape architects to be licensed before they can practice. Formal training for landscape architects is the first step. Those interested in landscape architecture study for a degree in landscape architecture from an accredited college or university. Upon graduation, they gain experience as an apprentice for a professional architect. Finally, the landscape architect must pass a state licensing examination. For most landscape architects, education does not end. Many seek further degrees to improve their skills.

Landscape Designer

Landscape designers are trained in the art of design and the science of growing horticultural plants. Landscape designers work primarily with

1-10. Landscape designers are trained in the art of design and the science of growing horticultural plants.

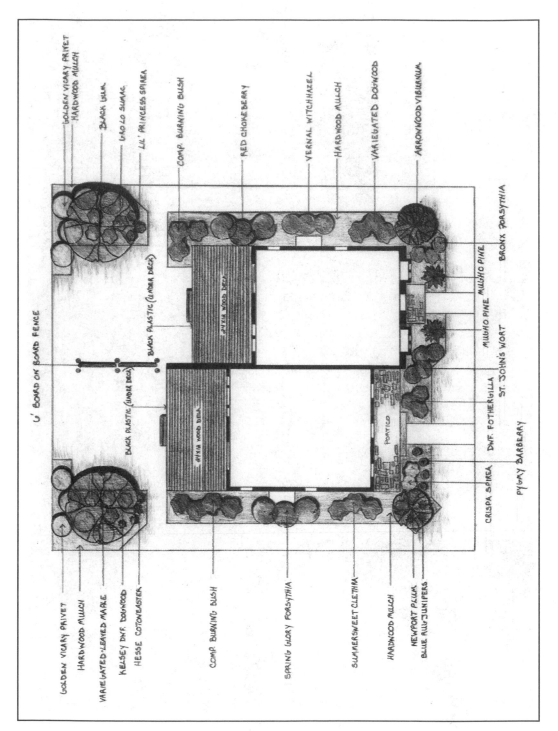

1-11. An example of a landscape design.

residential home designs and small commercial sites. They are often employed by landscaping companies or by garden centers and nurseries that offer landscape installation services. A knowledge of plant identification, cultural requirements for plants, construction practices, and the principles of design are required to be a successful designer. Landscape designers must also develop their personal skills. They must effectively communicate with the client about the landscape plan and with construction crews to see that the job is installed as designed.

Formal education beyond high school is needed for landscape designers. Some landscape designers gain their education through an associate's degree from a community college. Others earn a bachelor's degree in ornamental horticulture from a four-year college or university. Further education is helpful.

LANDSCAPE CONSTRUCTION

Once a design has been drawn for a landscape project, work can begin on construction. *Landscape construction* is the segment of landscaping that involves the installation of materials identified in the landscape design. Construction projects range from being very simple, such as planting a tree, to very elaborate. Large projects may involve moving soil, installing drainage systems, building permanent structures, such as walls, walks and drives, and planting numerous plants.

1-12. Landscape construction is the segment of landscaping that involves the installation of materials identified in the landscape design.

LANDSCAPE CONTRACTOR

The construction of the project is performed by a ***landscape contractor***. Landscape contractors are hired to install the landscape. Their job is to transfer the design provided on paper to the actual landscape. Therefore, landscape contractors must be able to read and understand the landscape plans.

The landscape designer and the contractor may work for the same company. Sometimes, the contractor hires a designer. Sometimes, the contractor is trained in landscape design. The important thing is that the contractor fully understands what the designer has intended with a design. It is equally important that the contractor communicate with the designer when part of the plan simply will not work. A good working arrangement eliminates many problems during the installation.

There are many aspects to the landscape contractor's job. Like any business, landscape contractors advertise their work and try to build a professional image with the public. They develop business contracts with clients. Contractors may be responsible for obtaining building permits, and they must install projects in accordance with municipal codes. Contractors ensure that the materials called for in the landscape plan are ordered and that the necessary equipment is available and in working order. Landscape contractors must also hire qualified workers to do the physical installation.

Landscape contractors learn the profession while on the job and through school. It is common for an individual to start in this field as a crew member. As a crew member, they gain practical experience. They can also

1-13. The landscape supervisor provides leadership to the crew. (Courtesy, Church Landscape)

improve their understanding of plant care, plant identification, business skills, construction practices, and landscape design through formal education at a community college or university. Additional training programs for landscape professionals are available through state and national landscape associations.

LANDSCAPE SUPERVISOR

Landscape workers are usually organized in groups or crews. A *landscape supervisor* or crew chief has responsibility for the crew. The landscape supervisor provides leadership to the crew. This individual assigns tasks to the workers and usually works alongside them. Teamwork among the workers is extremely important. Working well with one another improves the quality of work as well as the speed in which it takes to complete a job.

LANDSCAPE MAINTENANCE

Landscape maintenance is the care and upkeep of the landscape materials after installation. Landscape maintenance includes tasks, such as mowing grass, fertilizing landscape plants, pruning landscape plants, applying pest controls, planting and weeding flower beds, removing leaves in the fall, cultivating soil, and applying mulch to landscape planting beds.

1-14. Landscape maintenance is the care and upkeep of the landscape materials after installation.

The goal of a good landscape maintenance program is to keep the landscape as attractive and functional as intended in the original landscape design.

Most landscape companies focus on either construction or maintenance. There are several reasons for this. The specialized equipment required for each type of work differs. The workers are trained to do specific types of work and are familiar with certain equipment. Also, the types of projects performed call for different scheduling of workers. Some landscape companies do both construction and maintenance. However, those companies usually have some landscape crews assigned to construction and others to maintenance.

Landscape maintenance involves all types of landscape projects. A large portion of contracted landscape maintenance work is performed on large landscapes surrounding commercial office buildings, apartment buildings, townhouse associations, condominiums, etc. Most homeowners rely on professionals to do the more difficult installation and then maintain the landscape themselves. Other homeowners hire landscape professionals to attend to the upkeep of their landscape. Golf courses and large gardens requiring constant maintenance often employ workers year round.

1-15. Maintenance involves weed control in planting beds.

REVIEWING

MAIN IDEAS

Landscaping is challenging work centered on improving the appearance of land. Landscaping begins with a landscape plan or design. Landscape design is the practice of creating a plan to make the best use of available space in the most attractive way. The landscape plan is developed by either a landscape architect or a landscape designer. Landscape architects tend to work with large-scale landscape designs while designers concentrate on residential landscape projects. Knowledge in plant materials, plant cultural requirements, the principles of art, and interrelationships between people and their surroundings is valuable to architects and designers.

Landscape construction is the segment of landscaping that involves the installation of materials identified in the landscape plan. Installation projects range from planting woody landscape plants to building fences, walls, and patios. The landscape contractor is the one hired to install the landscape as specified in the landscape plan. Landscape supervisors lead crews working as a team to complete the job.

Landscape maintenance is the care and upkeep given to a landscape after installation. Some tasks include mowing turf, pruning woody plants, fertilizing landscape plants, and removing leaves in the fall. Most companies focus on landscape construction or landscape maintenance.

QUESTIONS

Answer the following questions using correct spelling and complete sentences.

1. What is landscaping?
2. Why is landscape design important?
3. How do landscape architects and landscape designers differ?
4. What are some skills beneficial to architects and designers?
5. What does landscape construction involve?
6. What are some jobs of a landscape contractor?
7. What does landscape maintenance involve?

CHAPTER SELF-CHECK

Match the term with the correct definition. Write the letter by the term in the blank provided.

a. landscape designer   d. landscape contractor   g. landscape design
b. landscape construction   e. hardscape   h. landscape architect
c. landscaping   f. landscape maintenance   i. landscape supervisor

_____ 1. Leader responsible for the landscape crew

_____ 2. Creating a plan to make the best use of available space in the most attractive way

_____ 3. An individual trained in making landscape plans with greater emphasis on large areas

_____ 4. An individual trained in making landscape plans with emphasis on residential landscapes

_____ 5. A company hired to install landscape projects

_____ 6. The care and upkeep of a landscape after installation

_____ 7. The installation of landscape materials identified in a landscape plan

_____ 8. The part of the ornamental horticulture industry that involves the beautification of outdoor terrain and, to some extent, interior settings

_____ 9. The portion of landscaping that involves physical features

EXPLORING

1. Interview local landscapers on the various aspects of their jobs. Learn the scopes of the businesses. Do they undertake design work, construction work, maintenance work, or a combination of these? Ask what landscapers like most about their work and what they dislike.

2. Visit a university or community college that offers a program in landscape architecture or landscape design. Find out what course work is recommended to obtain a degree.

2

Working with the Customer

Before a design is drawn, a shrub is planted, or a blade of grass mowed, an agreement must be reached between the customer and the landscaper. Without an agreement, how would the customer know what services were to be provided and at what cost? How would the landscaper know what work is to be performed?

Reaching an agreement is necessary in the business world. How is this accomplished? It happens when the landscaper makes an effort to communicate in a cooperative way with the customer. This open communication usually starts with a meeting between the designer and the customer.

2-1. Working with customers requires good communication skills.

OBJECTIVES

1. Explain how to meet the client
2. Describe how to determine the client's needs and desires
3. Identify concepts in making a sale
4. Identify supportive materials in making a sale
5. Explain the difference between a proposal and a contract
6. Describe how to maintain customer relations through follow up procedures

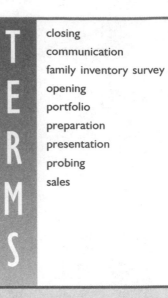

T
E
R
M
S

closing
communication
family inventory survey
opening
portfolio
preparation
presentation
probing
sales

LANDSCAPING BEGINS WITH A SALE

Landscaping is a service industry. The landscape company provides the client with a well-planned design, a professionally installed landscape, or maintenance of the client's landscape. Fair dealings with the customer and quality work are beneficial to both the customer and the landscaper. The customer receives quality services and goods in exchange for money. The landscaper generates money to maintain a healthy business and wins endorsements that lead to additional jobs later.

THE SALES PROCESS

Of course, the landscaper must first persuade the client to purchase services. Landscape projects begin with the sales process. *Sales* is the exchange of goods or services at a price mutually agreed upon by the parties involved. The one landscape employee in the best position to make

STEP 5: THE FOLLOW-UP
Reinforce customer's decision to purchase service.
See that installation and billing are timely.
Provide advice on care of landscape materials.
Strengthen relationship with customer.

STEP 4: THE CLOSING
Secure an agreement with the customer to purchase the service.

STEP 3: THE PRESENTATION
Introduce services to satisfy customer needs.
Use portfolio to demonstrate quality of work.
Answer questions about work to be done.

STEP 2: THE OPENING
Develop a strong rapport.
Define customer needs.
Complete family inventory survey.

STEP 1: PREPARATION
Develop knowledge of landscape service.
Prepare a portfolio.
Secure an appointment.
Develop a sales strategy.

2-2. Five steps to a landscape sale.

a sale is the designer. It is the designer who applies the wants and needs of the customer to a landscape design. The designer also knows through experience what work the company can perform.

Other employees of landscape businesses are involved directly or indirectly in sales. It is common for the owners of businesses to be actively involved in the sales process. In some companies, the owner is the sales person. The owner has direct contact with the customer and relates the customer's needs. Crew leaders and workers also contribute to making sales. Their professionalism and the way they conduct themselves on the job attract the attention of potential customers. Sometimes, their contact with potential customers leaves either a positive or negative impression.

Making the sale is a problem-solving process. Sales differ because of the people involved and their needs. Knowing this, the designer must be flexible as the sale unfolds. An understanding of the sales process enables the designer to adjust to the challenge presented with each customer. Completing a successful sale usually depends on executing five steps in the sales process.

Step I: Preparation

The saying "Prior planning prevents poor performance" holds true in the sales process. A prepared sales person will anticipate the questions and concerns of the customer and address them accordingly. *Preparation* involves a number of factors before the sale is actually conducted.

First, new customers need to be located. In the landscape industry, it would be better to say the landscape company needs to be located. This is because the customers usually make the initial contact with the landscape company. These customers need landscape services they cannot or do not want to do themselves. They may need a complete landscape installed. They may want an area of the existing landscape improved.

2-3. Many customers learn of landscape services through the telephone book and make the first contact by telephone.

It is however, up to the landscaper to market their company to potential customers. Many customers learn of the company from telephone book advertisements, through newspaper advertisements, word of mouth, or from flyers distributed by the company. Landscape companies can also promote their services by doing work for house contractors, placing signs at construction sites (i.e., "Landscaping by AJB Landscape Company"), sponsoring community events, or participating in home shows. Established landscapc companies, known for high quality work, often survive entirely by referrals and repeat customers and do little advertising.

2-4. This landscape company promotes its work by placing a sign in a newly completed landscape.

Once the contact is made, the designer has the responsibility of setting up an appointment with the customer. Typically, the meeting is held at the customer's home so the designer can see the site being discussed. Prior to the meeting, the designer will develop a sales strategy based on what is known about the customer's needs. The designer must also be prepared to explain the landscape goods and services available for sale to the customer.

Step 2: The Opening

Opening a sale is the first meeting of the designer and customer. The opening of a sale has two primary purposes. One is to develop a strong rapport or a relationship of agreement and harmony with the customer. The other is to define the needs of the customer through carefully planned

2-5. Greeting the customer with a smile creates a good first impression.

questions. The opening phase takes place during the first meeting with the customer.

The initial meeting with the customer is critical as it provides the first impressions about the salesperson and the professionalism of the company. First impressions are lasting impressions. Poor impressions at the first meeting are difficult to change. Some things contribute to making a good impression. Examples are politeness, dressing according to the situation, smiling, acting confidently without being arrogant, speaking clearly, showing an interest in what the customer has to say, and looking the customer in the eye.

Throughout the meeting it is important to communicate with the customer. Effective **communication** requires that both individuals participate in exchanging information. This gives both parties an opportunity to get to know one another. The result is an easing of tension and awkwardness and a building of trust.

After the initial introductions, build rapport with light conversation before diving into the business at hand. The weather, sporting events, and holidays are topics in which a wide range of people take interest. In fact, when strangers meet they often talk about something both have in common, such as the weather. As they become more comfortable with one another they move on to other topics. Experience helps designers determine the appropriate time to move on to the purpose of the visit.

At this point, it is helpful to probe for customer needs. **Probing** is a practice of thoroughly investigating a customer's wants, needs, and problems. Probing involves asking appropriate questions through a customer

2-6. Probing involves asking careful questions to learn more about the customer's landscape needs.

interview to discover the needs. Knowing the needs of the customer allows the salesperson to adjust their sales effort to address those needs. If the sale is made, the landscaper is better able to provide the exact goods and services that will meet the needs uncovered during the probe.

2-7. This family is completing a family inventory survey.

Landscape design is complex and there are many factors to consider during the design process. Therefore, a written family inventory survey is a useful tool in the probing process. The *family inventory survey* is a form on which the customer provides information on factors that affect the landscape project. Sometimes, it is helpful if the designer is present. On other occasions, the family can complete the survey as the designer analyzes the site. A third possibility is to let the family complete the survey at their leisure and return the survey to the designer before design work begins.

FAMILY INVENTORY SURVEY

FAMILY MEMBERS:

Name	Age	Sex	Hobbies
_____	_____	_____	_____
_____	_____	_____	_____
_____	_____	_____	_____
_____	_____	_____	_____
_____	_____	_____	_____
_____	_____	_____	_____

PUBLIC AREA (front of the house):

Driveway needs _____

Number of cars owned by family _____

Off-street parking needed _____

Entry garden _____

Landscape lighting _____

Privacy from the street _____

Structures, such as fences, walls, brick pavers, etc. _____

OUTDOOR LIVING AREA (rear of the house):

How much time do you want to spend maintaining the landscape?

      Minimal _____   Moderate _____   Quite a bit _____

What are your gardening interests? Describe preferences.

    Vegetable garden _____

    Perennial garden _____

    Annual flowers _____

    Rose garden _____

    Small fruits (raspberries, strawberries, grapes, etc.) _____

    Large fruits (apples, peaches, etc.) _____

What favorite plants would you like included in the design? _____

_____

_____

_____

_____

List any plants you do **not** want in your landscape: _____

_____

FAMILY INVENTORY SURVEY (continued)

What size groups do you anticipate entertaining? _____
    Patio _____   Deck _____
    Patio materials (brick pavers, flagstone, concrete, etc.)_____
    Permanent seating _____
Will you have a grill? _____
    Gas _____   Gas line from the house? _____
    Charcoal _____
Sink _____   Water _____   Electrical outlets _____   Storage _____
Swimming pool _____
    Portable _____
    Permanent _____   Size _____   Shape _____
        Decking _____   Material _____
        Enclosure _____
            Lighting _____
            Dressing facility _____   Storage _____
Lawn Games _____
_____

SERVICE AREA:

Vegetable garden _____   Size _____
Compost bin _____   Cold frames _____
Greenhouse _____   Size _____
Lawn and garden tool storage _____   Size? _____
Dog run _____   Size _____   Dog house _____
Clothesline _____   Permanent _____   Portable_____
Garbage cans _____   Number _____   Preferred location _____
Play area for children _____
    Outdoor gym _____   Size _____
    Preferred surface material (sand, wood chips, grass, etc.) _____
    Shade desired_____
Other features you would like included with your landscape:
    Statuary _____
    Water features _____
        Fountain _____   Pool _____   Fish _____   Aquatic plants _____
    Bird features _____
        Feeder(s) _____   Bath(s) _____   House(s) _____
        Bird attracting plants _____
Other notes or comments: _____
_____
_____
_____

Step 3: Presentation

Presentation is the step where the designer introduces the service or product that meets the customer's needs identified earlier in the sales process. The presentation should do three things. It should introduce the service or product the landscaper can provide to solve the landscape need. It should convince the customer that the plan suggested by the landscape company will work. Third, it should create a desire in the customer to buy the goods and services offered by the landscape company.

Customers will buy landscaping services if the solutions offered meet their needs. Therefore, the designer must direct his or her presentation to appeal to the customer's needs. The designer must be honest with the customer about the product or service. Claims of benefits to the customer must be both possible and believable. Also, presentations conducted in an upbeat, positive way contribute to successful sales.

2-8. This designer is using portfolio materials to help the customer visualize landscape possibilities.

Supportive materials are extremely useful during the presentation. A *portfolio* of design work and photos of previous landscape projects can be shown to a customer. When the customer sees the landscaper's work, they can more easily determine if they will benefit. It is also helpful to provide a list of references or former customers. These materials add credibility to the designer's claims by showing the quality of the work performed. The landscaper also demonstrates an openness about the work performed. After viewing portfolio materials and contacting references, the customer feels more confident in the services they are buying.

2-9. It is up to the designer to convince the customer they will receive high quality service for the price they pay.

During the presentation, it is likely the customer will want to discuss the cost of the landscape project. Rough figures for previous jobs can help to answer those questions. A truly accurate figure for the entire project is difficult to provide until the design is drawn.

The amount of money the customer is willing to invest in the landscape influences the design. Many people envision a beautiful landscape and are shocked to learn what their ideas cost to install. During these situations, it is up to the designer to reinforce the value of the service. It is also helpful for the designer to establish the customer's financial limits. Having openly discussed the budget for the landscape project, the designer can adjust the design work accordingly.

Step 4: Closing

The *closing* of the landscape sale interview is the agreement between the customer and the designer to begin work on the design. Usually, this will happen after the designer has reviewed the type of work the company has done and offered some ideas for the customer's landscape.

In the landscape industry, it is a common practice to complete the design work and meet with the customer again to go over the costs of installation. For the design itself, some designers may charge an hourly rate, while others may charge a flat fee. It is also a common practice to provide a free design if the landscape is installed by the designer's company. Regardless of the design fee structure, the customer should be asked to sign a contract for design work to be completed.

During a second interview, the designer meets with the customer to discuss the details of the design. Along with the design, the designer should present a prepared proposal for landscape services. The detailed, written proposal helps the customer understand exactly what services and costs are being agreed upon. At this point, the designer can explain the plan and field questions regarding details of the design and installation costs. Adjustments to the landscape plans can be made, if necessary, to satisfy the customer. The next step in the sale is to obtain a signed contract for the construction of the landscape project.

There are differing methods to close a landscape sale. In some cases, the designer may, in a straight forward manner, want to request that the customer buy their services. This method is simple and direct. An example is, "Would you like me to begin the design process for your new landscape?"

A second method is the assumed close. In this case, the designer takes for granted the customer is going to buy his or her services. This closing is common when the reputation of the landscape company precedes the

---

AJB Landscapes, Inc.

September 7, 1998

LANDSCAPE PROPOSAL

Front Entry Walk and Courtyard:

Remove and dispose existing concrete front walk.

■ Pour concrete to enlarge the front step to be surfaced in bullnosed pattern bluestone.

■ Construct the front entry walk and courtyard out of patterned bluestone, as designed.

$11,780.00

Public Area Foundation Plantings:

Remove and dispose of existing plant material that is dead or in decline.

■ Prepare planting beds with premium blend compost.

■ Install the following plant material:

3 Bigleaf Wintercreeper Euonymus 18"	15 Assorted Hosta 1 gallon
1 Winged Euonymus 36"	1 White Fringetree 6'
11 Dense Yew 30"	3 Cardinal Hydrangea 24"
1 Clump Linden 12'	1 European Black Alder Transplant
5 Juddi Viburnum 30"	3 Miss Kim Lilac 30"
2 Canadian Hemlock 7'	1 River Birch 18'
3 Dwarf Fothergilla 24"	165 sq. ft. Assorted Perennials 1 gallon
1 Shadblow Serviceberry 8'	655 sq. ft. Pachysandra 'Green Carpet' 3" pot
3 'Green Velvet" Boxwood 18"	

$13,220.00

Outdoor Living Area Plantings:

Prepare planting beds with a premium blend compost.

2-10. A landscape proposal.

AJB Landscapes, Inc.

September 7, 1998

LANDSCAPE CONTRACT

AJB Landscapes, Inc. agrees to furnish and install the items specified on order number 44908 dated August 29, 1998 in the sum of $20,460.00.

—Twenty Thousand Four Hundred Sixty and 00/100 dollars—

Payment is to be made as follows:

$6,820.00 Down payment due with contract
$6,820.00 Due at start up
$6,820.00 Due upon completion

AJB Landscapes, Inc. shall not be responsible for "Acts of God" or any other conditions beyond their direct control, but otherwise guarantees all material specified herein for a period of one year unless neglected by the purchasers.

Authorized Signature _____
AJB Landscapes, Inc.

Accepted _____

_____

Date _____

2-11. A simple contract for work to be performed.

sales interview. Sometimes, the customer will make comments early in the sales interview indicating that the designer's services will be purchased. In these situations, the designer may simply say, "When would you be available to meet again to go over the preliminary design work?"

A third closing involves the summary of the sales interview. Major points of the sales presentation are restated by the designer. The summary may go something like this: "Let me summarize our discussion. Once I receive your family inventory survey, I will design a landscape plan that

2-12. Signing a contract completes the sale.

2-13. The follow-up helps to retain customer loyalty and to achieve future sales.

will be attractive, require low maintenance, and is functional. Two weeks from now, we will meet again to discuss details of the plan and make changes if you feel some are necessary. Also, at that time I will provide you a proposal for installation costs."

Step 5: The Follow-Up

Throughout the landscape project, it is important to communicate with the customer. Remember, the designer is providing a service to the customer. The service being sold is not completed in one day. Often, landscape projects last several months. Continued contact with the customer ensures the wants and needs of the customer are met.

Follow-up after the sale is complete is equally important. This helps retain customer loyalty and to achieve future sales. Quality workmanship and follow-up procedures create new customers by referral and result in repeat customers. To create a positive influence and build a strong relationship with the customer, certain activities should occur:

- Work is completed as scheduled.
- Bills are handled in a timely fashion.
- Advice on plant care is given.
- Installation work is completed properly.
- The customer is frequently asked if they are satisfied with the work.
- Care is taken to avoid disturbing or damaging nonlandscaped areas and features.

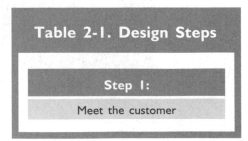

Table 2-1. Design Steps
Step 1:
Meet the customer

REVIEWING

MAIN IDEAS

Landscaping is a service industry including the design of landscape plans, the installation of new landscapes, and the maintenance of existing landscapes. The health of a landscape company depends on its ability to attract customers and sell them services. Usually, the sales or exchange of landscape services for a mutually agreed upon price rests upon the skills of the designer. The success of the designer often is determined by his or her understanding of the basic steps in the sales process.

Five steps identified in the sales process include preparation, the opening, the presentation, the closing, and the follow-up. Preparation involves planning for a meeting with the customer based on what is known at that time. The opening provides a chance for the customer and designer to get to know one another through open communication. In this step, the designer probes to learn more about the customer's needs and uses a family inventory survey as a tool. The presentation step is when the designer presents possible solutions for the customer's landscape needs. Use of portfolio materials is helpful during the presentation. At some point, the sales interview comes to a close with the signing of a contract for work. There are several methods to close a sale including the straight-forward method, the assumed close, and the summary. The fifth step involves follow-up procedures demonstrating a concern for customer satisfaction. Follow-up procedures build customer loyalty and lead to future sales.

QUESTIONS

Answer the following questions using correct spelling and complete sentences.

1. What is sales?
2. Why does the landscape designer often have the responsibility for conducting the sale?
3. What are the major steps of the sales process?
4. What are some ways landscapers can promote their business to attract customers?
5. Why is the opening critical in the sales process?
6. What is probing?

7. Why is the family inventory survey useful?

8. What takes place in the presentation portion of the sales interview?

9. What are three methods to close a sale?

10. What are some practices used in the follow-up sales step?

CHAPTER SELF-CHECK

Match the term with the correct definition. Write the letter by the term in the blank provided.

a. portfolio   d. presentation   g. communication
b. probing   e. sales   h. closing
c. opening   f. family inventory survey

_____ 1. An exchange of goods or services at a price mutually agreed upon by the parties involved

_____ 2. A form on which the customer provides written information on factors that affect the landscape project

_____ 3. Design work and photos of previous work that can be shown to a customer

_____ 4. The end of the landscape sale interview in which an agreement is reached between the customer and the designer

_____ 5. The step where the designer introduces the service or product that meets the customer's needs identified earlier in the sales process

_____ 6. Both individuals participate in exchanging information, which gives both parties an opportunity to get to know one another

_____ 7. When the designer and customer first meet and begin to get to know one another

_____ 8. A practice of thoroughly investigating a customer's wants, needs, and problems

EXPLORING

1. Role play a landscape sales interview in the classroom. Practice the five sales steps identified in this chapter. Arrange to have the interview videotaped so you can review your performance.

2. With the help of your teacher, identify a family that would like to have their house landscaped. Ask them to complete a family inventory survey that can be used in the design process.

3

Analyzing the Landscape Site

Imagine being asked to develop a landscape design for a house. The owner has invited you to look at the property. You ask yourself "What am I going to look for? What is important to note before I begin the drafting work? How am I going to remember what I see?"

Skill in analyzing the site can be the difference between a great design and one that fails miserably. This is because landscape design is more than a pretty drawing. A landscape designer's work involves live plants, complex soil characteristics, climate extremes, and of course, people and their interactions with the landscape.

3-1. Analyzing the site is critical to a well-planned design. (Courtesy, R.S. Hursthouse & Associates, Inc.)

OBJECTIVES

1. Describe equipment used in the drafting process

2. Explain the purpose of a site analysis sketch

3. Describe physical features to be recorded on a site analysis sketch

4. Describe climatic factors to be recorded on a site analysis sketch

5. Explain why views should be recorded on a site analysis sketch

TERMS

Ames lettering instrument
architect's scale
base plan
circle template
computer assisted design (CAD)
contour lines
drawing paper
elevation view
engineer's scale
erasure shield
French curve
grade
hardpan
hardware
macroclimate
microclimate
native plant
ornamental plant
plan view
plat of survey
site analysis plan
software
soil structure
soil texture
subsoil
topography
topsoil
video imaging

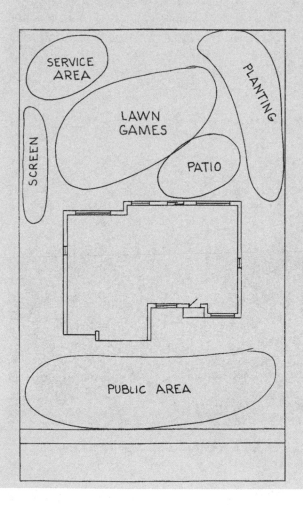

PREPARATION FOR THE DESIGN PROCESS

One key to successful landscaping is to consider the features of the site and the surrounding area. You will need to study the property before any design takes place. Designers note site characteristics, such as the drainage of water, the slope of the land, soil conditions, existing vegetation, views to and from surrounding areas, existing structures, and climate. Knowing what the site has to offer helps the designer enhance the positive features and correct the negative ones.

3-2. The landscaper of this project has taken the natural features of the site into account. (Courtesy, Church Landscape)

The design process begins with gathering information that is crucial for the design work. Client needs, as discussed in the previous chapter, are important. Also, preparation for the design work requires details, such as the dimensions of the house, the height of the windows, the size of the lot, orientation to North, etc.

THE BASE PLAN

The first drawing in the landscape design process involves a base plan. The *base plan* is a drawing of the house on the lot. This drawing can be on a large sheet of paper or entered into the computer. Include doors and windows, drawn to scale, on the base plan. The base plan shows the plan view of the house as it sits within property lines. The *plan view* is a view

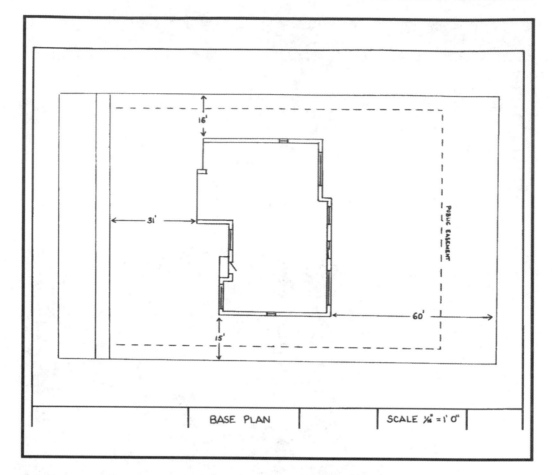

16'

31'

PUBLIC EASEMENT

60'

15'

| BASE PLAN | | SCALE ⅛" = 1' 0" |

3-3. The base plan shows the plan view—house situated on the lot.

from above looking down as opposed to a drawing of the front of a house known as the *elevation view*.

Include physical features on the base plan, such as the driveway, patio, walks, and fences. You can obtain much of this information from the plat of survey homeowners receive with the purchase of a home. A *plat of survey* is a legal document indicating the exact locations of physical structures on a piece of property and the exact dimensions of the property. Also, try to obtain a blue line copy of the house plans. The blue line gives valuable information concerning the floor plan, room usage and sizes, and the locations and sizes of doors and windows, as well as room usage. Visit the site to obtain exact measurements that may not be included on the plat of survey or the house plans.

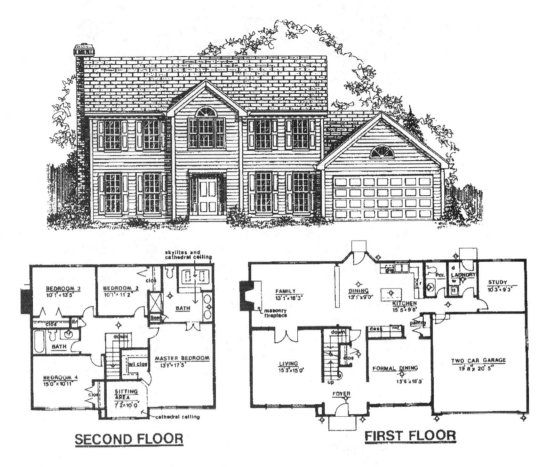

3-4. A house shown from the elevation view with the floor plan.

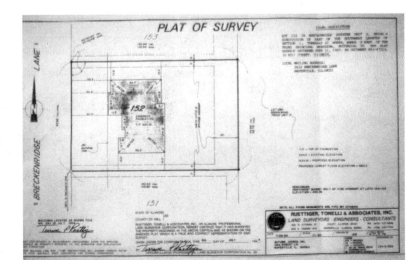

3-5. The plat of survey is a legal document indicating exact locations of physical structures on a piece of property.

THE DESIGN PROCESS

Landscape designs may be produced with the simplest equipment or sophisticated computer technology. Whether low tech or high tech equipment is used, the needs of the customer and the principles of design must be followed in the design process.

COMPUTER ASSISTED DESIGN (CAD)

Computer technology is one of the fastest growing segments of the information age. "Internet" and "Cyberspace" are common words in the vocabulary of young people. As the cost of technology continues to decrease and computers become simpler to use, more landscape designers will use them in their design work.

The term *computer assisted design (CAD)* refers to the use of computer hardware and software to produce drawings. *Software* is the programs (instructions) which make the equipment function. *Hardware* describes the computer equipment. Hardware includes input devices which allow the designer to enter information into the computer. These devices may include a standard computer keyboard, mouse, pen plotter, and more.

Video imaging is a technique that uses computer technology to superimpose a landscape design over a photograph of the customer's undeveloped landscape. Video imaging software may require a scanner, a special camera and input device, or a video input device. A computer specialist should be consulted when hardware is being selected for a video imaging system. Documentation on minimum hardware requirements is provided with the software by most CAD and video imaging software suppliers.

3-6. Landscape designs may be produced with video imaging using computer technology.

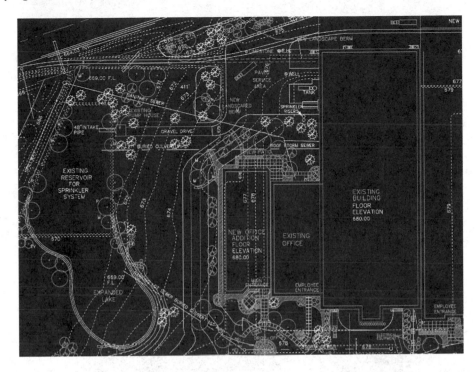

3-7. A CAD site plan with contours and design. (Courtesy, LANDCADD Division of Eagle Point Software)

Designers need training and practice to master computer design systems. However, the principles of design and the procedures covered in this book should be followed. A CAD system is a tool to help the landscape designer. One of the major advantages of a CAD system is the ease with which designs can be edited to satisfy changes desired by the customer.

3-8. A CAD perspective view of a hole on a golf course. (Courtesy, LAND-CADD Division of Eagle Point Software)

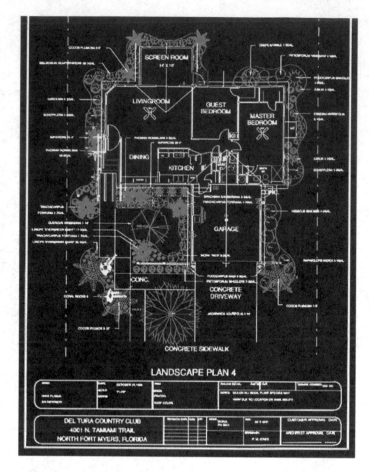

3-9. A CAD planting plan for a residential site. (Courtesy, LAND-CADD Division of Eagle Point Software)

DRAWING THE PLAN

Many residential designers prefer to draw plans by hand. The drafting equipment needed is inexpensive. Many designers are comfortable with pencil and paper designs. In addition, customers of residential projects seldom require drastic changes to plans. Small changes can easily be made by hand.

A simple, low cost setup might include the following drafting equipment:

Drawing board — At least one side must be true and the surface must be smooth (minimum size 20″ × 24″).

T-square — The working edge of the T-square must be straight and 90 degrees to the edge of the drawing board. When drawing, hold the T-square firmly to the edge of the board. Use the top edge of the T-square to draw horizontal lines.

3-10. Attractive, functional landscape plans can be produced using low cost drafting equipment.

Drawing paper — White vellum or tracing paper is commonly used. Drawing paper is translucent. Lines can be seen through the paper. Many sizes are available. Use the T-square to line up the top edge of the paper on the drawing board. It is important that the paper is square. Then, fasten the free corners with small pieces (1 to 2 inches in length) of drafting tape, which is similar to masking tape. Smooth the paper from the center with your fingernails to avoid smudging the paper and secure the remaining corners. Check the squareness of the paper after it has been secured, and make adjustments if needed.

Drafting tape — Drafting tape is used to secure drawing paper because it is less sticky than masking tape.

Drawing pencils — Select medium grade pencils for drawing: 3H, 2H, H, F, HB, and B. 3H grade pencils have harder lead than a B pencil and, thus, provide a lighter line. HB pencils can be used effectively for most drawing. Always keep your pencil sharp to maintain uniform lines. Hold the pencil at a 60-degree angle to the paper. Another tip is to pull the pencil across the paper rather than pushing the pencil. Roll the pencil slowly between your thumb and forefinger. Rolling the pencil helps to maintain a uniform line.

Triangles — Two triangles commonly used are the 45-degree triangle and the 30-degree × 60-degree triangle. Hold the triangle firmly on the top side of the T-square and use the edge to draw 90-, 60-, 45-, and 30-degree lines. Be sure to hold the T-square snug to the side of the drawing board as you draw.

Eraser and erasure shield — Use these tools to remove unwanted lines. The erasure shield is a thin metal plate used to protect lines while erasing. To avoid a messy, smudged drawing think about every line before it is drawn and erase completely when necessary.

Scale — For landscape design purposes, the architect's scale is recommended. The ***architect's scale*** can easily be used for scale measurements of 1/16", 1/8", and 1/4". It is also preferred because the homeowner can use a ruler to read the plan. The other scale used is the engineer's scale. The **engineer's scale** is divided by tenths and is used to produce 1/10, 1/20, 1/50, 1/100 scale drawings. It is useful to have an engineer's scale on hand to convert plat of survey measurements, normally drawn using an engineer's scale, to the base plan. Never use the edge of the scale to draw lines.

Circle template — This instrument is used as a guide to draw circles and curves on the landscape plan.

Compass — The compass is used to make large circles and curves not possible using the circle template.

French curves — Irregular curves can be drawn with the French curve.

Ames lettering instrument — The Ames lettering instrument is used to draw light parallel guidelines for lettering. The space between the lines can be adjusted depending on the size of letters desired. Place a well-sharpened pencil in a hole and slide the lettering instrument along the top edge of the T-square. Move the pencil to the next hole and repeat the process.

Drawing a Plan to Scale

Base plan drawings are made to scale. **Scale** is a measure of dimensions. Scale allows the designer to shrink the house, the lot, and the landscape plan to a size that is manageable and will fit on a piece of paper. The preferred scale for landscape design work is 1/8 inch. That means that 1/8 of an inch on the plan represents 1 foot at the site. Another way to express this is one inch on the plan is equal to 8 feet at the site (1 inch equals 8 × 1/8 or 8/8s). By following a strict 1/8 inch scale all measurements will be accurate. Scales of 1/4 inch and 1/16 inch are also commonly used for landscape design work.

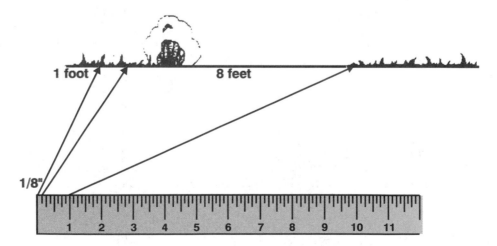

3-11. Scale is a measure of dimensions. One foot in the landscape would be drawn 1/8 of an inch wide on paper at 1/8 inch scale.

SITE ANALYSIS

It is important for the designer to visit and study the landscape site and to record observations. Several visits often reveal information that might be overlooked with just one visit. Visits at different times of the day and under different weather conditions are helpful. Materials needed during these visits might include a clipboard, pencil, 100' measuring tape, camera, and an accurate drawing of the house and the lot. Sometimes, notes can be recorded on a duplicate of the plat of survey. Photographs taken of the site are great as a reference during the design process.

Carefully transfer observations made during the visits to a site analysis plan. The **site analysis plan** is a piece of paper with an accurate sketch of the house and lot on which observations are recorded. Trace the base plan through to the site analysis paper. The site analysis plan can then be referred to throughout the design process.

Some of the features to be noted on a site analysis plan follow.

ORIENTATION OF THE HOUSE

Note on the site analysis plan the orientation of the house on the lot. Knowing which direction is north is vital to designing a functional plan. The exposure of walls to the sun's rays influences plantings. The orientation of the house is a factor in locating activity areas. Orientation of the house also has tremendous impact on plant selection and location due to shade requirements or exposure to wind.

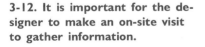

3-12. It is important for the designer to make an on-site visit to gather information.

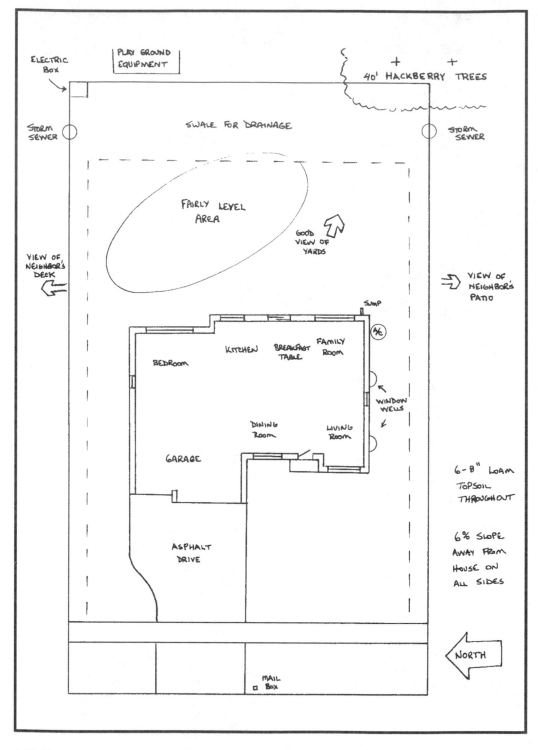

3-13. The site analysis plan consists of an accurate sketch of the house and lot on which observations are recorded.

THE LAY OF THE LAND

The lay of the land in terms of hills, valleys, and flat areas is referred to as **topography.** Note on the site analysis plan the topography of the site to be landscaped. This can be done with the use of arrows and written notes. It is also helpful to obtain plans from the developer or soil survey agencies that show the topography of the site with contour lines. Surveyors use **contour lines** to represent the vertical rise or fall of the land. Each line represents a certain elevation. The lines are labeled in a break in the line or on the high side of the contour. Each contour line connects all of the points of equal elevation on the map. Steep slopes are shown by closely spaced lines. Gentle slopes are identified by more widely spaced lines.

3-14. Measure the height and width of windows during the site analysis.

The natural **grade** or slope of the land is usually changed to some extent when a home is built. Changing the grade usually results in a change to the natural drainage patterns. If not addressed, the outcome can be flooded basements. Another problem that can arise is poorly drained soils. Most plants require well-drained soils to survive. Poorly drained soils limit the types of plants that can be grown.

Study the grade of the land surrounding the house. Determine the drainage patterns. Ask yourself questions regarding the drainage. Does water flow quickly away from the structure? Are there areas on the lot

3-15. Heavy equipment used in construction can seriously damage soil structure and drainage patterns.

3-16. Construction equipment has compacted this soil greatly slowing water drainage.

where water stands after a rainfall? Do the neighboring properties present a drainage problem? Will drainage tile or regrading be required?

Heavy construction equipment damages soil structure. This is especially true when wet soils are involved. Often a *hardpan* or densely, compacted layer of soil under the soil surface results. Hardpans inhibit the flow of water through the soil. They can also inhibit root growth. You will find that many construction companies have little knowledge or concern for soil and the importance of soil for healthy plant growth.

One goal of landscaping is to limit changes to the natural land form and slope of the property so the new landscape remains consistent with the surrounding properties. Drastic changes to the site can make the property "stick out like a sore thumb." Note on the site analysis features of the land, such as a large flat area, a rock outcrop, or estimated percent of slope. These notes will influence the design of the three major landscape areas addressed in later chapters.

3-17. Note the predominant land form in the region where the home is located. (Courtesy, University of Illinois Cooperative Extension Service)

In different parts of the country, the natural appearance of the terrain differs. For example, the northeastern states tend to be wooded and hilly, plains and woodlands dominate the midwestern states, and the Rocky Mountain states are rocky and dry. Within each region, there are a variety of terrains. Wherever the house may be located, the landscape should be designed to give the house the appearance that it belongs with the landscape. Well-designed landscapes provide a natural setting for the structures. As the site is analyzed, observe the predominate land form in the region and in the area surrounding the house.

SOIL

The soil found on the landscape site provides plants with water, air, nutrients, and support. These characteristics, important to plant growth, vary with the type of soil. Both soil texture and soil structure influence the availability of water, air, and nutrients for plant growth. *Soil texture* is the proportion of different sized particles in the soil described as sand, silt, and clay. *Soil structure* is the arrangement of soil aggregates in the soil. Soil with poor drainage, low nutrient-holding ability, and poor water-holding ability can lead to the death of the plants. Use this information to select plants based on the soil conditions or to amend the soil.

The soil found near the surface, known as the *topsoil*, is most valued for healthy plant growth. Depending on the location in the country, the topsoil may be a few inches to several feet deep. Most plant roots are found in the top two feet of soil and benefit from a thick topsoil layer. It is in the topsoil layer that the best combina-

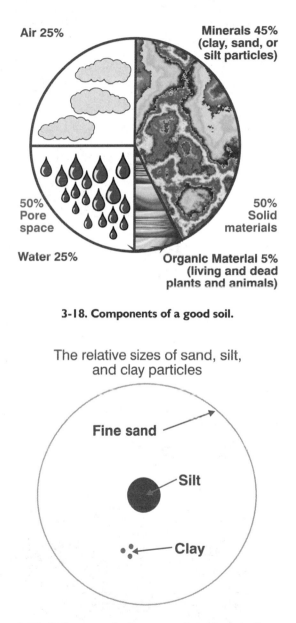

3-18. Components of a good soil.

The relative sizes of sand, silt, and clay particles

3-19. Soil texture is the proportion of sand, silt, and clay particles in the soil.

Table 3-1. Characteristics of the Various Soil Classes

Soil Property	Sand	Silt Loam	Clay
Looseness	Good	Fair	Poor
Air Space	Good	Fair to Good	Poor
Drainage	Good	Fair to Good	Poor
Tendency to Form Clods	Poor	Fair	Good
Ease of Working	Good	Fair to Good	Poor
Moisture Holding Ability	Poor	Fair to Good	Good
Fertility	Poor	Fair to Good	Fair to Good

tion of nutrients, air, and moisture for plant growth is found. Even large trees have most of their roots in the top two feet of soil. The topsoil is usually dark in color due to a high content of organic matter. Organic matter consists of decomposed and partially decomposed plants and animals.

Below the topsoil is a lighter colored layer of soil known as the *subsoil*. Subsoil can vary in color based on soil series, from yellow to brown to red. The subsoil is considered of much lower quality than topsoil for growing plants. It lacks a good combination of nutrients, air exchange, and moisture, and the amount of organic matter is very low.

Grading of soil around house construction sites disturbs the layers of soils. A common practice is to remove the topsoil, construct the home, and return the topsoil when construction is completed. Although good in theory, it often results in the damage to soil structure and the complex relationships between the soil layers. As is often the case, a homeowner

3-20. This topsoil is dark in color due to a high percentage of organic matter.

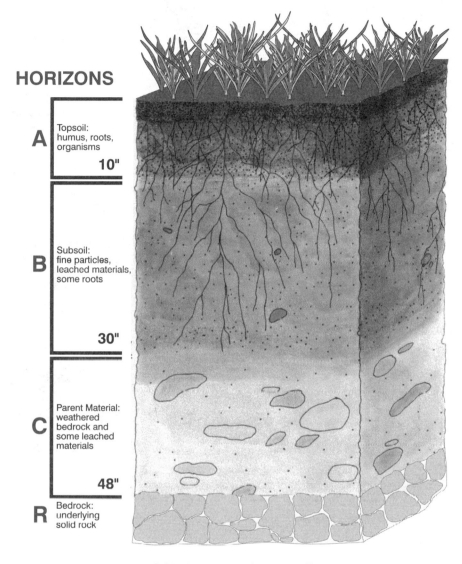

HORIZONS

A Topsoil: humus, roots, organisms
10"

B Subsoil: fine particles, leached materials, some roots
30"

C Parent Material: weathered bedrock and some leached materials
48"

R Bedrock: underlying solid rock

3-21. A diagram of a soil profile.

is left with a thin layer of topsoil in which to grow their plants. Some of the same problems can occur if the landscaping project itself calls for the moving of large amounts of soil.

Note on the site analysis plan the type of soil. Determine the texture of the soil and the depth of the topsoil and record this information on the plan. It is also a good idea to have the soil tested by a university extension office, the United States Soil Conservation Department, or a private soil-testing service for nutrient levels and textural classification.

3-22. A common construction practice by developers is to remove and stockpile topsoil until work is complete.

3-23. Topsoil is returned to a site and spread over the subsoil.

EXISTING VEGETATION

Existing vegetation includes native plants or ornamental plants found in the landscape prior to construction. *Native plants* are those growing naturally, not introduced by people. *Ornamental plants* are those planted by people for the attractive characteristics they possess. Determine the value of these plants and make note on the site analysis plan. Native plants are often valued for the natural appearance they can give to a landscape. Sometimes, existing ornamental trees and shrubs are large or especially beautiful and cannot be replaced. The designer must judge whether it is cost effective to save the existing plants and whether the plants fit into the design. In some cases, the recommendation is to transplant existing vegetation from one part of the site to another.

Inspect existing plants to determine their value. Identify the plants. Some plant species have greater ornamental value than others. Correct identification will reveal the potential size of the plant, health problems, and other attributes related to plant quality. The age of the existing plant is important. Older, more mature plants may be in decline. Consider the shape and form of the plants. One-sided or oddly shaped plants are not as valuable as full, symmetrical plants.

Construction crews must be careful not to disturb drainage patterns or compact soil if existing vegetation is to be preserved. Native plants often die within a few years if not protected from construction traffic or from changes in drainage patterns. A good example involves old oak trees in the Midwest. People pay top dollar for a lot with large oak trees on which to build their home. Construction traffic compacts the soil around the tree roots, roots are cut when installing basements and utilities, and the grade is altered affecting drainage patterns. Two, three, six years after the home is completed the homeowners are left wondering why their beautiful trees are dying.

3-24. Developers have placed fencing below the drip line of this existing Green ash (*Fraxinus pennsylvanica*) to protect the tree and its roots during construction.

3-25. The oak trees in this photograph are dying as a result of damage to the root zone during construction of the house.

NATURAL FEATURES

Rocks, earth, and water found on the site are considered natural features. When worked into the designed landscape, they add to the visual appeal. While conducting the site analysis, determine which natural features have value and are to be preserved. The challenge in the design process is to incorporate these features into the plan without losing their natural appearance. Avoid any changes to the site that destroy the natural character of the land.

CLIMATE

Climate greatly influences the landscape design and plant selection. Climate is broken down into two categories, macroclimate and microclimate. *Macroclimate* concerns the temperature, precipitation, humidity, and wind over large areas or regions. *Microclimate* is the temperature, precipitation, humidity, and wind on the landscape site.

Research on the macroclimate is extremely helpful in the landscape design process. Note the average temperatures in summer and winter for the region. The low temperature determines which plants can be grown based on their ability to withstand cold. The summer high temperatures play a role in determining how best to achieve a comfort level for the people. The amount of annual precipitation also influences the selection of plant materials and decisions on the need for an irrigation system. Plants grown within regions with high humidity tend to have more disease problems than those in dryer climates. Also, note on the site analysis the prevailing wind direction. The landscape can be designed to take advantage of cool summer breezes and to block cold winter winds.

3-26. The walls enclosing this courtyard influence the microclimate and the type of plants that can be grown.

3-27. A designer studying the views from a property.

The microclimate is influenced by buildings, plants, and landscape structures. Each of these or a combination of these can alter the typical macroclimate conditions. For example, a planting area surrounded on two or three sides by the walls of a building often allows for the planting and survival of plants adapted to warmer climates. The walls protect the plant from freezing winds and cold temperatures.

VIEWS

Study and make note on the site analysis plan views to and from the landscape site. Those living in a house will frequently look away from their property to the surrounding areas. If some views are particularly attractive, make note of them. Views worth maintaining might include golf courses, nearby woods, mountains or bodies of water, and well-maintained landscapes. These views can add to the value of the property and to the pleasure of the

3-28. The view across these backyards is attractive and is one that should be preserved.

3-29. Some views are not attractive, such as this cluttered yard.

owners. Other views may be eyesores, such as a parking lot, a well-traveled road or expressway, or even a neighbor's yard.

The other major views to consider are those from off the property. People generally approach the public area of the house in one or two directions. Note on the site analysis plan these directions so the view of the home can be enhanced. In other cases, views from off the property may not be welcome to the homeowner. Maybe a neighbor's deck is in line of sight with a large window or the owner's own deck. Public traffic that has open views of the backyard living area may need to be screened to maintain the owner's privacy.

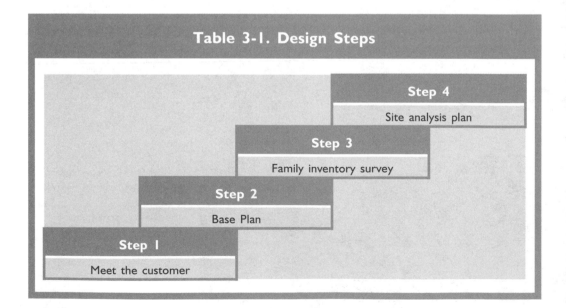

Table 3-1. Design Steps

	Step 4
	Site analysis plan

Step 3
Family inventory survey

Step 2
Base Plan

Step 1
Meet the customer

REVIEWING

MAIN IDEAS

The design process begins with the gathering of information from the client and the site. The first drawing is the base plan showing the house as it is situated on the lot. This is drawn to scale, usually 1/8 or 1/4 inch equals one foot. Designers draw plans using simple equipment or computer assisted design (CAD) systems. The base plan is then used as a guide for the site analysis plan.

The site analysis plan is a record of observations made on a piece of paper with an accurate sketch of the house and lot. The information recorded on the site analysis plan is obtained during visits to the site. Some observations to be recorded are the grade or slope of the land, which affects drainage of water, soil type and quality, which influences plant growth and water drainage, and existing vegetation. Occasionally, it is worthwhile to try to save plants on the site during the construction process. Also noted on the site analysis survey are natural features, the macroclimate and microclimate, and good and poor views.

QUESTIONS

Answer the following questions using correct spelling and complete sentences.

1. What is the base plan?
2. What are the advantages and disadvantages to drawing a landscape plan by hand?
3. What are the advantages and disadvantages of using computer assisted design equipment?
4. What is the site analysis plan?
5. Why is a site analysis plan important?
6. What should be noted on a site analysis plan?
7. Why is the grade around a house important?
8. What are the soil characteristics that should be noted?
9. What notes should be recorded in terms of existing vegetation?
10. How do macroclimate and microclimate differ?
11. Why are views to and from a landscape site important?

CHAPTER SELF-CHECK

Match the term with the correct definition. Write the letter by the term in the blank provided.

a. topsoil   e. scale   i. plat of survey
b. soil texture   f. T-square   j. grade
c. site analysis plan   g. plan view   k. base plan
d. microclimate   h. ornamental plants   l. drawing paper

___ 1. Planted by people for the attractive characteristics they possess

___ 2. A piece of drafting equipment held firmly to the drafting board and used to draw horizontal lines

___ 3. A piece of paper with an accurate sketch of the house and lot on which observations are recorded

___ 4. The proportions of sand, silt, and clay particles in the soil

___ 5. The drawing of the plan view of the home oriented on the lot

___ 6. The soil found near the surface

___ 7. The slope of the land

___ 8. A view of the house and landscape from above looking down

___ 9. A legal document indicating the exact locations of physical structures on a piece of property and the exact dimensions of the property

___10. A measure of dimensions

___11. Translucent white vellum or tracing paper used for drafting landscape plans

___12. The temperature, precipitation, humidity, and wind on the landscape site

EXPLORING

1. Select a house in need of a landscape design. Obtain a plat of survey for the house and visit the site for additional measurements. Use the information collected to draw a base plan from the plan view. Practice the drafting tips discussed in this chapter.

2. Go to the house site identified in Exploring Activity 1, and make observations related to the grade, soil characteristics, climate, natural features, and views. Using the base plan, trace the house and lot through to another sheet of paper. This will serve as the site analysis plan. Record your observations on the site analysis plan. You may want to use colored markers to represent different observations.

4

Designing the Landscape

If you were to ask 100 artists to paint the same view of a street scene, would any 2 of the paintings be the same? It is doubtful. Each artist views the scene differently. The colors they use would vary. Their brush strokes would differ. Even the painting style (modern art, impressionist, etc.) would differ. Is it possible then that all 100 of the paintings would be attractive? Of course, it would be possible.

The same holds true in designing the landscape. Each landscape design project may have multiple solutions to the design. As you design your landscapes, do not worry about the design being perfect. Follow the guidelines in this book and do your best to provide a functional and attractive landscape plan for the homeowner.

4-1. This house appears to belong in the landscape. (Courtesy, Church Landscape)

OBJECTIVES

1. Describe the three major areas of a residential landscape

2. Explain the elements that make up the three main areas of design

3. Identify family activities that occur in the three areas of design

4. Describe rules of landscape design as applied to the public area

5. Explain landscape design rules for the outdoor living area

6. Identify points of emphasis in the design areas

T
E
R
M
S

corner planting
deck
doorway planting
enclosures
focal point
garden accessory
high interest planting
outdoor living area
patios
private area
public area
service area

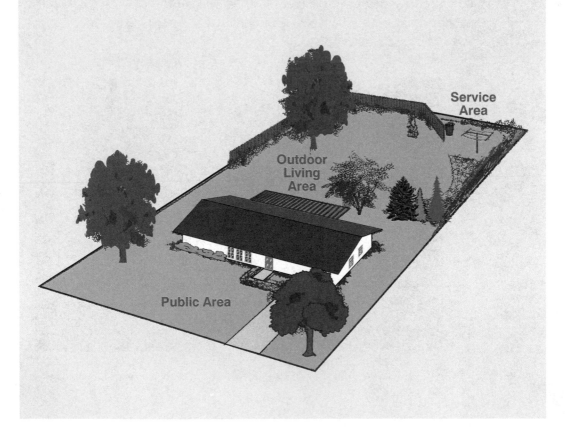

Service Area

Outdoor Living Area

Public Area

THE MAJOR DESIGN AREAS

Before work with the pencil and paper begins, it helps to have a good understanding of landscape areas to be designed. The good residential landscape design has three main areas: the public area, the outdoor living area, and the service area. Understanding the purpose of each area aids the designer in creating a landscape plan that will meet the needs of the customer. Different functions or activities are designated to occur in each of these areas.

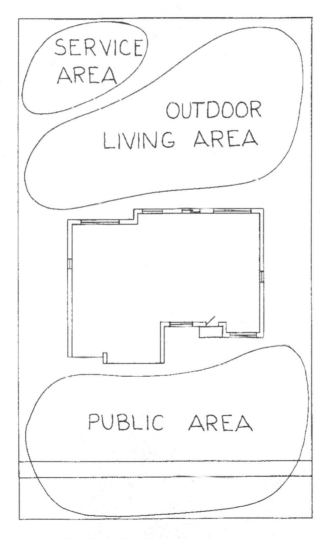

4-2. The home landscape has three main areas.

THE PUBLIC AREA

The **public area** is the portion of the property that is in full view of the public. It includes the area between the house and the road. It provides people their first impression of the house. For that reason, the public area is designed with the appearance of the house in mind. In the movies, you often see one or two star actors. The stars are surrounded by a supporting cast of many other actors. In a similar way, the house is the star of the public area, surrounded by a supporting cast of landscape elements (trees, shrubs, etc.). In the movies, the supporting cast never outshines the star. In the landscape, the house should outshine all landscape elements.

Design the public area so people passing by look at and appreciate the house. A well-designed landscape improves the appearance of the house and focuses attention on the front door. The front door is the most important aspect of the public area. The front door is the **focal point** or point of emphasis of a well-designed landscape. The focal point captures the attention of the viewer.

Keep three main goals in mind as you design the public area for a house:

1. Soften the architectural lines of the house.

2. Frame the house with trees.

3. Maintain open lawn areas.

Houses are artificial structures placed in natural settings. Standing alone, they appear rigid. The lines produced by the architecture of the

4-3. The house should outshine all landscape elements.

4-4. The vertical lines of this house need to be softened with plantings.

house are straight. Vertical lines created at the corners of houses are particularly harsh in appearance. Make it a priority to design the public area so the sharp architectural lines are softened with plant materials.

Study the architecture of the house to be landscaped. Note the dominant architectural lines. Consider the masses of the house. It is sometimes helpful to sketch the house in the elevation view. Properly locate the windows, doors, and porches on the drawing. Then, indicate the dominant lines and masses on the sketch with colored pencils.

The dominant lines of the house should be repeated in the plant materials. Select trees and shrubs with horizontal branching habits if the house has dominant horizontal lines. Houses with dominant pyramidal forms call for trees with pyramidal growth habits. Only houses with pyramidal forms should have trees with pyramidal growth habits in the

4-5. Select trees and shrubs that repeat the dominant lines of the house.

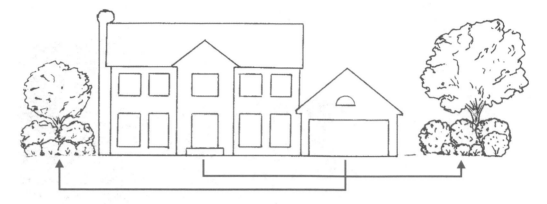

4-6. Repeat the architectural masses of the house at the opposite side of the house with masses of plant materials.

public area. This practice improves the appearance that the house belongs with its surroundings.

The dominant architectural masses of the house contribute to visual balance or imbalance of the house. Study the masses and determine how proper placement and massing of plant materials can achieve better balance. Strive to design landscape plantings that repeat the architectural masses at the end of the house opposite of the planting. For example, the right side of the house might appear as a large blocky mass. In this case, a large blocky mass of plants should be installed to the left side of the house. This reversal of location promotes a balanced view.

Architectural detail of the house influences the landscape design. Different-sized windows, randomly located shutters, wrought iron railings,

4-7. Design simple plantings when the house has abundant architectural details.

roof supports, and changes in building materials and colors lead to a busy appearance. When the house has abundant architectural details, avoid adding to the visual confusion. Design simple plantings with neutral green colors and rounded forms. Houses with equal-sized, evenly spaced windows or with little detailing permit more variety in the landscape plantings.

Four elements that make up the public area are 1) walks, driveways, and parking areas; 2) tree plantings; 3) shrub plantings; and 4) lawn or

4-8. Walks and drives make up one element of the public area. (Courtesy, R.S. Hursthouse & Associates, Inc.)

ground cover areas. Together, the elements of the public area contribute to a functional and attractive landscape.

Walks, Driveways, and Parking Areas

The walks and driveway are important considerations in the design process. They need to be functional, permitting easy access to the house. Well-designed walks and drives appear to blend into the landscape. Poorly designed walks and drives draw attention away from the house.

The entry walk leads guests to the front door. Therefore, it should follow

4-9. Avoid designing walks that divide the lawn area or that snake through the lawn.

4-10. Here is a driveway that also serves as an entry walk.

a direct line and be wide enough for two people to walk side by side. Careful design prevents the walk from attracting the attention of the viewer. Sometimes people try to get "fancy" with their entry walk by making it serpentine through the front lawn. The unusual shape of that type of walk actually calls attention to itself. Also, walks that bisect the lawn take away from the overall appearance of the house. Lawns that are undivided give a more spacious appearance and provide an attractive setting for the home. The best walk design is one that parallels the front of the house and connects with the driveway.

Large expansive driveways and circle drives can draw attention from the home. These drives often dominate the view of the landscape by their size alone. Design the driveway so it will meet the needs of the customer without being excessive. A driveway for a single car should be a minimum 10 feet wide. A driveway for two cars should be 18 feet wide. Driveways that also serve as a walk, connecting the entry to the street, should be 11 feet, 8 inches wide. Circle drives need to be 14 to 18 feet wide depending on the curve.

Frame the House with Trees

Trees play many roles in the landscape. In the public area, well-positioned trees frame the house much as a picture frame frames the picture. Most people view the house at roughly a 30- to 45-degree angle. Therefore, locate trees so they will frame the house at a 30- to 45-degree angle from the street. Refer to the site analysis plan for the primary direction of traffic passing the front of the house. Sometimes, the house cannot be framed

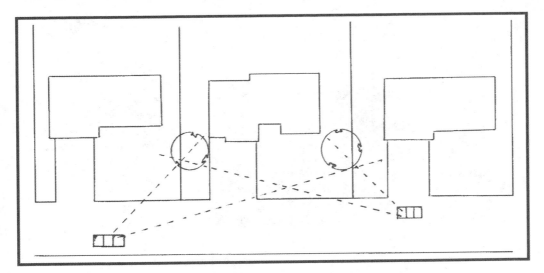

4-11. Frame the house with trees at a 30- to 45-degree angle from the street.

from more than one direction. Choose the direction from which most people will view the house.

The sizes of the framing trees are also important. Select large trees whose mature size will match the size of the house. For instance, a two-story house requires larger trees for effective framing than a single-story house. Trees in scale with the house will help to balance the overall view. Also, select trees for this purpose that have growth habits that repeat the dominant lines of the house.

Trees have other functions in the public area. They can provide shade in the summer. They can also be used to mask or screen awkward archi-

4-12. This house has been framed with trees.

4-13. Within only ten years these poorly placed trees have screened the view of the house and its front door.

tectural features. For example, a tree could be used to screen a point where brick color changed slightly as the result of an addition to the house. Other examples of awkward features include a large roof mounted antenna, a satellite dish, an awkward roof line, or a chimney. However, trees should not block the signals to a satellite dish.

Shrub Plantings

Shrubs are used in the public area to tie the house to the landscape. They help to soften the vertical lines of a house and hide the foundation. Softening of architectural lines can be accomplished by placing shrubs at the foundation of the house. Use foundation plants at the corners of the house and at the doorway. They are also helpful in hiding the foundation walls or in breaking up a broad expanse of wall. Because evergreen plants

4-14. Shrubs are used in the public area to tie the house to the landscape. (Courtesy, Church Landscape)

4-15. Plants pruned in unnatural shapes do not belong in the public area.

lend color to the landscape throughout the year, they often work well as foundation plants. However, deciduous plants also work effectively.

Select foundation plants that have natural forms that will complement the architectural style of the house. Plants with natural, open forms soften architectural lines. A common mistake is the failure to consider the mature size of the plants used. As a result, the homeowner is forced to prune the plants frequently to prevent them from covering windows, walks, and doors. The resulting appearance is a series of plants pruned into tight, geometric shapes that do little to soften architectural lines. Avoid this mistake by drawing plants at their mature size on the landscape plan.

Severe pruning of foundation plants contributes to another common mistake. Many people share a mistaken belief that plants pruned into green meatballs, poodle bushes, and other unnatural shapes improve the appearance of the house. These do not belong in the public area. Their unusual shapes grab the viewer's attention from the house. The regular pruning also places stress on the plants by reducing total leaf-surface area.

If the house has wide overhangs, locate the plants at least one foot beyond the drip line of the house. Plants located beneath the overhangs often do not get enough light or water.

Corner Plantings

Special attention needs to be given to plants placed at the corners of the house. These plants are referred to as *corner plantings*. Use plants with rounded forms, and arrange them in group plantings. The grouping should consist of several different plant species that complement one another. It is a good practice to select plants for corner plantings that will not grow taller than two-thirds the distance from the ground to the eaves.

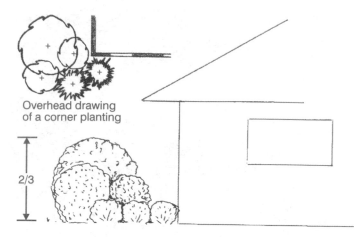

Overhead drawing
of a corner planting

2/3

4-16. Select plants for corner plantings that will not grow taller than two-thirds the distance from the ground to the eaves.

Selecting and placing plants that cause the viewer's eye to step down from the tallest plant to the shortest plant is an effective technique. Corner plantings contribute greatly to the overall appearance of the house. They help unite the house with the landscape. This is accomplished by softening of the harsh vertical lines created by the corners of the house. A well-done corner planting provides a scene whereby the house blends into its natural surroundings. Corner plantings hide the foundation of the house. The stepping down from the tallest plants also leads the viewer's attention to the front door.

Doorway Plantings

Another important planting arrangement, known as the ***doorway plantings***, is located on either side of the entry door. These plantings may be identical if the architecture of the house has formal balance. Most houses,

4-17. Shorter plants near the doorway draw the eye toward the door of this North Carolina landscape.

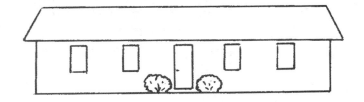

4-18. The doorway plants are usually no taller than one-fourth to one-third the distance from the ground to the eaves.

however, have informal or asymmetrical balance. In the case of houses with asymmetrical architecture, use different plantings on either side of the doorway.

Use shorter plants for doorway plantings. To determine the height of the plants, follow a line from the threshold of the door to a point at the corners of the house that is two-thirds the distance from the ground to the eaves. Choose plants that have a mature height at or below this line. The doorway plants are usually no taller than one-fourth to one-third the distance from the ground to the eaves. Placing of the taller plants at the corners and shorter plants at the doorway has the visual effect of drawing the viewer's eye toward the door. The outline of the corner and doorway plants sloping to the door draws the attention of the eye inward.

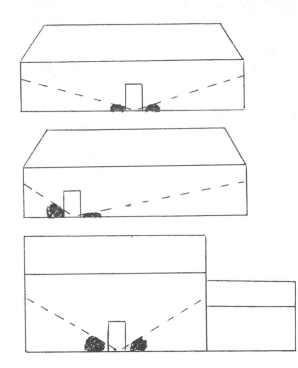

4-19. The height of corner and doorway plants can be determined by drawing a line from the point two-thirds the distance from the ground to the eaves at each corner to a point at the center of the threshold.

Another way to draw attention to the door is to use specimen plants. Specimen plants due to their high visual quality help pull the viewer's eye toward the door. They also provide high visual interest to visitors as they approach the doorway.

Lawn Areas

Lawn or grass areas unite all elements of the public area. The lawn also provides a broad expansive setting for the house. These qualities improve the overall appearance of the landscape and the house. It is important to maintain a large unbroken expanse of lawn area. Avoid dividing the lawn with walks, drives, and island plantings. Place all shrubs in planting beds. Shrubs scattered throughout the lawn create a design that appears unorganized.

4-20. The lawn serves to unite all elements of the public area and provides a broad expansive setting to the house. (Courtesy, Western DuPage Landscaping, Inc.)

THE OUTDOOR LIVING AREA

The outdoor living area is designed differently than the public area for several reasons. The **outdoor living area** includes all the property to the rear of the house except the service area. It is out of sight of the public. For this reason, some landscapers call this area the **private area.** Views in the outdoor living area tend to be away from the house. Therefore, the house is not the focus of attention. Instead, the design of the outdoor living area focuses on utility and beauty. The outdoor living area is designed with the family's gardening interests and entertainment activities taken into consideration. Several design elements satisfy the needs and interests of the family. They include the following:

4-21. The outdoor living area is designed with games and entertainment in mind.

- ■ **Enclosures** including fences, walls, or plants create walls for the outdoor living room.
- ■ **Surfaced areas** such as walks, paths, sitting areas, patios, and decks comprise one element of the outdoor living area.
- ■ **Plantings** of shrubs, trees, perennials, annuals, and ground covers enhance the appearance of the outdoor living area.
- ■ **Garden accessories** used to add interest include sculptures, pools, fountains, rocks, furniture, and lighting.

The outdoor living area has grown in importance over the years. More people are spending a greater proportion of their leisure time to the rear of the house. This trend has resulted in a greater desire from customers to landscape their outdoor living area. The lifestyle of the customer, whether it is entertaining guests or providing room for the play of children, calls for well-designed outdoor living space. Consider the outdoor living area as an extension of the indoor living space. The landscape is a room. Trees and the sky function as the ceiling. Plants and fences serve as the walls. The ground is the floor.

The Ceiling

The ceiling in the outdoor living area involves overhead features. Except in heavily wooded lots the sky composes most of the ceiling. This is rightfully so, as the sky is a beautiful feature that should be enjoyed. Maintain open areas in the design to view the sky. Trees provide the next

4-22. The sky composes most of the ceiling in the outdoor living room.

most common ceiling element. The limbs of shade trees planted near the patio become part of the ceiling in the outdoor living room. Trees also provide shade for a play area or the patio. Studies have shown there is a psychological comfort to be gained relaxing by a tree. If given a choice, people will sit near a tree with overhead protection rather than sit in a wide-open area. Patio umbrellas and other physical structures protect people from the sun's rays and provide a sense of overhead protection.

4-23. Trees provide a sense of overhead protection. (Courtesy, R. S. Hursthouse & Associates, Inc.)

The Walls

The walls or **enclosures** of the outdoor living room serve several purposes. They help to define space. They screen views. They provide privacy. They can serve as backdrops to flowering plants, and they can provide

4-24. Enclosures of columnar plant materials contribute to the natural appearance of the landscape.

protection from winds. Base the location and height of enclosures on the information gathered through the site analysis survey. The height of the enclosure may vary depending on its function. For privacy purposes and wind protection, an enclosure of 6 feet or more is recommended. Other functions, such as defining space or screening a vegetable garden, could be accomplished with shorter enclosures.

Enclosures can be established with plant materials. Plant materials are frequently used because of their natural appearance in the landscape. Plant materials have a softer appearance than the physical structures. In addition, establishing an enclosure with plant materials is less expensive than enclosures made of other materials. One disadvantage of using plant material for screens is they take up ground space. A columnar plant 6 to 10 feet tall will likely take up 4 to 6 feet of ground space. Because of their width, enclosures with plant materials should be limited to larger spaces.

Design masses of one type of vertical plant material to establish the enclosure. A mix of different species conflicts with the principles of design discussed in chapter six. Shrubs grown close to one another as clipped or unclipped hedges form living walls. A clipped hedge requires pruning several times a year to maintain the desired shape. Clipped hedges have a formal appearance. An unclipped hedge is allowed to grow naturally and is considered low maintenance.

Wood fences are another popular enclosure solution. Wood fences are particularly popular in the western states. A fence often is the most efficient way to provide enclosure. Fences take a small amount of square footage, thus, maximizing yard space. Another advantage is fences are useful in keeping animals from entering or leaving the yard.

Different fence styles can be used in the outdoor living area for different purposes. For example, a small solid fence might be used to enclose the

4-25. Wood fences are popular for enclosure purposes. (Courtesy, Illinois Landscape Contractors Association)

vegetable garden or screen garbage cans, while a wood board on board fence might enclose the property. Also, consideration must be given to the effect fences might have on breezes that cool the living area. Fence styles that let air pass are sometimes desirable for this purpose.

Fence construction influences the design of the landscape. Never have two different fence types or sizes meet at the corner of the yard. The obvious difference between the two attracts the viewer's attention. Also, when installing a fence, see that the top of the fence is level. In the case of hilly terrain, step the fence down the hill. A level fence projects a sense of stability.

A third material used for enclosure purposes involves stone or brick. Walls constructed of these materials give a sense of permanence. Cost of walls constructed of these materials is high, but maintenance is very low. Walls tend to easily blend into the landscape.

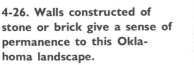

4-26. Walls constructed of stone or brick give a sense of permanence to this Oklahoma landscape.

The Floor

The floor or surface of the outdoor living area is made of many materials. The most common surfacing material is a grass lawn. Other surfaces include ground cover plants, organic mulches, inorganic mulches, concrete, stone, and brick pavers. Surfacing materials can be used to strengthen the bed pattern designs. Base the selection of the material on the function it is to serve. For instance, grass is attractive, green, cool, and soft, making it a good play surface. Unfortunately, it requires regular care. Brick pavers, flagstone, and concrete are hard, durable materials that lend themselves well to walks and patios. Ground covers and mulches function well as low elements in planting beds. They fill spaces between trees and shrubs and tie the differing units together.

4-27. Pavers lend them-selves well to walks and patios.

4-28. Decks are wooden surface areas raised above the ground. (Courtesy, R.S. Hursthouse & Associates, Inc.)

4-29. Locate the patio or deck adjacent to the house and so it can be easily accessed through a door to the house. (Courtesy, R.S. Hursthouse & Associates, Inc.)

4-30. This simple walk connects the patio with the public area. (Courtesy, R.S. Hursthouse & Associates, Inc.)

Nearly every house built today is constructed with a patio or deck in mind. *Patios* are built with hard permanent materials and are level with the ground. Brick pavers, concrete, and flagstone are common surface materials for patios. *Decks* are wooden surface areas raised above the ground level. Cedar, redwood, and wood treated to resist decay are used in deck construction. Decks require more maintenance than patios. Washing and staining a deck every three to four years, depending on the severity of the weather and the wood used, extends the life of the deck.

Patios and decks serve as a transition from the interior of the house to the outdoors. Also, because of the activities that take place on a patio or deck (cooking meals, entertaining guests, etc.), ease of movement is important. Locate the patio or deck adjacent to the house. This will allow it to be easily accessed through a door to the house. It is preferable to locate the patio or deck nearest to the kitchen if

4-31. The pattern design of this patio is the same as the bed pattern style used in the rest of the living area.

more than one door is available. Sometimes they are located a short distance from the house, but are connected to the house with a surfaced walkway.

Walkways serve to make passage in and around the landscape easy. Brick pavers, concrete, flagstone, gravel, wood chips, and cross sections of logs are some materials used for walkways. Walkways designed to connect the public area to the outdoor living area allow guests to reach the patio or deck without entering the house. Walkways also make movement around the landscape easier for the homeowner.

The patio or deck is the center of activity in the outdoor living area. Therefore, the pattern design of the patio or deck should dictate the bed pattern style used in the rest of the living area. If the patio has lines 90 degrees to the house, use 90-degree bed patterns for the planting beds. Also, locate plantings and enclosures to benefit those on the patio or deck. High interest plantings within view of the patio or deck provide enjoyment for the viewers

Plantings

Plants in the outdoor living area serve many functions. The primary function of plants is to provide pleasure for the homeowner. Well-designed shrub borders provide viewer interest from the deck or patio, as well as from indoors. Annual and perennial gardens give a splash of color to the landscape. Trees provide shade and a ceiling for the outdoor living space.

Some plantings called *high interest plantings* are designed to capture the attention of the viewer and to provide interest to the garden. Place high interest plantings in full view of the patio or deck. In locating these high interest plantings, also consider the views from the inside. Carefully designed plantings provide interest for those inside throughout the year.

Garden Accessories

Garden accessories are items in the landscape that attract attention and provide interest. Because they draw the attention of the viewer they have limited use in the public area. Remember, one of the rules of landscaping is to make the house the center of attention. However, in the outdoor living area, garden accessories can be used as focal points. Some accessories used with great success include sculptures, pools, and lawn ornaments.

4-32. A high interest planting is placed close to this patio. (Courtesy, R.S. Hursthouse & Associates, Inc.)

It is not required that a design have garden accessories. Sometimes, the customers request accessory placement in the landscape. When asked to utilize garden accessories in the landscape, work them into the plan

4-33. Garden accessories include statues and water features.

where they can be fully appreciated. It is often effective to locate accessories within the high interest planting area. Avoid locating the accessories haphazardly in the design.

THE SERVICE AREA

Areas to the rear or the side of the house set aside for strictly functional purposes make up the *service area*. Garbage cans, garden storage sheds, clotheslines,

4-34. Pots planted with annuals and perennials make good movable garden accessories.

compost piles, and vegetable gardens are some activities that occur in a service area. Most service area activities are screened from view due to the nature of the activities. Work the service area activities into the rest of the plan. For example, the vegetable garden and compost pile could fit nicely inside a planting bed.

PLAY AREAS

Design play areas to blend in with the landscape. If placed in the center of the yard they attract attention due to the size of the structures and bright colors of the toys or equipment. It is best to place the play areas where they are less noticeable. At the same time be sure to design an

4-35. This play area has been located away from the patio and the high interest planting area. (Courtesy, R.S. Hursthouse & Associates, Inc.)

4-36. This youngster is protected from the elements by well-placed plants. (Courtesy, R.S. Hursthouse & Associates, Inc.)

open line of site to the patio and from a room indoors. In sunny, warm climates provide overhead protection with well-placed shade trees.

REVIEWING

MAIN IDEAS

The residential landscape has three major areas of design. The areas are the public area, the outdoor living area, and the service area. Each is designed differently based on the functions the area will serve.

The main purpose of the public area design is to enhance the appearance of the house. Three main practices help to achieve a more attractive public area. The first is to soften the architectural lines of the house. Design the landscape with foundation plantings at the corners and doorway. Shrubs at the corners should be no taller than two-thirds the distance from the ground to the eaves. Those at the doorway should be no taller than one-fourth to one-third the distance from the ground to the eaves. Select foundation plants based on their mature size, growth habit, and their design qualities. Second, frame the house with trees. In doing so, use trees with growth habits that reflect the dominant lines of the house. Third, maintain a broad expanse of lawn. Open uncluttered lawn area provides a grand setting to the house and ties other landscape elements together.

The design goals for the outdoor living area revolve around the family's interests and entertainment needs. Consider the outdoor living area to be an extension of the indoor living space. The ceiling of the outdoor living room consists of the sky, trees, and artificial elements. The walls or enclosures of the room include living plant materials, wood fences, and stone or brick walls. Enclosures serve several functions that include furnishing a backdrop for flowering plants, providing privacy, screening views, and defining space. The major flooring material in the outdoor living room is grass. Some other materials used are mulches, concrete, brick pavers, stone, and wood. Durable flooring material is used for decks and patios. Locate decks and patios close to the door leading into the house.

The service area is the portion of the property used for utility purposes. Some common activities are storage of garbage cans, clotheslines, work sheds, and vegetable gardens. Often this area is screened from view due to the nature of the activities.

QUESTIONS

Answer the following questions using correct spelling and complete sentences.

1. What are the three main goals in designing the public area?
2. How are foundation plants used in the public area?
3. Why is it important to consider size in the selection of foundation plants?
4. What role do trees have on the public area?
5. How do the major architectural lines of a house influence plant selection?
6. What is the advantage to keeping open lawn in the public area?
7. What are some examples of materials that make up the ceiling, walls, and floor of the outdoor living area?
8. What functions do enclosures serve?
9. Where should patios and decks be located? Explain why.
10. What function does the service area have?

CHAPTER SELF-CHECK

Match the term with the correct definition. Write the letter by the term in the blank provided.

a. outdoor living area
b. focal point
c. public area
d. patios

e. high interest plantings
f. garden accessories
g. corner plantings

h. doorway plantings
i. decks
j. service area

____ 1. Plants placed at the corners of the house
____ 2. Located on either side of the entry door

____ 3. Built with hard permanent materials and level with the ground

____ 4. Areas to the rear or the side of the house set aside for strictly functional purposes

____ 5. Items in the landscape that attract attention and provide interest

____ 6. Plantings designed to capture the attention of the viewer and to provide interest to the garden

____ 7. Point of emphasis of a well-designed landscape

____ 8. All the property to the rear of the house except for the service area

____ 9. Wooden surface areas raised above the ground level

____10. The portion of the property that is in full view of the public

EXPLORING

1. Tour a residential neighborhood. Ask yourself a series of questions:

   Does the public area design show off the house?

   Do the homeowners use rounded plant forms to soften architectural lines?

   Are the lawns broad and expansive?

   Has an effort been made to frame the house with trees?

   Are the doors the focal point of the designs?

   Are the doorway plants one-fourth to one-third the distance from the ground to the eaves?

   Do the growth habits of the plants repeat the dominant lines of the houses?

   Are the views of the houses balanced by reversing the plant masses?

2. Visit the backyards of family or friends. Ask yourself?

   Is the patio or deck large enough for the entertainment needs?

   Is the patio or deck located near a rear entry to the house?

   Are poor views screened from view?

   Are there interesting plantings within view of the patio or deck and the indoors?

   Are the bed patterns for the plantings the same as the outline of the patio or deck?

5

Starting with a Plan

Ask landscape designers what they like about their work and you might get many different answers. Some would say they like working with the customers. Some enjoy the creativity that goes into a beautiful landscape design. Others might love the challenge offered with each new job. All would agree that they like to see their contribution in transforming an empty landscape into one that is lush and green.

Getting to the final lush, green landscape requires a plan. The plan itself can be broken down into a number of steps. The beginning steps in creating a useful landscape plan are discussed in this chapter.

5-1. A functional landscape begins with planning.

OBJECTIVES

1. Describe how activity areas can be organized with goose egg plans

2. Describe bed patterns for landscape plantings

3. Explain how to locate trees in the plan

4. Explain how to plan an energy efficient landscape

5. Identify the first steps in creating a landscape design

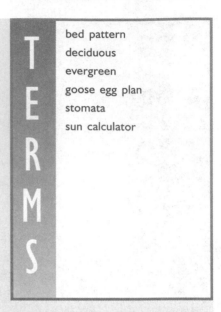

T
E
R
M
S

bed pattern
deciduous
evergreen
goose egg plan
stomata
sun calculator

BEGINNING THE DESIGN WORK

Once information has been gathered, work can begin on creating a design. The family inventory survey completed by the customer provides information on their wants and needs. The site analysis survey shows features on the site that will influence the design. Together with the base plan, they provide enough information to begin creating a design.

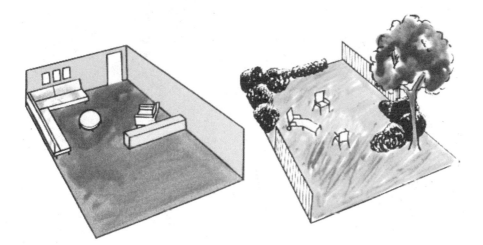

5-2. Consider the lot as room. (Courtesy, University of Illinois Cooperative Extension Service)

As work on the design progresses, apply three considerations:

1. Consider the lot on which the house sits to be like a room. A well-designed landscape becomes an extension of the indoor living space.

2. Consider the floor plan of the house. Locations of various rooms within the house impact the design of the landscape. For instance, locating a patio near the family breakfast area is very practical. Also, placing a high interest planting within view of those seated in the living room increases the value of the landscape.

3. Consider the landscape as viewed by neighbors and those who pass by.

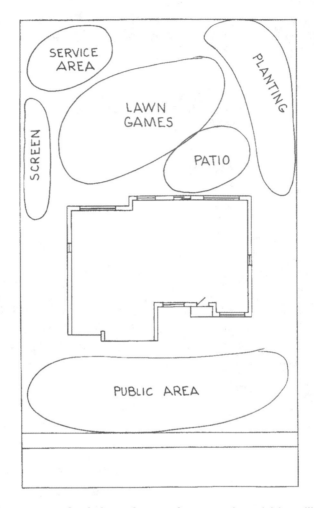

5-3. A goose egg plan helps to locate where certain activities will occur.

GOOSE EGG PLANNING

Plan the location where activities will occur to achieve a well-organized landscape. It is important to understand that various activities are best located in different areas of the landscape. A good way to organize activity areas is to quickly draw small sketches of the house and the lot similar to the dimensions on the base plan. Each of these might only be 4 to 5 inches in size. Then, sketch rough ovals or circles on the small drawings to represent activities. These odd shapes are referred to as the **goose egg plan**. Some examples of activities or land uses sketched on the plan include lawn games, play areas for children, patio or deck, vegetable garden, plantings, shed, screen, water garden, service area, and public area.

Try to be open-minded when working on the goose egg plan. Consider a wide range of possible solutions. Exact, detailed work will come later. In fact, it is better to let yourself be creative. Forcing yourself to work quickly is often helpful in this step.

After several sketches are made, look at the plans carefully and choose the plan that appears to be the most practical. Some things to consider are whether the activities are compatible to one another. For instance, you would not want the children's play area right next to the patio. You would not want the patio located away from an entry to the house either. Also, consider how the microclimate, macroclimate, soil conditions, views, and existing vegetation might affect each activity. It would be a mistake to locate a vegetable garden in the shade of existing trees or to obscure a beautiful view with plantings.

The value of the goose egg plan is it provides a general guide for the landscape design. It encourages the designer to be creative. It is not a rigid plan. If something does not work, the plan can be changed so it will work. All design work that follows reflects the location of the activities sketched in the goose egg plan.

ESTABLISHING BED PATTERNS

The design step that follows goose egg planning is the establishment of bed patterns. The bed patterns form the framework for the design. A **bed pattern** is a border that outlines where plants are planted. The border separates the lawn from the plantings within the bed. By placing all shrubs, ground covers, perennials, and annuals within a planting bed, maintenance in and around the plants is kept to a minimum. Imagine how much extra work would be involved to control weeds and cut grass if shrubs, ground covers, and annuals were planted at random on the property. Also, by locating plants within a planting bed it is much easier to follow the principles of design that will be discussed in chapter 6.

5-4. A bed pattern is a border that outlines where plants are planted and separates the lawn from the plantings within the bed.

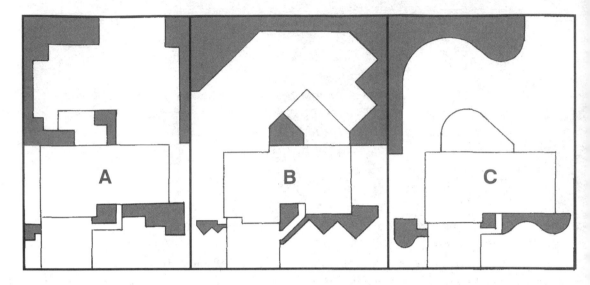

5-5. The three main bed pattern styles are (A) straight lines at 90 degrees to the house, (B) straight lines at 45 degrees to the house, and (C) curved lines.

The eyes of the viewer tend to follow the outline of the bed patterns. Therefore, it is important to design bold patterns that are consistent throughout the landscape. Three main styles are commonly used for bed patterns. They are curved lines, straight lines at 90 degrees to the house, and straight lines at 45 degrees to the house.

The lines of a curved plan flow smoothly through the landscape and lend themselves well to a natural appearance. Design bold curves. Little squiggles through the landscape confuse the viewer and lack clear definition. Often, this style is a mix of arcs and straight lines tangent to those arcs.

The 90-degree patterns reflect the architectural lines of the house. They give the impression of greater control over the landscape. Many famous formal gardens benefit from the symmetrical look provided by 90-degree bed patterns. Symmetrical landscapes have the same bed patterns and plants on each side of an axis. Select 90-degree patterns for a formal, rigid look to the landscape. Bed patterns of 90 degrees do work in the home landscape and with asymmetrical designs, as well. As with the curved bed patterns, these should be designed to appear bold.

The 45-degree patterns also reflect the architectural lines of the house. However, the 45-degree lines can be used to provide an asymmetrical look to the landscape. The asymmetrical appearance created with 45-degree patterns tends to have more interest for the viewer than the formal, 90-degree plan.

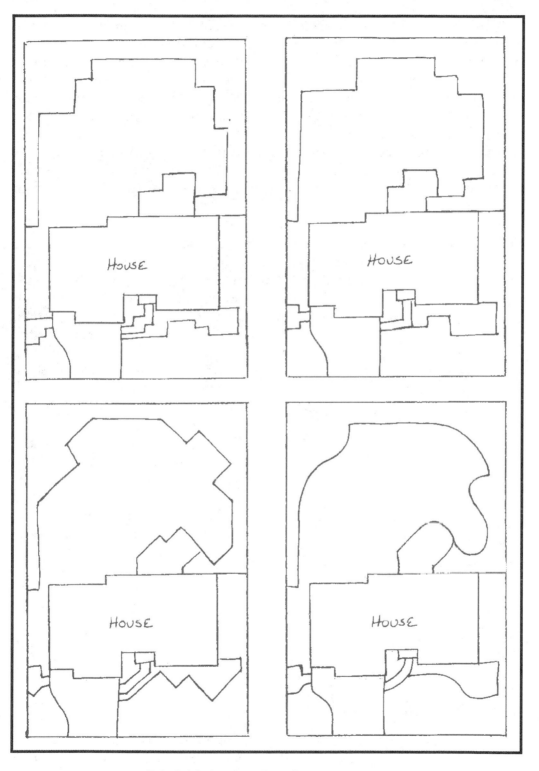

5-6. Quick sketches of possible bed patterns.

Start by drawing rough sketches of possible bed patterns. Sketch the house and the property lines. Several of these could be drawn on a standard size sheet of paper. Now, try different bed pattern ideas including the curved, 90-degree and 45-degree styles. Use the goose egg plan as a guide for locating the various activity areas. Work quickly taking no more than a few moments for each. Be consistent with your patterns. Only one style of bed pattern should be used for the outdoor living area or the public area. Changing a bed pattern style within one of those areas appears disruptive. Since it is unlikely anyone could view both the outdoor living area and the public area at the same time, the bed pattern style used in each area may differ.

After a number of sketches have been drawn, choose the best plan for the landscape project. Ask yourself if the plan addresses the needs of the family. Does it have visual interest? Are the bed patterns appropriate for the site or will changes need to be made?

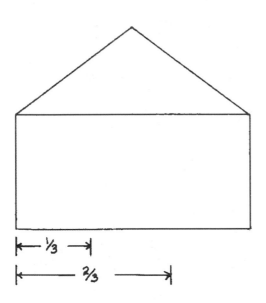

5-7. On wall surfaces devoid of architectural features, begin the bed pattern one-third or two-thirds the distance across the wall.

The pattern selected is then enlarged and placed on tracing paper laid over the base plan or entered into the computer. You may find that during this transfer process you will need to make slight adjustments to your bed patterns. During this phase, take care to draw accurate lines.

Whichever style is used, start and finish the planting beds at architectural features of the house. Some examples are the edge of a window, a jog in a wall, and a change in building material. On wall surfaces lacking architectural features, begin the bed one-third or two-thirds the distance across the wall. Also, draw bed patterns to meet the house or another physical structure at a 90-degree angle to the structure. This touch gives a clean appearance and keeps maintenance low.

DESIGNING PATIOS, DECKS, WALKS, AND DRIVES

Design surfaced areas to follow the same pattern as the planting beds. If the bed pattern style used in the outdoor living area is curved, the deck or patio should have curves in its outline as well. A square patio conflicts

5-8. Design patios and decks to follow the same pattern as that used in the planting beds. (Courtesy, R.S. Hursthouse & Associates, Inc.)

visually with curved bed patterns. Where the home has an existing deck, it may be advisable to let its shape dictate the style of bed patterns used.

Refer to the family inventory survey to help determine the size of the deck or patio. The minimum size should be 300 square feet. Of course, if the family entertains large groups, you will want to design a larger surface area. Calculate the square footage of the surface area drawn with the bed patterns and make adjustments as necessary.

Also, at this stage of the design process locate walks or pathways. A walk from the public area to the outdoor living area is often necessary. Guests do not have to trek through the house for outside functions. Furthermore, a surfaced walk is easier to walk across than grass. Usually, this type of walk is located on the garage side of the house. Walks in the landscape can be narrower than public walks or walks to the front door. Two feet in width is acceptable. Stepping stones with grass between the stones also make an effective walk.

5-9. The minimum size of a patio should be 300 square feet. (Courtesy, University of Illinois Cooperative Extension Service)

LOCATING TREES IN THE PLAN

The customer may be fortunate to have existing trees on the property. However, most new homes do not have older trees if they have any trees at all. Usually, it is up to the landscaper to install trees. Trees provide shade, a backdrop to the house, screening of poor views, framing of good views, and a sense of permanency to the landscape.

Trees are the largest element of the landscape. Locate them on the plan once the bed patterns have been established. At this point do not select the specific trees. Selection of specific trees comes later in the design process. Rather, choose the location of the tree and a basic size — small, medium or large. The location and size should be determined by family needs and site conditions. Some examples of where to place trees include: a patio that requires shade from a tree, a poor view that can be screened only with the placement of a tree, and the main approach to the house, which calls for framing with trees.

5-10. Trees provide shade, a backdrop to the house, screening of poor views, framing of good views, and a sense of permanency to the landscape. Shown are River Birch, *Betula nigra*, in fall color.

DESIGNING AN ENERGY EFFICIENT LANDSCAPE

Trees have a tremendous impact on the microclimate around a house. When carefully located, trees soften harsh weather conditions. The result is an improved comfort level for the family. Also, energy requirements to heat and cool the house can be reduced.

Deciduous trees, or those that lose their leaves in the fall, can be used to cool the microclimate in the summer. The leaves of these trees reflect some radiant heat energy back into the atmosphere. Some heat energy is

5-11. Shade trees help to keep this house cool in the heat of summer.

absorbed by the tree through evapo-transpiration. In this case, water evaporates from the leaves through the pore openings, called **stomata**, in the epidermal layer of the plant tissue. As it does so, heat energy is absorbed and the air temperature is lowered. This cooling effect is similar to the way perspiration serves to cool your body. Under a large shade tree, the temperature can be 15 to 25 degrees cooler than in the sun. In addition, the shade produced by trees on the outside walls of the house keeps the interior cooler than if the walls were exposed to the sun's rays.

PROTECTION FROM THE SUN'S HEAT

The first step in locating trees in the landscape for cooling purposes is to learn the direction from which the sun's rays hit the house. The

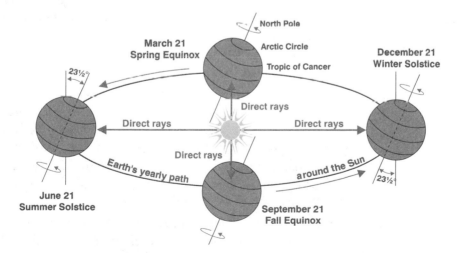

5-12. The rotation of the earth on its axis and its orbit around the sun cause seasonal change.

5-13. Deciduous trees allow the sun's rays to warm the house in the winter.

angle of the sun changes with the seasons. As the earth rotates on its axis the seasons change.

In the winter months, the sun is farther south on the horizon. The sun's rays hit primarily the south wall. By allowing these winter rays to hit the house and enter windows on the south wall, the interior of the house is warmed. *Evergreen* trees, or those that keep their leaves year round, planted south of the house would block these rays, while deciduous trees would let most of the rays pass.

In summer, the sun is farther to the north. The walls that receive the greatest amount of radiant energy in the summer months are the east and west walls. As the sun rises, the rays hit the east wall. However, blocking these rays is not necessary due to the cooling that takes place at night. Between 11:00 a.m. and noon the sun's rays hit the south wall with intensity. Consider placing a deciduous tree to shade the east end of the south wall or the south end of the east wall during that period. An evergreen in this location would block wanted rays in the winter months.

The sun hits its highest point in the sky at noon. The angles of the rays are very steep. Most of these rays hit the roof of the house. The amount of radiant energy absorbed by the south wall at noon is very small. It is not until 1:00 p.m. to 2:00 p.m. that the sun descends and the rays begin to hit the west wall. At around 4:00 p.m. the sun reaches its greatest heating capacity. The heat absorbed by the west walls during this time is transferred into the house throughout the night. Place shade trees within 25 feet of the house to block the rays hitting the west wall between 3:00 p.m. and 5:00 p.m. Here again, use deciduous trees.

The *sun calculator* can be used to help locate trees in the landscape. Slide a copy of the calculator under the tracing paper. Be sure the calculator is oriented correctly in terms of north and south. Then, center the calculator

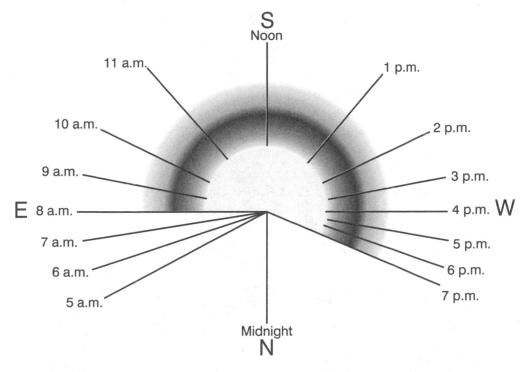

5-14. The sun calculator can be used to help locate trees in the landscape.

on the wall or area (e.g., patio, play area) to be shaded. Locate your trees within the angles suggested to block the sun's rays for a particular time.

WIND PROTECTION

Trees also reduce the impact of harsh winds in the winter. Groups of evergreen trees planted in the path of the prevailing winter winds effectively

5-15. Evergreen trees, such as these Douglasfir, *Pseudotsuga menziesii,* **planted in the path of the prevailing winter winds effectively cut the wind chill. (Courtesy, University of Illinois Cooperative Extension Service)**

cut the chill of the wind. In much of the United States, the prevailing winter winds come from the north and northwest. Trees can be carefully located to block the prevailing winter winds that strike a house. The loss of heat is reduced resulting in lower heating costs. Another benefit is the wind speed is slowed, causing snow carried by the wind to fall to the ground rather than drift around the house. Benefits are also gained in the summer. Well-placed trees slow the wind speed and reduce the drying effect of hot summer winds.

The extent of wind protection can be calculated. A row of trees or shrubs provides protection for a distance twenty times the height of the plants. Measure the height of the windbreak and multiply by twenty. For example, a ten-foot high windbreak would provide protection for a distance of two hundred feet (10 × 20 = 200 feet).

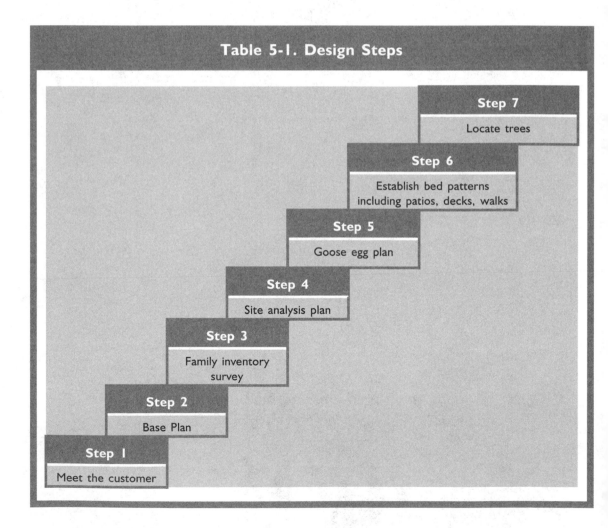

Table 5-1. Design Steps

Step 7
Locate trees

Step 6
Establish bed patterns including patios, decks, walks

Step 5
Goose egg plan

Step 4
Site analysis plan

Step 3
Family inventory survey

Step 2
Base Plan

Step 1
Meet the customer

REVIEWING

MAIN IDEAS

Goose egg planning is a step in the landscape design process that helps the designer locate where activities will occur in the landscape. Goose egg planning involves quick sketches of ovals or circles that represent the activities. The location of activities and the activities themselves are influenced by the family inventory checklist and the site analysis survey.

Bed patterns are established following the goose egg planning. Bed patterns form the framework for the design. Shrub plantings, flowers, and ground covers are placed within planting beds. Three main bed patterns are used for planting beds: curved lines, straight lines 90 degrees to the house, and straight lines 45 degrees to the house. Quick sketches of possible bed patterns are drawn. The bed pattern best suited for the landscape project is selected and transferred to the master plan.

Trees are the largest element of the landscape. They are located on the plan after the bed patterns are established. Consider their use as shade providers, backdrops to the house, screens of poor views, and frames for the house when locating them. The sun calculator is helpful in locating trees for an energy efficient landscape.

QUESTIONS

Answer the following questions using correct spelling and complete sentences.

1. What considerations are important as the initial landscape planning takes place?
2. Why is it important to organize the location of landscape activities?
3. How are goose egg plans developed?
4. Why are bed patterns important?
5. What are the major bed patterns?
6. How can trees be located in the landscape to shade areas from the sun?
7. What can be done to reduce heat loss in the winter months?

CHAPTER SELF-CHECK

Match the term with the correct definition. Write the letter by the term in the blank provided.

a. goose egg plan
b. evergreen

c. bed patterns
d. deciduous

e. stomata
f. sun calculator

____ 1. A border that outlines where plants are planted

____ 2. Trees that keep their leaves year round

____ 3. Trees that lose their leaves in the fall

____ 4. Tool used to help locate trees for an energy efficient landscape

____ 5. Rough sketches of ovals or circles to represent locations of activities

____ 6. Leaf openings

EXPLORING

1. Using the family inventory survey and the site analysis plan developed in the previous chapters, practice goose egg planning. Sketch a small version of the house on the lot. Reproduce this drawing. Now, based on the material provided, quickly draw four or five goose egg plans. Try to be creative as you sketch these plans.

2. Select the best goose egg plan. If there is not one that appears functional, draw some more. Next, using the small sketches of the house on the lot try drawing bed patterns that will accommodate the goose egg plan you have selected. Try two to three sketches of each of the three main bed pattern styles.

3. Transfer the bed pattern that you consider to be the best to the base plan drawn previously. Take care when enlarging, to draw the bed patterns accurately.

4. Locate trees on your plan. Use the sun calculator to place trees for an energy efficient landscape.

6

Using the Principles of Art

What is art? The *American College Dictionary* defines art as the production or expression of what is beautiful, appealing. We are familiar with art in the form of paintings and music. Painters apply colors to canvas as an expression of beauty. Musicians compose sounds that are appealing. Both types of artists follow guidelines established by countless artists that have preceded them over the centuries.

How are art concepts applied in landscaping? As with painters and musicians, landscapers over the centuries have defined rules, which if followed, result in beautiful, appealing landscapes. In this chapter, the principles of art, as applied to landscape design, will be examined.

6-1. Beautiful landscape settings result from following the principles of art as shown in this Florida landscape.

OBJECTIVES

1. Describe the design qualities of plants
2. Explain the principles of design as applied to the landscape
3. Explain the impact of line and form in design work
4. Explain how texture influences designs
5. Explain the visual impact of colors as a design quality

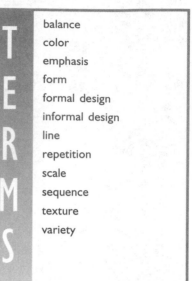

T
E
R
M
S

balance
color
emphasis
form
formal design
informal design
line
repetition
scale
sequence
texture
variety

THE ART AND SCIENCE OF GROWING PLANTS

Horticulture is often defined as the art and science of growing plants. Landscaping is the segment of horticulture pertaining to the art and science of growing plants in an outdoor setting. The science of growing plants involves botany and soil science. Plants are living organisms. Understanding what plants need to perform in certain situations and how to successfully grow them is a science.

6-2. An understanding of plant growth and care is important to assure that the plants provide long-lasting pleasure in the landscape. (Courtesy, Illinois Landscape Contractors Association)

The art of landscaping deals primarily with visual art. Arranging plants and other design elements in a way that is pleasing to the eye is an art. Attractive landscapes can be achieved by following basic rules or the principles of art. These principles are the same as those considered by artists who paint and sculpt.

Selecting plants for use in the landscape is based on the ability of a plant to grow in certain situations and the principles of art and design. As a result, the plant selection process is often the most time-consuming step in producing a design. The plants used must fit with all the other elements of the design in a way that is attractive. The major design qualities to consider in selecting plants for the landscape are line, form, texture, and color.

6-3. Natural and artificial features in the landscape have line.

LINE

Everything in the landscape has **line** whether it is natural or artificial. The outlines of trees and shrubs have line. The edge separating lawn and planting beds has line. The patterns in patio and deck materials have line. Line gives the viewer's eye direction and movement. Whatever its source, the viewer's eye follows the line. For example, the eye may move up and down following the line of upright plants or the corner of a house. The eye follows the horizontal lines of spreading junipers. It also follows the outline of an entire mass planting.

6-4. The observer's eye follows the outline of an entire mass planting.

6-5. The eye tends to follow the outline of this planting and the outline of the foregound shrubs.

Line creates emotional and psychological responses from the viewer. Vertical lines are severe and when used in excess, cause a feeling of tension and nervousness. Horizontal lines, on the other hand, provide a relaxing, pleasant emotional response. Doctors have been known to send patients with nervous breakdowns to ocean resorts or on cruises as therapy. The horizontal line where the sky meets the sea has a therapeutic, calming effect on the patient's nerves.

6-6. Horizontal lines, such as where the sky meets the ocean are relaxing and pleasant.

FORM

Form is the three-dimensional shape of the plant. The lines formed by the trunk and branches contribute to the form of the plant. Examples

6-7. Common plant forms: (a) horizontal: Pagoda Dogwood, *Cornus alternifolia*; (b) vase: American Elm, *Ulmus americana*; (c) columnar: Lombardy Black Poplar, *Populus nigra* 'Italica' ; (d) oval or oblong: American Sweetgum, *Liquidambar styraciflua*; (e) rounded: Bradford Callery Pear, *Pyrus calleryana* 'Bradford'; (f) weeping: Weeping European Beech, *Fagus sylvatica* 'Pendula'; (g) Pyramidal: Littleleaf Linden in youth, *Tilia cordata*;

6-8. Form is the three-dimensional shape of the plant. Pictured is Annabelle Smooth Hydrangea, *Hydrangea arborescens* 'Annabelle.' (Courtesy, Midwest Groundcovers)

of forms or plant shapes include: columnar, oval, pyramidal, round, vase, and weeping. Extreme forms, such as columnar plants, have high visual energy. High visual energy implies the ability of a plant to attract attention. The more extreme the form, the more attention the plant will attract.

Different plant forms affect the viewer in different ways. Upright forms, common with many evergreens, provide accent to a design. They draw your attention. Upright forms are difficult to use in the landscape because they are so visually active. Horizontal or spreading forms emphasize the breadth of space. They are less visually active forms. Rounded forms are the most common forms found in nature. They lend themselves well to groupings and mass plantings.

Plant forms greatly influence a landscape design. Avoid using all one type of form as the landscape can appear very monotonous. It is a good

6-9. Upright forms provide accent to a design. Shown is a Blue Colorado Spruce, *Picea pungens* 'Glauca.'

6-10. Shrubs with rounded forms are common and lend themselves well to group plantings. Shown is a species of Cotoneaster.

practice to use a majority of rounded forms. Using the rounded forms helps to establish a natural, informal appearance to the landscape. Add a few of the more extreme plant forms to the design for variety and interest.

TEXTURE

Texture is another design quality of plants to consider. Simply stated, *texture* is the appearance of a plant in terms of coarseness or fineness,

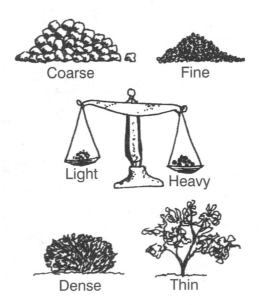

6-11. Texture is the appearance of a plant in terms of coarseness or fineness, roughness or smoothness, heaviness or lightness, denseness or thinness.

6-12. The texture of a plant is based largely on the leaves. (Pictured is an ornamental grass.)

roughness or smoothness, heaviness or lightness, denseness or thinness. Coarse-textured plants have a higher visual energy than fine-textured plants. Coarse-textured plants appear closer to the viewer than they really are, while fine-textured plants appear more distant.

Both leaves and branches determine a plant's texture. Coarse textures result from large leaves and twigs, dull leaf surfaces, short petioles, and entire leaves (entire leaves lack serrations or sinuses). Smaller leaves and twigs, glossy leaf surfaces, long petioles, and cut leaves contribute to fine-textured plants.

There are some rules of design to keep in mind as you consider the texture of plants. Monotony results if all the plants in the landscape have similar textures. Therefore, use some variation to

6-13. Coarse texture results from large leaves, short petioles, and a dull leaf surface as in this Elm, *Ulmus species.*

add interest. It is most pleasing to the eye if changes in texture take place gradually. A smooth transition from finer textured plants to coarser textured plants is preferred. Never place an extremely fine-textured plant next to a coarse plant.

The designer can also create a different feel in the landscape by selecting plants based on plant textures. Because coarse-textured plants have high

6-14. The textures of the iris and the hosta in this landscape are in sharp contrast with one another. (Courtesy, Midwest Groundcovers)

6-15. The feathery leaves of this Baldcypress, *Taxodium distichum* give it a fine texture.

visual energy and appear closer to the viewer, they should be used in larger settings. If coarse-textured plants were used in a small setting, such as a courtyard, they would make the courtyard appear even smaller. Use finer textured plants in small landscape settings or when the viewer is close to the planting, as in a patio seating area.

COLOR

Color is the final design quality of plants to consider. It has the greatest appeal or visual impact of all the design qualities. The primary concern when considering plant color is the leaves.

6-16. The primary concern when considering plant color is the leaves. (Shown is Lantanaphyllum Viburnum, *Viburnum x rhytidophylloides*.)

The source of **color** is light. Sunlight contains wavelengths of different lengths including x-rays, gamma rays, microwaves, ultraviolet waves, and visible light. Visible light has all the colors to which we are familiar. When visible light hits an object, light waves are either absorbed by that object or reflected. When light hits a green leaf, all the wavelengths are absorbed except green light wavelengths. The green wavelengths are reflected into the viewer's eye.

The colors of visible light are divided into two major groups — warm colors and cool colors. Warm colors

6-17. Color has greater visual impact than other design qualities.

Table 6-1. Colors		
	Warm Colors	**Cool Colors**
Colors	yellow, orange, red	blue, green, violet
Energy	high visual energy	low visual energy
Human response	striking, cheerful, stimulating, appear to advance toward the viewer	restful, peaceful, relaxing, appear more distant to the viewer

6-18. Foliage with warm colors has high visual energy and appears closer to the viewer.

include yellow, orange, and red. People find warm colors to be striking, stimulating, and cheerful. They have high visual energy. Cool colors have lower visual energy. They include violet, blue, and green. Cool colors invoke a feeling of restfulness and peacefulness. As with the other design qualities, the designer can select plants to create a desired effect. Plants with red-green, yellow-green or black-green foliage have high visual energy and appear

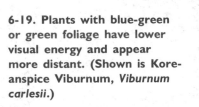

6-19. Plants with blue-green or green foliage have lower visual energy and appear more distant. (Shown is Koreanspice Viburnum, *Viburnum carlesii*.)

6-20. Design the landscape plan using mostly green-leafed plants, which provide an atmosphere of restfulness.

closer to the viewer. Those plants with blue-green or green foliage have lower visual energy and appear more distant.

The main purpose of using plants in the landscape is to provide a natural, green setting that creates an atmosphere of restfulness. Therefore, design the landscape plan using mostly green-leafed plants. For variety and interest, plants with warmer leaf colors can be used. However, be careful in using plants with yellow, maroon, bronze, or variegated leaves. They can easily dominate a landscape. In the public area, they draw attention from the most important feature of the landscape — the house. A good rule to follow is to use at least nine green plants for every one plant that has the visually active, warm leaf colors.

PRINCIPLES OF DESIGN

A well-designed home landscape has a look of oneness. The elements of the design flow together and create a unified view. The plants do not stand out as individuals, nor does an individual plant "scream for attention." The aim of a well-designed landscape is to attract and hold the attention of the viewers. The design appears organized, and the various parts flow together.

How do you achieve a unified landscape design? Unity in the landscape is accomplished by applying principles of design to the design qualities: line, form, texture, and color. In other words, the designer can create unity by selecting plants based on their qualities of line, form, texture, and color.

6-21. A unified landscape planting is accomplished by manipulating line, form, texture, and color and by applying principles of design. (Courtesy, University of Illinois Cooperative Extension Service)

The selection is based on the principles of art or design. The principles of design referred to in this book include repetition, variety, balance, emphasis, sequence, and scale.

> *Repetition* — Simplicity is another way to express this concept. Keep the plantings simple by repeating forms, textures, and colors of the plants throughout the design. The repetition of the design qualities of plants contributes to unity in the landscape.

6-22. Repetition is accomplished by repeating the lines, forms, textures, and colors of the plants throughout the design.

> **Variety** — If every plant in the design was the same or if all the plants shared the same line, form, texture, and color the view would be boring. Therefore, provide variety or contrast in the design by selecting some plants with different qualities from the

6-23. Provide variety in the design by selecting some plants with different qualities of line form, texture, or color from the mass of plants.

mass of plants. Variety in the plantings contributes interest to the design.

Balance — Balance implies equilibrium whether the design is formal or informal. ***Formal designs*** are symmetrical and have the same

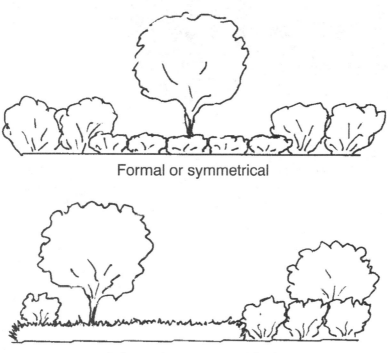

Formal or symmetrical

Informal or asymmetrical

6-24. Balance is an equilibrium of landscape elements, which provides a sense of stability.

6-25. The landscape for this house has a formal design with the same plantings on each side.

6-26. This small planting shows informal balance.

plantings on each side of a view. Formal designs give a feeling of stability. *Informal designs* are said to be asymmetrical and have different plants and different sized plants on each side of a view. Although the plantings differ, the visual weights of these

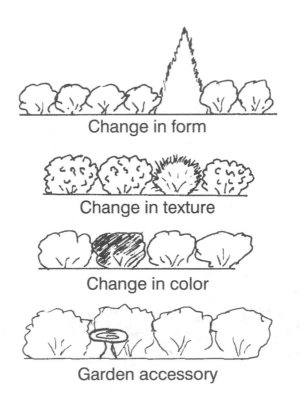

Change in form

Change in texture

Change in color

Garden accessory

6-27. Emphasis is achieved with changes in form, texture, color, or with garden accessories.

plants balance one another. Informal balance has a more dynamic appearance.

The style of the house also influences whether the landscape in the public area should be formal or informal. Design plantings to be the same on either side of the entrance of houses with formal architecture. With houses having informal architecture, use different plantings on each side of the entrance.

Emphasis — Emphasis indicates dominance of some elements of the design over others. Select some plants with visually active qualities (extreme lines, forms, coarser textures, warm colors) to serve as accents in certain areas of the design.

6-28. The visually active qualities of this European White Birch, *Betula pendula* **provides emphasis to the design.**

Sequence — Sequence is the uniformity of change from one item in the landscape to the next. Change of at least one quality of

6-29. Sequence is gained through the uniformity of change of form, texture, or color from one item in the landscape to the next.

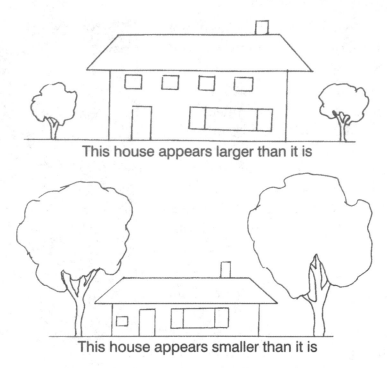

This house appears larger than it is

This house appears smaller than it is

6-30. Scale is the proportion of one object to another.

6-31. Because this Tuliptree, *Liriodendron tulipifera*, dwarfs the house, it is out of scale.

form, texture, or color from one area of the planting to another gives transition.

Scale — Scale is the proportion of one object to another. It sometimes means the relationship of an object with a designated standard, such as a building or a person. It can also apply to the size of one object in relation to another in a planting. Use landscape elements to which people can relate. For example, it is difficult to relate to the size of a giant redwood and feel comfortable, whereas, a smaller tree with limbs closer to the person creates a comfortable feeling.

REVIEWING

MAIN IDEAS

Landscaping involves the principles of art and the science of growing plants. The landscape designer must therefore be knowledgeable in both areas. Selecting plants based on their design qualities and their ability to survive is often the most time-consuming step in the landscape design process.

Landscape design is a visual art. The principles of design applied to landscape designs are the same as those applied to other forms of visual art. The major qualities of design are line, form, texture, and color. Line is the outline of the elements in the landscape. The eye follows the lines of landscape elements. Vertical lines are severe, while horizontal lines are restful. Form is the three-dimensional shape of a landscape element. The more extreme the form, the more visually active it appears. Texture is the appearance of a plant in terms of coarseness or fineness, roughness or smoothness, heaviness or lightness, denseness or thinness. Coarse-textured plants have high visual energy and appear closer to the viewer. Fine-textured plants have low visual energy making them ideal for small landscape settings. Color is the design quality that gains the most appeal. Warm colors, red, orange, and yellow are stimulating and cheerful. They have high visual energy. Cool colors consisting of blue, violet, and green have lower visual energy and are restful.

Applying principles of design to the design qualities results in unity. The designer can select plants and artificial design elements based on their qualities of design while following principles of design. Repetition is accomplished by repeating lines, forms, textures, and colors of the plants throughout the design. Variety is provided in the design by selecting some plants with different qualities of line, form, texture, or color from the mass of plants. Some areas of the design can be emphasized by selecting plants more visually dominant over other plants. Sequence is the uniformity of change from one item in the landscape to the next. Scale is the proportion of one object to another.

QUESTIONS

Answer the following questions using correct spelling and complete sentences.

1. How is landscaping both an art and a science?
2. What is line?

3. What is form?

4. How do plant characteristics affect the quality of coarseness or fineness?

5. How do warm and cool colors influence the viewer of a landscape design?

6. How is unity in the landscape accomplished?

7. What are the principles of design? Define each.

8. What are the major design qualities to consider in plants and artificial design elements?

CHAPTER SELF-CHECK

Match the term with the correct definition. Write the letter by the term in the blank provided.

a. color   d. variety   g. repetition
b. scale   e. sequence   h. form
c. texture   f. line

_____ 1. Accomplished by repeating lines, forms, textures, and colors of the plants throughout the design

_____ 2. The greatest appeal or visual impact of all the design qualities

_____ 3. The appearance of a plant in terms of coarseness or fineness, roughness or smoothness, heaviness or lightness, denseness or thinness

_____ 4. The three-dimensional shape of the plant

_____ 5. Gives the viewer's eye direction and movement

_____ 6. Contrast in the design achieved by selecting some plants with different qualities from the mass of plants

_____ 7. The proportion of one object to another

_____ 8. The uniformity of change from one item in the landscape to the next

EXPLORING

1. Take a walk around your neighborhood or school and try to identify features in plants that contribute to the plant's texture, form, and color. Why do some plants grab your attention before others?

Selecting Plants for the Design

Imagine baking a homemade apple pie from scratch without any knowledge of ingredients. You cannot identify flour, sugar, eggs, lard, apples or other food products in the kitchen. Even if you could identify them, you would not know the amounts to use. Would you use wheat flour, soy flour, rye flour? In addition, you would need to know the reason for adding specific ingredients. Would you use lard for the crust or the filling? It is safe to say that without knowledge of the materials your pie would be a disaster.

The major ingredients in the landscape are plants. Instead of baking a pie, the landscaper is creating an attractive and functional landscape. Knowing the materials with which to work and the reason for using certain plants for certain situations has an immense impact on the final product.

7-1. Plants are the major building blocks of this Washington landscape.

OBJECTIVES

1. Identify qualities to consider in selecting trees for the landscape

2. Explain how landscape plants are categorized

3. Describe plant nomenclature and its importance

4. Explain how soil conditions and climate influence plant selection

5. Identify uses for shrubs

6. Describe how to best use flowers in the landscape

7. Explain how to locate and draw plants on the landscape plan

8. Explain how to select plants to fit landscape needs

9. Describe how a plan is labeled

TERMS

annual
cultivar
foundation plant
genus
ground cover
group planting
hardiness
hedge
ornamental grass
ornamental tree
perennial
plant nomenclature
screen
shade tree
shrub
shrub border
species
specimen plant
tree
variety
vine

PLANTS: BUILDING BLOCKS OF THE LANDSCAPE

The residential landscape is made of different elements. There are the plant materials and physical structures. Of the two, plants are the most important. Plants are considered the major building blocks for a landscape. Physical structures in the landscape, such as patios, walls, and fences, are often needed to serve specific landscape functions. When they are well built, they are attractive. It is up to the landscape designer to determine the best selection and use of plants and physical structures.

7-2. Thousands of plants are available for use in the landscape. The designer of this landscape has used a variety of trees, shrubs, annuals, ground covers, and perennials.

In the design process explained in this book, the actual selection of the plant species, varieties, and cultivars is one of the last steps. A landscape designer has literally thousands of plants from which to choose for use in the landscape. How does the designer go about determining which plants to use? First, the designer must decide what function a plant has in the landscape. Is it to be a tree or a shrub? How large should the plant be? Is the plant to blend in with others or is it to be of high interest to attract attention? Also, plants are living organisms. How is the selection of plants influenced by the conditions a plant must have to live and be healthy? These are some questions a designer must answer before selecting specific plants to serve specific functions.

PLANTS TYPES

It helps to know a little about the plants used for landscape purposes. Plants are available in thousands of different shapes and sizes for landscape use. Each type of plant serves a different purpose in the landscape.

Tree — A tree can be defined as a single-stem, woody, perennial plant reaching the height of 12 feet or more. An exception to this rule involves some trees, such as birches and alders, which are often grown with multiple stems that increase their ornamental value. Some trees are grown with limbs to the ground, such as beeches, firs, pines, and red maples. Also, trees may be deciduous or evergreen.

7-3. Trees are single-stem, woody, perennial plants reaching the height of 12 feet or more. Shown is a Red Maple, *Acer rubrum*, in fall color.

Shrub — Shrubs are multi-stem, woody plants that do not exceed 20 feet in height. In general, shrubs are about as tall as they are wide. They may be deciduous or evergreen. There are many types of shrubs from which to choose, including viburnums, honeysuckles, spireas, hollies, junipers, and yews.

7-4. Shrubs are multi-stem, woody plants that do not exceed 20 feet in height. Pictured is *Forsythia* 'Meadowlark.' (Courtesy, Midwest Groundcovers)

Ground cover — Ground cover may be woody or herbaceous. It forms a mat less than 1 foot high covering the ground. Grass is the most common plant used as a ground cover. Other common ground covers include English ivy, periwinkle (vinca), euonymus, and Japanese spurge (pachysandra).

7-5. Ground covers are woody or herbaceous plants that form a mat less than one foot high covering the ground. Pictured is Japanese spurge, *Pachysandra terminalis*. (Courtesy, Midwest Groundcovers)

Vines — Vines are woody or herbaceous (soft stemmed) plants that require some type of support. They may climb on objects or creep along the ground. Some ornamental vines include Boston ivy, wisteria, and clematis.

7-6. Vines are woody or herbaceous (soft stemmed) plants that require some type of support. Shown is Boston ivy, *Parthenocissus tricuspidata*.

Annuals — Annuals are herbaceous plants that live for one growing season and are valued for the color their flowers or ornamental foliage adds

7-7. Annuals are herbaceous plants valued for the color their flowers or ornamental foliage adds to the landscape.

to the landscape. Common annuals are impatiens, marigolds, petunias, coleus, and zinnias.

Perennials — Technically, a perennial is a plant that has a life cycle of more than two growing seasons. They may be woody as with trees and shrubs or herbaceous. In the landscape industry, the term perennial refers to herbaceous plants with life cycles of more than two years grown for their display of flowers or foliage. Some popular perennials are daylilies, peonies, lilies, and iris.

7-8. In the landscape industry, perennial refers to herbaceous plants with life cycles of more than two years grown for their display of flowers or foliage. Pictured is the yellow *Coreopsis verticillata* 'Moonbeam' and the orange Poppy, *Papaver species*. (Courtesy, Midwest Groundcovers)

Ornamental grasses — Ornamental grasses are valued for their textures and colors that add interest to the landscape. Some ornamental grasses are annuals, others perennials. Some grow best in warm climates, while

7-9. Variegated Chinese Silver Grass, *Miscanthus sinensis* **'Variegatus', is a warm season grass grown for its ornamental value. (Courtesy, University of Illinois Cooperative Extension Service)**

others prefer cool climates. Use of ornamental grasses has grown in popularity in recent years.

PLANT NOMENCLATURE

There are so many trees, shrubs, ground covers, vines, annuals, and perennials, how does one begin to learn how to tell one plant from another? A good place to start is with plant nomenclature. ***Plant nomenclature*** is the naming of plants. Horticultural plants have two types of names, common names and botanical names. Plants often have more than one common name. For instance, the tuliptree may also be known as yellow poplar, tulip magnolia, tulip poplar, and whitewood depending on where you are in the United States. The number of common names can lead to confusion when people from different regions refer to the same plant by different names.

In 1753, Carl von Linne (Linnaeus) of Sweden ushered in the beginning of the binomial system of naming plants. The binomial system of naming plants reduces confusion. All plants today, including landscape plant materials, are given a binomial name. This means each plant has two Latin names. The first of the two names is the genus, and the other is the specific epithet. So, the tuliptree, known by many different common names, can be clearly identified by its Latin name, *Liriodendron tulipifera*. The advantage to the binomial system is it is recognized and used by horticulturists around the world.

Most landscape customers know plants by their common names. In communicating effectively with the customer, the landscaper must know

7-10. In communicating effectively with the customer, the landscaper must know the common names of plants.

the common names of plants. However, it is equally important for the landscaper to be able to identify plants by their botanical name. This is especially true when ordering plants from nurseries, when reading professional literature, or when talking to people in the landscape industry from other regions of the country.

The **genus** is a closely related group of plants comprised of one or more species. Plants with the same genus are more similar to one another than with plants of other genera. Classification is based largely on the structure of flowers and fruit and to some extent leaves, buds, roots, and stems. The generic name is written with a capital letter and underlined or italicized. For example, sugar maple, silver maple and other maples are more similar to one another than they are to plants of other genera. Therefore, they share a generic name. It is *Acer*.

The **species** is composed of plants that show characteristics that distinguish them from other groups in the genus. The species can pass distinct characteristics from one generation to the next. The specific epithet is written in lower case and underlined or italicized. There are many maples in the genus *Acer*. Some of these are distinct from the others. Although all the maples carry the *Acer* genus, the specific epithets differ. For instance, the specific epithet for the red maple is *rubrum* and the specific epithet for the Japanese maple is *palmatum*.

A group of plants within a species that show a significant difference from other plants in the species is termed a **variety**. The difference is inherited from the previous generation through sexual reproduction. The variety follows the specific epithet and is written in lower case and underlined or italicized. A thornless variety of honeylocust is written as follows: *Gledtisia triacanthos* var. *inermis* or *Gledtisia triacanthos inermis*

Another group important to the landscape industry is *cultivar*. Some plants have distinguishing characteristics from the other plants in the species but do not transfer those characteristics to their offspring through sexual reproduction. Instead, they must be propagated asexually, possibly through grafting or cuttings. For example, the Crimson King Norway Maple with maroon leaf color is distinct, but cannot pass on the unique feature through sexual reproduction. Since it is technically different from a variety, it is written with each word of the cultivar name capitalized and with single quotations. The correct name is written as *Acer platanoides* 'Crimson King.'

7-11. Autumn Purple White Ash, *Fraxinus americana* 'Autumn Purple', **is a cultivar selected for outstanding fall color.**

SELECTING PLANTS

One of the first things to consider in the selection of plants for the landscape is the appearance of the plant. Quality plants are said to have a four-season value. That means the plant has attractive qualities at any time of the year. This includes showy and possibly fragrant flowers, good-looking, healthy foliage in the summer, beautiful fall color and fruit effects, and winter interest created by the branching structure or bark color. Quality plants also have a symmetrical form or shape. However, plants should not be selected on their appearance alone. Other factors need to be considered.

TREES

Trees are the largest and most permanent plant material used in the landscape. Some shade trees may grow 100 feet tall and some may live for hundreds of years. Because of their size, fewer trees are used in the landscape than shrubs or ground cover plants. A large residential landscape may only have 5 to 10 trees. The same landscape may have 50 or more

7-12. Shade trees are described as large trees, with spreading canopies, such as this Silver Maple, _Acer saccharinum_.

shrubs and hundreds of ground cover plants. Proper selection of trees for the landscape involves the line, form, texture, and color, (discussed in chapter 5) that contribute to an aesthetically pleasing landscape. Proper selection is also important in terms of the future health and vigor of the tree. Selecting trees tolerant of the growing environment results in an attractive landscape many years after the trees have been installed.

When selecting a tree, consider the function it is intended to serve. Some trees lend themselves well to specific uses. Large trees, with spreading canopies, such as sugar maples, red oaks, and tuliptrees, make good _shade trees_. Shade trees are preferred for use in residential lawns, parks, and along streets. Trees that are smaller and have high ornamental value are often called _ornamental trees_. Some ornamental trees include flowering dogwood, flowering crabapples, redbud, and Japanese maple. Ornamental trees are suggested for smaller areas and when high visual interest, such as a display of flowers in spring, is desired.

During the design process, allow for the mature size of the tree. Avoid placing a large tree too close to the house. The view of the house may be

7-13. Smaller trees with high ornamental value, such as this flowering crabapple (_Malus sp._), are often called ornamental trees.

blocked as the tree grows or structural damage may be caused. Also, avoid planting large trees below power lines and telephone wires. The lines and wires can be damaged as the tree grows. Trees beneath power lines are frequently pruned severely by utility companies to protect the wires.

Decide if the trees are to stand alone or if they are to form a group. If grouping is desired, place the trees closer to one another. Grouping of visually active, upright evergreens including spruce and fir is often desired to soften the visual effect of an individual tree.

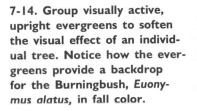

7-14. Group visually active, upright evergreens to soften the visual effect of an individual tree. Notice how the evergreens provide a backdrop for the Burningbush, *Euonymus alatus*, in fall color.

Select trees that are hardy. **Hardiness** refers to the ability of a tree to withstand cold temperatures. Trees have differing abilities to survive in areas in the United States. Southern magnolia, *Magnolia grandiflora*, can survive in the warm southern states, but is not tolerant of the cold winter temperatures of the northern states. Hardiness zones in the United States have been established. The U. S. Department of Agriculture Plant Hardiness Zone Map is useful in deciding what trees will survive in your region.

To benefit from the plant hardiness zone map, begin by identifying what zone the landscape is within. For example, Champaign, Illinois is in zone 5 where the average minimum winter temperature is between –20 and –10 degrees Fahrenheit. Then, read the literature that states what zone the trees you are considering can survive. If they match, the tree is tolerant to the average minimum temperature in that zone. Usually, trees survive over several zones. For instance, Southern magnolia grows in zone 6 with average minimum temperatures of –10 to 0 degrees Fahrenheit and in warmer zones. It would not be a good choice for the zone 5 Champaign, Illinois landscape that gets below –10 degrees.

Hardiness of trees is more important than just survival. Some trees valued for outstanding spring floral displays, such as flowering dogwood

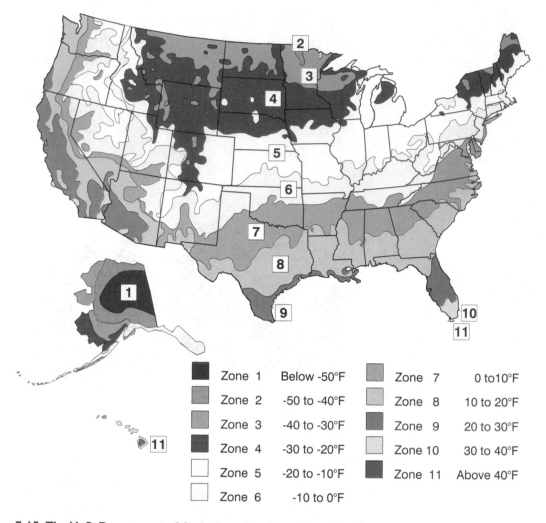

Zone 1	Below -50°F	Zone 7	0 to 10°F
Zone 2	-50 to -40°F	Zone 8	10 to 20°F
Zone 3	-40 to -30°F	Zone 9	20 to 30°F
Zone 4	-30 to -20°F	Zone 10	30 to 40°F
Zone 5	-20 to -10°F	Zone 11	Above 40°F
Zone 6	-10 to 0°F		

7-15. The U. S. Department of Agriculture Hardiness Zone Map is useful in selecting trees based on tolerance to cold temperatures. The map shows the average annual minimum temperatures of 11 zones.

and magnolia, may grow in cold climates. Unfortunately, the flower buds are not as hardy as the tree. In cold winters, the flower buds are sometimes the only parts of the tree damaged.

Avoid using trees that are known to be messy. Messiness may be in the form of fruit, peeling bark, and easily broken twigs that litter the landscape. Some varieties of crabapples, honeylocust, and sweetgum produce large numbers of fruit that require cleaning. Sycamores and hickories have peeling bark that forms debris below the tree. Siberian elms have

7-16. Although ornamental, the fruit of some trees are known to be messy.

7-17. Lombardy Black Poplars, *Populus nigra* 'Italica', are short-lived trees.

brittle twigs that break easily in winds and fall to the ground. Messy trees increase the labor needed to maintain the appearance of the landscape.

Another consideration is the life expectancy of trees. Some trees, like oak, beech, and Douglasfir, can be expected to live hundreds of years. Others, including some types of poplars, elms, maples, and cherries, are short lived. Some of these trees may show signs of decline after only 15 to 20 years in the landscape. Short-lived trees tend to be fast growing. While fast growth is desirable to someone in a new landscape, it does have drawbacks. Fast growing trees have weaker wood and are more likely to suffer storm damage.

Choose trees resistant to disease and insect problems. If a tree has beautiful characteristics, but is susceptible to insect infestations and diseases, its value is reduced. Some trees are vulnerable to certain problems, while others are not. American sycamores suffer from a fungal disease called *anthracnose*. A tree similar in appearance, the London planetree, is resistant to anthracnose. Selecting the London planetree over the American sycamore will reduce problems later. Some crabapple cultivars are terribly susceptible to apple scab, which can defoliate a tree. Other cultivars are

7-18. The American Sycamore, *Platanus occidentalis,* **at the center of this photograph is slow to leaf out due to anthracnose.**

resistant to apple scab. The smart designer selects trees known to be relatively disease free. The paper birch has been decimated in some parts of the country by an insect known as the bronze birch borer. If a birch must be included in the design, use birches resistant to the insect attacks, such as the river birch.

Trees may suffer physiological disease. A common problem involves the pH of the soil. pH is a measure of acidity or alkalinity of a soil. The pH scale ranges from an extremely acid reading of 1 to an extremely alkaline reading of 14. A neutral reading is seven. Most plants prefer a soil pH between 5.5 and 7.0. If the pH is outside that range, nutrients become unavailable to the plant. Without the ability to absorb certain nutrients, the plant sickens, the leaves show symptoms of discoloration (often yellowing), and the tree may die. It is much wiser to select trees that tolerate the soil pH found on the site than to change the pH of the soil to accommodate the tree.

Select trees that tolerate the moisture level in the soil. Most trees prefer loose, well-drained soils. If you have a situation where the soil is wet and the conditions cannot be easily corrected, select trees that will tolerate those conditions, such as bald-cypress, red maple, and river birch. In

7-19. This Pin Oak, *Quercus palustris,* **shows signs of nutrient deficiency due to high soil pH.**

7-20. The thorns on this Cockspur Hawthorn, *Crataegus crusgalli*, could be dangerous.

other cases, the soil may be sandy and prone to dry quickly. Use trees tolerant to dry soils, such as hackberry, honeylocust, and pines.

There are other considerations when selecting trees. Avoid using trees with thorns that could present safety hazards in certain settings. Native honeylocusts and some hawthorns have dangerously sharp thorns. Consider the rooting habits of the trees. The roots of Norway maples grow at the surface of the ground. This makes it difficult to grow grass or other plants beneath the tree. Also, consider the density of the shade cast by the tree. Honeylocusts are open, allowing sunlight to reach the ground and permitting grass growth. On the other hand, Norway maples, American elms, and other trees create dense shade making it difficult to grow grass or other plants

7-21. The shade of this Norway Maple, *Acer platanoides*, is dense and prevents grass growth below.

underneath. Some plants can also be selected to attract wildlife to the landscape. Birds in particular are attracted to the edible fruit of some trees and shrubs.

A final consideration involves the harsh growing conditions found in many urban centers. A consideration for plant selection in these areas is the tree's tolerance to pollution and salt. Ginkgo, red oak, and littleleaf linden are examples of trees tolerant of pollution. Honeylocust, goldenraintree, and green ash are three trees with salt tolerance. They would be appropriate where de-icing salts are used.

SHRUBS

Shrubs have multiple functions in the landscape. They can be used as specimen plants, group plantings, hedges, screens, foundation plants, or shrub borders. Select shrubs on their intended use. Also, consider their flowers, foliage, branching habits, and their suitability to the growing conditions. Many considerations discussed in the selection of trees apply to the selection of shrubs. A definition for different uses of shrubs follows:

7-22. This Ginkgo, *Ginkgo biloba*, shown in fall color is very resistant to pollution damage making it a good tree for city streets.

Specimen plants — A specimen plant displays outstanding form, texture, and color. Because of its qualities, it can stand alone. When placed with other plants in a grouping, it should be planted so it can be seen and enjoyed as an individual plant.

7-23. This Rhododendron displays outstanding characteristics and could be used as a specimen plant. (Courtesy, Midwest Groundcovers)

Group plantings — Group plantings consist of several different species of shrubs. The importance of each individual plant is lower within group plantings than it is with a specimen plant. The individuals of each species are located so they will overlap slightly with each other to form a mass or there may be some space left between the plants.

Interest in the design can be raised by the numbers of materials used. Use odd numbers of materials to create interest for the viewer. Design the plan using three, five, and seven shrubs together.

Hedges — Hedges consist of all one type of shrub. They define space, they tie other landscape elements together, and they may screen views. Some hedges are 20 feet tall while others may be only 1 foot in height. Hedges can be clipped for a formal appearance or they can be unclipped for an informal, natural look.

Screens — A screen is a solid mass of one type of shrub. It serves as a living wall that effectively blocks views. The ideal shrubs for use as screens are tall, narrow, upright plants.

Foundation plants — Foundation plants are shrubs placed around the foundation of the house. They help tie the house to the landscape by softening the corners, and they block the view of the foundation. It is best to use shrubs that do not get very large.

Shrub borders — A mass of many shrubs on the border of the property is called

7-24. Group plantings consist of several different species of shrubs and trees.

7-25. This clipped Eastern Arborvitae, *Thuja occidentalis*, hedge defines space, ties other landscape elements together, and screens views.

7-26. This row of rose shrubs serves as an effective screen. (Courtesy, Midwest Groundcovers)

7-27. Foundation plants are shrubs placed around the foundation of the house.

a shrub border. Shrub borders help to create the outdoor living room, screen views, and serve as a backdrop for annual and perennial flowers. Unlike the group planting, draw all the shrubs in the shrub border to touch or overlap one another to form a single mass.

7-28. A mass of many shrubs on the border of the property is called a shrub border. (Courtesy, R.S. Hursthouse & Associates, Inc.)

7-29. Flowers have high visual energy and must be used with caution in the residential landscape.

FLOWERS

Annual and perennial flowers provide an accent of color to the landscape. Accent is special emphasis provided by striking or prominent features of the landscape plants or structures. The bright flower and foliage colors are visually appealing. Because the colors attract the attention of the viewer, they must be used with caution.

Limit your use of flowers to the outdoor living area or in small numbers near the entry way in the public area. Remember, the house is the most important feature of the landscape. Bright-colored flowers can easily attract the attention of the viewer, which should be directed to the house. Flowers placed between foundation plants, lining driveways, and in island beds in the front lawn divert attention from the house and are considered poor design. A few flowers placed by the front door are acceptable as the flowers help to call attention to the door.

7-30. A few flowers placed by the front door help to call attention to the door.

7-31. Plant flowers in full view of the patio, deck, or interior rooms. (Courtesy, R.S. Hursthouse & Associates, Inc.)

In the outdoor living area, plant flowers in full view of the patio, deck, or interior rooms. Here, flowers can be enjoyed without detracting from the house. Again, be careful not to overwhelm the viewer with color. Use the flowers to create high interest areas within the design. Overuse of flowers disrupts the relaxing effect of the landscape achieved through the use of green plants.

It is best to use flowers in combination with woody plants. Design flower borders to be planted in front of woody plant materials or physical structures, such as fences or walls. The woody plants with green foliage provide a backdrop for the flowers. Place the taller flowers to the rear of the flower border and the shortest plants to the front. Plant the flowers in drifts of the same varieties. Drifts of color are bold in appearance and easy to "read." Avoid mixing individual flower varieties and colors within

7-32. This design has the flower border planted in front of a fence. (Courtesy, University of Illinois Cooperative Extension Service)

7-33. Plant flowers in drifts of the same varieties.

a flower bed. The spattering of different colors in a flower bed is difficult for the viewer to process because of its busy appearance.

Angled or incurved flower beds work best for designing a flower border. The bed pattern itself creates interest. Design the flower border to be no more than 5 feet in depth. This allows for easy maintenance, and view of all the flowering plants. The principles of design discussed in Chapter 6 apply to flower borders as well as woody plants. Warm color flowers are powerful and should be used sparingly in small landscapes as they tend to close in on the viewer. Also, observe the principle of sequence, and select flowers with colors that will provide a smooth transition from one

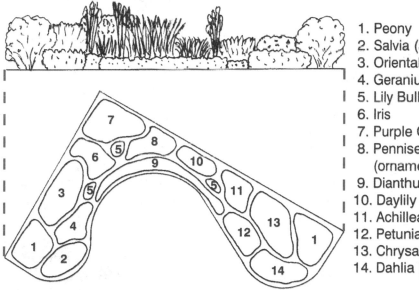

1. Peony
2. Salvia (annual)
3. Oriental Poppy
4. Geranium
5. Lily Bulbs
6. Iris
7. Purple Coneflower
8. Pennisetum (ornamental grass)
9. Dianthus
10. Daylily
11. Achillea
12. Petunia (annual)
13. Chrysanthemum
14. Dahlia (annual)

7-34. Angled or incurved flower beds work best for designing a flower border.

7-35. These tulips provide a welcome splash of color to the landscape in the spring. (Courtesy, Church Landscape)

drift to the next. Place coarse-textured flowering plants at the ends to provide strength and to frame the flowers in the incurve.

Flowers are seasonal. Their flower displays often provide only a few months of color. The length of time a flower bed shows color can be extended by applying a color rotation. With color rotation, there is a cycle of several floral displays in one growing season. In spring, the flower bed may display flowers of spring flowering bulbs, such as tulips, narcissus, and hyacinths. When the bulbs finish flowering, they are replaced with annuals including petunias, marigolds, and impatiens. A third planting occurs as temperatures drop in the fall. The fall bed might display chrysanthemums or ornamental cabbage.

DRAWING PLANTS INTO YOUR PLAN

Now that you have a greater understanding of the materials used in landscaping and their functions, you can begin design work with plants. Plant size is the next consideration in the design process. Bed patterns have been established in previous design steps. Now, draw the trees and shrubs on the plan. Locate all of the plants, except those trees placed in the lawn, within the planting beds. On the first draft of the landscape plan, draw circles that represent the different trees and shrubs. Detailed plant symbols can be drawn as the final plan is completed. A rough draft of the plan allows for erasures and some messiness as you try different solutions to the plan.

Draw the shrubs at their mature size in the planting beds. For instance, if you want a grouping of 6 foot shrubs, draw 3/4 inch (the same as 6/8 at 1/8 inch scale) circles using the circle template. Careful measurements obtained during the site analysis are very helpful in determining the size of foundation plantings. Too often, people place shrubs in the landscape while they are small without knowing that the plant has a natural tendency

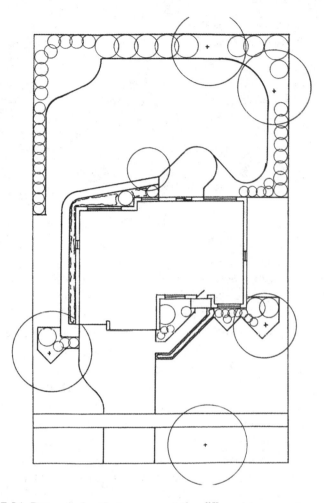

7-36. Draw circles that represent the different trees and shrubs at their mature size in the planting beds.

to get quite large. Some trees are extremely large at maturity. It is acceptable to use symbols smaller than the mature size of the larger trees to provide an easy-to-read plan.

Locate plants in the planting bed by placing the larger shrubs toward the back of the bed. Smaller plants should be placed in front of these. The smallest plant material should be to the front of the planting. Also, group plants of the same species by slightly overlapping your symbols. Shrubs that are planted close enough to one another to form a massing create a more attractive view than individual shrubs scattered throughout the planting bed.

Once the size of the plants has been decided, determine if the plants are to be evergreen, deciduous, or broadleaf evergreen. Then, assign each

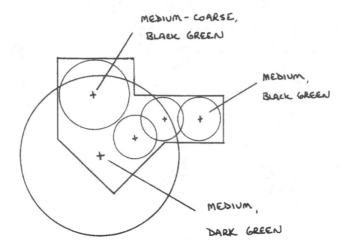

7-37. Assign each plant or grouping of one species a desired texture and color.

plant or grouping of one species a desired texture and color. Abbreviations for textures include: C – coarse, MC – medium coarse, M – medium, MF – medium fine, and F – fine. Abbreviations for colors include: G – emerald green, BLG – blue-green, YG – yellow-green, RG – red-green, GG – gray-green, and BG – black-green. As you choose these plant characteristics, keep the principles of design in mind.

The following step is to select the plants that fulfill the description you have established in the previous steps. Refer to reference books that describe woody plant materials. For example, you may have decided that the plan calls for a grouping of 6 foot shrubs that are of medium texture and emerald green. Looking at the reference materials, you find that the compact American cranberrybush viburnum (*Viburnum trilobum compactum*) and dwarf winged euonymus (*Euonymus alatus compactus*) are two plants with these characteristics. Consider other factors, such as hardiness, shade requirements, fall color, etc. before making your final choice.

7-38. Select the plants that fulfill the description you have established in the previous steps.

7-39. Use symbols to represent different types of plants on the final plan. (Courtesy, University of Illinois Cooperative Extension Service)

PLANT SYMBOLS

Up to now, all of your work has been rough and your plan is probably a bit messy. At this point, tape a piece of quality vellum over your rough plan. Take care to center the drawing. Trace the house walls and paved areas through to the clean paper. Now, trace the bed patterns. Slight changes may be necessary at this point to make a more functional and attractive design. The last items to trace are the plant symbols.

It is helpful to use symbols in your design work that represent the different types of plants. The symbol styles used vary from one designer

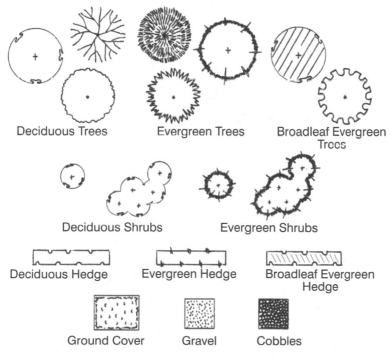

Deciduous Trees   Evergreen Trees   Broadleaf Evergreen Trees

Deciduous Shrubs   Evergreen Shrubs

Deciduous Hedge   Evergreen Hedge   Broadleaf Evergreen Hedge

Ground Cover   Gravel   Cobbles

7-40. Examples of plant symbols.

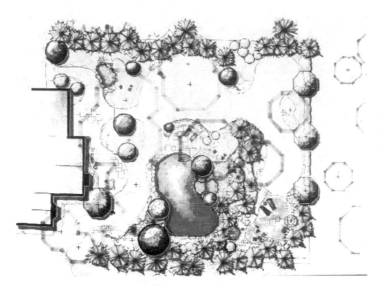

7-41. A plan drawn with final plant symbols. Notice how the color enhances the appearance. (Courtesy, R.S. Hursthouse & Associates, Inc.)

to the next. Most designers have developed their own symbols over the years. The style you adopt is not as important as whether the plan is easy to read and attractive. Keep in mind that many plans sell primarily because the customers find them attractive.

Use different symbols for the different types of plants in the plan. Draw evergreen plants, deciduous plants, broadleaf evergreens, ground covers, and vines with their own symbols. Be sure to indicate the center of all trees and shrubs. The plan can also be easier to read if the larger trees are drawn with a darker line than the smaller plants. The darker line gives the appearance of the tree providing a canopy over the other plants. Color can be added to the plan to provide higher interest.

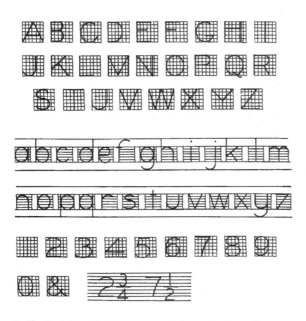

7-42. A style of letters and numbers that can be used for labeling.

LABELING

On the final plan, it is important to provide information that will make the plan easier to read. One piece of information that is critical is accurate labeling of the landscape materials. Try to keep the plan neat while labeling. Print

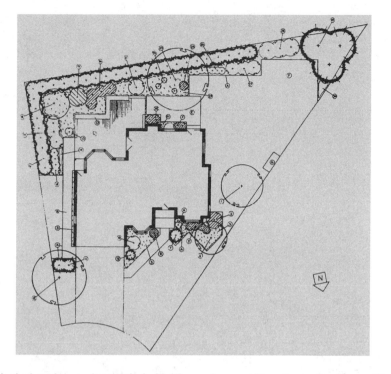

7-43. This design shows plants labeled with numbers and hardscape features with letters.

clearly, using upper case letters. Hand printing gives a personal touch to the plan. Labeling with computerized programs has benefits as well; the plan is often easier to read. Also, label the plan in an organized manner. The logical way to label is to begin at one point of the plan and move in a clockwise fashion. Each plant species can be assigned a number that corresponds to a master list to the side of the design. One list might be for plants alone. Another list could be used to identify hardscape features.

Other information needs to be identified on the plan. Note the client's name for whom the design is prepared in a title box. This might appear

THE THOMAS RESIDENCE		
SCALE: 1/8"=1'0"	APPROVED BY:	DESIGNED BY: PENTONY
DATE: 1/15/98		REVISED:
SHEET TITLE:	LANDSCAPE PLAN	
		DOCUMENT NUMBER:

7-44. An example of the title box for a plan.

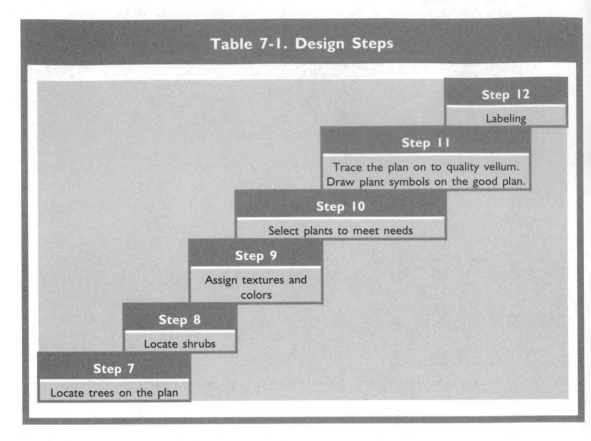

Table 7-1. Design Steps

Step 12
Labeling

Step 11
Trace the plan on to quality vellum.
Draw plant symbols on the good plan.

Step 10
Select plants to meet needs

Step 9
Assign textures and
colors

Step 8
Locate shrubs

Step 7
Locate trees on the plan

as 'The Thomas Residence.' Record the scale at which the design was drawn (for example, scale: 1/8 inch = 1'0"). Also, date the plan and include the designer's name. In an open area on the plan, indicate which direction is north in relation to the site. Any number of arrow symbols can be used.

REVIEWING

MAIN IDEAS

Plants are the major building blocks of the landscape. The plants used include trees, shrubs, ground covers, vines, annuals, and perennials. All plants have been given a Latin name. The two-part Latin name consisting of the genus and the specific epithet eliminates confusion that occurs with common names. The genus and species names are given based on the similarity of flowers, leaves, stems, and fruit.

Trees are the largest element of the landscape. Trees are placed on the landscape plan before other plants. A number of considerations go into the selection of specific trees. Consider the principles of design (line, form, texture, and color), the mature size, hardiness, and life expectancy. Consider the messiness, growth rate, insect and disease resistance, and pollution and salt tolerance of the tree. Also, consider soil conditions, safety factors, such as thorns, and shade effect.

Shrubs are used in greater numbers than trees. They also have many purposes. Specimen shrubs are those that are outstanding in their qualities of form, texture, and color. Group plantings consist of several different species of shrubs. A hedge is a row of shrubs that define space and may be clipped or unclipped. Shrubs of all one species that block a view are screens. Foundation plants are those planted in front of the house foundation. Shrub borders consist of many species of shrubs that have similar form, texture, and color creating the look of oneness.

Flowers add color to the landscape. Because of their bright colors, they need to be used with caution to avoid dominating the landscape. Avoid placing flowers in the public area as they divert attention away from the house. In the outdoor living area, place flowers in drifts within the shrub border. The shrubs provide a backdrop for the flowers.

Begin placing landscape plant materials on the rough draft of the plan using circles to represent the plants. Draw the circles to scale to establish the size plants needed. Next, assign qualities of design including texture and color to each plant or plant group. Once the plant characteristics have been established, use reference materials to select specific plants. On the final plan, draw the plant materials with symbols that help to differentiate the plant types.

QUESTIONS

Answer the following questions using correct spelling and complete sentences.

1. What are the types of plants used in the landscape? Describe each.
2. Why is the binomial system of plant nomenclature important?
3. How do varieties and cultivars differ?
4. What factors must be considered in selecting trees?
5. What are the major uses of shrubs in the landscape? Explain each.
6. Why is it difficult to use flowers in the public area?
7. Why is it important to draw plants at their mature size on the landscape plan?
8. What are the steps for selecting plants for the design beginning with the drawing of circles to choosing plant names?
9. Why are symbols used to represent different plant types?

CHAPTER SELF-CHECK

Match the term with the correct definition. Write the letter by the term in the blank provided.

a. hardiness   e. hedges   h. shade trees
b. genus   f. cultivar   i. annuals
c. shrubs   g. tree   j. ground cover
d. foundation plants

_____ 1. Refers to the ability of a plant to withstand cold temperatures

_____ 2. Plants that have distinguishing characteristics from the other plants in the species, but do not transfer those characteristics to their offspring through sexual reproduction

_____ 3. Multi-stem, woody plants that do not exceed 20 feet in height

_____ 4. A single-stem, woody, perennial plant reaching the height of 12 feet

_____ 5. Large trees, with spreading canopies, such as sugar maples, red oaks, and tuliptrees

_____ 6. Shrubs placed around the foundation of the house

_____ 7. All of one type of plant that can be clipped for a formal appearance or left unclipped for an informal, natural look

_____ 8. Herbaceous plants that live for one growing season and are valued for the color their flowers or ornamental foliage adds to the landscape

_____ 9. A closely related group of plants comprised of one or more species

_____10. Woody or herbaceous plants that form a mat less than 1 foot high covering the ground

EXPLORING

1. Locate plants on your rough landscape plan. Draw circles to scale to represent the trees and shrubs.

2. Determine if the plants are to be evergreen, deciduous, or broadleaf evergreens. Then, decide what texture and leaf color each type of plant should have.

3. Based on the sizes, textures, and colors established in the previous steps choose plants to fill the needs of your design. Use reference books to help you with the plant selection. Also, minor changes, such as adjusting size, texture, and color requirements, are permitted as you follow this process.

4. Place a piece of good quality vellum paper over your rough draft. Trace the design including the house, walks, driveway, patio, bed patterns and plants. As you trace the plants, use symbols that represent the different plant types.

8

Pricing the Plan

Money. Is money important to you? It probably is to landscape customers. Money, often hard earned, gives people an opportunity to have landscape work performed on their property. Naturally, customers would like the best materials available, quality service, and timely results for their money. Most customers will approach several landscape companies in search of the best price.

Money is definitely important to the landscaper as pay for services performed. Money received pays for salaries and other business expenses. Money allows the landscaper to stay in business. But what if the landscaper consistantly prices the work too high? Work may be lost to competitors. This chapter centers on methods of pricing landscape construction work.

8-1. Landscaping is a business.

OBJECTIVES

1. Define estimates and bids

2. Explain how to cost out a landscape plan

3. Describe landscape specifications

4. Calculate amounts of landscape materials identified in a plan

5. Determine how to estimate labor requirements

6. Explain how to mark up prices to allow for overhead, contingency costs, and profit

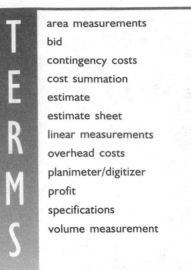

TERMS

area measurements
bid
contingency costs
cost summation
estimate
estimate sheet
linear measurements
overhead costs
planimeter/digitizer
profit
specifications
volume measurement

DETERMINING THE PRICE OF LANDSCAPE PROJECTS

Work for the designer is not limited to the design of the landscape plan. The landscape designer is also involved in determining the price of landscape work. Pricing of landscape work involves two common business procedures. The two terms used for these procedures are the estimate and the bid.

ESTIMATE

An *estimate* is an approximate price for the work to be done. The estimate includes the cost for materials and labor. The materials needed for the project must be counted. The number of workers required and the time it takes them to complete the project are also calculated. Experience in the industry is of great help to the designer in determining an estimate, because the designer must anticipate the costs for the entire project. Depending on the importance or the size of the project, the designer may spend anywhere from minutes to hours to complete an estimate.

The estimate is presented to the customer as a proposal as discussed in chapter 2. The price quoted in an estimate is flexible. The final cost to the customer may change as actual costs are learned. Sometimes, the landscape installation takes longer than expected or additional materials are needed that alter the cost of the project. It is important for the customer to understand that the price may change because of these unanticipated

8-2. Shown are the designer and the owner of a landscape company discussing the price of a landscape project.

costs. The advantage of the estimate is it gives the customer an idea as to the cost of the landscape project.

BID

A **bid** is a fixed price placed on the landscape work to be done. A bid differs from an estimate in that the bid price cannot be changed once it is accepted without the agreement of the customer. Bids are common when more than one company is competing for a particular project. Each company may prepare and submit a bid based on their estimated costs. Usually the low bid wins the customer's business.

Because bidding is competitive, landscapers must take care not to lower their offer so much that they lose money. Over the long term, landscape companies that lose money through low bids lower the value of the landscape industry. If it happens often enough, the companies go out of business. Therefore, landscapers must take great care to perform accurate calculations for bids to assure a fair profit.

LANDSCAPE SPECIFICATIONS

To establish the accurate pricing of a job, the designer must first specify what the project includes. **Specifications** are written descriptions of landscape materials, work, and time schedules for a project. Specifications include the details of the project. Some examples are the size of each plant, the number of plants, the depth of the mulch, instructions for soil amendments, and the installation techniques for the patio.

The quality of landscape materials can vary widely. Individual plant species of the same size may command different prices. A 3-inch Sugar Maple, *Acer saccharum*, is less expensive than a patented cultivar, such as the Green Mountain Sugar Maple. Of course, the Green Mountain Sugar Maple has been selected for outstanding characteristics. The price of the tree also hinges on the care it received while it was being grown. A high-quality Green Mountain Sugar Maple pruned properly during its development will have an attractive and sound branching structure. The same type of maple not given equal attention could have a poor branching structure making it less valuable.

The quality of landscape materials extends to the hardscape materials. Wood and stone used in the landscape are available in different grades of quality. The highest grades hold the highest prices. Similarly, highly skilled laborers can demand higher prices based on the superior quality of their work.

Although specifications are in writing, it is usually necessary to verbally express these to the customer. The additional explanations clear up speci-

8-3. The value of plant material depends on the variety selected as well as the manner in which it was grown.

fications that may be unclear to the customer. It also gives the landscaper the opportunity to explain the differences in quality of materials and work.

ESTIMATE PREPARATION

The preparation of an estimate can be made easier with a landscape construction **estimate sheet.** An estimate sheet is a form for calculating prices. It helps if the same form is used for each project. Many landscapers use computer spreadsheets to speed the preparation of estimates. On the estimate sheet, the designer can record material descriptions, quantities, material costs, labor costs, cost for site preparation, and total costs. Table 8-1 shows a sample estimate sheet. Consider the wide range of material costs and prices from one region to another as you study the sample estimate sheet.

CALCULATING COSTS

A number of factors need to be taken into account in calculating installation costs. They include labor costs, material costs, overhead costs, contingency costs, and profit.

1. The anticipated cost for both labor and materials should be listed in detail. Use the actual wages the employees will be paid and the cost of the materials purchased wholesale.

2. **Overhead costs** are the general costs in running a business. Examples include: mortgage or lease payments, legal fees, utilities, insurance, office expenses, and maintenance of equipment. To obtain the overhead multiply the total for labor and materials by 20 percent.

Table 8-1. A Sample Estimate Sheet

LANDSCAPE CONSTRUCTION ESTIMATE SHEET

JOB NAME   DATE
JOB LOCATION   DESIGNER
JOB DESCRIPTION

Description	Quantity	Material Unit Cost	Total Material Cost	Total Labor Cost ($15.00/hr)	Total Labor and Material Costs
Plant List					
Acer saccharum, 'Green Mountain,' 3" B&B	3	275.00	825.00	90.00	915.00
Fothergilla gardenii, 3 gallon container	12	16.00	192.00	60.00	252.00
Sod	235 yds	1.10	285.50	81.25 (.25/yard)	438.75
Hedera helix, 'Thorndale,' 3" pot	300	0.58	174.00	45.00	219.00
Construction Materials					
Finish grading of site				525.00	525.00
Brick pavers, 6 cm	1230	1.61	1,980.30		1,980.30
Sand, construction grade, 2" deep	3 tons	5.00	15.00		15.00
Gravel, grade 8, 3" deep	4 tons	6.00	24.00		24.00
Landscape fabric, 3' × 50' roll	3 rolls	9.95	29.85		29.85
Patio installation	300 sq. ft.		369.50	900.00 ($3/sq. ft.)	900.00
Florida cypress mulch, 4" deep	10 yds	36.95		90.00	459.50
Subtotal Costs (total materials and labor costs)				$1,791.25	$5,758.40
	Overhead Costs (subtotal material and labor costs × 20%)				$1,151.68
	Contingency Costs (overhead + subtotal materials and labor × 10%)				$691.00
	Cost Summation (subtotal material and labor costs + overhead + contingency)				$7,601.08
	Profit (cost summation × 20%)				$1,520.22
	TOTAL (cost summation + profit)				$9,121.30

3. A ***contingency costs*** should be figured into all jobs. This accounts for theft of materials on the work site, mechanical breakdowns, rainouts, etc. The contingency charge may vary from job to job. An accepted charge is to multiply the overhead plus labor and materials by 10 percent.

4. Add the labor, materials, overhead, and contingency charges to obtain a ***cost summation.***

5. ***Profit*** is the amount of money the landscaper receives after deducting all costs of the project. The mark up for profit is included on the estimate sheet. A fair mark up for profit is 20 percent. Multiply the cost summation by 20 percent to determine the profit.

6. Total cost for the project is the addition of the summation costs and the profit.

MATHEMATICAL COMPUTATIONS FOR THE LANDSCAPE

LABOR REQUIREMENTS

The landscaper calculates the amount of time required to complete a job. The unit of measurement for time is hours. Labor requirements are calculated on how many hours are required to do a specific function, whether it is by an individual or a crew. This calculation is applied to all phases of the planting plan in order to estimate the amount of time the job will take to complete. The size and capability of the landscape crew largely determines the amount of time required.

An example for calculating a sod job follows. Each landscape crew member installs 100 sq. yd. of sod per hour. Divide the total number of yards of sod needed for the landscape job by 100 sq. yd. per worker hour. The total number of hours required to install the sod is calculated with a simple formula.

$$\frac{\text{sq. yd. of sod needed}}{100 \text{ sq. yd. per worker hour}} = \underline{\hspace{2cm}} \text{ total worker hours to install sod}$$

How many worker hours will be needed to install 1,500 square yards of sod?

$$\frac{1,500 \text{ sq. yd. of sod needed}}{100 \text{ sq. yd./per worker hour}} = 15 \text{ total worker hours to install sod}$$

Similar labor calculations would be made for grading soil, planting trees and shrubs, installing brick patios, and other construction tasks. Estimating landscape costs requires basic mathematical skills. Besides counting the total number of plants to be installed, the designer needs to be able to determine accurate measurements for hardscape materials. This involves linear, area, and volume measurements.

8-4. Edging is measured in linear feet.

8-5. Sod is measured by the square yard or yard.

LINEAR MEASUREMENTS

Linear measurements are the measurements made of a line. Linear measurements are one-dimensional. Most linear measurements are made in feet, referred to as linear feet. A common linear measurement in the landscape involves edging for the planting beds. The total length of the bed outline needs to be learned before edging materials can be purchased or a cost estimated.

Measurement of linear feet on a design is done with a scale. It usually involves making a series of measurements and adding them to get a total. On plans with curving lines, a nylon string is sometimes used. The string is laid over the curving lines, straightened, and measured with a scale.

AREA MEASUREMENTS

Area measurements are those made of the surface. They are two-dimensional. The common units of area measure are square feet and square yards. An example of the use of area involves the number of square yards (yards for short) of sod required for a lawn. Other examples include the number of square feet in a brick patio and the number of square feet to be planted with ground covers.

Area measurements require the use of a scale and some basic geometry. Some examples follow:

1. Areas of rectangles and squares are equal to the length times the width.

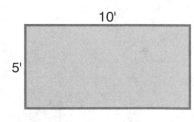

L × W = Area
10' × 5' = 50 square feet

2. Areas of triangles are equal to ½ the base times the height.

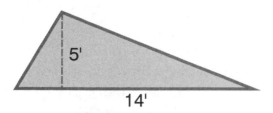

½ × (base × height) = Area
½ × (14 × 5) = 35 square feet

3. Areas of circles are equal to the radius squared times pi. The radius (r) is half the diameter of the circle, and pi is a constant at 3.14.

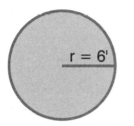

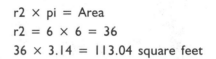

r2 × pi = Area
r2 = 6 × 6 = 36
36 × 3.14 = 113.04 square feet

VOLUME MEASUREMENTS

Volume measurements are the measure of size or amount in three-dimensions. The units of measure for volume in landscape applications are cubic feet or cubic yards (yards for short). Some materials measured by volume include soil, sand, gravel, and mulch. A common problem is determining the number of cubic yards of mulch needed to cover the planting beds. This type of problem requires some computations. Mulch is usually spread 3 to 4 inches deep, but is sold by the cubic yard.

The space that is measured is most often contained in a rectangle. The volume of a rectangle is learned by multiplying the length × the width × the height.

8-6. Peat moss is sold by the cubic foot.

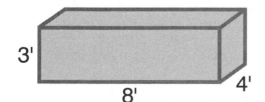

Length × width × height = volume
8' × 4' × 3' = 96 cubic feet

Planimeter/Digitizer

Some landscape companies use a computer device called a ***Planimeter/ Digitizer*** to accurately and quickly calculate linear feet, area, and volume. The device saves a great deal of labor by reducing hand measurements. By moving the arm of the Planimeter/Digitizer from various points on the design, linear feet, area, and volume are calculated. Because of the expense of the device, it is used primarily with large landscape plans.

8-7. This person is using a Planimeter/Digitizer to cost out a plan.

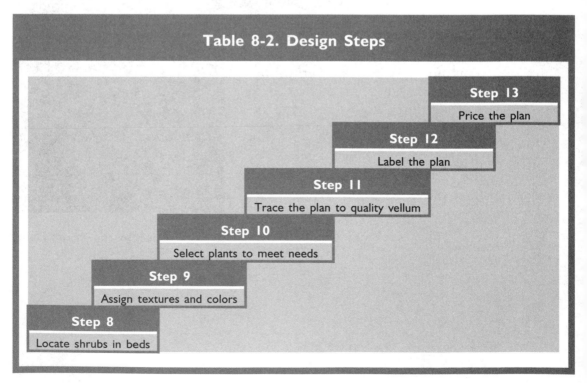

Table 8-2. Design Steps

| Step 13 |
| Price the plan |

| Step 12 |
| Label the plan |

| Step 11 |
| Trace the plan to quality vellum |

| Step 10 |
| Select plants to meet needs |

| Step 9 |
| Assign textures and colors |

| Step 8 |
| Locate shrubs in beds |

REVIEWING

MAIN IDEAS

Landscaping is a business in which money is exchanged for landscaping services. The designer of the landscape plans is usually the one with the task of pricing a project. An approximate price for the project can be given to the customer as an estimate. The final price may change from the original estimate if unforeseen costs arise. A bid, on the other hand, is a fixed price that cannot be changed without the consent of the customer. Bids are used when more than one landscaper is competing for a particular job.

The landscaper must specify what is involved in the landscape project. Specifications include written descriptions of landscape materials, work, and time schedules for a project. Some details of the project to be listed as specifications are the size of each plant, the number of plants, the depth of the mulch, instructions for soil amendments, and the installation techniques for the patio. Specifications can be placed on an estimate sheet. Overhead and profit are included on the estimate sheet along with material totals and costs.

In determining landscape costs, the landscaper must be able to use basic mathematical computations. Three common measurements are linear, area, and volume. Linear measurements are one-dimensional. Area measurements are two-dimensional and units used are square foot and square yard. Volume is the measure of space in three-dimensions. Units of measure associated with volume are cubic foot and cubic yard. A computer device called a Planimeter/Digitizer is used to measure linear feet, area, and volume.

QUESTIONS

Answer the following questions using correct spelling and complete sentences.

1. What is the difference between an estimate and a bid?
2. How do specifications relate to estimates and bids?
3. Why is it important to add overhead costs to the price of the project?
4. What is considered a fair profit?
5. Why are mathematical calculations important in preparing a landscape project estimate?
6. How are linear measurements made?
7. How are area measurements made?
8. How are volume measurements made?
9. What is a Planimeter/Digitizer?

CHAPTER SELF-CHECK

Match the term with the correct definition. Write the letter by the term in the blank provided.

a. volume measurements   e. profit   h. Planimeter/Digitizer
b. bid   f. estimate   i. overhead
c. estimate sheet   g. specifications   j. area measurements
d. linear measurements

_____ 1. Measurements made of the surface that are two-dimensional

_____ 2. A form used for calculating prices for each project

_____ 3. The general costs in running a business

_____ 4. An approximate price for the work to be done

_____ 5. One-dimensional measurement of a line.

_____ 6. The amount of money the landscaper receives after deducting all costs of the project

_____ 7. A fixed price placed on the landscape work to be done

_____ 8. Computer device used to accurately and quickly calculate linear feet, area, and volume

_____ 9. Written descriptions of landscape materials, work, and time schedules for a project

_____ 10. The measure of size or amount in three-dimensions

EXPLORING

1. Develop your own estimate sheet and price your landscape plan. Practice your skills in measuring linear feet, area, and volume. Use landscape supply company catalogs and nursery catalogs to obtain material prices. Your instructor can help you with pricing for labor. Do not forget to add overhead costs and a profit to your total. Are you surprised with your results?

2. Visit with local landscapers. Ask them how they go about preparing bids and estimates. What techniques do they use to ensure that their overhead costs, contingency costs, and profit are covered?

9

Preparing the Site for Planting

Once a landscape has been planned, proper installation is needed. The planting plan must be carried out. A landscape often includes more than plants. Fences, paved areas, walls, lighting, and other features may be used to enhance a landscape. Proper installation of these features makes a landscape attractive, long lasting, and functional for the homeowners.

What tools and equipment are going to be needed? Where are the trees and shrubs to be planted? Where are existing utility lines located? Will grading be required? What is the condition of the soil? These are some of the questions that need to be answered when preparing the site for planting.

9-1 Establishing landscapes includes landforms, pavements, constructed features, water, and plantings.

OBJECTIVES

1. Interpret specifications of a planting plan
2. Identify landscape construction tools and equipment
3. Measure and calculate the slope of a hillside
4. Establish proper elevations and grade a landscape site
5. Locate existing utilities
6. Determine the need for soil cut and fill
7. Describe staking the landscape site
8. Determine the texture and percolation characteristics of the soil
9. Describe proper landscape bed preparation
10. Discuss the elements necessary for good plant growth

TERMS

acidic
alkaline
berm
capillary water
cut
fill
final grade
grading
gravitational water
hardscape
hygroscopic water
infiltration
J.U.L.I.E.
landscape construction
leaching
nursery
nutrient
percolation
permeable
pH scale
planting bed
planting plan
pore spaces
rough grade
soil
soil amendments
soil structure
soil texture
staking the site
terrain

LANDSCAPE PLANNING AND CONSTRUCTION

Landscape plans for newly constructed homes may call for grass, trees, shrubs, fences, and patios. Landscape workers, not house construction workers, perform construction work outside the house. The same general design and construction steps apply in landscaping the yard as in building a new house. Developing a house plan starts the house construction process. After developing a planting plan, the outdoor phase of landscape construction is ready to begin. *Landscape construction* is the execution of the planting plan and installation of hardscape features.

9-2. A tree spade may be needed to install large trees.

Landscape contractors do many more tasks besides planting trees and shrubs. Today, they must also construct and install a variety of hard goods, such as patios, decks, walks, fences, walls, and fountains. The term *hardscaping*, first used during the 1970s, describes installing nonplant landscape features, such as fences, patios, walks, pools, and walls. Some landscape contractors may specialize in only one or two types of landscape installation. However, most landscape contractors plant trees, shrubs, install patios, and build fences.

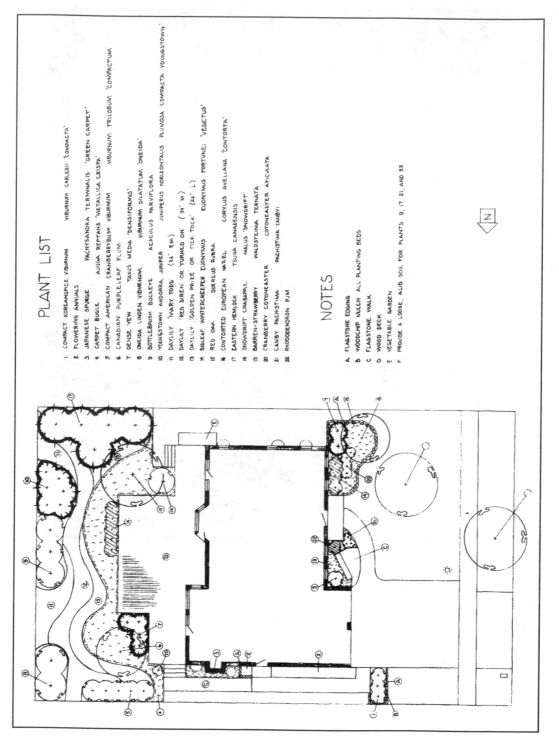

PLANT LIST

1. COMPACT KOREANSPICE VIBURNUM — VIBURNUM CARLESII 'COMPACTA'
2. FLOWERING ANNUALS
3. JAPANESE SPURGE — PACHYSANDRA TERMINALIS 'GREEN CARPET'
4. CARPET BUGLE — AJUGA REPTANS 'METALLICA CRISPA'
5. COMPACT AMERICAN CRANBERRYBUSH VIBURNUM — VIBURNUM TRILOBUM 'COMPACTUM'
6. CANADIAN PURPLELEAF PLUM
7. DENSE YEW — TAXUS MEDIA 'DENSIFORMIS'
8. ONEIDA LINDEN VIBURNUM — VIBURNUM DILATATUM 'ONEIDA'
9. BOTTLEBRUSH BUCKEYE — AESCULUS PARVIFLORA
10. YOUNGSTOWN ANDORRA JUNIPER — JUNIPERUS HORIZONTALIS PLUMOSA COMPACTA YOUNGSTOWN
11. DAYLILY 'MARY TODD' (24" EM)
12. DAYLILY 'RED SIREN' OR 'TURNED ON' (34" M)
13. DAYLILY 'GOLDEN PRIZE' OR 'TICK TOCK' (26" L)
14. BIGLEAF WINTERCREEPER EUONYMUS — EUONYMUS FORTUNEI 'VEGETUS'
15. RED OAK — QUERCUS RUBRA
16. CONTORTED EUROPEAN HAZEL — CORYLUS AVELLANA 'CONTORTA'
17. EASTERN HEMLOCK — TSUGA CANADENSIS
18. SNOWDRIFT CRABAPPLE — MALUS 'SNOWDRIFT'
19. BARREN-STRAWBERRY — WALDSTEINIA TERNATA
20. CRANBERRY COTONEASTER — COTONEASTER APICULATA
21. CANBY PACHISTIMA — PACHISTIMA CANBYI
22. RHODODENDRON P.J.M.

NOTES

A. FLAGSTONE EDGING
B. WOODCHIP MULCH ALL PLANTING BEDS
C. FLAGSTONE WALK
D. WOOD DECK
E. VEGETABLE GARDEN
F. PROVIDE A LOOSE, ACID SOIL FOR PLANTS 9, 17, 21, AND 22

9-3. Planting plan for a residence.

THE PLANTING PLAN

The landscape designer talked with the homeowner about their specific outdoor needs, desires, and problems. The landscape designer through the design process developed a *planting plan* which shows the exact location for plant materials, includes a plant materials list, and hardscape features. Contours and spot elevations may also be shown on the planting plan. Landscape contractors use the planting plan to install the hardscape features and plant the trees, shrubs, and flowers as illustrated.

Nurseries grow many different varieties of trees, shrubs, and bedding plants used by the landscape contractor. In the past, most landscape companies grew the plant material, drew the plans, and installed the plants. Today, many landscape companies specialize in only one phase of the landscape business.

LANDSCAPE TOOLS AND EQUIPMENT

Landscape contractors need a wide variety of tools and equipment to prepare the site for planting and to install plant materials. Proper preparation and installation techniques are essential in executing the planting plan. If the landscape contractor does not have a particular tool or piece of equipment, it may have to be rented or that portion of the job subcontracted.

When using tools or operating equipment, safe practices should be followed. Follow manufacturers' guidelines for operating equipment and power tools. Tools and equipment must be maintained and kept clean if they are to save time and function properly. Some good tool and machine operation tips include:

- Read and follow owner's manual recommendations

- Perform daily maintenance procedures.

- Check the condition of the tool or equipment before starting.

- Warm up the engine before operating.

- Operate at safe speeds.

- Check instrument readings while in operation.

- Select the proper tool or machine for each job.

Framing square

Combination square

Hacksaw

Wheelbarrow

Level

Shears

Circular saw

Soil ball cart

Cutter mattock

Sabre saw

Electric drill

Garden trowel

Chainsaw

Rotary spreader

Mallet

Crosscut saw

Garden hoe

Garden rake

Leaf rake

Shovel

Spade

Masonary trowel

Claw hammer

Bow saw

Skid-steer loader

Backhoe with front-end loader

9-4. Some tools and equipment used in landscape construction.

SITE CHARACTERISTICS AND THE PLANTING PLAN

Implementing the planting plan, while dealing with the unique characteristics of a site, is the responsibility of the landscape contractor. The landscape designer worked within the boundaries of nature when altering the landforms. Usually, there will be some alteration needed at the site.

TERRAIN

The landscape site is seldom flat. Areas that appear to be level usually do slope in one direction or the other. **Terrain** describes the rise and fall of land (hills and valleys). **Topography** is a record of an area's terrain. Some slope is necessary to allow excess surface water from rain and snow to drain. Medium to large hills allow the landscape designer many opportunities to create unusual landscapes. Many outdoor activities need flat surfaces, while slopes can provide interesting visual experiences in the landscape.

A landscape contractor shows a slope as a percent relating the vertical rise of the land to the flat horizontal distance. Use the following formula to determine the slope.

$$\frac{\text{Vertical Distance}}{\text{Horizontal Distance}} \times 100 = \text{percent slope}$$

Measuring a Slope

Use a 48-inch level and a yard stick to measure slope. Put one end of the level on the hillside (slope) and raise the other end until the bubble is in the center of the leveling vial. The level will now be level with the earth surface. Use the yard stick and measure the distance from the ground to the bottom edge of the level. Measure both distances in inches, not feet. Determine the percent slope of the hill with this formula.

9-5. One slope measuring technique.

$$\frac{\text{Vertical Distance}}{\text{Horizontal Distance}} \times 100 = \text{percent slope}$$

Example: A vertical distance of 15 inches was measured using the 48-inch level.

$$\frac{15}{48} \times 100 = 31 \text{ percent slope}$$

A transit and target rod is another method used by landscape contractors to measure a slope.

Landscape Activities and Slope

The ideal and the maximum slope percentage for several common components in the landscape are shown in Table 9-1. These are not exact percentages, but serve as a guide to determine how dif-

9-6. Landscape planting beds and lawn on a slope.

Table 9-1. Recommended Slope Percent for Different Landscape Components

Landscape Component	Ideal Slope Percent	Maximum Slope Percent
Decks and patios	$1/2$ to 1	3
Lawns	2 to 3	5
Walks	1 to 4	8
Driveways	1 to 10	11
Slopes with landscape plants	20 to 30	50
Wheelchair ramp	3 to 5	8
Steps	33 to 50	66

ferent slopes can be used in the landscape. The percentages are also a guide for changing the slope with grading to allow for different activities.

SURVEYING

In the past, landscape surveying dealt with marking property boundaries and dividing farm land into small city lots for home construction. Today, surveying skills help establish the elevation of patios, the leveling retaining wall foundations, and the layout of drainage systems according to the landscape plan. These skills can also help the landscape contractor establish the correct slopes for a variety of outdoor activities. The transit and target rod surveying instruments are used to determine the present elevation and establish new ones.

Proper drainage of surface water is essential to a well designed landscape. Most plants do not grow well in poorly drained soil. Install an underground drain tile system to remove the extra water from the soil. Surveying skills can help the landscaper correctly grade drainage tile trenches to provide good water flow in the tile.

9-7. Transit and target rod used to establish elevation.

Standing water from excessive surface runoff can result in temporary ponds that limit the use of the landscape site. Use surveying instruments to construct slopes that will direct water away from buildings and into natural drainage areas. Establish a 1 or 2 percent slope to help surface water drain from the house, patio, walk, and driveway.

LOCATING UNDERGROUND UTILITIES

Two days before starting a landscape job, the crew supervisor should call the Joint Utility Location and Information Exchange, *J.U.L.I.E.* J.U.L.I.E. will find and mark all underground utilities at the construction site. Most state laws require contractors to call J.U.L.I.E. before digging.

GRADING

Grading involves the moving of soil and the reshaping of the land.

9-8. Underground telephone lines in a landscape bed marked with flags.

Adding soil to the landscape site is called a *fill* or filling. Removing soil from the site is known as a *cut.* Grade the site to improve drainage patterns, to create an interesting land appearance, and to ensure healthy plant growth. Grading can also make sites with steep slopes more useful for a variety of outdoor activities. Landscapers follow the planting plan and cut and/or fill to establish the desired grade recommended on the plan.

Remove and stockpile the topsoil at the construction site before starting any major grading projects. The subsoil can then be reshaped using a skid-steer loader or a backhoe with a front-end loader to create the rough grade. The *rough grade* is establishing the approximate grade or slope of the terrain that should closely parallel the proposed final grade. The *final grade* is leveling to a smooth appearance by breaking the soil clumps into marble-sized particles, which makes the surface suitable for planting and seeding. It is the elevation of the soil surface after completing all grading operations. Rough grading an area will change the natural drainage patterns and can severely damage existing tree root systems. Keep the on-site topography in harmony with the surrounding properties.

9-9. A skid-steer loader being used to level the soil to rough grade at a construction site.

Establishing adequate new drainage patterns should be the number one priority when rough grading a landscape site. Surface water should drain away from buildings but cannot be diverted onto neighboring property. Grade the soil around homes so that there is a 2 to 4 percent slope away from the house to reduce the chance of flooding or seepage into the

9-10. Poor land-scape grading cre-ates small ponds of water.

structure. Construct concave depressions or channels called swales to carry surface water away from buildings. Some sites may need catch basins and drain tiles installed to improve drainage.

After completing the rough grade, spread a 3- to 6-inch layer of topsoil, from the stockpile, on the rough graded subsoil and establish the final grade. Use a transit and target rod to measure the exact final grade elevation prior to planting grass seed or plants. The elevation in feet will be found on the landscape planting plan.

This grading should be done when weather conditions are dry. The soil structure can be destroyed if heavy equipment is used on wet soil. Rototill the soil to break up soil clumps into marble-sized particles before smoothing the surface. Small areas can be hand raked while box-scrapers or gills will be needed for large landscape sites to smooth the surface and establish the final grade.

Special Landscape Effects

Proper grading to the designer's plan can create many special landscape effects. The plan may call for mounds of soil called **berms**. Berms give a flat landscape site an added dimension of height and change the ordinary into the unusual. A berm of any significant size requires large quantities of soil. If the berm is to be mowed, usually the slope will not exceed 33 percent. Berms provide interesting landforms immediately useful and visible in the landscape. Ponds are another example of special landscape effects

9-11. Berms add interest to the landscape.

created from grading. People often enjoy the sight and sound of water in the landscape.

STAKING THE SITE

Landscape plans usually do not have measurements. The construction supervisor must use a scale and measure the exact location of each plant. Most landscape plans are drawn using a $1/8'' = 1'- 0''$ architect scale. The supervisor using the $1/8''$ scale takes measurements to determine the exact location of each plant on the plan. Transferring the measurements from the planting plan to the outside ground to show the location of each plant is the next step.

9-12. A landscape crew beginning to install plant materials after the site has been staked.

The landscape supervisor will usually stake the site the day before the crew is scheduled on the job. To **stake the site,** the plant name is written on small wooden or plastic stakes and the stakes are driven into the ground to show the exact center of each planting hole. This shows the crew members where to dig and what to plant. Besides staking plant material location, the supervisor will also locate the patio, walls, fences, and other hard material with stakes.

SOIL

Soil means different things to different people. Some people think of soil as dirt, the material to wash from clothes or sweep up from the floor. To an agronomist or soil scientist, **soil** is that part of the earth's crust in which the root system of a plant grows. Soil supplies mineral elements and water and provides a means of support for plants throughout the world. Mineral particles and organic matter make up the solid part of soil, while the holes in the soil are called **pore spaces**.

9-13. Nearly half of a plant grows under the ground. (Courtesy, Agricultural Research Service, USDA)

SOIL FUNCTIONS

Compare soil to a sponge used to wash a car. The sponge has solid parts but it also has many holes that can fill with water. An ideal soil will have 50 percent solid material and 50 percent pore space. When the sponge is dry, its holes are filled with air, but when dipped in a bucket of water the air is replaced with the water. The pore spaces in soil can hold water, air, or some of both. Plant roots not only need water but also air for good growth. Therefore, the best soil for plant growth will have its pore space half full of water and half full of air. The total pore space is not as important as the size of the pore space (hole). Small pore spaces hold water while the larger ones hold air. Mineral particles that make up the soil will determine the size of the pore spaces.

Drainage

When there is rainfall, water either enters the soil or flows off the soil as surface drainage. A soil with good texture and structure will absorb a great deal of rainfall. The process of the water soaking into the soil is known as *infiltration.* Once in the soil, the water moves downward. The downward movement of water through the soil is known as *percolation.* In heavy rainfall, the pore spaces of soil fill up more quickly than water can drain through the soil. When this occurs, and all pore spaces are filled with water, the soil is considered saturated. Additional rainwater forms puddles or flows downhill on the surface of the soil. A quality soil that allows water movement by infiltration and percolation is said to be *permeable.*

Water found in soils is placed into one of three categories. The categories are gravitational water, capillary water, and hygroscopic water.

After a rain, much of the water drains down through the soil through the pore spaces. This is called *gravitational water* because gravity pulls the water down. The water ends up in the ground water below the soil surface. Gravitational water flows quickly through sandy soils that have large pore spaces and more slowly through clay soils with tiny pore spaces.

As gravitational water moves through the soil, it carries with it dissolved minerals, chemicals, and salts. This process is known as *leaching.* The soil texture will determine how quickly minerals, chemicals, and salts are

Soil particles

Pore spaces

9-14. Pore spaces are the openings between solid soil particles.

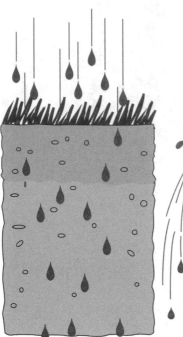 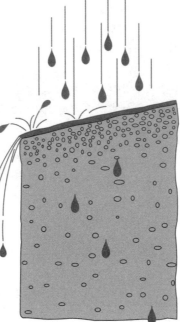 

Soil with high organic matter content and good structure permits water

Hard-packed surface soil plus impermeable subsoil prevents absorption.

Rock layer prevents water from soaking deeply into soil.

9-15. Permeable soil allows water to infiltrate and percolate.

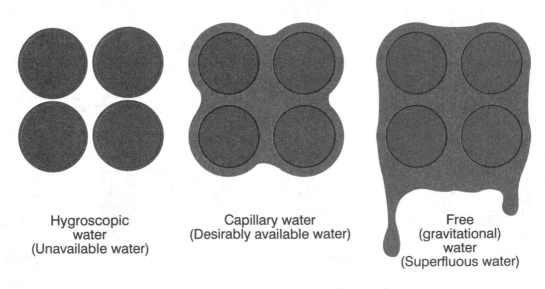

Hygroscopic water
(Unavailable water)

Capillary water
(Desirably available water)

Free
(gravitational)
water
(Superfluous water)

9-16. Three types of water are found in soils.

leached, or washed, through a soil. Because of leaching, plants grown on sandy soils need more frequent fertilizer applications.

Capillary water is a second type of water. It is also the water that plants are most able to use. ***Capillary water*** is the water held between the soil particles against the force of gravity. This water can move through a soil upwards or sideways by capillary action. As surface soil dries out, some water moves up into the open pore spaces by capillary action. Clay soils have a greater number of pore spaces than sandy soils. Therefore, they hold more capillary water.

A third type of soil water is called hygroscopic water. ***Hygroscopic water*** is the water that forms a thin film around individual soil particles. Even the driest soils have hygroscopic water. Plants are unable to absorb and use this type of water.

Air

Air is also found in the pore spaces. Roughly 25 percent of the total soil volume will be air. After a rain, many of the pore spaces are filled with water. As that water drains away, air fills the pore spaces. In dry soils, air may take up the majority of the pore spaces. Sandy soils with large pore spaces tend to be well-aerated. Clay soils with their tiny pore spaces often are not well-drained and have a smaller percentage of air.

Most plants perform best when there is a balance between water and air in a soil. Sandy soils are loose and well-aerated, but do not hold water very well. Clay soils hold water, but are not well-aerated. Soils that have a mix of sand, silt, and clay tend to be both well-drained and well-aerated, which is good for plant growth.

SOIL STRUCTURE

Sand, silt, clay, and organic matter particles in a soil combine with one another to form larger particles of various shapes and sizes. These larger particles are often referred to as soil aggregates. The way in which soil aggregates are arranged is referred to as ***soil structure.*** There are eight categories of soil structure, including blocky, columnar, crumb, granular, platy, prismatic, single grain, and massive.

Soil structure affects water and air movement in a soil, nutrient availability for plants, root growth, and microorganism activity. The pore spaces

Granular

Crumb

Platy

Prismatic

Massive

Columnar

Blocky

Single grain

9-17. Soil structure categories.

created by the larger soil particles are larger than those in-between individual particles of sand, silt, or clay. This allows for greater air and water movement, better root growth, and open passageways for small animals. The aggregates are also better able to hold water and nutrients.

Soil structure can be destroyed. A major cause of damage is driving heavy equipment over wet soil. Damage is also caused by working soil when it is either too wet or too dry. These conditions lead to the clay particles clogging up the pore spaces. The soil becomes compacted, very dense, and when it dries, it becomes very hard. It is very difficult for most plants to survive in a soil whose structure has been destroyed. Soil structure can be improved by adding organic matter.

Soil Texture

The mineral particles of soil are arranged according to size from very fine to very coarse. *Soil texture* refers to the proportion of sand, silt, and clay particles. Clay describes the smallest soil particle usually less than .002 mm in diameter. Sand particles are large compared to clay with a diameter from .05 to .5 mm. Silt particles are smaller than sand, but larger than clay particles, and have a diameter from .002 to .05 mm. Soil texture affects the retention of water and the rate that water moves into the soil after a rain. Loam soils have approximately equal parts of sand and silt with a low percent of clay. Most landscape plants grow best in a loam-type soil.

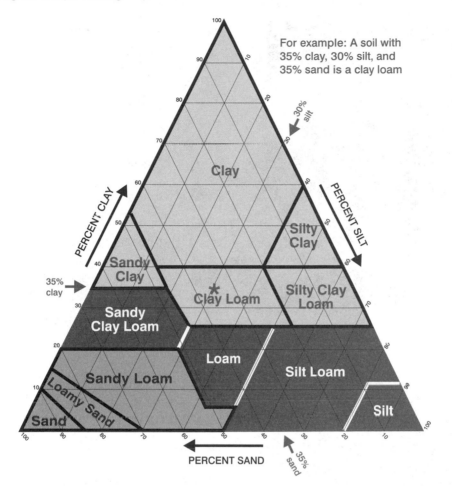

For example: A soil with 35% clay, 30% silt, and 35% sand is a clay loam

9-18. The soil triangle is used to describe the soil texture.

SOIL PROPERTY	TEXTURAL CLASS		
	Sand	Silt Loam	Clay
Aeration	excellent	good	poor
Cation Exchange	low	medium	high
Drainage	excellent	good	poor
Erodibility (by water)	easy	moderate	difficult
Permeability (by water)	fast	moderate	slow
Temperature (spring)	warms fast	warms moderately	warms slowly
Tillage	easy	moderate	difficult
Water-Holding Capacity	low	moderate	high
Resistance to Compaction	excellent	good	poor

9-19. Soil properties influenced by soil texture.

9-20. Soil high in sand content holds little water and has a gritty feel.

9-21. Topsoil partially spread after grading at this site.

Topsoil and Subsoil

Before or during construction, grading will usually disturb the original soil. Therefore, very little natural topsoil will be found at the surface. Although the spreading of topsoil following grading may have been accomplished, this layer is usually quite thin. The root system of landscape plants may penetrate 12 to 24 inches in favorable soils.

The excavated material from grading differs from topsoil. It has not been subjected to the mellowing effect of plant roots. It does not have the abundance of soil microbes feeding on dead roots and underground stems. Sandy soils have a low water-holding capacity and are subject to wind erosion. These soils are generally low in nutrients because rainfall has leached the important nutrients from the sand.

Alkaline soils occur throughout drier regions, wherever internal soil drainage is poor. Applying an acid formulation of fertilizer can improve nutrient availability on alkaline soils. Saline soils usually occur on coastal plains where the salt water penetrates. Selecting landscape plants that like saline soils may be the best solution to this problem.

BED PREPARATION

The *planting bed* describes the area in the landscape where shrubs and flowers are planted. Remove all sod and grass from the new landscape planting beds before planting shrubs. Never place sod and soil dug from the planting hole on the existing lawn. Put the soil in a wheelbarrow or on a piece of plywood to make the cleanup after tree and shrub planting quick and easy. It is best to back fill the planting hole with the same soil that came from the hole, no soil amendments added. *Soil amendments* are materials added to the soil to improve drainage, moisture holding ability, and aeration. Sulfur and lime products are commonly used to adjust soil pH.

9-22. A 2-inch layer of peat moss has been applied to this planting bed before rototilling.

Very poor clay soil at the landscape sites may require the addition of sand or peat moss to improve soil aeration and drainage. First, cover the existing soil with a 2-inch layer of peat moss followed with a 2-inch layer of sand. Rototill the planting bed to mix the sand and peat into the top 6 inches of soil.

Many cities recycle grass clippings, landscape waste, and newspapers and sell this compost. This decomposed waste can be used to improve poor soil instead of using peat moss. For best results, always plant shrubs and flowers in a well-prepared planting bed.

NUTRIENTS REQUIRED FOR PLANT GROWTH

Nutrients are chemical substances that support the life processes. Plants require 16 elements for good growth. Some elements come from the air, others from water, and the rest from the soil. Plants use large quantities of nitrogen, phosphorus, and potassium, the three primary or

Table 9-2. Essential Elements Required by Plants

OBTAINED FROM AIR AND WATER		
Carbon Hydrogen Oxygen		

OBTAINED FROM THE SOIL	Element	Chemical Symbol	Available Form
Primary or macronutrients	Nitrogen	N	NO_3^-, NH_4^+
	Phosphorus	P	$H_2PO_4^-$, HPO_4^{--}
	Potassium	K	K^+
Secondary nutrients	Calcium	Ca	Ca^{++}
	Magnesium	Mg	Mg
	Sulfur	S	SO_4^{--}
Minor or micronutrients	Iron	Fe	Fe^{++}, Fe^{+++}
	Manganese	Mn	Mn^{++}
	Copper	Cu	Cu^{++}
	Boron	B	$H_2BO_3^-$ and others
	Zinc	Zn	Zn^{++}
	Chlorine	Cl	Cl^-
	Molybdenum	Mo	MoO_4^{--}

macronutrients, but need smaller amounts of the three secondary nutrients. Plants require very small amounts of the minor or micronutrients for good growth.

Landscape plants like other plants require 16 elements for healthy growth and development. Air and water supply plants with three of the necessary elements—hydrogen, oxygen and carbon. Among the remaining 13 elements, calcium and magnesium will usually be present to some extent in most soils. However, in acid soils, the supply is so limited that lime must be added to reduce the soil acidity and improve availability.

Large quantities of potassium, commonly called potash, may be present in the soil, but often this potash is not available for plant use. Light, frequent applications of potash will supply plants with this valuable ele-

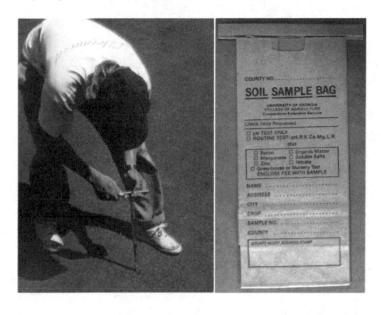

9-23. Collecting a soil sample (left) and a soil sample bag (right).

ment. Growing plants require more nitrogen than any of the other nutrients. Most fertilizer mixtures contain nitrogen, phosphorus, and potassium. Plants, especially evergreens, growing on alkaline soils may lack iron and have yellow-green foliage. Apply a soluble form of iron to yellow turf and change its color to bright green.

Soil testing shows the ability of the soil to supply the essential nutrients necessary for good plant growth. After testing the soil, apply a fertilizer containing the nutrients recommended by the soil test. Over application of nutrients can occur when no soil testing is done. Always read and follow all the directions on the fertilizer label.

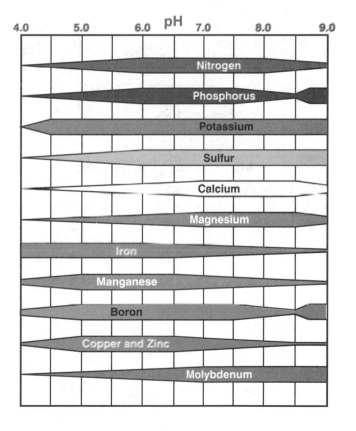

9-24. Nutrient availability as influenced by soil pH.

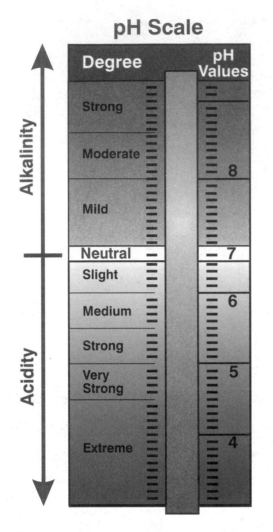

9-25. Soil pH is the degree of acidity, alkalinity, or neutral.

SOIL pH

Soil scientists use a 14-point *pH scale* to explain the acidity or alkalinity of soil. On this pH scale, the middle number 7.0 is neither acid nor alkaline but neutral. Soil with a pH below 7.0 is *acidic* while soil pH over 7.0 is *alkaline*. A soil sample with a pH of 2.0 is more acidic than a sample with a pH of 6.5. Soil scientists called agronomists test soil samples in a laboratory to find the exact pH. Once the pH is identified, amendments can be used to raise or lower it.

The "p" of pH is always a small letter while the "H" is always a capital letter. Agronomists use the pH scale to simplify the reporting of acidity and alkalinity. In a laboratory, the agronomist measures the hydrogen ion concentration of a soil sample to be $H+ 10^{-5}$, but will report the soil pH as 5.0. Lemon and tomato juice have an approximate pH of 3.0 while the pH of soap is about 9.0. Most landscape plants grow best when the soil pH is between 5.5 and 7.0.

Nutrients are most available when the pH is in that range. Needle evergreens, such as junipers and pines, require an acid soil between 5.0 and 6.0. The same holds true for most broadleaf evergreens.

Soils in the eastern part of the United States are generally acid, below 5.5, while those soils in the southwest will usually be alkaline, above 8.0. Midwest soils tend to be in the 6.0 to 7.5 ideal range. Materials can be added to modify the soil pH. When soil tests indicate a low soil pH (below 5.5), add ground limestone to raise the pH into the normal range. Soils with a pH above 8.0 need sulfur compounds, such as ammonium sulfate, added to reduce the pH into the normal range.

REVIEWING

MAIN IDEAS

The landscape crew supervisor must identify the locations of all plants required at the landscape site. The crew supervisor must transfer all measurements from the planting plan to the landscape site.

Contour lines on the planting plan show the rise and fall of the land. Different terrains suggest different kinds of use for the site. Use a level and a yard stick or transit and target rod to determine the percent slope at a landscape site. Planting plans use solid contour lines to indicate changes from the original land elevations. A cut will remove soil from the landscape site while a fill will add soil to the site.

Proper landscape bed preparation is essential for good plant establishment and growth. Improve poor soil by adding peat moss or other organic material. Use soil tests to determine the need for fertilizer applications in the planting bed. There are 16 elements necessary for good plant growth. Three come from air and water while the remaining 13 come from the soil.

QUESTIONS

Answer the following questions using correct spelling and complete sentences.

1. What is a planting plan and how is it used?

2. What does the term terrain mean?

3. Describe two ways to determine the percent slope of a hill.

4. How does a landscape contractor know where underground utilities are located?

5. What is the difference between rough grade and final grade?

6. What is a landscape berm?

7. What is percolation?

8. What is a soil triangle?

9. What are soil amendments used for when preparing a planting bed?

10. What are the three primary nutrients and their chemical symbols?

CHAPTER SELF-CHECK

Match the term with the correct definition. Place the letter in the blank provided.

a. berm   d. staking the site   g. target rod
b. contour line   e. grading   h. plant nurseries
c. planting plan   f. terrain   i. landscape construction

____ 1. Developed by the landscape designer

____ 2. The crew supervisor does this the day before the landscape crew starts the job

____ 3. The rise and fall of land

____ 4. The smoothing of the soil surface

____ 5. This instrument has numbers on it and is used to determine the elevation of a given site

____ 6. Mounds of soil that create special effects in the landscape

____ 7. These lines on the planting plan show how the terrain changes elevation

____ 8. Landscape plant material is grown at this location

____ 9. The execution of the planting plan and installation of hardscape features

EXPLORING

1. After drawing a simple landscape plan, practice staking it out at school or home.

2. Measure several hills at school and around town and determine the percent slope.

3. Borrow landscape plans from a contractor and study the contour lines and determine if cuts or fills will be required.

4. Describe major outdoor activities and determine the best slope of each activity.

5. Prepare a landscape bed at school or home before planting shrubs and flowers.

6. Collect a soil sample and send it to a laboratory for testing.

10

Installing Plant Materials

People like to see attractive outside areas. They like to see healthy green plants and beautiful flowers. Everyone admires a well-kept lawn. A beautiful landscape does not just happen. It must be planned and properly installed.

Who selects the trees and shrubs planted around new homes? What are B&B, BR, and container-grown plants, and how do they differ? What steps should the landscape contractor follow when planting trees and shrubs in the landscape? Why use mulches in landscape planting beds? Where in the landscape should flowers be planted? What is a geotextile and why should it be used? These and many more questions will be answered in this chapter on installing plant materials.

10-1. A beautiful landscape must be properly installed. (Courtesy, Church Landscape)

OBJECTIVES

1. Identify the harvesting methods used by nurseries

2. Define xeriscape

3. Describe steps in proper tree and shrub planting

4. Install ground covers and vines

5. Plant flowers in a bed or border

6. Install bed edging

7. Demonstrate proper landscape fabric installation

TERMS

annual

anti-transpirant

balled and burlapped (B&B)

bare root (BR)

bedding plant

bed edging

container grown

container nursery

drought tolerance

field nursery

flower bed

flower border

geotextile

ground cover

guying

hardy plant

herbaceous plant

landscape fabric

mulch

perennial

root circling

soil ball

staking

stomata

sunscald

tender plant

transpiration

vine

water requirement

winter burn

xeriscape

Balled & Burlapped plant

Planting hole a minimum of 12 inches wider than soil ball. Cut twine and push burlap back. Form a saucer at the base of the tree and fill with 3" of mulch.

Tree supported by guying

HARVESTING METHODS USED FOR LANDSCAPE PLANTS

Planting plans show the plant by name and its location on the plan. Designers recommend planting balled and burlapped (B&B), bare root (BR), or container-grown plants depending on the time of year and the budget for each landscape job. A ***container nursery*** grows nursery crops to marketable size in containers. A ***field nursery*** grows nursery crops to marketable size in fields. Field nurseries make B&B and BR plant material available. Evergreen shrubs best survive transplanting in the landscape if grown as B&B or container plants. Plant nurseries sell small and medium-sized trees and shrubs as B&B, BR, or container plants. However, large trees transplant best by the balled and burlapped method.

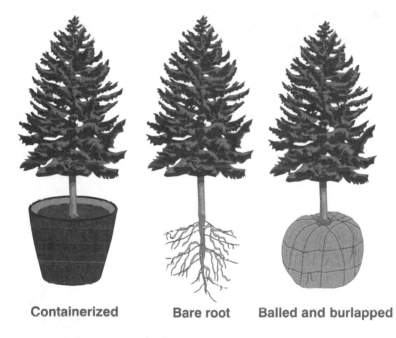

Containerized   **Bare root**   **Balled and burlapped**

10-2. Landscape plants can be sold in containers, bare root, or balled and burlapped.

BALLED AND BURLAPPED PLANTS

Before the 1960s, trees grown in a farm field were hand dug, keeping a ball of soil around the root system. Covering the soil ball with burlap,

10-3. Balled and burlapped trees being planted. (Courtesy, Church Landscape)

to hold the soil and roots together, completed this harvesting technique. The term **balled and burlapped (B&B)** describes this tree harvesting method. Large, power tree spades are used to dig and transplant trees with a trunk diameter of 4 to 12 inches. Using hydraulics, these machines dig trees by pushing three or four large spades into the soil. Balled and burlapped trees should be planted in the spring or fall.

BARE ROOT PLANTS

Another popular harvesting technique called **bare root (BR)** describes digging the trees without taking soil from the field. Small and medium-sized trees and shrubs transplanted as bare root have a high survival rate. Most rose bushes and fruit trees sold today use the bare root method. However, most narrowleaf and broadleaf evergreens do not survive when transplanted using the bare root method. Careful attention should be taken not to allow the sun to burn the roots of landscape plants. This root dessication can be prevented by always covering the roots with

10-4. Machine used to dig bare root plants in a nursery.

a piece of burlap during the installation process. Dormant shrubs are usually sold bare root and should be planted in the spring.

CONTAINER GROWN PLANTS

Today, many plants are grown in plastic, peat, or recycled newspaper containers. The containers may be filled with a soil-based medium which contains topsoil or a soilless medium that contains organic and inorganic materials. **Container grown** describes this cultural method. Container

10-5. Container grown nursery stock.

grown plants are easy to handle and move and provide protection for the plant's root system. Container plants grow in confined planting areas, not open farm fields. They can be planted any time during the year when the ground is not frozen.

Bedding Plants

Flowers to be installed in the landscape beds are usually sold already growing and ready to begin blooming, rather than from seed. Flowers in this form are called **bedding plants.** The containers these plants are grown in can be plastic

10-6. Pansy in an individual container.

or manufactured from organic compounds such as peat moss. The majority of bedding plants are grown in plastic cell packs which are designed to fit into large plastic flat trays.

Herbaceous plants are non-woody plants, such as annuals, bulbs, perennials, turfgrass, and certain vines that die back to the ground each year. Bulbs are classified depending upon their time of planting, time of blooming, and temperature tolerances. Bulbs are sold loose from soil. Vines and vegetatively propagated turfgrasses are usually available in containers.

PLANT INSTALLATION CONSIDERATIONS

Factors to consider when installing plants include water requirements, growth rate, hardiness, and nutrient and pH needs.

WATER REQUIREMENTS

Water requirement refers to the amount of water plants need to live and grow. Some plants need more water than others. Increasingly, plants that need less water are being selected in landscaping.

Drought tolerance is the ability of a plant to live and grow with low amounts of moisture. The climate in the area being landscaped is important in plant selection. Plants that need an abundance of water should be used in places with high natural moisture.

10-7. Landscapes in arid areas often use native, water efficient plants, such as cactus.

GROWTH RATE AND MATURITY

Plants grow at different rates and to different sizes. Plant selection for a landscape must consider the growth of plants. A plant that is very small when planted may grow into a large plant at maturity.

Trees and shrubs are classified by height and spread. Height is how tall a plant grows. It is the vertical space needs of a plant. Some dwarf shrubs grow only a few inches in height. Trees may reach a hundred feet or more. Plants should be selected and placed in a landscape on the basis of mature height.

Spread is the size and fullness of the canopy. It is the horizontal space needs of a plant. Trees may have huge canopies. Small shrubs may have only a few inches of spread. The space available to achieve the purposes of the landscape must be considered. Masses of annuals with little spread may require placing the plants close together.

HARDINESS AND OTHER ADAPTATIONS

Hardiness refers to how well a plant is suited to the climate. Some plants withstand cold; others do not. Some plants require full sun; others will grow well in partial sun or shade. Low-growing plants set underneath taller plants must be able to grow in less than full sun.

Hardiness zones have been established based on plant temperature tolerance. The 11 zones are based on the average minimum temperatures that plants can survive. When a tree or shrub is assigned a hardiness zone rating, it should survive the winter in that zone or any zone having a higher numbered rating. See Figure 7-15.

Plants must be able to tolerate salt in some locations. Two examples include coastal areas near saltwater and along highways where salt is used to control snow and ice.

NUTRIENT AND PH NEEDS

Plants vary in nutrient and pH requirements. Soil analysis determines the nutrients available in the soil. Part of preparing the site for planting includes soil tests. Matching the plants to the natural available nutrients and pH reduces cost.

SOURCES OF INFORMATION IN SELECTING AND INSTALLING PLANTS

Good information is needed to help in selecting and installing plants. Landscape designers and landscape contractors need to know plant materials. The important information about plants includes:

- common and scientific names
- whether the plant is deciduous or evergreen
- height and spread of the plant
- growth, training, and trimming requirements
- characteristics of flowers and fruit, if any
- hardiness zone
- pest resistance and problems
- sun requirements (full sun, partial sun, or shade)
- water requirements
- life span (perennial, biennial, or annual)
- others, such as poisonous foliage, thorns, and potential problems from roots, leaves, and flowers or fruit.

Information about plants is presented in charts that summarize the major features of the species. **Appendix B, Plant Materials List, includes information on common plants used in the landscape by classification.** Reputable local nurseries often have useful information. Agriculture offices at land-grant universities and cooperative extension services usually have information and specialists who can help with plant selection and installation guidelines.

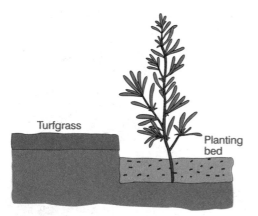

Turfgrass

Planting bed

10-8. Lowering the planting bed to catch moisture is one technique to help make efficient use of available water.

USING XERISCAPING

Xeriscape is water conservation through creative, appropriate landscaping and water management. The water qualities of an area are determined, and plant materials are selected accordingly. Turf areas are limited and can be replaced with materials such as ground covers, mulches, or hardscape features. An efficient irrigation system may be installed to provide supplemental water. Soil improvements allowing for better moisture penetration and water holding capacity are used. A soil test will be needed. Regular maintenance is needed to preserve the plantings and conserve water.

Water Zones

Water zones are areas in a landscape based on the amount of water needed by the plants. Irrigation may be needed if natural moisture supplies are inadequate. Three zones are typically used:

- **Very low water zone**—The very low water zone usually requires no water beyond what is naturally available, except to establish the plants. Plants that are being established may need irrigation. Plants in the very low water zone need to be selected for low water need. Annual flowering plants are not appropriate because of their high water need. Native shrubs, cacti, and other species are often best.

- **Low water zone**—Plants in the low water zone usually need more water than what is available naturally. Some irrigation is needed. Shrubs, ground cover materials, and limited annuals may be appropriate.

- **Moderate water zone**—The plants in the moderate water zone typically need supplemental water. Focal points in the landscape and areas of high use near entrances are in this zone. Annuals and other succulent materials may be used.

Careful Planning

Xeriscaping requires careful planning and installation. A soil analysis is needed to determine nutrient needs. An efficient irrigation system should be selected and properly installed. The amount of turfgrass is limited. (Most turfgrass requires large amounts of moisture.) The use of annual flowering plants is limited. Drought-tolerant perennial flowers and ornamental grasses should be selected. Mulch should be used to cool the surface, prevent erosion, and conserve soil moisture.

PREPLANTING INFORMATION

Successful tree and shrub planting starts with proper care during shipment and ends with correct planting techniques. To prevent drying out and burning of leaves, cover trees with tarpaulins or plastic sheeting when transporting on open trucks or trailers. Failure to properly protect trees and shrubs during transport is a major reason for plant death after planting.

Spring planting has been the standard practice in the landscape business for years, especially when most trees were sold as bare root plants. The short spring season may not allow the landscape contractor time to install all the scheduled landscape projects. Many contractors plant in the fall using B&B or container-grown plants to increase landscape sales.

Some trees and shrubs do not transplant well in the fall in zones 1-6. Therefore, spring planting is recommended. Avoid fall planting of broadleaf evergreens, birches, Bradford Callery pear, hollies, oaks (except pin oak), silver linden, sweetgum, sour gum, and tulip trees. In zones 7-11, most trees and shrubs are planted year around.

Avoid summer planting, especially, during hot, dry periods. However, many landscape contractors find it necessary to install plants in the summer to complete all their projects. Successful summer planting requires adequate irrigation by the homeowner.

GUIDELINES FOR SELECTING TREES

The general appearance of a tree will reveal much about its quality and potential for success when transplanted. Is the trunk straight and is the crown symmetrical? Does the tree show signs of current season growth? Signs of viability include expanding buds, new leaves, and elongated shoots. Are there any signs of disease or insect damage? Shade trees should have a strong, well-defined central leader with equally spaced branches forming a symmetrical crown. Trees having multiple leaders, crossing, rubbing, or overly-crowded branches have not been pruned properly and are less valuable.

Discolored, sunken, or swollen areas in the trunk are additional signs to look for when selecting a tree. Bark cuts and scrapes are also undesirable. Trunks with visible wood borer damage and those showing signs of sunscald or cracking should be avoided.

Trees purchased as container-grown should be well-rooted and firmly established in their containers. The root mass should retain its shape and hold together when removed from the container. However, if the roots circle and form a dense web, the tree may be pot-bound. Pot-bound plants are often under stress.

10-9. Balled and burlapped (B&B) plants ready for shipment.

The rootball size for balled and burlapped (B&B) trees is based on the trunk diameter. The American Association of Nurserymen has determined the sizes necessary for tree recovery after transplanting.

Appropriate Rootball Sizes for Balled and Burlapped Trees

Trunk Diameter (inches)	Minimum Rootball Diameter (inches)
½	12
¾	14
1	16
1¼	18
1½	20
1¾	22
2	24
2½	28
3	32
3½	38

The soil ball should not be excessively wet or dry and should be securely held together by burlap, twine, or possibly a wire basket. The trunk should be centered in the rootball and should not move independent of it.

Bare root (BR) trees should be stored in a cool, shady area with their roots protected from drying by packing or burlap. Their root system should be damp and flexible. When bare root trees are ready to be planted in the landscape, their root systems should continue to be protected until they are actually placed in the ground. Exposure of the roots to the sun should be limited as much as possible.

PLANTING TECHNIQUES FOR TREES AND SHRUBS

Different landscape contractors may use different planting methods. The following techniques describe common methods of transplanting trees and shrubs.

BALLED AND BURLAPPED PLANTING TECHNIQUES

The *soil ball* is the soil surrounding the root system, which has been balled and burlapped. Always dig the planting hole a minimum of 12

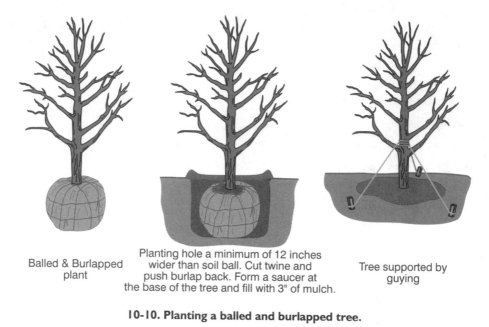

Balled & Burlapped plant

Planting hole a minimum of 12 inches wider than soil ball. Cut twine and push burlap back. Form a saucer at the base of the tree and fill with 3" of mulch.

Tree supported by guying

10-10. Planting a balled and burlapped tree.

inches larger than the soil ball of the tree or shrub. This will allow a minimum of 6 inches of space between the soil ball and the edge of the planting hole in which new roots can expand. Research has shown that the larger the hole, the better. The top of the soil ball should be level with the surface of the new planting hole and the bottom of the hole should be flat. This allows the tree or shrub to be planted at the same depth as it was originally growing in the nursery. To prevent plant death from root rot, never plant a tree in a hole that is deeper than the height of the soil ball.

When planting B&B stock, carefully place the plant in the hole without removing any burlap or twine and check the hole for proper size. Grasp the plant by the soil ball when handling it. Always untie and remove all twine from around the plant stems before you are ready to plant. With the B&B shrub in the hole, pull the burlap back from the top of the soil ball and push it down between the soil ball and the walls of the planting hole. This will prevent the burlap from acting as a wick, removing moisture from the root ball. Note that synthetic, "burlap look-alike" plastic material should be removed completely before planting.

CONTAINER GROWN PLANTING TECHNIQUES

Before placing a container grown plant in the hole, remove the container. Invert the container plant and tap the container edge on a solid object. The soil ball will slide out of the container. Take care not to disturb the

10-11. If the container plant's roots are circled at the edge, cut these roots with a knife and spread them at the bottom.

root system. One problem with plants grown in containers is root circling. *Root circling* is when the plant's root sytem has become too long for its container. If the plant is pot bound, cut the roots at the edge with a knife and spread them before planting. Place the soil ball in the hole and check for proper hole diameter and depth. Position the plant in the hole with the best looking side toward the main viewing point.

BARE ROOT PLANTING TECHNIQUES

Follow the same general installation guidelines when planting bare root rose bushes, fruit trees, or other bare root plants. Remove the thin plastic covering around the roots and discard any sawdust or other moisture-holding material found inside the plastic bag. Dig a hole as deep as the longest root and at least 12 inches in diameter. The bark or stem of a bare root plant will usually have a stain marking the level of the original field height. The tree or shrub should be planted at the same depth as it was growing in the nursery. After removing the soil from the planting hole, make a cone-shaped pile of soil in the bottom center of the hole. Rest the plant

10-12. The harvesting method used for the landscape plant determines the shape of the planting hole.

Bare root
Hole mounded on bottom

Balled and burlapped
Flat on bottom

10-13. Correctly planted flowering tree. Note the saucer around the tree for holding water.

10-14. Small tree with two support stakes.

crown, the junction of roots and stem, on top of this soil cone. Carefully spread the secondary roots to their natural shape. Back fill the hole tamping the soil to remove any unseen pockets of air. Construct a saucer by creating a small berm around the edge of the planting hole to hold irrigation water and clean up the planting area.

BACK FILLING THE HOLE

Break up all large soil clumps with a shovel before using them to back fill the hole. Partially back fill the hole with existing soil and carefully tamp the soil around the root system, but do not pound the soil. Continue back filling the hole tamping the soil to help prevent air pockets from forming around the root system. After completing the filling operation, construct a soil saucer, slightly larger than the root system, with the extra soil from the hole. Fill the saucer with water and let it slowly wet the root system and surrounding soil. The saucer will help retain rain or irrigation water for use by the tree or shrub.

SUPPORT BY STAKING OR GUYING

Some new research shows that the trunk of a young tree is strengthened if it is allowed to sway in the wind. However, trees 6 to 12 feet tall may require additional support after planting. Give this support by driving two or three long wooden stakes next to the soil ball and attach a wire between the stakes and the tree trunk. Protect the soft trunk tissue by covering the wire with a short piece of rubber hose. This method of support is called *staking*.

Note that shrubs rarely require additional support.

Newly planted trees more than 15 feet tall need cables or wires attached to the tree trunk and to three equally-spaced stakes driven around the tree base for support. The wires between the stakes and the tree trunk are split in the middle with a turnbuckle, which is used to adjust the wire or cable tension. The tree trunk should be protected by covering each wire with a short piece of rubber hose. This support method is called ***guying***. Guying cables need to be visibly flagged for safety.

WATERING PRACTICES

Newly transplanted trees and shrubs require deep and thorough watering for the entire first year after planting. Homeowners may forget to water trees and shrubs regularly after planting. The following watering technique will thor-

10-15. Bracing a tree by guying.

oughly wet the soil 12 inches deep and is an easy way to provide adequate soil moisture for most plants. Slowly empty a 5-gallon bucket of water in the soil saucer of shrubs. Use two 5-gallon buckets of water on large shrubs and trees. Instruct homeowners to continue this weekly watering practice for the first growing season on all landscape plants when no rainfall has occurred during the week. Most landscape contractors only water plants once after installing them. The homeowner should then assume the watering responsibility and should continue weekly watering for the first growing season.

FERTILIZER AND ANTI-TRANSPIRANT

Most landscape contractors do not fertilize trees and shrubs at the time of planting. Over fertilization can cause more stress to newly transplanted trees than no fertilization. Shade trees may require minor pruning of dead or broken branches at planting time.

One way of reducing water loss is to spray the plant with an anti-transpirant. An ***anti-transpirant*** seals the stomata and helps prevent leaf scorch or leaf burn. The ***stomata*** are pore openings in the epidermal layer of

10-16. Newly transplanted tree with trunk protected with tree wrap.

plant tissue where transpiration occurs. *Transpiration* is the loss of water from the plant through the leaves in the form of water vapor. After planting evergreen shrubs, they should be sprayed with an anti-transpirant to reduce water loss. Application of an anti-transpirant will also help reduce transplant shock when applied to evergreens at the time of planting.

TRUNK WRAPPING

Many landscape contractors wrap tree trunks with a heavy paper, tree wrap material to reduce the possibility of sunscald and to protect them from rodents or other pests. *Sunscald* or *winter burn* describes a condition in which bark blisters from the intense winter sunlight.

Start wrapping the paper spirally around the trunk from the ground level and continue up to the first branch. Securely attach the tree wrap paper to the trunk with twine or tape. Never damage the trunk if it can be avoided.

PLANTING TECHNIQUES FOR GROUND COVERS AND VINES

Ground cover refers to a woody or herbaceous plant that forms a mat less than 1 foot high covering the ground. It is generally regarded as a special purpose plant. A *vine* is a woody or herbaceous plant that climbs naturally with some type of support or creeps along the ground.

GROUND COVER INSTALLATION

Most ground cover plants have a maximum height of 12 inches. In the past, ground covers were used mainly on steep banks to hold soil and reduce erosion. For years, landscapers also recommended ground covers under trees or in other shady areas where grass would not grow. Today, ground covers are an important part of a well-designed home landscape planting. They are a living mulch that will cover the soil and reduce weed growth in landscape planting beds.

Since ground cover plants do not have much individual form, their design form is determined by the shape of the landscape bed. Most ground covers are perennial plants that grow year after year without replanting. Most are also evergreen plants, keeping their leaves all year; however, a few are deciduous and drop their leaves in the winter. Some ground covers have showy flowers; while others have interesting and unusual leaf colors or patterns.

Ground covers are often used instead of grass to cover the soil. Ground covers improve the appearance of the ground, hold the soil, and prevent erosion on steep slopes. They may be difficult to establish and completely cover an area. Frequent watering, during this establishment stage, will speed the spread of the ground cover plants. Weeds can be difficult to control in the ground cover bed during the establishment stage. Pulling weeds by hand from between the plants may be the only effective method of control. Herbicides that control most weeds will also kill the desirable ground cover plants.

Table 10-1. Calculating Amounts of Groundcover

NUMBER OF PLANTS NEEDED	
Specified Distance Apart	Multiply area to be covered (sq. ft.) by:
4" o.c.	9.0
6" o.c.	4.0
9" o.c.	1.78
12" o.c.	1.0
15" o.c.	0.64
18" o.c.	0.44
24" o.c.	0.25

Spacing of the plants will help determine how quickly or slowly the soil will be completely covered. Most ground covers are planted 8 to 12 inches o.c. The term "o.c." stands for "on center" or the distance between the center of one plant and the center of the next plant. Appendix B, Plant Materials List, provides specific spacing requirements for ground covers.

Many ground covers will grow faster than low-growing evergreens. Do not plant fast-growing ground covers (English ivy, *Hedera helix;* crown vetch, *Coronilla varia;* or honeysuckle, *Lonicera sempervirens*) in the same planting bed with slow-growing evergreens.

VINE INSTALLATION

A landscape plant whose stem requires support for upright growth is called a vine. They may be deciduous or evergreen. In many parts of the country, vines are not as popular today as in the past. Vines, especially in the north, require more care than most other landscape plants. Use vines for overhead protection, over a patio or other areas, as an alternative to shade trees. Plant vines next to walls and fences to soften their harsh construction lines. Many vines are planted for their beautiful flowers or colorful fruit.

A decorative support called an arbor or trellis can be used to support the weak stems of climbing plants. Climbing plants have three different methods of support: tendrils, twining, or holdfasts. Small special stems called tendrils, wrap around the support structure and help many climbing plants stay on the trellis. Some vine plants hold onto the support structure by twining or simply wrapping their entire stem around the support. Other vines have developed special root-like structures, called holdfasts, on their stems that penetrate wood, brick, or mortar to secure the plant to the wall or fence.

Vines growing on brick or wood homes can cause structural damage. The holdfast structures of the vine can weaken the brick wall by damaging the mortar between the bricks. Thick-growing vines may hold extra moisture around wood window frames and cause the wood to rot. In the south, the Virginia creeper (*Parthenocissus quinquifolia*) is a fast-growing vine that can smother shrubs and large trees in the landscape.

Clematis is one of the most popular vines in the country. Large, fragrant, white, blue, red, or purple flowers can add interest to any landscape. The stems containing the red-orange berries of the American bittersweet vine add color to dried, fall floral arrangements.

PLANTING TECHNIQUES FOR FLOWERS IN THE LANDSCAPE

Vivid flower colors contrasted with green shrubs attract attention to the landscape. Homes built before 1950 contained large flower beds in the front yard. Bright-colored flowers attract the public's eye and can detract from the total home appearance. Today, designers normally place the flower beds in the backyard where they can be enjoyed close up by family and friends. Planting flowers in the private area also adds many colorful features to the landscape.

10-17. Vivid flower colors attract attention.

FLOWER BORDERS, BEDS, AND GROUPS

Flowers in front of shrubs in a planting bed create a *flower border* with the shrubs providing the back drop. A *flower bed* is a planting bed that only contains flowers. Tall-growing flower varieties should be planted at the back of the flower bed and short varieties at the front edge. Flower bed design should be kept simple. Try to plant groups of the same flowers together.

Annual flowers are plants that germinate from seed, grow to maturity, flower, and produce seed in one growing season. Annual flowers give the landscape quick color at a reasonable price. They can also be used in perennial flower beds to help maintain color throughout the year. Annuals planted in the spring will die each fall and need to be replanted each spring. *Perennial* flowers are plants that live for more than two growing seasons. Perennials may be placed in subgroups of herbaceous or woody types.

Plants can be further classified by temperature tolerance. *Tender plants* are more sensitive to temperature extremes than *hardy plants*. Hardy bulbs

10-18. Annual flowers in shady area.

planted in the fall will flower each spring for many years. Plant tender bulbs and tubers in the spring for summer flowering but dig up in the fall before frost and store inside through the winter. Planting time, plant cost, and general maintenance requirements should be considered by the designer when selecting the best flowers for each landscape job. Appendix B provides cultural information for annual and perennial flowers used in the landscape.

Perennial Gardens

One of the fastest growing segments of landscaping is the perennial garden. Perennials offer a vast array of colors and textures. The proper

10-19. Perennial flower bed.

10-20. Perennial gardens are often used to add color and beauty to the private area.

choice of perennial plant material can mean beautiful blooms from spring, through summer, and into the fall.

There are several considerations when selecting a site for a perennial garden. The amount of sun or shade the site is exposed to plays an important part in plant selection. The amount of sun the site receives during the day must be known. Another key is proper drainage. The site selected should have good drainage so the plants do not sit in standing water. A good way to determine if the site has good drainage is to dig a hole at the site and fill it with water. Let the water drain and fill the hole again. If the water drains out at less than 1 inch per hour, the drainage will need to be improved, or plant material that will thrive in wet conditions must be selected.

After the site has been selected and the needs have been determined, the perennial bed pattern shape can now be laid out. An easy way to accomplish this is to lay a garden hose or rope on the ground in the desired shape of the garden. The shape of the bed should be in harmony with the rest of the landscape. If other landscape beds are curved, the perennial bed should be curved. If they are straight or 45 degree angles, the perennial garden should be also. For ease of maintenance, design planting beds to be no deeper than 5 feet.

The selection of plant material is the most important decision for the perennial garden. Perennials are available in a variety of colors, sizes, and flowering times. In addition, sun requirements and drainage needs have to be considered. Colors and sizes that create a balanced garden should be selected. A number of groupings of plants generally look better than single plants spread throughout the garden. Taller plants should be placed towards the rear with shorter ones toward the front. There should be a plan used when selecting plant material.

Generally, perennials are planted in the spring or in the fall. Site preparation should begin some time before the actual planting. The bed should be tilled about 6 inches down and the soil mixed thoroughly. Organic material such as peat moss or leaf compost should be added. The soil should be kept loose until planting. Soil should be tested in order to determine fertilizer requirements and pH.

Flowering Bulbs/Tubers/Corms

Plant hardy flowering bulbs, such as tulips (*Tulipa* sp.), daffodils (*Narcissus* sp.), and hyacinths (*Hyacinthus* sp.), in the fall. They will give the landscape added color the following spring. In cold climates, plant tender plants, such as canna (*Canna* sp.) in the spring and enjoy their glorious blooms through the summer. Come fall, dig up the bulbs and tubers and store them through the winter for planting next spring. Appendix B provides cultural information for bulbs and tubers used in the landscape.

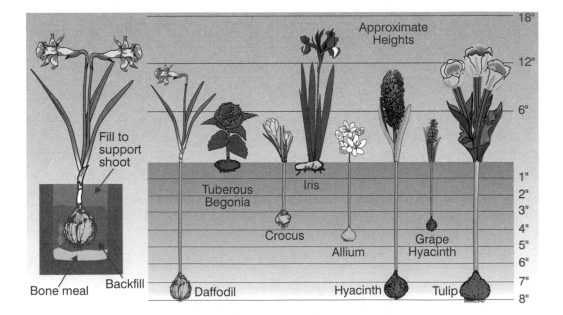

10-21. Planting technique for bulbs and tubers. Spring flowering bulbs can be planted from September through early November in a sunny, well-drained location.

FLOWER PLANTING

Flowers grow best in well-prepared beds. The planting bed should be free of all turf. Organic matter, such as peat moss, leaf compost, or manure, should be added and tilled into the top 6 inches of the soil to improve soil texture and increase water holding capacity.

Some flowers require full sun, while others need a shady planting location. Always know the different kinds of flowers and their individual growth requirements. Plant them in the right place. Some flowers can survive a variety of planting conditions while others cannot.

10-22. Flowers should be planted in beds that have been well-prepared.

AFTER PLANTING CARE

Flower beds need hand watering and require regular weeding. Without an intense maintenance program, flower beds look terrible. Immediately after planting, apply a herbicide to prevent weed seeds from germinating in the flower bed. As with all pesticides, always read and follow the label directions. Weed seed germination can also be reduced or prevented by using a mulch around the individual plants.

Fertilize flower beds once or twice a year by applying a liquid flower fertilizer when watering. Follow the manufacturer's recommendations for proper mixing. Over fertilization has killed more flowers than under fertilization. Follow the label instructions for additional applications throughout the season. When in doubt about whether to fertilize or not to fertilize flowers, do not fertilize.

FINAL PLANTING STEPS

Edging the planting bed and applying a landscape fabric can enhance any landscape project and eliminate weed growth. Many different types of landscape mulch are available. Installing mulch along with the final cleanup of the job site will complete the landscape installation process.

BED EDGING

Bed edging is the area where the landscape bed joins the lawn area. The landscape area may be naturally edged or may have a permanent, finished edge. Use a sharp spade to make a clean, crisp line between the grass lawn area and the landscape bed. Naturally edged beds look great right after the edging but need frequent touch up to keep them looking good. A variety of materials are available to put a permanent, finished edge on the landscape bed. This type of edging minimizes hand trimming and helps contain mulches, such as stone and bark, within the bed area. It will also help to keep more water in the planting beds by slowing surface runoff.

Plastic, steel, aluminum, pavers, timbers, and treated wood are used as bed edging materials. During the last 10 to 15 years, the most widely used edging materials have been heavy duty polyethylene/vinyl types. These edging materials have a variety of shapes, such as the common round bead tops and a series of horizontal groves, v-lips, or fins on the bottom help

10-23. Natural-edged bed without plastic or metal edging.

prevent frost heaving. Vinyl edging sizes vary, but 4 inches wide by 20 feet long is the normal size. A variety of thicknesses are available.

Steel edging provides a more permanent edge, but at an increase in cost. Commercial landscape sites usually specify steel edging on the landscape planting plans. Steel landscape edging material is sold in 4 inch widths with thicknesses of 1/8, 3/16, or 1/4 inch and lengths of 10, 16, or 20 feet.

Aluminum edging is available in similar sizes to the steel edging. It comes in several colors—natural, black, green, bronze and black. Special stakes hold all edging materials in the soil and prevent the edging from heaving out of the ground during freezing and thawing conditions.

Treated landscape timbers 4" × 6" × 8' provide a different bed edging effect.

10-24. Edging installed around landscape planting bed.

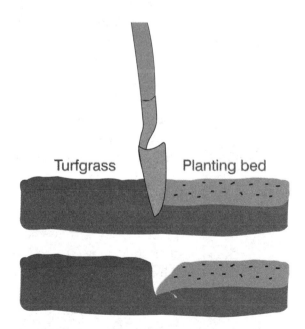

Turfgrass   Planting bed

10-25. The sharp drop in a natural-edged bed will slow rhizome turfgrasses and stop bunch grasses from spreading.

The inability to construct curved bed edges is a main difference between wood and other edging materials. Large landscape projects can use railroad ties for bed edging. However, railroad ties may appear too large in the average home landscape.

Installation

Dig a trench deep enough to bury the edging with ½ to ¾ inch exposed above the mulch. Follow the manufacturer's directions to install the stakes provided with the edging. Drill ½-inch diameter holes through railroad ties. Drive 3-foot long reinforcing rods into the soil to secure the ties to the site. Heavy clay soils or when using landscape timbers may only require a 3/8-inch hole and 18" depth.

LANDSCAPE FABRIC

Landscape fabric is a plastic sheet placed in the landscape bed to reduce weed competition with the landscape plants. Solid, black plastic sheets were used in the 1970s. The solid sheets prevented air and water movement into the soil. Modern landscape fabrics, called geotextiles, have replaced the solid plastic sheets. *Geotextiles* are woven strips of plastic landscape fabric that allow the movement of air, water, and fertilizer into the soil. Some landscape fabrics also contain herbicides to control weeds. Landscape fabric is covered with mulch after installation.

Clear the area to bare soil and unroll the fabric over the planting bed. If placed over an existing bed, cut an "X" over each plant, slip plants through the opening and push fabric under the plant base. If placed over a new bed, roll fabric over the soil and cut an "X" for each hole where the plant and its roots will be placed. Fold excess fabric under and cover it with a minimum of 4 inches of mulch. Do not leave any fabric exposed since it will deteriorate after prolonged exposure to direct sunlight.

10-26. Landscape fabric is used to prevent weed growth in the landscape bed.

LANDSCAPE MULCH

Landscape mulch covers the soil or landscape fabric in planting beds. *Mulch* is the material used around plants to reduce water loss, prevent weed growth, keep soil temperatures uniform, or prevent erosion. Mulching improves the general appearance of planting beds. Organic and inorganic mulch give the landscape designer or contractor two major kinds of mulch from which to choose. Spread the mulch uniformly 1 to 4 inches deep in the planting bed area.

10-27. Bark mulch also can prevent weed growth in planting beds.

Organic Mulch Materials

Organic mulches come from material that was once living—ground tree bark, pine needles, rice hulls, peat moss, wood chips, corn cobs, and cocoabean hulls. One drawback of organic mulches is they deplete the soil of nitrogen as they decompose. Each region of the country produces several different kinds of organic mulch materials. Therefore, many of these mulch materials will not be available in all parts of the country. While organic mulches have a very pleasing earthy appearance, they decay quickly in the landscape. Normally, beds require a yearly top dressing with new mulch to keep them looking good. Large-particle mulches last longer. Organic mulch should be replenished periodically, but the landscape fabric should last for years.

10-28. Wood mulch spread at the base of a tree to control weeds and keep soil moist.

10-29. Pine needle mulch is popular in the southeastern United States.

Inorganic Mulch Materials

Inorganic mulches, called aggregates, come from materials that were never living. Inorganic mulch materials are more permanent and seldom require top dressing with new mulch. Gravel, crushed stone, sand, and brick chips furnish the landscape contractor a variety of materials to choose from.

To complete the planting operation, clean up the planting site by removing debris from the planting holes and discarding plant containers. Landscape construction jobs may require a crew to work for several hours or many days at one job site. Each day brings a crew new challenges and opportunities to provide customers a beautiful and functional landscape.

10-30. Gravel is an inorganic mulch used in landscape beds.

REVIEWING

MAIN IDEAS

Landscapers install bare root, balled and burlapped, or container grown plants in the home landscape. Follow these simple rules when transplanting trees and shrubs. Always use a clean sharp spade. Dig the hole a minimum of 12 inches larger than the soil ball size. Plant the tree so the top of the soil ball is level with the soil at the site. Remove any plastic containers from the soil ball before planting. Remove twine from around the trunk of the tree. Spray evergreens with an anti-transpirant to reduce water loss.

Plant flowers in flower beds or flower borders. Hardy bulbs should be planted in the fall to give the landscape color in the early spring. Always prepare flower bed soil before planting the flowers. Use a herbicide to control weeds in flower and landscape beds. Mulch flower beds to reduce hand watering.

Edge planting beds to create a crisp line between the lawn area and the bed. Plastic, steel, aluminum, pavers, timbers, and treated wood make excellent bed edging. Install a landscape fabric to prevent weed growth in the planting bed. Mulches add the finishing touch to a well-designed and installed landscape bed. Organic mulches, such as bark or wood chips, give the bed a natural look. Gravel mulch will last many years without any additional maintenance.

QUESTIONS

Answer the following questions using correct spelling and complete sentences.

1. What is the difference between bare root, balled and burlapped, and container grown plants?
2. What is xeriscape?
3. How deep should the hole be when planting a tree or shrub?
4. Why should an anti-transpirant be used after planting evergreen shrubs?
5. What is sunscald?
6. How many ground cover plants are needed for 10 sq. ft. if they are spaced 6" o.c.?

7. What is the difference between a flower bed and a flower border?

8. Why install bed edging around landscape planting beds?

9. What is the purpose of landscape fabric?

10. What are the two major kinds of landscape mulch? What are the advantages of each?

CHAPTER SELF-CHECK

a. guying   e. flower bed   i. gravel
b. sunscald   f. stomata   j. flower border
c. geotextile   g. pine needles
d. container grown   h. hardy bulbs

____ 1. Holes that let air and water into the leaf

____ 2. Trees and evergreens grown in plastic containers filled with a special soil mix

____ 3. Attach cables between the tree trunk and a stake to support the newly transplanted tree

____ 4. Many landscape contractors wrap tree trunks with a paper wrap to prevent damage from the sun

____ 5. A landscape planting containing flowers, not shrubs

____ 6. This material should be installed under mulch to prevent weed growth in landscape planting beds

____ 7. A landscape planting containing both flowers and shrubs.

____ 8. An organic type mulch.

____ 9. An inorganic type mulch.

____10. Planted in the fall and flower the next spring.

EXPLORING

1. Go to a garden center and identify bare root, balled and burlapped, and container-grown plants.

2. Apply an anti-transpirant material to flower and vegetable transplants in your home garden.

3. Install plastic edging and landscape fabric in landscape beds at school or home.

11

Installing Patios, Decks, and Walks

Patios and decks connect the interior rooms with the outdoor landscape. They serve as outdoor dining rooms, game areas, or a place to relax. They must be designed large enough to handle the normal amount of traffic with overload capability built into the surrounding landscape.

Walks are the pathway entrance to and from the residence. They are built to eliminate cutting across lawns or corners. The primary walkways should be wide enough so two people can walk side-by-side. Secondary walkways only need to accommodate one person.

What materials can be used to construct a patio? How large should the patio be? What kinds of brick are available for patio construction? How do you install a concrete patio? Why use "treated" wood when building a deck? These and many other questions will be answered in this chapter.

11-1. A deck connects the interior rooms with the outdoor landscape.

OBJECTIVES

1. List advantages and disadvantages of surfacing material

2. Determine patio size for a family of four

3. Describe the different materials used to construct patios

4. Demonstrate the techniques in installing concrete walks and patios

5. Know the installation steps for paver blocks

6. Describe wood-treating techniques to prevent rot

7. Identify deck components and correctly size each

8. Calculate dimensions for outdoor steps

TERMS

accelerator
baluster
beam
broom finish
cement
cleat
cubic yard
cure
deck
deck boards
eased
exposed aggregate
float
form
joist
patio
paver blocks
paving
plate compactor
retarder
riser
screeding
soft paving
tread
trowel

LANDSCAPE PAVING

Covering the soil with a hard surface material to prevent soil erosion and compaction from traffic is called *paving*. Aggregates are often used for paving. Gravel or concrete driveways can prevent soil compaction problems. Sidewalks and patios provide a strong surface for people traffic in the home landscape. Grass or other plant materials cannot provide a permanent surface for either car or people traffic. Paving materials can be divided into two groups—hard paving and soft paving materials. As the name implies, hard paving includes such materials as poured concrete, brick, stone, tile, and wood.

11-2. Modern concrete patio.

Soft paving materials lack the solid form that hard paving materials provide. Many landscapers use the term loose aggregates to describe soft paving. Soft materials may be very durable but may require more maintenance to keep them looking good in the landscape. To prevent injuries, use soft paving materials in children's play areas. Install soft surfacing materials for walks and drives that get little traffic. These materials can also be used as a temporary surface before installing a permanent, hard surface material.

The following loose aggregate materials provide soft paving surfaces: wood or bark chips, sand, gravel, and ground-up car tires. Ground-up car tires will not make a good driveway paving surface. However, they can provide an excellent paving material under children's playground equip-

11-3. Installing a slate patio. (Courtesy, R.S. Hursthouse & Associates, Inc.)

11-4. A playground covered with wood chips.

ment. Use loose aggregate material for little-used garden walks and drives. Rake occasionally to keep the loose aggregate materials looking good.

Hard surfaces provide the home landscape with a strong, durable, low-maintenance surface suitable for many different activities. However, the sun can heat hard surface materials limiting daytime use. Some hard surface materials are very slippery when wet and may present additional hazards. The cost of material and installation for hard surfacing is high.

The landscape contractor will guide the homeowner in selecting the patio surfacing material and will also suggest guidelines for overall patio size. You cannot build too large a patio, but it is easy to build one that is too small. Landscapers recommend the following guidelines for patio design. All sides of a well-designed patio should be at least 8 feet long. A good patio for a family of four will contain at least 300 square feet of

surface area. Consider both guidelines as minimum recommendations and increase them as money
and space allow.

Entrance walks and other
heavy traffic walks should be 3
feet wide while secondary paths
can be 2 feet wide. Again, consider
the above sizes as minimums and
increase as the situation demands.

THE PATIO

Before 1960 in the United
States, few families spent time
outside in the backyard. As
Americans started moving outdoors into the backyard during the
late 1950s and the early 1960s,
the patio was born. The patio provided the hard surface needed to
keep family members' feet out of
the grass and mud and prevented
chair and table legs from sinking
into the ground. Shortly after creating the patio, the American people began grilling hot dogs, ham-
burgers, and steaks on the patio
grill. The house contractor built
many of these new patios from
concrete before the landscape contractor was hired.

A *patio* provides a hard surface outdoors for a variety of family activities, such as eating, danc-
ing, playing games, or just

**11-5. A walk in the outdoor living area con-
structed with pavers. (Courtesy, Pavestone
Company, Dallas, TX)**

11-6. Flagstone patio on concrete base.

Table 11-1. Patio Construction Materials

Construction Material	Material Cost	Aesthetic Quality	Durability and Life	Maintenance and Upkeep
Gravel	very low	low	medium	high
Concrete	medium	low	high	low
Brick over sand	medium	high	medium	medium
Patio pavers over sand	medium	medium	medium	medium
Flagstone over sand	high	high	medium	low
Brick over concrete	high	high	very high	low
Wood decks	high	high	medium	medium
Clay tile over concrete	very high	very high	low	low
Flagstone over concrete	very high	high	medium	low

relaxing and talking. The patio can be constructed from a variety of building materials and several different construction techniques can be used for each material.

The cost of construction for patios will vary with the different building materials. Gravel will cost the least; flagstone over concrete will cost the most. The homeowner and the landscaper will decide which material to use and how to construct the patio.

11-7. Concrete blocks filled with soil and planted with grass seed provide a living driveway.

CHOOSING THE RIGHT PATIO MATERIAL

The shape of a patio may dictate the choice of building material. It is difficult to build a patio with curved edges out of brick or flagstone, but concrete will easily conform to many odd-shaped layouts. If the site is hilly, a wooden deck may be more appropriate than leveling the site and building a concrete patio.

11-8. Deck on a steep hill-side.

Most people think brick patios are beautiful, while a concrete patio is very ordinary. Each material has a different aesthetic quality. A concrete patio will last a long time, but one made from inexpensive patio stones may need replacing in five years.

Yearly maintenance requirements will also affect the selection of patio materials. Wood will need frequent treatment with preservatives to keep the boards looking good and prevent rot. A brick-over-concrete patio will last for 30 or more years with very little yearly maintenance. Cost is usually the major factor in selecting the best patio material for each landscape site.

After the customer selects the patio material, the landscape contractor must correctly install the patio. Some landscape contractors do not install all types of patios, but subcontract this work to other companies. The subcontractor works directly for the landscape contractor and only completes a small part of the total landscape work. Many companies specialize in building brick or flagstone patios, while others only construct wood decks.

CONCRETE PATIOS

Concrete is the most popular patio surfacing material. It is easy to install and can be poured into almost any desired shape. Low maintenance and durability make concrete a good choice when selecting patio surfacing materials. Mix sand, gravel, cement, and water together to create concrete. *Cement*, the "glue" that holds the sand and gravel together, is a mixture of lime, clay, iron, and silica. Most communities have ready-mix concrete companies that mix and deliver concrete in large trucks to the building site. A chemical reaction changes the soupy liquid mixture into a solid form a few hours after pouring. Temperature and humidity will affect this chemical reaction, but nothing can stop it. When the concrete truck arrives, be ready to pour and finish the concrete.

11- 9. Pouring ready-mix concrete.

FORMS CONSTRUCTION

Use 2" × 4" boards to construct wood forms before pouring concrete walks or patios. Set the forms so the top edge of the 2" × 4" is the desired surface height of the finished concrete pad. Steel or wood stakes hold the 2" × 4" in place while pouring concrete. Most walks and patios will be 3½ inches thick, the same as the actual thickness of the form. Many landscape contractors "paint" the wood forms with motor oil before pouring concrete to prevent it from sticking to the boards.

Locate the patio site and dig out any existing lawn. Excavate the site to a depth of 6 inches below the finish surface of the patio. Shovel a

11-10. 2" × 4" forms before pouring concrete walk.

2½-inch layer of crushed gravel called road pack or hardcore as a base in the excavated patio site. Use a plate compactor to compact the gravel. A *plate compactor* is a mechanical plate vibrator used to compact base materials and pavers. It has a small gasoline engine that vibrates the heavy steel plate tamping the base material.

MIXING CONCRETE

Most concrete is prepared at a plant and delivered to the construction site in trucks that continue the mixing process until delivery. Small job amounts can be mixed with a portable mixer or by hand in a large tub or wooden box. Generally, ready-mixed concrete is used for all jobs requiring one or more cubic yards of concrete.

EQUIPMENT FOR CONCRETE WORK

Elaborate equipment is not needed for mixing and placing concrete, although, for efficient work, certain simple tools are essential. They are:

■ Water and pail for handling water and washing tools.

■ Square-pointed shovels for turning and mixing.

■ Tamp for compacting concrete or foundation bases.

■ Steel plan wheelbarrow for moving aggregates and concrete mixtures.

■ Mixing box or platform if concrete is mixed by hand for small jobs.

■ Screed (straightedge board) for leveling concrete.

■ Wood float and trowel for finishing concrete.

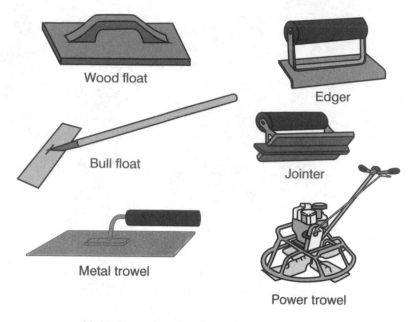

Wood float

Edger

Bull float

Jointer

Metal trowel

Power trowel

11-11. Examples of tools used in concrete work.

ORDERING AND POURING CONCRETE

Ready-mix companies sell concrete by the cubic yard. A ***cubic yard*** is a volume measurement 3 feet wide, 3 feet long, and 3 feet high. There are several ways to compute the quantity of concrete necessary for a patio. One easy way is multiply the length and width of the patio to find the square feet and divide this answer by 80 square feet per cubic yard. A patio 24 feet long and 10 feet wide will require 3 cubic yards of concrete.

$$24' \times 10' = 240 \text{ sq. ft.} \qquad \frac{240 \text{ sq. ft.}}{80 \text{ sq. ft./cu. yd.}} = 3 \text{ cu. yd. concrete}$$

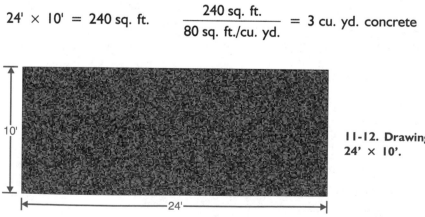

11-12. Drawing of a patio, 24' × 10'.

When ordering ready-mixed concrete, give the following information:

1. Use to be made of ready-mix. Will it be used for patio, walk, or driveway?

2. Amounts of exposure the concrete will receive. Will it receive severe exposure, normal exposure, or mild exposure?

3. Amount of ready-mixed concrete needed.

FORMS

A *form* is a frame or mold that holds liquid concrete to shape until it has set. The forms for concrete must be strong and rigid to prevent sagging, bulging, and spreading.

Forms may be removed easily without the concrete sticking to them if they have been coated on the inside with crude oil before they are used. All pieces of concrete should be removed from forms before they are used again.

11-13. Form with plastic and steel reinforcement ready for placing a concrete slab. (Note bracing to keep form from warping or collapsing under the pressure from the weight of the wet concrete.)

REINFORCING CONCRETE

The tendency of concrete to crack has been an accepted problem in construction. To reduce cracking, landscapers incorporated metal wire mesh when pouring concrete. Wire mesh will not prevent concrete from cracking, but will hold the cracked pieces together. Wire mesh can also rust and discolor the concrete.

Today, many landscapers use plastic fibers instead of metal wire mesh to add strength to the finished concrete. Fibrillated polypropylene fibers, bundles of interconnected strands, reduce the formation of shrinkage cracks and increase the tensile strength of the concrete slab. Fibermesh® is a popular brand of polypropylene fiber. The fibers are engineered exclusively for concrete use. When the bundles of fibers are added to the concrete mix, at the rate of 1½ pounds per cubic yard, the mixing action causes them to open and separate into millions of individual fibers. The fibers are uniformly distributed throughout the concrete in all directions, providing effective secondary reinforcement for shrinkage crack control. The fiber will not rust or stain surfaces, is noncorrosive and alkali-proof, and will not affect the finishing characteristics of concrete.

PLACING CONCRETE

The ready-mix truck will pour the concrete in the constructed forms. Use shovels to move the concrete and fill the forms. Level the concrete surface by working a 2" × 4" straight edge across the narrow sides of the patio form. This leveling technique is called screeding. Screeding will move the excess concrete from high spots and fill in the low spots. When the concrete starts to get hard, use a bull float to make the surface smooth and work the large aggregates down from the surface. Use an edger to put a curve on the edge of the concrete next to the forms.

A concrete mixture should be placed in the forms when it is thoroughly mixed. Concrete will begin to set within 30 to 45 minutes after the water is added. A shovel or thin board may be used to work the mixture against the forms. A powered vibrator is used for larger jobs. It can be rented from an equipment rental business.

Several stages of hardening take place as concrete *cures*, gets hard. The slower the concrete cures, the stronger the patio. Cover newly poured concrete for at least seven days with a sheet of plastic to slow the curing process. The initial hardening takes only a few hours. Several days later, the concrete goes through a second curing stage and gets harder. After one month, concrete completes a third curing stage. No traffic should be allowed on the concrete during the first and second stages of curing, about three

11-14. Finishing a concrete driveway.

to seven days. After this time, the forms can be removed and light traffic will not damage the concrete. Heavy traffic should not be permitted until concrete has cured for one month.

Concrete poured in the summer may cure too fast. Ready-mix companies can add a chemical *retarder* to slow this hardening process. Cold winter temperatures may slow the curing process too much, causing the water to freeze before the concrete hardens. Chemicals called *accelerators* are added to speed the hardening process.

FINISHING CONCRETE

A *float* is a tool used for initially smoothing the surface of liquid concrete after screeding. A metal *trowel* is a tool used to bring a thin film of cement to the top after the concrete has initially set, making a very smooth surface. This film of cement does not wear as well as a cement and sand mixture, and is slippery when wet.

11-15. Concrete finished, ready to cover.

Concrete can have a variety of surface finishes depending on the wants and needs of the customer. A glassy smooth surface may look great, but it can be very slick when wet and may reflect light into nearby buildings. Drag a broom over the concrete just before it hardens to create a rough, nonskid **broom finish** on the surface.

Many landscapers expose the gravel used to make the concrete by washing away some of the cement just before the concrete hardens. *Exposed aggregate* can create an unusual patio from ordinary concrete. Skill is needed to know when to expose the aggregate. Washing too early can destroy the concrete. If you wait too long, the concrete may be too hard to remove the cement particles. Timing is very important.

REMOVING FORMS

Forms are removed when new concrete has set sufficiently so it will not be damaged in the process. Ordinarily, during warm weather, two or three days should be sufficient for forms to remain in place for walls and small objects. In cold weather, the forms should remain in place about twice as long.

In determining when to remove forms, weather, temperature, and nature of the work must be considered. In no case should the forms be removed until, by careful examination, the concrete has thoroughly set and there is no danger of it breaking apart or becoming damaged. It is often an advantage to leave the forms in place during curing to help retain moisture in the concrete.

CONCRETE WALKS AND DRIVEWAYS

Walks and driveways are carefully planned for attractiveness and use. Walks are built for convenience and to eliminate cutting across lawns or corners. Walks are of great importance to both the utility and beauty of the landscape.

Here is how to construct a walk:

1. Estimate the quantities of cement and aggregates or ready-mix that will be required. Most walkways are 36 to 48 inches wide and 4 inches thick.

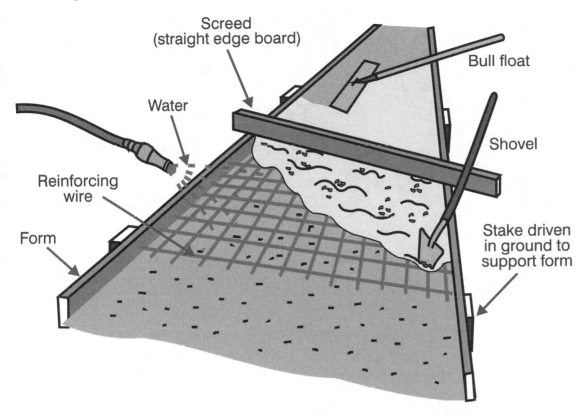

11-16. Procedures in placing a concrete walk include keeping the soil moist, working with the concrete with a square-point shovel, striking with a two-by-four, and using a bull float to smooth the surface.

2. Prepare a level, well-drained, compact base. Build up the base so the top of the walk will extend 2 inches above the ground.

3. Use two-by-fours for side forms. Use stakes to hold the forms in position. Level tops of forms so the concrete will be of the desired thickness; ordinarily a thickness of about 4 inches is sufficient. A slight slope to one side of 1/8 inch per foot will allow water to drain off rapidly.

4. Place partition strips at intervals of 4 to 6 feet.

5. Level with a screed (straight edge board).

6. Finish with a wooden float.

7. Cover with plastic after the concrete has hardened slightly. Cure for at least seven days.

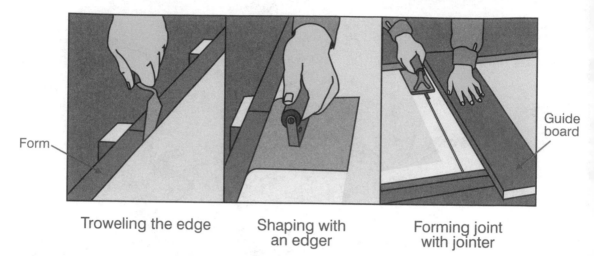

Form

Guide board

Troweling the edge   Shaping with an edger   Forming joint with jointer

11-17. Finishing a walk involves using a trowel to separate wet concrete from the form, using an edger to slightly round the edge, and using a jointer to make a joint.

A good driveway is attractive and serviceable. The arrangement and location of a driveway should be planned with care. Driveways for single vehicles are 9 to 10 feet wide. Most are made of concrete 4 to 6 inches thick. A compact, well-drained base is more critical for driveways than walks.

The center of the base should be 1 inch higher than the edges, and the base should be rounded uniformly so the concrete will have a uniform thickness of 6 or more inches. Use 2" × 6" lumber for side forms. Level the forms and stake them securely. Place partitions about 20 feet apart and allow space for the expansion and the contraction of the concrete. Add reinforcing wire once the forms are in place. Strike off so the center will be 1 inch higher than the outer edges. Finish and cure similarly to walks.

PAVER BLOCKS

Many companies manufacture paver blocks and bricks. *Paver blocks* are specially made units constructed from compressed concrete into many types, styles, colors, and sizes. The concrete mixture is compacted under extreme pressure and high frequency vibrations to give the finished paver a compressive strength of 8,000 psi. The pavers have a maximum water

11-18. Patio constructed using paver blocks.

absorption of 5 percent and resist freezing and thawing cycles. Paveloc® Industries, Inc. and Unilock® license manufacturers throughout the country to produce concrete pavers. The most common size of pavers available is 2 3/8 inches thick, 8 inches long, and 4 inches wide. Pavers can be cut using any masonry saw or by hand using a brick chisel. Wood, aluminum, steel, or plastic edging must be used on all sides of the surface when laying the paver blocks.

Mark off the area and remove any existing turf from the site. Excavate the site to a depth of 7 inches below the finished surface. Prepare the base using a 2½-inch layer of crushed gravel. Use a plate compactor to

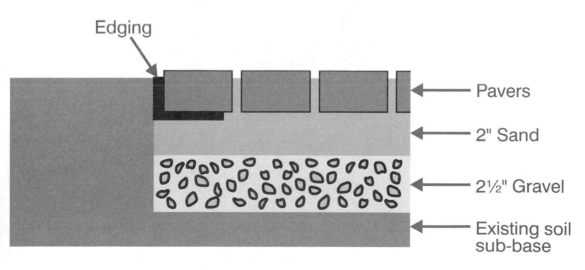

11-19. Cross-section of paver installation technique.

compact the gravel. Landscape fabric can be placed over the gravel to help keep the entire paver surface uniform by lessening individual pavers or areas from being heaved during freezing and thawing conditions.

Install edge restraints to keep the pavers in place. BrickEdg® by Oly-Ola Sales, Inc. and Permaloc aluminum edging are specially made for this purpose. Landscape timbers or railroad ties can also be used. Next, add a 2-inch layer of sand. Take special care to level (screed) this sand layer.

Place the pavers in position starting in a corner. Cut pavers as necessary for the edges. Level the pavers and fill the joints with coarse sand. Use a plate compactor for final compaction going over the top of the pavers in several different directions. Sweep more dry, coarse sand into the cracks between the pavers. Rinse off the excess sand with a gentle spray from a water hose to complete the job.

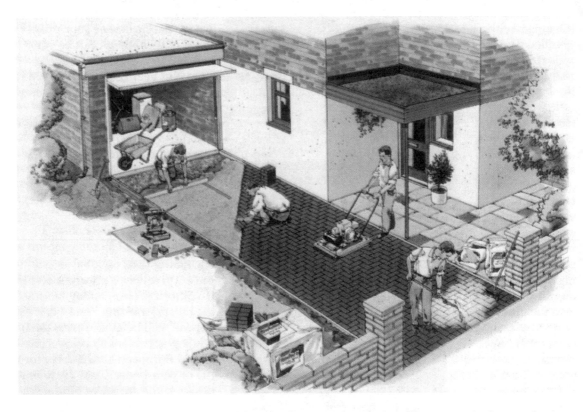

11-20. The steps to installing pavers are: (1) mark and excavate the site, (2) prepare the base and compact, (3) install edge restraint, (4) screed the sand base, (5) lay pavers starting in a corner, (6) cut pavers as necessary, (7) fill the joints with coarse sand, (8) use a plate compactor for final compaction of the pavers, and (9) sweep more sand into joints and rinse off with a gentle spray from a hose. (Courtesy, Pavestone Company, Dallas, TX)

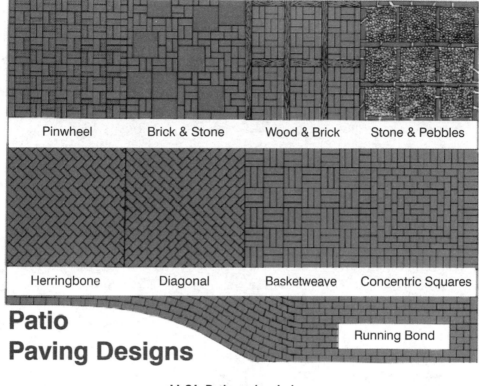

Pinwheel   Brick & Stone   Wood & Brick   Stone & Pebbles

Herringbone   Diagonal   Basketweave   Concentric Squares

Patio Paving Designs

Running Bond

11-21. Patio paving designs.

BRICK PATIOS

Bricks have been used in construction for thousands of years. Clay dug from a hole in the ground is heated in a kiln to several thousand degrees for several days. Different clays will create different colors of brick. The standard brick size is 3¾ inches wide by 2¼ inches thick and 8 inches long. Bricks made from clay will last hundreds of years in the landscape. Lay bricks on a sand base using the same technique as used when installing concrete pavers. Never use house bricks for constructing surfaces.

Bricks can also be laid over a bed of concrete. This technique is twice as expensive as placing the bricks on a sand base. Dig out the site to a depth of 7 inches and pour a 3½-inch concrete base. After the concrete base has hardened, cover it with a 1-inch bed of mortar. Gently place each brick in the mortar and use a level to create a flat surface. Leave a ¼-to ½-inch space between the bricks. Fill these cracks the next day by sweeping a dry mixture of mortar and sand into each crack. Use a fine stream of water to wet the dry mortar mix and complete the brick installation.

DECKS

Deck describes a patio with a wooden surface area raised above the ground level. Decks first became popular during the late 1960s as a way of adding outdoor living space on hillside lots. However, many decks today are built on level ground. Decks can be built just inches high or elevated well above the ground. They may be freestanding or attached to the home or other buildings. Decks can even be built on a second-story above a garage, carport, or other roofed structure. The landscape site may suggest the use of a wooden deck instead of other patio materials.

Usually, the deck is the same height as the house floor so people can walk onto the deck without stepping up or down. A bilevel deck can solve the problem of small changes in elevation from the house floor to the yard. The upper deck will be level with the house floor and the lower deck only one step above the yard. Wooden steps connect the two deck levels.

11-22. Elevated deck.

Redwood and bald cypress are two naturally decay-resistant woods. High price and limited availability make them poor choices for deck construction. Other woods can be used when treated with chemicals that discourage decay and insect infestation. These chemicals are forced into the wood by a high-pressure treatment technique.

Today, Southern yellow pine is pressure-treated with Wolman® chromated copper arsenate (CCA) to reduce decay. Wolmanized® or CCA treated lumber can be hazardous to humans during the construction of a deck. However, follow a few simple safety precautions to reduce these hazards.

SAFETY PRECAUTIONS WITH CCA TREATED LUMBER

- Wash hands after handling CCA treated wood and before eating
- Wear a dust mask when cutting and sawing treated lumber
- Use CCA lumber only on outside projects
- Never use CCA lumber on an inside construction project
- Never burn wood scraps; take them to a sanitary landfill
- Never construct a food preparation area with CCA lumber

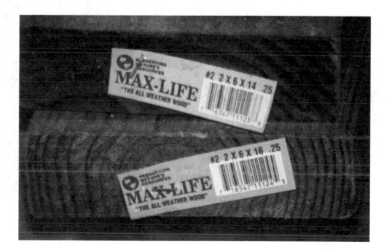

11-23. Treated lumber label.

CONSTRUCTION TIPS

- Always nail a thinner board to a thicker board
- Drive nails in the deck board at a slight angle, toward each other, for greater holding power
- When toenailing, stagger opposing nails so they pass each other
- Nails and other hardware should be hot-dipped, zinc-coated

- To reduce splitting, drill a pilot hole about three-quarters the diameter of the nail

- For maximum holding power, use spiral-shank nails or deck screws

- The nail should penetrate the thicker piece of lumber twice as deep as the thickness of the thin piece of lumber.

- Blunt the nail point with a hammer to reduce the chances of splitting the wood

Deck boards are held together with special fasteners created just for heavy-duty outdoor use. Nails are identified by a "d" designation, which stands for penny. A 16d nail is called a 16-penny nail. Use spiral-shank, galvanized nails that "screw" into wood when driven with a hammer. These nails are also called deck nails.

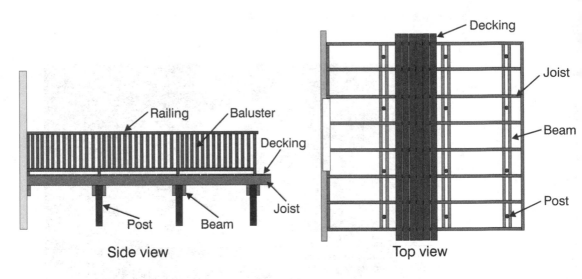

11-24. Parts of a deck.

Galvanized buglehead screws (deck screws), similar to the black drywall screws, can also be used when building decks. These screws have a #2 Phillips head and are installed with an electric drill or screw gun. Install large lag screws for major structural connection on the deck. Use a wrench or socket to install lag screws with a square or hex head. Always use washers and predrill the holes to reduce the splitting of wood when installing lag screws.

DESIGN

Decks are made up of five major parts—posts, beams, joists, decking, and railings. The three basic considerations when selecting building materials and deck design are function, structural stability, and appearance.

Dig holes for support posts 48 inches deep, place CCA treated 4" × 4" or 6" × 6" posts upright in the hole. Use a level to keep the posts plumb while filling the holes. Fill the hole with a bag of dry premixed concrete. Wet the dry concrete mix around the post to start the chemical curing of the concrete.

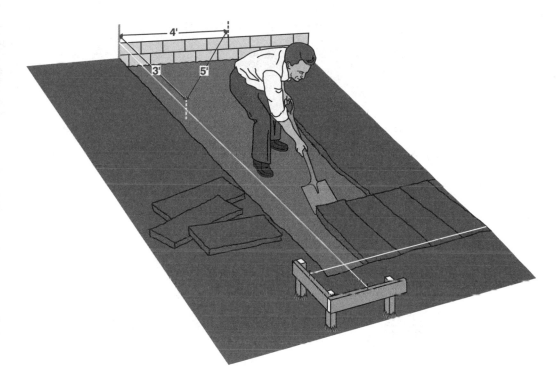

11-25. Layout and site preparation for deck or patio construction.

Use Tables 11-2 and 11-4 to select the correct post size and spacing. *Beams* are 2-inch thick boards, 8- to 12-inches wide, which connect the posts and provide the support for the joists in deck construction. *Cleats* are the short boards attached to the posts for the beams to rest on. *Joists* are run at a 90-degree angle to the beams and are usually spaced 16- or 24-inches "on center" (o.c.). Use Table 11-3 for joist size and spacing.

Table 11-2. Minimum Beam Sizes

Length of Span (ft.)	Spacing Between Posts (ft.)						
	4	**5**	**6**	**7**	**8**	**9**	**10**
6	(2) 2 × 8s	(2) 2 × 8s	(2) 2 × 8s	(2) 2 × 10s	(2) 2 × 10s	(2) 2 × 10s	(2) 2 × 12s
7	(2) 2 × 10s	(2) 2 × 10s	(2) 2 × 10s	(2) 2 × 10s	(2) 2 × 10s	(2) 2 × 12s	(2) 2 × 12s
8	(2) 2 × 10s	(2) 2 × 10s	(2) 2 × 10s	(2) 2 × 12s	(2) 2 × 12s	(2) 2 × 12s	(3) 2 × 12s
9	(2) 2 × 10s	(2) 2 × 10s	(2) 2 × 12s	(2) 2 × 12s	(2) 2 × 12s	(3) 2 × 12s	*
10	(2) 2 × 10s	(2) 2 × 12s	(2) 2 × 12s	(3) 2 × 12s	(3) 2 × 12s	*	*
11	(2) 2 × 12s	(2) 2 × 12s	(3) 2 × 12s	(3) 2 × 12s	*	*	*
12	(2) 2 × 12s	(2) 2 × 12s	(3) 2 × 12s	(3) 2 × 12s	*	*	*

*Beams larger than 2 × 12 recommended. Consult a designer for appropriate sizes.

Deck boards cover the joists and provide the flooring surface of a deck on which people walk and where furniture is placed. Always install the deck boards with the bark side up to reduce cupping action as the boards weather. Several different sized deck boards are available. Deck boards are also available with squared edges or rounded edges called **eased**-edges.

Table 11-3. Maximum Allowable Spans for Deck Joists

Joist Size (inches)	Joist Spacing (inches)	
	16	**24**
2 × 6	9'-9"	7'-11"
2 × 8	12'-10"	10'-6"
2 × 10	16'-5"	13'-4"

Table 11-4. Minimum Post Sizes

Height (ft.)	Load Area (sq. ft.) = Beam Spacing × Post Spacing				
	48	72	96	120	144
Up to 6	4 × 4	4 × 4	6 × 6	6 × 6	6 × 6
Up to 8	6 × 6	6 × 6	6 × 6	6 × 6	6 × 6

Vertical loads figured as concentric along axis.
No lateral loads considered.

Eased-edged deck boards resist splitting and look better. Deck boards will usually be either a 2" × 6" (1½ inches thick by 5½ inches wide) or a five-quarter, 5/4 × 6" (1 inch thick by 5½ inches wide). Most deck boards are made from Southern pine or Douglasfir.

Install deck boards using deck nails or buglehead screws. Separate the deck boards using a nail as a spacer or set the boards 1/8 to 1/4 inch apart. Use a small block of wood to uniformly space the boards. Trim the edge of the deck boards, after nailing, to create a straight line. Do not allow the deck boards to overhang the deck support member by more than 1½ inches.

Next, install the posts for the railing. The support posts can also be used for the railing support. Standard railing height is 36 inches above

11-26. Installing deck boards.

11-27. Deck built around trees. Cut the hole in the deck large enough to allow for future tree growth.

the deck surface. The vertical pieces of wood between the top and bottom rails are called *balusters*. Place the balusters 6 inches apart.

STEPS

Patios, decks, and walks may have several levels or they may be used in combination. Steps are necessary to allow access to or to connect these different levels. The material selected by the designer for the steps usually matches the levels being connected. However, the surface area should take into account that outdoor steps can become slippery when wet.

There are two basic components of steps. The *riser* is the elevating vertical part of a step and the *tread* is the level part of the step on which the foot is placed. The slope of the incline of steps should be 33 to 50 percent. In unusual situations, an incline up to 65 percent is acceptable. Steps in a landscape should be constructed to allow the user to maintain a natural stride pattern. The steps should be constructed so that the total length of two risers and one tread is 26 inches. As the tread dimension increases, the riser dimension decreases. The formula for calculating dimensions for outdoor steps is Tread + 2 Risers = 26". Therefore, a riser of 7 inches would have a tread of 12 inches, or a riser of 5 inches would have a tread of 16 inches.

11-28. Parts of steps.

REVIEWING

MAIN IDEAS

Grass or other plant materials cannot provide a permanent surface for vehicular or people traffic. Hard surface and loose aggregate materials provide a durable surface for high traffic areas in the home landscape. The patio became popular in this country during the early 1960s. A patio must be large enough for the family's outdoor activities. Concrete, manufactured paver blocks, brick, and flagstone are popular construction materials for home patios.

A patio made from wood is called a deck. Decks can be constructed level with the ground or elevated well above the ground. They may be freestanding or attached to the home. Construct the deck using redwood, bald cypress, or treated lumber. Follow all safety precautions when using CCA treated lumber. Always consult engineering charts when selecting posts, beams, and joists for deck construction. Deck boards now are commonly sold as 5/4- × 6-inch boards. Their edges can be square or eased.

QUESTIONS

Answer the following questions using correct spelling and complete sentences.

1. What size should a patio be for a family of four people?
2. Why may it be necessary to build a deck instead of a patio?
3. What are four different kinds of paving materials available?
4. What is screeding concrete?
5. Why use treated lumber when building a deck?
6. What are the two basic components of steps?

CHAPTER SELF-CHECK

Match the term with the correct definition. Place the letter in the blank provided.

a. pressure-treated   d. plate compactor   g. bilevel deck
b. loose aggregate   e. screeding   h. beam
c. retarder   f. ready-mix

____ 1. A mechanical vibrator used to compact base materials and pavers

____ 2. Concrete delivered in a large truck to the construction site

____ 3. Deck with two or more levels

____ 4. Material added to concrete poured in the summer

____ 5. Leveling the sand before placing the patio bricks

____ 6. Large boards attached to the deck posts, which will support the joists

____ 7. Soft paving materials that can provide a temporary surface in the home landscape

____ 8. Technique used on lumber so it will resist decay

EXPLORING

1. Examine your patio or a neighbor's. Describe the building materials. Is this patio the correct size?

2. Talk to a landscape construction company and visit a site where they are building a deck.

3. Try finishing a small concrete pad using a bag of premixed concrete. Make a wooden form, from 2 × 4s, 2 feet square. Use correct concrete-finishing tools.

12

Installing Fences and Walls

Fences and walls serve to enclose a section of the landscape. They may provide protection or privacy. They can change the climate of a small area by reducing wind or the sun's rays. They may serve safety or engineering needs by holding back soil on a slope or enclosing an electrical transformer. They can mark the property boundary. They are the walls in the outdoor room of the landscape design.

Why install a chain link fence in a backyard? From what materials can a retaining wall be made? Why put weep holes in concrete retaining walls? What is a microclimate? How do fences and screens differ? How deep should a fence post hole be dug? What material should be used when backfilling around fence posts? What is a restrictive covenant and how is it important when building fences? What is a mortarless block wall system?

12-1. A fence can provide privacy in the outdoor living area.

245

OBJECTIVES

1. List reasons for fences and walls

2. Discuss microclimate and its importance in the landscape

3. Know the different parts used to construct fences

4. Describe the popular types of enclosures used in the landscape

5. Be able to install fence posts properly

6. Describe the different materials used in constructing retaining walls

7. Be able to install retaining walls properly

8. Describe mortarless block wall construction techniques

TERMS

bay
covenant
enclosure
fence
frost line
gate
gate post
infill
line post
main post
microclimate
mortarless block wall system
ordinance
pilaster
post
retaining wall
screen
wall
weep hole
wrought iron

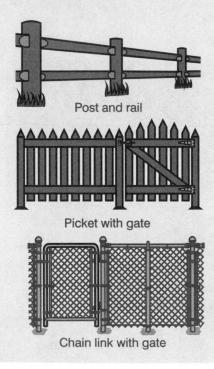

Post and rail

Picket with gate

Chain link with gate

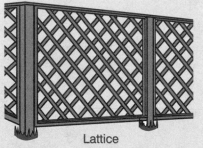

Lattice

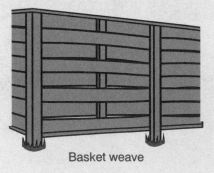

Basket weave

LANDSCAPE FENCES AND WALLS

Landscapers use the term *enclosure* to describe both fences and walls used in the landscape. A *fence* is an enclosure having posts, rails, and infill usually constructed from wood, metal, or plastic. Concrete, brick, stones, and blocks are used to construct more substantial enclosing elements called walls. A *wall* is an upright structure serving to enclose, divide, support, or protect an area.

MAJOR REASONS FOR FENCES AND WALLS

- protect property
- provide security for children and pets
- ensure privacy
- create sound barriers
- maintain microclimates
- screen objectionable views
- mark property lines

Fences can serve any or all of the above purposes in the home landscape. Fences should solve specific problems in

12-2. A louvered fence screens the air conditioner units, but allows good air circulation.

12-3. Wrought-iron fence sections around the front yard.

12-4. A painted, wooden rail fence is decorative in this landscape.

the yard. Do not build fences just to build fences. Keep fences as a background for landscape planting. Do not let them become the main attraction. Some fence materials may require constant painting and maintenance.

The temperature, precipitation, humidity, and wind of a small area, such as a backyard, is called a **microclimate**. Well-designed fences will allow cooling breezes into the yard, but prevent strong, cold winds. A strong, prevailing wind can make an outdoor living area unusable or at best uncomfortable much of the year. A wall constructed near the patio can deflect the wind and allow greater use of the outdoor area. Glass or plastic fence materials are usually used around swimming pools to control unwanted cool winds.

12-5. This split-rail fence defines property lines.

Fences are usually constructed along the property line for both security and visual privacy. Walls can be constructed on the property line or inside for the same reasons. Many landscapers use the term **screen** to describe a fence or wall used to create only visual privacy in the landscape. Screens do not have to be on the property line, but can be moved closer to the patio for increased privacy. Screens will not provide security or property protection.

Plant material can also provide the homeowner with the same visual privacy that fences do. However, living screens are usually 4 to 6 feet wide, while

12-6. A preassembled plastic, basket weave fence.

fences are 4 to 6 inches wide. Small city properties usually do not have the space necessary for living screens.

12-7. A natural board-on-board fence with evergreens planted in front of sections.

Fence materials should be similar to the house construction materials. Ideally, brick homes should have matching brick outdoor walls. Wood fences look best when used around homes constructed of natural wood. Size restrictions of the lot and budget limitations may prevent using identical home and fence construction materials.

LEGAL CONSIDERATIONS
WHEN BUILDING FENCES AND WALLS

An ***ordinance*** is a governmental regulation or statute. City ordinances and building codes cover the location, size, and construction of fences and walls within the city limits. Many cities restrict all fences or walls to a maximum of 6 feet in height in the backyard. Some cities limit fence height in the front yard to 4 feet. City ordinances usually do not regulate the type of fence material used.

12-8. Chain link fence provides security around this electric transformer.

A ***covenant*** is an agreement made between two or more parties to do or keep from doing a specific thing. Many subdivisions have restrictive covenants that regulate fence construction within the subdivision. Some covenants regulate the fence material, while others restrict the height and location of all fences in the subdivision. Some people believe chain-link fences are not beautiful and do not want them in the subdivision.

FENCES

Wood, plastic, and metal fences can be built on site or preassembled sections can be erected. Preassembled fence sections are built in a factory and are ready to install without additional construction. Today, landscape companies usually install preassembled sections of fence. Most fence sections are either 4 or 6 feet high and usually 8 feet long.

FENCE PARTS

Wooden fences have posts, rails, and infill. A ***post*** is a strong upright material that supports a fence. Two kinds of posts are typically found: main and line.

A ***main post*** is at a corner or a gate. The post to which a gate is attached is known as a ***gate post. Line posts*** are between corner and gate posts. Rails are the horizontal supports between posts. Most fences with infill have two rails. Rails are sometimes known as stringers. Some fences are built only of rails attached to posts.

The distance between two posts is known as a ***bay. Infill*** is the material fastened to the rails that ensures security and privacy. Infill may also be known as screening. With fences that have a public view, the rails are put on the inside. Rails are often on the outside of a decorative patio or backyard fences.

A ***gate*** is a movable barrier in a fence. Most gates are attached with hinges on one side. A latch on the side opposite the hinges holds the gate securely fastened. Some latches may have locks that help prevent unauthorized entry. Gates are typically designed using similar material to the fence structure.

A common metal fence used in commercial and residential landscapes is the chain link fence. This is usually an all-metal fence. It is a strong

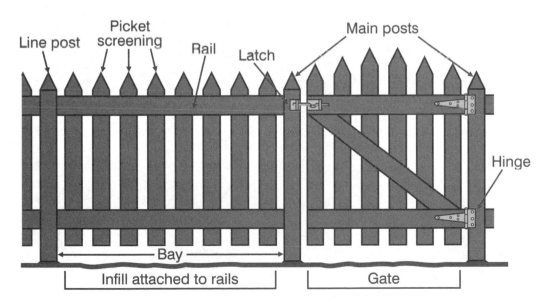

12-9. Major parts of a picket fence.

fence that can be constructed in various heights. Chain link fences offer full visibility of the protected areas.

Chain link fence fabric does not come in preassembled pieces. The wire fabric is galvanized number 9- or 11-gauge wire. Set 1½-inch pipe posts, 2½ feet deep, in holes that are 10 feet on center. Backfill the holes with concrete. Install a top pipe rail before stretching and attaching the wire chain link fabric to the pipe frame.

The fence material may be galvanized steel, aluminum, or vinyl-coated steel mesh. Only galvanized posts and rails should be used. A top rail may be used with only a tension wire at the bottom. The mesh wire must be stretched taut between the posts. Specially-made bands and post tops are used with chain link fences. Purchase preassembled gates.

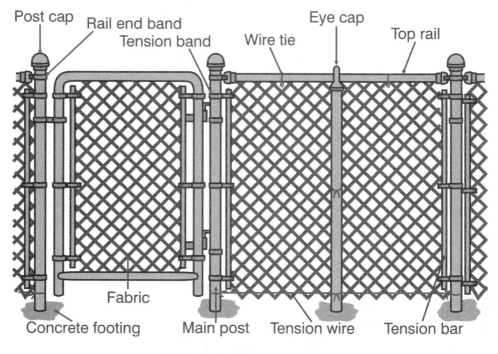

12-10. Parts of a chain link fence.

FENCES IN THE LANDSCAPE

A white, picket fence defines property and controls pets and children without creating a closed-in feeling. The original, split-rail fence built in the early 1700s did not use posts. Today, either two or three rails are

12-11. Natural-wood picket fence built on site.

12-12. Ornamental picket fence with large wooden posts.

held up with posts. This fence provides a visual backdrop for landscape planting and defines property lines. The basket-weave fence is a very popular style throughout the country. It is an interesting and beautiful fence that provides total privacy and security for children and pets.

Boards, 6 to 8 inches wide, made of wood or plastic are used to construct the modern board fence. The boards can be next to each other to provide a solid screen or spaced to allow air circulation, while still providing good visual privacy. Wood fences require constant painting or staining to keep them looking neat and clean. Plastic fence material looks like painted wood but does not require maintenance.

Table 12-1. Popular Types of Enclosures

Type	Description	Use in the Landscape
WOOD FENCES	made of natural wood or plastic, build on site or buy preassembled sections	
Board on Board	wood or plastic, usually 6" wide board, 6' high, painted or natural stain, construct on site or buy preassembled	privacy, security, screen objectionable views, create microclimates, sound barrier
Solid board	wood, usually 6" to 10" wide, 6' high, painted or natural stain, construct on site or buy preassembled	privacy, security, screen objectionable views, create microclimates, sound barrier
Basket weave	wood or plastic, very thin boards, 6' high, painted or natural stain, usually preassembled	privacy, security, screen objectionable views, create microclimates, sound barrier
Picket	3' to 4' high, wood or plastic, usually painted to match color of house	security for children and pets, mark property lines
Rail	wood or plastic, rough split and stained or finished painted boards, 2 or 3 rails	mark property lines
Louvers	6" wide boards angled to restrict view but permit air movement, natural or painted	privacy, security, screen objectionable views
CHAIN LINK	galvanized fabric, $1^1/_2$" pipe posts	
Standard Mesh	galvanized or aluminum fabric, not a good background for shrubs	security, mark property lines
Colored Mesh	wire covered with black or green vinyl coating to improve the look	security, mark property lines
Plastic/Metal Inserts	inserts fit all standard fabric	security, mark property lines, privacy, screen objectionable views
WROUGHT IRON	solid, square pieces of wrought iron, heavy and very expensive	
Hollow Tubing	hollow steel or aluminum tubing used instead of solid wrought iron, posts 1" square, upright tube $^1/_2$" square	security, mark property lines

(Continued)

Table 12-1 (Continued)

Type	Description	Use in the Landscape
MASONRY WALL	very large and massive, used on large building sites, not in a small backyard	
Plain Concrete Block	4" thick blocks with 8" blocks used to create columns every 16 feet	privacy, security, sound barrier, create microclimates
Brick	variety of kinds and colors, if possible match brick used in house, can curve to create interest	privacy, security, sound barrier, create microclimates
Poured Concrete	6" thick wall, use forms	privacy, security, sound barrier, create microclimates

Wrought iron is an iron that contains some slag and very little carbon. It is resistant to corrosion, tough, and ductile. Wrought-iron fences have been used around cemeteries for hundreds of years. Use wrought iron as a see-through fence when security and beauty are required. Today, large estates have installed hollow steel or aluminum tubes that look like the old-fashioned wrought iron. This new fence material is less expensive than the old material. However, this type of fence is still very expensive. Large, brick posts, 2 or 3 feet square, can be used to create an interesting and unusual fence to show property lines. Decorative accessories, such as scrolls, finials, and ball caps, are available to match wrought-iron fences.

12-13. Concrete blocks are used to construct this wall-type fence.

12-14. Modified picket fence in Alaska.

Walk gates and large industrial gates are available that match the style of the wrought-iron fence. This type of fence will enhance the beauty of a swimming pool while providing the needed security.

INSTALLING FENCE POSTS

Locate and verify all property boundaries before installing fences on or near the property line. Start fence construction by locating one corner post hole. Stretch a line from this post to the end of the fence. Measure 8 feet and mark the center of each post hole.

Setting posts involves digging holes, positioning the post in the hole, and placing fill around the post. Holes can be dug with a power auger or with hand diggers. Dig the hole with the center below the on-center location of the post on the line. The line will need to be slightly pushed to one side for digging.

A guideline is to make the depth of holes for wood posts in ornamental fences one-third the height of the post above the ground plus 6 inches. If a post is to extend 6 feet above the ground, use an 8-foot (or slightly longer) post and dig the hole 30 inches deep (24

12-15. Hand digging a fence post hole.

inches for post and 6 inches for gravel underneath post). In colder climates, the depth of the hole is determined by the frost line. The *frost line* is the maximum depth that the ground will freeze in winter. The bottom of the post must extend below the frost line so it does not heave during freezing and thawing conditions. The diameter of holes depends on the size of posts and the fill to be used.

12-16. A 2-person power auger used to dig post holes.

Use a 6-inch hand auger or clam shell post hole digger to dig several post holes. In hard soil conditions or on large jobs, a gasoline-powered auger can be used. Dig a clean hole, try not to make the hole wider than 6 inches. This will help support the post and fence. After setting the post, fill the hole with dry concrete mix and let the concrete cure for several days before constructing the fence.

12-17. Use a level to position the post.

12-18. Fill hole with dry concrete mix after positioning.

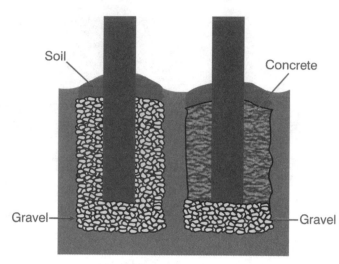

Soil

Concrete

Gravel

Gravel

12-19. This shows holes around posts filled with gravel that has been tamped (left) and concrete (right). (Note the layer of gravel in the bottom of the hole below the end of the post.)

Use a level to position the post vertically in the hole. Hold the level on two sides of the post to be sure it is vertical. Fill is the material placed around a post in the hole. Either concrete or gravel may be used. Many people prefer concrete because of post stability. Holes for posts where concrete is used as fill should be 50 percent larger than holes filled with gravel. Holes for 4-inch posts where gravel is used for fill should be 8 inches in diameter (12 inches for concrete). Six-inch posts should have holes that are 12 inches (gravel fill) and 18 inches (concrete fill) in diameter. The bottom of the hole should be filled with 6 inches of gravel or crushed stone. The gravel will allow moisture to escape and make the wooden post last longer. Backfill the hole one-half full with a dry mixture of concrete. Pour a bucket of water into the hole to moisten the concrete mixture. Fill the hole to the top with more dry concrete mixture and wet with more water. Check and make sure the post is still vertical after filling the hole. The concrete can also be mixed with water before placing it in the hole. Use one bag of premixed concrete for setting each post.

12-20. Original style of split-rail fence.

RETAINING WALLS

A *retaining wall* is an enclosure constructed to retain or hold soil in place. Well-constructed retaining walls can increase the available flat ground on hilly landscape sites. A variety of materials are available to construct a retaining wall. Poured concrete has been used for years for constructing retaining walls. Use railroad ties or treated landscape timbers to create strong but aesthetically pleasing walls. A variety of modern concrete block retaining wall systems are available. These new blocks are mortarless and easy to install. They come in a several different surface textures and colors.

Masonry constructed walls require a 12-inch wide by 12-inch deep poured concrete footing below the frost line. Concrete blocks or decorative bricks can be laid on top of this footing using mortar to hold the block together. Every 16 feet down the wall, a large square column called a pilaster is constructed. A *pilaster* is a rectangular support or pier projecting partially from a wall. The pilasters provide a visual break in a long wall and structurally support the wall.

12-21. A 6" × 6" landscape timber retaining wall.

CHOOSING THE TYPE OF RETAINING WALL

The height and strength required, shape, drainage, and cost are all factors when the designer selects a particular type of retaining wall. solid walls require footings, bracing, and reinforcement. The architecture and other parts of the hardscape features can affect the type of wall to be used also.

Sometimes a retaining wall serves a special purpose in the landscape. For example, the grade may have been raised around an existing tree. If the tree is to be saved, a retaining wall will have to be built around its base holding it to the original grade. This special purpose retaining wall will need vertical tiles set in a radial pattern beneath the dripline of the tree with crush stone underneath. The crush stone extends into the base of the retaining wall at the original grade. If the lawn area has been lowered around a tree, it will also need a retaining wall to hold the original grade.

Before beginning construction, analyze the site and develop a general layout and plan. Design the wall so surface water will flow around the ends of the wall, not over the top. Check all local building codes, lot lines, and buried utility lines before starting construction.

CONCRETE WALLS

Concrete walls are strong but are not beautiful. Water pressure can build up behind solid walls and can push them over. When building a solid wall, it is important to provide an exit for water trapped behind the wall. Every few feet down the wall, holes are made through the wall to release the built-up water pressure. These holes are called **weep holes** as water will weep through the wall. Few landscape contractors build retaining walls using poured concrete.

12-22. **Concrete retaining wall.**

RAILROAD TIE WALLS

Build railroad tie walls by stacking the ties on top of each other or placing the ties upright in a trench. Ties are treated with creosote to prevent rotting and measure 6 inches wide by 8 inches high and 8½ feet long.

12-23. Railroad tie retaining wall.

Most landscapers construct railroad tie walls a maximum of 4 feet high. Taller walls can be built, but they require additional bracing, called deadman, set into the hillside. Note that creosote can irritate the skin. Always wear long sleeve shirts and gloves when handling railroad ties.

Place the first railroad tie on level, compacted soil. Drill three, 11/16 inch diameter holes at a slight angle through each tie (a hole at each end and one in the middle). Drive a 3-foot long, 5/8 inch diameter reinforcing rod into the soil to hold the first row of ties. Set each row of ties back 1-inch from the row below. This will slant the wall into the hillside and provide greater support for the ties. Stagger the ties like brickwork. Continue drilling three, 11/16 inch diameter holes in each railroad tie. Use 6-inch long, 5/8 inch diameter, reinforcing rods to hold the ties together. Pole

12-24. Use of dead-man timbers extending back into the hillside to support the wall.

12-25. Installing reinforcing rods.

barn nails (40-penny) can also be used to hold the ties in place. Predrill all holes to prevent splitting the ties.

POST WALLS

Post or ballard walls offer variety in the landscape design. They are usually constructed with landscape timbers or railroad ties. They are installed by digging a trench. The posts are cut and placed side-by-side in

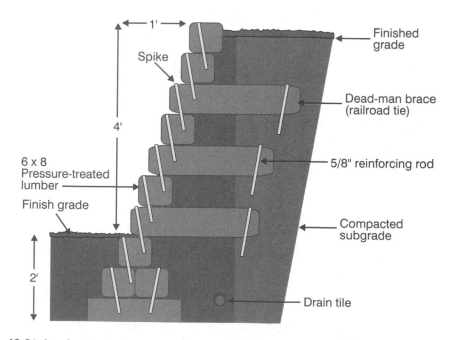

12-26. Landscape timber or railroad tie wall construction using dead-man bracing.

12-27. Retaining wall constructed by placing the railroad ties or posts vertically in the ground. Note that the tops can be even or uneven (as shown).

the trench. The top of the posts can be even or uneven depending on the appearance wanted by the landscape designer. After the posts are in proper position, the trench is backfilled. This can be done with soil and gravel layers or with equal amounts of concrete on both sides.

When installing post walls, generally there is as much post under ground as there is above ground. Higher post walls will require larger diameter posts. Weep holes may be needed to allow excess water to drain from behind the wall.

MORTARLESS CONCRETE BLOCK WALL SYSTEM

Mortarless block wall construction systems became popular in the 1980s. A *mortarless block wall system* uses precast concrete blocks, with various surface textures and colors, stacked on top of one another without mortar to hold them together. One popular block system is called Allan Block®. These blocks are $7^5/_8$ inches high, 12 inches deep, and $17^5/_8$ inches

12-28. A mortarless retaining wall system is attractive in this landscape.

long. A junior size that is 7½ inches long is also available. They are stacked on top of each other without using mortar to hold them in place. The built-in interlock is provided by a raised front lip and notched bottom. It provides built-in set back and a tight wall with clean lines. The Keystone® mortarless block system uses special reinforced fiberglass pins to hold each block in place. Both block systems automatically establish the necessary setback angle, lock each course of blocks together, and provide some built-in drainage through the wall.

Measure the wall length and multiply by the average height to compute the surface square feet of wall. Multiply the total square footage by 1.4 to find the total number of blocks needed. Retaining walls less than 4 feet high do not require a concrete footing. Concrete footings will be needed on walls higher than 4 feet.

12-29. Curved landscape flower bed created using mortarless blocks.

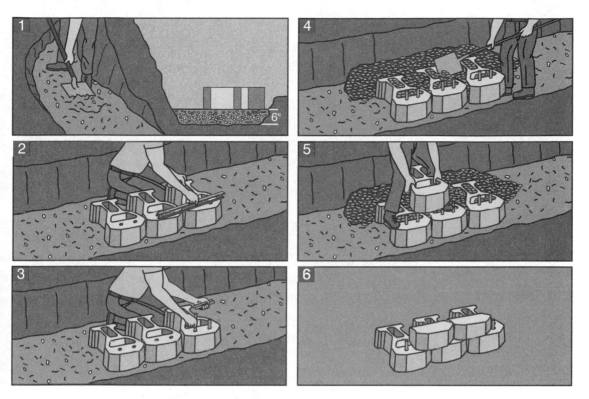

12-30. Diagram of installation technique for a Keystone® mortarless block wall system.

Dig and level the bottom of the footing. Compact the base of the footing before adding a 3-inch layer of pea gravel. In heavy soil conditions, install a plastic drain tile behind the base course of blocks to remove

12-31. Mortarless block wall systems are often used to create raised planting beds or to provide transition in topography of the land.

water. Place blocks side by side on the prepared foundation. Level each block from side to side and from front to back. Check level often and use a string line to keep the wall straight. Carefully backfill with pea gravel around the base blocks and pack the gravel to lock the blocks in place.

Backfill behind the base course and each successive course with sand or pea gravel. Clay or topsoil are not recommended as backfill. Fill the voids in and between the blocks with the pea gravel. Position the second and additional layers of blocks over the base course by staggering the edges to be in the middle of the block beneath it. The setback angle is automatically established by placing the block tightly against the front lip of the block beneath it. Backfill as each course is completed.

Curved and serpentine walls are easy to construct using the mortarless blocks. Inside curves are built by placing the front faces edge to edge and fanning the blocks to meet the curve. Taller walls require special design techniques; consult the block distributor for pre-engineered plans. Reinforced poured concrete or plastic landscape fabric can be integrated to provide strength for large-scale projects.

REVIEWING

MAIN IDEAS

There are several reasons for building fences in the home landscape. Privacy and security for children and pets are the most important reasons. However, well-designed fences also create sound barriers, screen off-site objectionable views, create microclimates in the yard, and mark property lines. No single fence material can do all of the above. The landscape designer and homeowner must decide which style fence to install.

Fences can be constructed on the property line or built away from the property line. The term screen usually describes fences or walls built inside the property line to create visual privacy. Check city ordinances and building codes for restrictions on location and size of fences. Some subdivisions also have restrictive covenants that not only regulate the size and location of fences, but may also restrict certain fence materials.

In the past, the board fence was not only the most popular fence but the only style of fence. Today, landscapers have a variety of fence materials to select from. The board fence may be made from plastic boards not natural wood, as in the past. When choosing fence materials and design, consider the amount of maintenance needed to keep the fence looking good in the future.

Select fence material that is similar to the house construction material. Natural wood fences look best next to wood-sided houses, not brick homes. Build fences that complement the general architectural style of the home. Use split-rail fences in the country not around a contemporary home. Wrought-iron fences are elegant and need large lots to effectively show them off. In some parts of the country, masonry walls are used as fences.

Retaining walls hold soil and provide additional flat areas in the landscape. Poured concrete walls are strong, but they are not beautiful. Stack railroad ties on top of each other to create an interesting retaining wall. Landscape timbers can also be used, instead of railroad ties, for wall construction. These walls are usually 4 feet or less in height. Install reinforcing rods to hold the ties or timbers in place.

During the 1980s, a new style retaining wall was developed called the mortarless block wall system. Plants throughout the United States manufacture concrete blocks with interesting surface textures and colors. These blocks are designed to stack on top of each other without using mortar to hold them together.

QUESTIONS

Answer the following questions using correct spelling and complete sentences.

1. What are five reasons for installing fences in the home landscape?
2. Define microclimate.
3. What is a screen used for in the landscape?
4. What is a restrictive covenant? Why is it important when designing and installing fences?
5. Name four different kinds of wood fences.
6. What are the two major types of metal fences?
7. How is water pressure from behind a retaining wall released?
8. How is a mortarless block retaining wall constructed?

CHAPTER SELF-CHECK

Match the term with the correct definition. Place the letter in the blank provided.

a. covenant   d. wrought iron   g. weep hole
b. pilaster   e. Allan block   h. pea gravel
c. retaining wall   f. chain link   i. enclosure

_____ 1. Walls constructed to hold soil and create flat surfaces in the landscape

_____ 2. Mortarless retaining wall block system

_____ 3. Columns built every 16 feet on brick walls

_____ 4. Holes in solid retaining wall to relieve water pressure

_____ 5. A fence that will provide security but is not beautiful

_____ 6. A beautiful fence that can provide security

_____ 7. Backfill around mortarless block wall systems with this material

_____ 8. Special rules that some subdivisions have restricting fence construction techniques

_____ 9. A term that describes both fences and walls used in the landscape

EXPLORING

1. Visit landscape sites where fences are being constructed.

2. Try installing several fence sections at home or school. Follow the steps discussed when installing the posts.

3. Visit a landscape site where retaining wall construction is taking place.

13

Using Light and Water to Enhance the Landscape

Lighting in the landscape provides safety for people, security for the grounds, and an enrichment to the night landscape. Dramatic focal points can be created in the landscape at night. Lighting also provides the homeowner with the necessary light to use the outdoor room at night.

Water features provide great visual impact in the landscape. Moving water is a great source of relaxation. A quiet reflecting pool mirrors the elements around it. Water features are focal points that enhance the landscape.

Landscape plants require adequate water to survive in the landscape. The water plants receive affects their growth and development. Determining when to water landscape plants is important in the maintenance of a healthy landscape.

13-1. Water appeals to the sense of sight and sound in the landscape. (Courtesy, R.S. Hursthouse & Associates, Inc.)

OBJECTIVES

1. Identify the major different lighting techniques available

2. Know the difference between high- and low-voltage

3. Decide when to use high- and low-voltage lighting systems

4. Determine the need for water features in the landscape

5. Identity the different materials used in pond construction

6. Describe the proper technique for installing a small lily pond

7. Recognize the requirements for an automatic irrigation system

8. Identify the major parts of an automatic irrigation system

TERMS

backflow prevention device

ecosystem

filtration system

ground fault circuit interrupter (GFCI)

high-voltage

irrigation controller

low-voltage

mirror lighting

night-landscaping

path lighting

photocell

pop-up rotating sprinkler

preformed pool

shadow lighting

silhouette lighting

spotlighting

sprayhead sprinkler

station

up-lighting

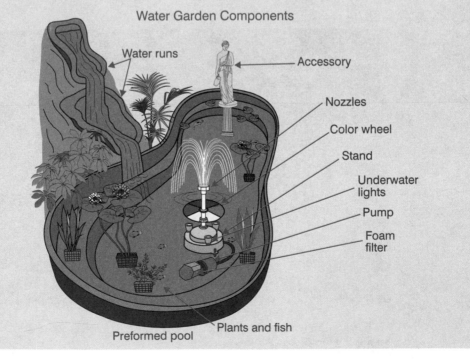

Water Garden Components

Water runs

Accessory

Nozzles

Color wheel

Stand

Underwater lights

Pump

Foam filter

Preformed pool

Plants and fish

LIGHTING THE LANDSCAPE

Safety, security, and enhancement of property are reasons for lighting the landscape around residential and commercial sites. Landscape lighting increases the usefulness of the landscape. Instead of having to move indoors when it gets dark, people can stay out and enjoy the outdoors. However, safety and security are the most important considerations when lighting business landscapes. While corporate and residential lighting needs may differ in degree, the desire for safety and attractiveness is the same.

Law enforcement agencies recommend lighted areas to deter criminal activities. *Photocells* are light sensitive switches that automatically turn security lighting on at dusk and off at sunrise. Security systems now include low-voltage lighting connected to motion detectors for increased

13-2. Night-lighting can enhance the landscape and improve safety for pedestrians. Note the light next to the palm tree's trunk.

safety around the home. For additional protection, new computerized timers can also vary the times lights go on and off.

For years, landscape lighting consisted of one or two spotlights attached to the back of the house. Today, modern, low-voltage lamps not only provide security, but also add beauty to the landscape. *Night-landscaping* describes the use of ornamental lighting to enhance the landscape after dark. Now, landscape designers can choose from hundreds of different style lamps to solve a variety of night-landscaping problems.

LIGHTING TECHNIQUES

There are six major night-lighting techniques—path, mirror, spotlighting, shadow, silhouette, and up-lighting. *Path lighting* or walk lighting offers improved safety for pedestrians while providing an interesting lighting effect in the landscape.

Mirror lighting technique uses reflected light on water to add interest in the landscape. To use *silhouette lighting*, shine a light behind the plant on a wall or other vertical surface. Viewers will only see the outline of the plant. Unusually shaped plants can provide dramatic lighting effects.

13-3. Path light next to garden steps.

13-4. Lighting used to highlight the shrubs in this landscape.

13-5. Up-lighting at the base of a tree.

Use **spotlighting** to direct attention to a specific object in the landscape. Do not overlight the object and wash away its unique colors and outlines. Creating a shadow of a plant on a wall or fence, called **shadow lighting**, can also give a dramatic effect. Shine the light through the plant and onto the surface. Place the lamp close to the plant and the shadow will be larger. Move the lamp away from the plant and the shadow will be smaller.

The **up-lighting** technique places a lamp at ground level which shines up at the base of a tree. This is a popular technique for business and commercial installations. Walk lighting and up-lighting are the most common lighting techniques in use today.

VOLTAGE SYSTEMS FOR OUTDOOR LIGHTING

Two main lighting systems are now available. **High-voltage** lighting systems use conventional 120-volt electricity while low-voltage systems convert the 120 volts to 24 volts. The high-voltage system allows for large lamps that produce more light in the landscape. Outdoor electric cable installation must conform to all local electric codes. These cables will usually be buried 18 inches underground by a licensed electrician.

Avoid using high-voltage sodium lights around landscape beds. Sodium lights give off a yellow cast making green plants appear unnatural in color. High-voltage mercury vapor lights give off a clear glow and work well for lighting large exterior walls that also have landscape plants.

Advantages of Low-Voltage Lighting

Low-voltage lighting systems run on 24 volts of electricity. By using 24 volts, it is safer, less costly, and adaptable to a variety of conditions.

Low-voltage systems have several advantages over 120-volt systems. Low-voltage systems may not have to be installed by an electrician. Low-voltage cable is buried 6 to 8 inches underground without using electrical conduit. Reduced voltage prevents electrical shocks even when touching the bare wires or accidentally cutting a buried cable with a garden tool.

Low-voltage lighting systems consist of three components. The heart of any low-voltage lighting system is the power pack. Operating off a standard 120-volt electrical outlet, the power pack converts the electrical current to a safe 24 volts for use by the lighting fixtures. Electric cables transmit the 24-volt electric current from the power pack to the individual lighting fixtures. Electric cable comes in a variety of wire sizes, 10- and 12-guage are the most common. Follow the manufacturer's recommendations on cable selection. Different lighting fixtures provide a unique lighting effect to a landscape.

13-6. High-voltage outdoor lighting illuminates this patio. (Courtesy, R.S. Hursthouse & Associates, Inc.)

13-7. Lights placed along a sidewalk to improve safety.

LOCATING LANDSCAPE LIGHT FIXTURES

Always use as few lights as possible to accent focal points that make the landscape and building unique. Today, the trend is toward a softer, more natural look in the landscape. Soft lighting may highlight specific features, such as plantings, walls, decks, or entrances. Avoid the runway look of light along walks. Place lamps close to walks and throw pools of light onto these surfaces.

13-8. Components of a low-voltage lighting system.

Try to locate landscape light fixtures either above or below eye level. Lighting fixtures can be incorporated into a retaining wall or under steps, or house eaves to accent design points. Good lighting can wash a landscape wall and highlight the uneven textures of the wall. Trees with white bark provide striking points of interest in the night landscape. Flower beds can be beautiful at night when properly lighted.

POWER PACKS

Power packs are available with various wattage ranges. Find the correct size of the power pack by adding the wattage of each bulb in the circuit. The power pack's rating should always be greater than the total lighting fixture wattage with all fixtures turned on. Controller options include manual, dusk-to-dawn, and timer-operated models. They also may have a remote control or built-in motion/heat sensors.

Timer-operated power packs automatically turn the lights on and off at a predetermined time. A photocell can turn the lights on at sunset and off at sunrise. Motion/heat sensor power packs use a timer that turns the lights on and off at predetermined times each day. However, if someone enters the protected area when the lights are off, the passive infrared motion sensor automatically turns the lights on for a set period.

INSTALLING LOW-VOLTAGE LIGHTING

City ordinances may require a licensed electrician install all outdoor lighting. Always check the local laws before working with electricity. Install a ground fault circuit interrupter (GFCI) device on all outdoor lighting equipment. A ***ground fault circuit interrupter (GFCI)*** is a safety device designed to protect people using electricity in areas that may be wet or have water. The GFCI will disconnect the electrical circuit when it detects a short or moisture.

13-9. Many different styles of lighting fixtures are available.

Begin at the power pack and stretch the cable to each light fixture. Install the cable by following the landscape's natural contour and barriers leaving 1 to 2 feet of extra cable at each fixture site to allow for future adjustments. Low-voltage cable is self sealing and weather resistant. It can be buried in the ground, covered with mulch, or hidden under shrubs or foliage. Assemble the fixture, as required, and connect it to the cable using the supplied connector. Push the fixture into place in the ground. Adjust the position of the fixtures, so they create the desired lighting effect.

SEVEN STEPS FOR HOME LANDSCAPE LIGHTING

- Evaluate the customer's landscape. Locate the focal points that need emphasis and plan the lighting around those points. Consider walks and driveways for safety and security lighting.
- Keep it simple. Try not to hang lamps from the top of large trees. Not only will installation be difficult, but replacing bulbs will also be difficult. Ground lights that shine into the trees can convey the same effect.
- Choose the fixtures. Some customers want the fixtures to blend into the landscape and be natural or not seen. Other customers want the lighting fixtures to make a statement and be very ornamental. Do not forget the weather. A beautiful fixture near the ground may be difficult to locate and avoid during snow removal.
- Select the bulbs. Large trees, large walls, and large parking lots will require larger-wattage bulbs. A clarity of brightness directs the eyes to the dominant point. From there, your eyes will drift to the rest of the landscape.
- Choose the correct wire size. Outdoor 12-gauge cable with a ground wire for high voltage is the standard in the landscape industry. Low-voltage cables are usually 10- or 12-guage.
- Choose a transformer or power pack. The transformer will convert the power from 120 volts to 24 volts. Add the wattage of all the bulbs in the circuit to determine the correct transformer size.
- Install the system. Use basic electricians' tools to install the lamp fixtures. Remember, electricity is always a potential danger. Bury low-voltage wire 6 to 8 inches underground. Make a drawing of where the wires lay, in case you want to do some digging in the future and as reference for the homeowner.

CARE AND MAINTENANCE

Low-voltage lighting systems require little care once installed. Occasionally, clean dirt, leaves, and other debris away from the fixtures. Periodically, check the fixtures for proper adjustment. Once a year, remove the bulbs and spray the lamp sockets with a silicone-base spray. Inspect the cable yearly for damage or fraying near the connection points. If a bulb burns out, replace it immediately. The voltage, a damaged bulb no longer uses, flows to the operating bulbs. This extra voltage can reduce the life of the remaining bulbs.

LIGHTING WATER FEATURES

13-10. Night-lighting increases the beauty of water features. (Courtesy, R.S. Hursthouse & Associates, Inc.)

Water features are especially interesting when lighted. Fountains look best when accented from under lighting. The water conducts the light and begins to glow. Colored or clear bulbs can be used to light water features. However, water and electricity, even with low-voltage systems, are hazardous. Follow all manufacturers' recommendations for proper installation of lamps in and around water features.

THINK SAFETY

Working at night, the landscape crew locates the lamp positions. During the next day, the crew permanently places the lighting devices in the landscape. Landscape crews should always have safety foremost on their minds while installing landscape lighting devices.

WATER IN THE LANDSCAPE

Many landscapers agree that water features in a landscape design are magic. A gently flowing stream, a cascading waterfall, or a peaceful lily pond can change a simple landscape into a breathtaking experience. The feature can be as formal as a circular fountain set into a patio area or as casual as a brook flowing through the backyard. In most home landscapes, the backyard provides the best location for water features. They should be in proportion to the landscape area.

WATER GARDEN PLANNING AND INSTALLATION

The most important consideration in water gardening is site selection. Most water plants need 6 to 8 hours of sun per day to thrive. The area should be level and not low where surface drainage would run into the pond. It should also be away from trees that would drop leaves into the pond in the autumn. The water garden should be placed where it can be enjoyed and viewed from areas frequented in the house or landscape.

A water garden is a closed *ecosystem*, a confined community. Included in this environment is water, air (oxygen and carbon dioxide), plants, and fish and snails. It is important that the environment be kept balanced. There needs to be good water circulation, oxygenating plants, proper plant coverage of the water surface, proper number of fish and snails, and proper maintenance. The smaller the pond, the more important these needs are. A common water gardening mistake is creating a pond that is too small.

13-11. Some water garden installation steps include (1) excavating and installing the pond liner; (2) grading the site for proper drainage; (3) installing power, lighting, and landscape plants; (4) planting water plants in containers or baskets; (5) acclimating fish to the pond's water temperature; (6) enjoying the plants and fish in the water garden.

Guidelines for proper balance in a water garden are:

- Circulate the water volume every 1 to 2 hours.

- Floating plants should cover 65 to 75 percent of the pond surface.

- Oxygenating and marginal/bog plants should number 1 plant per 2 sq. ft. of pond surface, taking into account that the total number of plants in the pond should cover 2/3 to 3/4 of the water surface.

- There should never be more than 1 inch of fish per 5 gallons of water (for example, 6 fish 5 inches long would require a pond with at least 150 gallons of water; $6 \times 5 = 30 \times 5 = 150$ gallons).

- There should not be more than 1 inch of snail per square foot of bottom surface area.

Water used to fill a pond may have elements that are harmful to plants and fish. City water may have chlorine, chloramine, or heavy metals. Chlorine will dissipate in 3 to 5 days. Chloramine needs to be treated and heavy metals neutralized. Country or well water may have nitrates or pesticides present. The best practice is to have the water tested. The water pH level is also important. A pH of 7.0 is best for fish and plants. The water pH should be tested and adjusted if necessary. It is best to treat or make adjustments to the water and wait 7 to 10 days before adding fish and plants.

Proper water circulation is important. The proper sized pump should circulate the entire water volume every 1 to 2 hours. A larger pump will be needed if the water garden has a waterfall, fountain, or other features which involves lifting water. Pumps are rated by gph (gallons per hour). The pump should be placed a minimum of 12 inches below the water surface. The out-take of the pump should be placed away from the intake for proper circulation. Some ponds may need a mechanical *filtration system*, a pump with a filter to remove impurities and keep the water clean and clear. A layer of gravel on the bottom can also provide a habitat for bacteria which will act as a biological filtration system.

Water plants are an essential part of a water garden. When plants are fully developed, they should cover between 2/3 and 3/4 of the water surface area. Most water plants such as water lilies prefer full sun for 6 to 8 hours per day to thrive. Plants that require containers should be placed at the proper depth. They should be fertilized once a month with pond tabs from spring to fall, and twice a month during hot weather. Brown or yellow growth should be clipped off down to the crown of the plant. It is also important to note that water lilies do not like too much turbulence. They need to be placed away from waterfalls and fountains.

Types of Ponds

Flexible pond liners can be used to create ponds of any shape and size. They come in various grades and quality, and in a range of prices. PVC (polyvinyl chloride) is the least expensive and the thicker grades are often guaranteed for 10 years. EPDM (ethylene propylene diene rubber membrane) is more expensive, but is generally considered much better material. The most important consideration is that the liner material be specifically intended for use in ponds. Some materials may contain chemicals that are harmful to plants and fish.

Preformed pools are ready-made pond shells of fiberglass or molded from plastic (polyethylene). They come in a variety of colors and shapes. Good support is crucial since the pressure of the water can warp the shell if it is not properly supported. Other materials such as concrete, nonabsorbent tile, or brick can also be used to build ponds.

To determine the approximate number of gallons (water volume) a pond holds, use the following formulas based on the shape of the pond:

Rectangular Pond: Length × Width × Depth × 7.5 = gallons

Oval Pond: Length × Width × Depth × 6.7 = gallons

Circular Pond: 3.14 × ½ Diameter × ½ Diameter × Depth × 7.5 = gallons

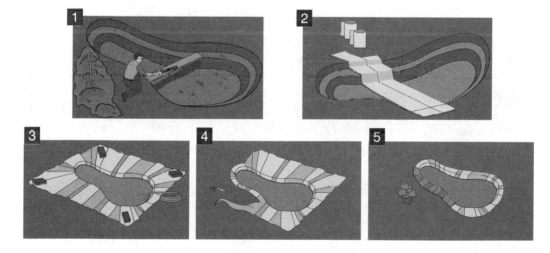

13-12. Pool installation steps using a liner include (1) excavate the site and remove any sharp objects; (2) spread sand over the bottom or cover the bottom with plastic or old newspapers; (3) drape the liner loosely in the pool with the edges anchored, and fill with water; (4) trim away excess liner, leaving an adequate flap around the edge at ground level; (5) line the perimeter with rocks or pavers to hide the liner edge for a finished look.

Pond Maintenance

If the pond water turns green, it is called an algae bloom. This is a natural occurrence. Treatment is usually unnecessary. An average algae bloom lasts for 10 to 14 days. It will disappear virtually overnight if the pond is properly balanced. Avoid fertilizing water lilies as long as the algae problem persists. Healthy water will often be slightly green. However, the water should be clear enough to see at least 6 to 8 inches below the surface.

Growing more aquatic plants can also help to inhibit algae. Algae needs sun to grow and reproduce. Water lilies and other desirable plants covering 2/3 to 3/4 of the pond surface will leave very little open water to catch the sun's rays. This is easily accomplished in mid-summer. However, early in the season before water lilies start to spread, algae will receive more of the sun's rays. As a spring control, floating plants like water lettuce (*Pistia stratiotes*) or water hyacinth (*Eichhornia crassipes*) can be added to help cover the pond surface. As the water lilies expand, excess floating plants can be removed. Note that water hyacinth can invade public waterways and is illegal in some states. Keep in mind that having some algae in the pool is normal.

A proper environment is needed for fish. Fish prefer cold water because it holds more oxygen. Do not overstock the pond with too many fish. Ideally, the proper number of fish can support themselves on natural food in the pond. This doesn't mean not to feed the fish. However, they should not be fed more than once a day and only as much food as they can eat in 5 minutes. Uneaten, nutrient-rich food acts as fertilizer for algae. Fish should be hungry enough to forage actively on natural food in the pond. In early spring and late fall, a low protein, high carbohydrate fish food should be fed. In the late spring to early fall, feed a high protein, low carbohydrate food. When the temperature reaches 40°F or below, do not feed the fish at all. Fish enter partial hibernation at 40°F.

During hot weather, water may need to be added to the pond due to evaporation. If more than 25 percent of the pond volume is added, it may be necessary to test and re-treat the water. In the autumn, leaves and other debris need to be kept out of the pond. A dip net can be used to remove leaves or a cover net stretched over the surface to keep out leaves and debris. Whenever organic matter collecting on the bottom gets to be about an inch thick, drain and clean the pond. The pump should be checked and cleaned, if necessary, on a regular schedule.

As temperatures cool in the fall, the water garden must be prepared for the coming winter months. Depending on the geographic location of the pond, winter can be anything from icy cold to relatively balmy. The pond's surface should be lowered 6 inches to allow room for the water to expand with freezing. The pump and any filters can be removed and cleaned or left running during the winter. If you choose to leave the pump running, it is important that it be raised to just below the surface of the water. Allowing the pump to circulate the water at lower depths is stressful to fish. If the pump is removed, a heater will be needed to keep the pond from totally freezing on the surface. A horse or cattle tank heater or bird bath deicer can be purchased and used.

The fish will not freeze to death if a pond freezes over solid. However, they can smother. Debris and organic material on the bottom builds up methane and other gases that must be allowed to escape. A small surface opening will allow for proper oxygen and gas exchange. If a pond is allowed to freeze over solid, do not break the ice with a blunt object. The ensuing shock waves can be stressful or deadly to fish. Heating a pan of hot water, placing it on the ice, and allowing it to melt through can create the needed opening. Once spring arrives and the water temperature reaches 50°F, fish can be fed a high carbohydrate, low protein fish food. When the water temperature reaches 70°F, a high protein regular type fish food should be used.

Water garden winter preparation checklist: (1) discontinue feeding fish; (2) remove leaves and debris, cover pond with a net; (3) turn off moving water features such as waterfalls or fountains; (4) lower pond depth; (5) remove and clean pump and filters or raise pump level; (6) install a heater to prevent freezing over; (7) remove tropical plants before the first frost; (8) cut off hardy submersible plants and place on bottom; (9) store hardy marginal/bog plants.

Water plants can be grouped into three basic types—hardy submersibles, hardy marginal/bog plants, and tropicals. Hardy means the ability to withstand cold temperatures. Different plant types need different preparations for winter protection. After the first frost, or when temperatures get down to 40°F, hardy submersibles should be cut off at the crown of the plant and placed on the bottom of the pond. Hardy marginal/bog plants need a dormant period. They may be placed in cold storage where the plants can go dormant without the container freezing solid. This type of environment may not be readily available. The other solution is planting them, container and all, with the top of the container at ground level in a planting bed. Tropical plants (non-hardy to zone 5) require indoor overwintering before the first frost. They can be submerged at the proper depth indoors in a fish aquarium. Some tropicals such as umbrella palm and dwarf papyrus can be grown as houseplants. When spring arrives and water temperature in the pond reaches 70°F, tropical plants can be placed back in the water garden at their proper depth.

RESIDENTIAL IRRIGATION SYSTEMS

Water is essential for good plant growth. In many parts of the country, rain will naturally provide the necessary quantity of water. However, in other parts, there is not enough water for good plant growth. Irrigation can supplement and furnish adequate water to plants. Properly designed and properly installed irrigation systems coupled with educated homeowners can save a large amount of water runoff and waste. There are cities and towns that now require municipal approval or licensing prior to installing a lawn or landscape irrigation system. The landscape designer should check with the local municipality for approval or permits.

DESIGNING AN IRRIGATION SYSTEM

To insure a complete and proper irrigation system design, a set procedure must be followed. The steps are (1) obtain site information, (2) determine the irrigation requirement, (3) determine water capacity and pressure, (4) select sprinklers and spacing ranges, (5) circuit the sprinklers into valve groups, (6) size pipe and valves and calculate total system pressure loss, (7) locate controllers and size wiring, and (8) prepare the final irrigation plan.

Site Information and Irrigation Requirements

The local climate is the main factor that will influence how much water will need to be applied for good plant growth. Evapotranspiration (ET) describes the loss of water from plant tissue, the soil, and the soil surface. The ET rate is affected by relative humidity, solar radiation, day length, air temperature, and wind velocity. Therefore, on a sunny, dry, windy, summer day plants will use larger quantities of water.

Most irrigation water is clean enough for human consumption. However, in some parts of the country waste water is used for irrigation. Some sprinkler manufacturers install a different colored sprinkler head on golf courses and other large turf areas where waste water is used for irrigation. This is to remind people that the irrigation water is not fit for human consumption.

Water Capacity and Pressure

The irrigation designer needs to know the flow in gallons per minute (gpm) available to the system and the working pressure (psi) at the point-

13-13. Proper irrigation can supplement available water for good plant growth.

of-connection. Static water pressure refers to the pounds per square inch (psi) of pressure in a closed system with no water moving. The static water pressure can be determined by using a direct pressure gauge reading or obtained from the water company. The water meter size is usually stamped or cast into the meter itself. The service line material (copper or galvanized), length, and size needs to be known in order to calculate pipe flow loss and working pressure. The line may be a different size than the meter.

Three calculations should be made and the most restrictive value be used as flow for the irrigation system. The pressure loss through a water meter should not exceed 10 percent of the minimum static pressure on the main side. The maximum flow through the meter for irrigation should not exceed 75 percent of the maximum safe flow of the meter. A water meter flow loss chart will be needed for these calculations. The velocity of flow should not exceed 5 to 7½ feet per second. A loss chart for the type and size of piping will be needed for this calculation.

Selecting Sprinklers

There are a number of different types of sprinklers and irrigation devices. The main types are sprayhead sprinklers, rotating sprinklers, bubblers, and drip irrigation devices. The size and shape of the areas to be irrigated and the types of plant material determines what type of sprinkler head will be used. Available water pressure and flow, local environmental conditions, soil type, and sprinkler grouping are other limiting factors. The goal is to select the type of heads that will cover the area properly using the least number of sprinklers.

Sprayhead sprinklers generally emit single or double sheets or fans of water in a fixed pattern. Types include shrub sprayheads, pop-up spray-

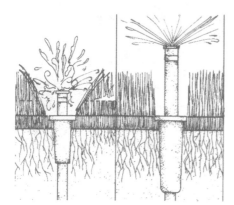

13-14. The well-designed head (right) will pop-up above plant material. The poor design (left) will not operate properly. (Courtesy, Rain Bird)

heads, and surface sprayheads. *Pop-up rotating sprinklers* have a single or pair of nozzles that raise and revolve to distribute water. In a large, open lawn area, rotary pop-ups can irrigate vast areas with substantially fewer heads than if sprayheads were used. Higher operating pressure is needed for rotating heads. *Bubblers* and *drip irrigation devices* produce short throw, zero radius, or ultra-low volume water distribution. These devices can irrigate a specific area without overthrow onto other plants or landscape features. A radius of 2 to 5 feet coverage is common with drip irrigation devices. This irrigation technique is used in parts of the country where irrigation water supplies are limited.

Sprinkler compatibility is important when circuiting sprinkler heads into groups that will be controlled by the same valve. Avoid mixing different types of sprinkler heads together on the same valve whenever possible. Different heads have different operating pressures and usually require widely varying operating times. Full-circle sprinkler heads water a complete circular area. Part-circle sprinkler heads distribute water on areas less than 360 degrees. Half-circle heads are used along a driveway, patio, property lines, or house.

Fifty percent, head-to-head, spacing is the most common spacing used in landscape irrigation. In cases where soil types, winds, low humidity, or high heat inhibit effective irrigation, closer spacing is recommended.

Once the designer chooses the equipment, proper spacing is the next step in the process. There are three major types of sprinkler spacing patterns and various adaptations for special situations. A triangular pattern is generally used where the area to be irrigated has irregular boundaries or borders that are open to overspray or do not require part-circle heads. A square pattern has equal sides running between four sprinkler head locations and is used when irrigating areas that are square or have borders at 90 degree angles to each other. The rectangular pattern is able to fit in areas with defined straight boundaries and corners.

The precipitation rate of heads selected should be calculated to determine if the rate will apply enough water during operating times and that the rate does not exceed the soil's absorption rate. The average precipitation rate is expressed in inches per hour. The formula is:

$$\text{Precipitation Rate} = \frac{96.3 \times \text{GPM}}{\text{S} \times \text{L}}$$

Where: 96.3 is a constant which incorporates inches per square foot per hour, gpm is the total gallons per minute applied to an area by the sprinklers, S is the spacing in feet between sprinklers, and L is the spacing in feet between rows of sprinklers.

Sprinkler Circuits, Valves, Piping

Sprinkler circuits are established by adding the gallons per minute (gpm) of similar heads in each area. Each circuit (valve group) cannot exceed the system flow limit established in step 3, determined water capacity and pressure. If the total is exceeded, an additional valve group will need to be added.

The designer will now need to locate the valves, mainlines, and lateral piping. Valves should be easily accessible for operation and service, and located where they will not interfere with normal traffic patterns. They should be located in the center of a sprinkler group to balance the flow and size of lateral pipe. Valve boxes are available for below ground installation. Valve and mainline locations should be kept in mind when circuiting sprinklers and drawing in lateral pipe lines.

The mainline pipe is heavier in construction, has constant pressure, and supplies water to the valve. The lateral pipe run from the valve to the sprinkler heads. The flow through the valve should not produce a loss greater than 10 percent of the static pressure available. The valve should be the same size as the largest pipe in the lateral it serves or no more than one size smaller than that pipe. The valve should not be larger than the pipe in the lateral, unless a high flow results from a split lateral.

Irrigation water can "backflow" through irrigation pipes into the water supply system and endanger public health. Most states require the installation of a ***backflow prevention device*** on irrigation systems. This device will prevent contamination of drinking water (potable water) by not allowing the irrigation water to flow backwards into the water supply.

13-15. A backflow prevention device is designed to eliminate the movement of irrigation water back into its potable water system source.

Controllers and Wiring

This is the electrical portion of the irrigation system design. ***Irrigation controllers*** regulate and control sprinkler systems. They have a day-of-the-week clock to regulate on which day water is applied, a twenty-four-hour clock to regulate the time of day sprinklers operate, and a station clock to control the time each valve group is turned on. Where multiple controllers are used, they should be located in groups if possible. A ground fault circuit interrupter (GFCI) should be used on the 120-volt electrical circuit used by the irrigation controller.

The term ***station*** describes a single electric switch in an irrigation controller. It turns on or off a solenoid valve which controls water flow to a single sprinkler circuit. Small controllers used in residential irrigation systems may have four to six separate stations. Between the controller and the solenoid valve that feeds the sprinklers, a network of valve low voltage control wires exists. Each valve is hooked up with two wires, a control or power wire and common or ground wire. It is important that wiring be properly sized.

Preparing the Final Irrigation Plan

The final irrigation plan is a diagram representing what the irrigation system should look like after installation. It will be used by the irrigation contractor as the system is installed. It should be drawn to scale with detailed explanations, a legend explaining the symbols, and show any major elevation changes. It will show all water and utility locations. The advantage to completing the final irrigation plan is the designer can ensure that complete coverage of the area to be irrigated has been achieved. The plan should also contain any special notes for specific requirements which must be met.

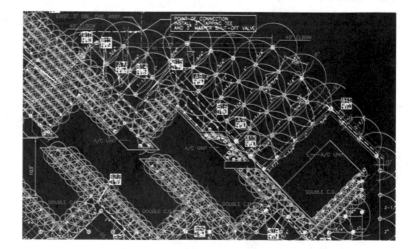

13-16. An irrigation design showing spray patterns and head placements. (Courtesy, LAND-CADD Division, Eagle Point Software)

REVIEWING

MAIN IDEAS

Landscape managers are discovering that outdoor lighting can enhance plantings and make turf, walkways, and gardens more visually pleasing at night. Besides providing beauty, safety, and security, lighting reinforces the image that property is well maintained. Many landscape contractors recommend low-voltage outdoor lighting systems because they operate on 24 volts instead of the standard 120-volt AC. Technological advances in low-voltage lighting have allowed manufactures to offer products equal in quality, if not better, than many high-voltage lights of just 10 years ago.

Always use as few lights as possible in the landscape. Good lighting can accent trees, shrubs, and flowers. Safety and security are other reasons for lighting the landscape. Install a ground fault circuit interrupter on all outdoor lighting equipment.

Water features provide the landscape with magic. Water features can be a formal fountain or a gentle brook flowing through the backyard. The sound of splashing water can mask noise made by nearby automobiles. Landscape pools are usually 18 inches deep. Heaters may be needed in fish pools in colder climates.

Underground sprinkler systems designed to water turf are popular in many parts of the country. These systems have timers that electrically turn on water valves in the irrigation system. Small sprinkler heads cover 4 to 12 feet diameter circles, while large heads can wet circles over 15 feet in diameter.

QUESTIONS

Answer the following questions using correct spelling and complete sentences.

1. What are three reasons for lighting a landscape?

2. Define the term night-landscaping.

3. Name six major night-lighting techniques.

4. What is the difference between high- and low-voltage lighting systems?

5. What is a ground fault circuit interrupter?

6. Why are water features important in the home landscape?

7. Name the five steps used when installing a pool with a liner.

8. Why may it be necessary to install a filtration system on a reflecting pond?

9. What are the major parts of an automatic irrigation system?

10. What is the purpose of a backflow prevention device in an irrigation system?

CHAPTER SELF-CHECK

Match the term with the correct definition. Place the correct letter in the blank provided.

a. ground fault circuit interrupter   c. path lighting   e. spotlighting
b. solenoid valve   d. preformed pool   f. silhouette lighting

_____ 1. Landscape pools made from plastic or fiberglass, ready to install in the home landscape

_____ 2. A special electrical device that disconnects electricity to outdoor lights if an electrical short develops

_____ 3. Lighting for walks and steps for safety considerations

_____ 4. Direct attention to specific plants or statues with landscape lamps

_____ 5. Electric valves that turn on sprinklers to irrigate turf

_____ 6. To shine a light behind a plant on a wall or other vertical surface to create an interesting pattern

EXPLORING

1. Talk with a local landscape contractor about pool and pond installation.

2. Visit several commercial buildings that use night-lighting. Describe the type of lighting system.

3. Visit a home landscape in your town that has a water feature. Take pictures and describe the water feature.

14

Watering, Fertilizing, and Mulching Woody Plants

Okay, you are a landscaper and you have just installed a landscape project. The customer pays you; the job is done, right? Not exactly, because landscape plants are living organisms, they require some care until they can take care of themselves. If the plants die, the customer will let you know and will want you to replace the dead plants at your expense.

If you are a smart landscaper, you will take the time to properly install the plants to reduce losses. You will probably check the plants occasionally as a follow-up procedure. In addition, you will leave instructions with the customer about how to care for the new plants. The question is how do you care for new plants?

14-1. Healthy, woody landscape plants require little care. The foreground shrubs are Swiss Mountain Pine, *Pinus mugo* var. mugo. (Courtesy, University of Illinois Cooperative Extension Service)

OBJECTIVES

1. Describe how woody plant biology influences maintenance practices

2. Explain recommended watering practices for woody landscape plants

3. Explain how woody landscape plants are fertilized

4. Identify mulches used in landscape practices

5. Describe how mulch is applied to the landscape

TERMS

broadcasting

chlorosis

desiccation

dry fertilizer

fertilizer capsule

fertilizer spike

inorganic mulch

microirrigation

mulching

organic mulch

respiration

root watering needle

root zone

soaker hose

soluble fertilizer

sprinkler

water bag

wilting

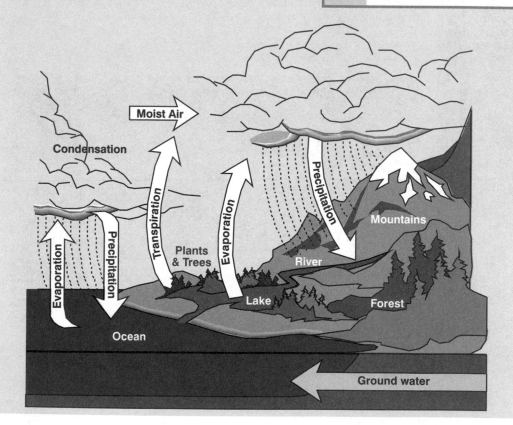

CARING FOR WOODY LANDSCAPE PLANTS

The health of woody landscape plants is worth maintaining for many reasons. One reason is it takes effort to install woody plants in the new landscape. Plants that die, particularly, well-established plants, are not easily replaced. Another reason is healthy plants are attractive plants. We appreciate the beauty of trees, shrubs, ground covers, and vines. Since these plants are expected to provide beauty in the landscape for many years, their health must be considered. Also, as plants' ornamental qualities increase with growth and maturity, they contribute to the real estate value of the house.

14-2. Healthy plants contribute beauty to the landscape. Shown is a Hick's yew, Taxus x media 'Hicksii,' hedge; Flowering Crabapples, *Malus species*; and Austrian Pine, *Pinus nigra* var. nigra.

BIOLOGY OF WOODY LANDSCAPE PLANTS

It is best to have an understanding of woody plant biology before caring for plants in the landscape. Woody plants are part of nature. In nature, they have adapted to specific climatic and growing conditions. Water and nutrients for plant growth and health are obtained through natural processes. Most water becomes available for plant use through precipitation. Nutrients are obtained from the mineral matter in soil and from the decay of organic materials.

In the landscape, woody landscape plants are often subjected to adverse growing conditions not found in nature. Compacted soils, poor soil drain-

14-3. Woody plants are adapted to climatic and growing conditions in nature that differ from conditions in the artificial landscape.

age, poor quality soil, and restricted areas for root growth, place stress on plants. Highway salts, air pollution, and competition from turfgrasses are other conditions that place stress on woody landscape plants. In addition, some plants are frequently used because they have high ornamental value, such as fall color, showiness of flowers, and growth habit. The selection often is not based on whether the plant is adapted to the growing conditions in the landscape. Placed in a stressful situation for which they are not well adapted, they often suffer, decline, and die.

Additional stress is placed on landscape plants during the transplanting process. Nursery plants, other than those grown in containers, are dug from the ground causing severe damage to the root systems. Some trees

14-4. Balled and burlapped plants may lose up to 95 percent of their feeder roots during the transplanting process.

might lose up to 95 percent of their feeder roots in the process. The trees are stored in holding areas before planting. Then, they may be planted under conditions unlike the ones in which they were growing. Their exposure to the wind and rain is changed and the soil type is probably different from the type in which their roots were growing.

One way to ensure healthy plants is to select plant species that do well in conditions offered by the site. Second, plants become established and grow more vigorously if the site has been well prepared before planting. Site preparation includes amending the soil or improving the drainage of water when necessary.

Stress affecting the health of woody landscape plants can sometimes be reduced with proper watering and fertilizing. Healthy plants are better able to defend themselves against diseases and insects than less vigorous plants. A good analogy is people and colds or flu. Most people catch a cold or flu when their immune systems are weakened. Perhaps, they have not gotten enough rest, they have not been eating a good diet, or they were improperly dressed in poor weather. These types of situations weaken their systems. The result is they are less able to fight off infectious organisms. The same is true with plants. Diseases more easily infect and insects are attracted to weakened plants.

14-5. Healthy plants, such as this Wayfaringtree Viburnum, *Viburnum lantana*, are able to defend themselves from disease and insect pests. (Courtesy, University of Illinois Cooperative Extension Service)

Energy and Woody Plant Life

Energy for plant life is produced through photosynthesis. The energy is in the form of sugar, or glucose. Live cells in the plant require a constant supply of energy to live and function. When an abundance of sugars are produced, trees convert the sugars into starches and oils. The starches and oils are held in reserve and converted back to sugars when needed. The level of stored energy in a tree influences its growth rate, reproduction, and defense capabilities. Woody plants with high energy reserves tend to be healthy plants.

Energy demands of a tree differ during the five main periods of growth in its life:

1. *Youth or juvenile stage.* A young tree has living cells throughout the plant. Photosynthesis must produce all of the energy demanded by the individual cells. The energy demands increase as the cells multiply and the tree grows.

2. *Development of leaves.* In the spring, trees form new leaves in which photosynthesis and the production of sugars will occur. During this period, trees use much of the energy, stored during the previous growing season, to produce the leaves. Disease or injury at the time of leaf development places great stress on the plant.

   The development of leaves is one of two periods in a tree's growth cycle when energy reserves are low. The other period of low energy is the fall when leaves drop. While the leaves drop, much energy goes to the formation of roots. At both times, optimal water levels are critical.

14-6. The two periods in a tree's growth cycle when energy reserves are at their lowest are in the spring when leaves and flowers are developing and in the fall when roots are being formed. (The tree on the far left of the left photograph is an Eastern redbud, *Cercis canadensis.* The tree to its right is a Flowering crabapple, *Malus* sp. The tree in the right photograph is an Amur maple, *Acer ginnala.*)

3. *High sugar producing period.* Photosynthetic activity is at its highest for six to eight weeks after the leaves have fully developed (late spring to early summer). The abundance of energy spurs new growth. Ninety percent of a tree's annual growth occurs during this time.

4. *Storage of energy.* After the leaves have become fully mature (mid-summer), the tree converts much of its energy being produced into starches and oils. The stored energy is essential as it improves a tree's ability to defend itself from disease.

5. *Dormancy.* Energy stored throughout the summer and early fall provides the tree with reserves to get through the winter.

What can we do to assist plants? First, an understanding of woody plant biology and how the production of energy promotes healthy plants is important in determining proper care. Knowing what conditions cause plant stress is critical. This is similar to medical practice, where doctors identify the problem before prescribing a treatment. Most of the time woody plants are fine without any treatments. In fact, many landscape plants have been 'nurtured to death' by people with good intentions.

Treatments by people to promote vigor and healthy growth of established plants include three common practices. They are watering, fertilizing, and mulching. The timing of water or fertilizer applications is usually more important than the applications themselves. Timing may make the difference in the life or death of woody plants. Applications, if needed, must be based on the plant's stage of growth and growing conditions rather than the timetable of the landscaper or homeowner.

14-7. Most woody landscape plants are fine without supplemental water or fertilizer.

WATERING

14-8. Newly planted trees need more care than established trees. Shown is Red Maple, *Acer rubrum*, in fall color.

Water is the basis of life. Hydrogen in water is a key nutrient in the photosynthetic process. Water is the carrier of dissolved nutrients from the soil into the roots. Water also sustains plant cells and keeps them turgid. Life processes in plants shut down when water is unavailable. That means, photosynthesis stops and energy production is halted. Obviously, stress to landscape plants will occur if water is scarce.

Newly transplanted landscape plants and firmly established landscape plants call for different watering practices. Newly transplanted trees and shrubs need special attention. They lose many of their roots in the transplanting process. It may take recently planted landscape plants three to six years to overcome the damage to their root systems. Until the plants recover, they need to be provided an adequate supply of water. On the other hand, large established trees and shrubs only need additional water in extreme drought conditions. Established trees and shrubs have extensive root systems that can pull water up through the soil from lower levels.

FACTORS AFFECTING WATERING

The weather is one factor that influences how often woody plants need to be watered. Cloudy, rainy, cool conditions reduce the need for water. Sunny, hot, windy conditions increase the demands for water. Landscapers and gardeners must monitor weather conditions to determine the need for watering.

Another factor affecting watering practices is the soil type. Water drains from sandy soils quickly; whereas, heavy clay soils hold water. Know the type of soil in which the plants are planted. Trees and shrubs growing in porous, sandy soil require more frequent watering than those in silty or clay soils.

A third factor is the plant. It is important to know the growing conditions to which landscape plants are adapted. Some plants are tolerant to dry conditions. Other plants perform well in wet soil conditions. Most plants, however, prefer moist, well-drained soils. Moist, well-drained soils have a balance of water and air in the pore spaces.

WHEN TO WATER

Observation skills and experience help people in determining when and if plants need additional water. The first plant symptom of insufficient water is wilting. **Wilting** is the drooping of a plant due to a lack of firmness in the plant tissues. Another early symptom is a loss of color or dullness to the leaves. If lack of water becomes severe, leaf tissues die and leaves can appear scorched. Leaves on some plants turn yellow and drop prematurely.

14-9. The Common Hackberry, *Celtis occidentalis,* **is very tolerant of drought conditions.**

Care must be taken because the symptoms for excessive dryness are the same as too much soil moisture. Stress symptoms appear during drought when there is no water available for the plant to absorb. In the

14-10. These Common Horsechestnut, *Aesculus hippocastanum,* **leaves are scorched due to a summer drought.**

case of too much soil moisture, most plants will show symptoms similar to those under drought conditions. Roots of plants die if the soil is saturated or waterlogged for long periods. This is because roots need oxygen. The oxygen is used in **respiration**, the chemical process in which root cells convert sugars into energy. Saturated soils have very poor air exchange with the atmosphere. If the roots die from lack of oxygen, the plant is unable to absorb the water it needs. It is best to allow soil to approach drying before watering. As the soil dries, oxygen replaces water in the soil pores.

One concern with newly planted trees in construction sites is the compaction of the soil from heavy equipment. This is a problem particularly with clay soils. The hole for the plant is dug. The plant is planted. Because the soil is so compacted, water does not drain from the hole. Unaware of the problem, the homeowner or landscaper waters the plant. The hole fills with water; the roots rot, and the plant dies. In these cases, it is important to provide drainage for the plants before planting. Two possible solutions to this problem include breaking through the hard-packed soil to allow drainage or installing drain tile.

A general rule for watering established woody landscape plants is to thoroughly soak the soil every two to three weeks during periods of drought. It is best to physically check the soil first to see if it is moist. This check involves digging 4 to 6 inches into the ground and feeling the soil. A dry feel would indicate a need to water. Newly planted plants need to be watered on a regular basis during the first few years after transplanting. In cold regions of the country, it is advisable to water landscape plants before the ground freezes. Available water in the soil in the winter helps to reduce damage caused by **desiccation**, water loss from tissues resulting in tissue death.

14-11. This photograph shows a tree being watered by letting the water trickle from the end of a garden hose.

HOW TO WATER

The key to watering is getting the water into the soil where the

14-12. Sprinklers can be used to water woody landscape plantings. (Courtesy, University of Illinois Cooperative Extension Service)

roots can absorb it. Water slowly so it will soak the soil rather than runoff the surface. To avoid runoff, it helps to build a soil saucer around the plants to hold water. Popular methods of watering include sprinkling, soaker hoses, watering bags, micro-irrigation systems, and soil needles. It is often enough to simply let water trickle out of the end of a hose until the soil around a plant is well moistened.

■ *Sprinklers*—Sprinklers water a large area. They are particularly useful in watering ground covers. If sprinklers are used, provide at least 1 inch of water at each watering. In average soils, 1 inch of water will soak the soil to a depth of 6–8 inches. The amount applied can be measured by placing a coffee can under the sprinkler and checking it periodically. Quite a bit of water is lost through evaporation when sprinklers are used.

■ *Soaker hoses*—Soaker hoses can be snaked through a landscape planting and hidden from sight with mulch. Soaker hoses, made of rubber, ooze water providing a slow application.

■ *Watering bags*—Watering bags are useful for newly transplanted trees located where watering is not easily done. Tiny holes in the bag allow the water to slowly seep into the ground.

14-13. The bag around this newly transplanted tree is filled with water.

■ *Microirrigation*—Microirrigation is a closed system characterized by low operating pressure and small orifice size. It has become popular particularly in areas that have a low annual rainfall. Calculations to determine the amount of water for each plant require the soil type and plant size. Special emitters and tubing deliver the prescribed amount of water to each plant. Once set up, this method of watering is efficient. Little water is lost to runoff or evaporation.

■ *Soil watering needle*—Soil watering needles supply water directly to the root zone of the plants. The needle is inserted a number of times around the tree or shrub to assure thorough watering.

14-14. This landscape technician is using a root watering needle to pump water directly to the root zone of the tree. The same equipment is used to apply soluble fertilizers.

FERTILIZING

Most trees and shrubs never need to be fertilized. They extract the nutrients they need from the soil. However, due to housing construction practices and landscape maintenance, fertilizers are sometimes very beneficial. Developers often leave housing sites with an abundance of subsoil low in fertility. These types of soils have low organic matter content. Fertility levels in landscape soils are not improved with high-maintenance landscapes. The natural process of nutrients being released into the soil by decaying plant parts is prevented with the removal of leaves, twigs, and grass clippings.

14-15. Plant litter that could provide nutrients to the soil through decay is often removed.

Woody landscape plants show signs of stress that can be reduced with fertilizer applications. Some signs to look for are growth slower than normal, twig dieback, earlier than normal fall color, and heavy seed set.

14-16. One symptom of stress is earlier than normal fall coloration. Shown is Sugar maple, *Acer saccharum*.

14-17. It is possible that watering and fertilizing could have saved this Norway maple, *Acer platanoides*. It was damaged by building construction.

14-18. The leaves of this Red maple, *Acer rubrum*, show signs of chlorosis due to a micronutrient deficiency.

An application of general purpose fertilizer can boost the energy production in the plant.

Sometimes, nutrient deficiencies occur. Nutrient deficiencies are often related to the pH of the soil. Extremes of pH in soils restrict the ability of some plants to absorb micronutrients. For example, pin oaks, *Quercus palustris*, develop chlorosis when grown in alkaline soils. ***Chlorosis*** is a yellowing of the leaves caused by the absence of chlorophyll. Iron deficiency is commonly associated with the chlorosis of pin oaks. The deficiency appears in pin oaks grown in high pH soils even if the soil is full of iron.

WHEN TO FERTILIZE

The best times to fertilize are in the spring of the year as the buds begin to swell and in the fall as the leaves drop. Spring applications provide the plants with nutrients when energy reserves are at their lowest. Nutrients applied in the fall are absorbed and stored until growth begins the following spring. Avoid fertilizer applications after mid-July as the nutrients encourage new growth at a time when the plants are naturally slowing in preparation for winter. Late season growth is soft and easily damaged by cold temperatures. Woody plants in need of fertilizers respond best if fertilized every three to four years.

Newly planted trees should not be given fertilizers. They are in the process of redeveloping their root systems. Soluble salts from the fertilizer can damage the young roots. It is recommended that only established landscape plants showing signs of stress receive fertilizer applications

HOW TO FERTILIZE

One key important to fertilizing is to deliver the fertilizer to the root zone. The ***root zone*** is the area in which roots are growing. Most tree roots are found in the top 2 feet of soil and extend one and a half times the width of the tree. The majority of small feeder roots, on which a tree depends for absorption of nutrients and water, are located in the top 12 to 15 inches of soil. Up to 60 percent of these feeder roots are outside the drip line of the tree.

Fertilizer can be applied to woody landscape plants in several ways. Dry fertilizer can be placed in the root zone. Soluble fertilizer is injected into the root zone. Dry fertilizer is broadcast over the ground. Soluble fertilizer is sprayed onto the foliage. Solid fertilizer capsules are placed in the trunk of a tree.

Dry Fertilizer in Holes

The method of using dry fertilizer involves placing dry fertilizer in the root zone of the plant. *Dry fertilizers* are most often sold in granular form. In this method, a series of holes 2 to 3 inches in diameter are made in the soil using an auger or punch bar. These holes are located under the drip line of the tree and 3 feet beyond the drip line. No holes are made closer than three feet to the trunk of the tree to avoid damaging major roots. The holes should be 2 feet apart and 12 to 15 inches deep. A large tree will require many holes so fertilizer is evenly distributed. The fertilizer is measured and placed in the holes. The holes are filled with water, then sealed with soil. This fertilizing method is time consuming and labor intensive.

The recommended amount of fertilizer depends on the size of the tree. Trees with diameters less than 6 inches should receive 5 pounds of 10-6-4 or 10-10-10 fertilizer for each inch. Trees larger than 6 inches in diameter should receive 10 pounds for each inch of diameter. These recommendations equal about ½ cup of fertilizer per hole.

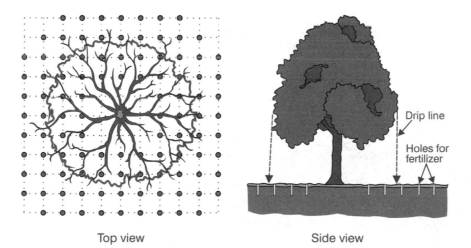

Top view   Side view

14-19. Proper placement of holes for dry fertilizer.

14-20. The owner of this tree used dry fertilizer spikes. They are shallow causing the death of grass above and rapid turf growth around the spike.

Dry fertilizer is also available in the market as fertilizer spikes. *Fertilizer spikes* consist of hardened fertilizer that is slowly released into the soil. The spikes are hammered into the soil around the tree to be fertilized. One advantage is they cut the labor of digging holes. However, they are difficult to place below the surface of the soil, and they tend to be expensive.

Soluble Fertilizer Injections

Soluble fertilizers can be in pumped into the ground around woody plants. *Soluble fertilizers* dissolve readily in water. The soluble fertilizer is dissolved. The soil needle is pushed into the ground. A hydraulic pump then forces the solution held in the tank through the needle into the root zone. A recommended rate of application calls for 30 pounds of 20-20-20 soluble fertilizer in 200 gallons of water. This method has advantages over dry fertilizers. The distribution of nutrients is more uniform, the nutrients are available to the plant immediately, the plant receives a good watering, and it requires less labor. Disadvantages are the equipment is relatively expensive, it can be difficult to push the needle into heavy clay soils, and soluble fertilizers leach or wash through the soil more quickly.

Broadcast of Fertilizer

Shrubs and ground cover plants are most often fertilized by broadcasting. *Broadcasting* involves the wide distribution of material on the surface of the

14-21. Shown is a soil needle used to inject soluble fertilizers into the root zone.

soil. The fertilizer dissolves and slowly works its way into the soil. Two to four pounds of 5-10-10 or 10-10-10 fertilizer per 100 square feet is recommended. The fertilizer should be applied when the foliage is dry and then watered immediately.

Soluble Fertilizers Sprayed onto Foliage

Foliage sprays using soluble fertilizers are effective when the leaves are young and during dry spells. The fertilizer nutrients are absorbed through the leaf tissues. Nutrients are quickly put to use in the leaves. Whereas, this method has some use with smaller landscape plants, it is impractical on the large scale.

Solid Fertilizer Implanted in Trunks

The method of inserting solid *fertilizer capsules* in the trunk of trees is primarily used for trees suffering from micronutrient deficiencies. Soil pH cannot be changed without damage to the roots, so the micronutrients are implanted in the tree. Holes are drilled in the trunk and the capsules are placed just under the bark. The nutrients dissolve in the sap and move up the tree. The major disadvantage of this method is it allows entry for disease and insect pests.

MULCHING

Mulching is the practice of spreading a material over the surface of the soil. Mulch reduces water loss, prevents weed growth, and keeps soil temperatures uniform. Quality mulches also contribute to an attractive landscape setting. In the case of organic mulches, the soil tilth can be improved as the mulch decays. The overall effect of mulches on landscape plants is very beneficial.

14-22. Mulching around trees helps prevent lawnmower damage to the trunk in addition to the other advantages discussed.

14-23. The crushed limestone mulch in this landscape is blinding and it raises the soil pH to levels harmful to plants. (Courtesy, University of Illinois Cooperative Extension Service)

SELECTING MULCHES

There are two major types of mulches. **Organic mulches** originate from plant material. Examples include wood chips, shredded wood bark, pecan hulls, and pine needles. **Inorganic mulches** have their source from materials that never were living. Some inorganic mulches are marble stones, volcanic rock, and river gravel. The availability of mulches varies from one region of the country to another.

Select mulches carefully. Choose mulches that are easily obtained, easy to apply, and inexpensive. Also, it is best to use mulches that complement

Table 14-1. Advantages and Disadvantages of Mulches

Advantages of Mulches	Disadvantages of Mulches
1. Suppress weed growth	1. Mulches cannot suppress large weeds
2. Maintain uniform soil temperature	2. Some mulches are flammable
3. Increase water holding capacity of sandy soils	3. Rodents and insects may live or overwinter in mulch
4. Increase aeration of heavy clay soils	4. Mulches may introduce certain plant diseases
5. Prevent and reduce surface erosion and soil compaction	5. Some mulches reduce nitrogen levels in the soil
6. Improve soil tilth	6. Mulches encourage slug and snail populations
7. Reduce evaporation of soil moisture	7. Mulches can prevent water from penetrating the soil
8. Create a desirable appearance	8. Mulches can be difficult to handle
9. Promote root growth in the upper 2" of soil	
10. Release nutrients for plant growth by increasing the breakdown of organic matter	

Table 14-2. Calculating Amounts of Mulch

CUBIC YARDS OF MULCH NEEDED	
Specified Depth	Multiply area to be covered (sq. ft.) by:
2"	.006
3"	.009
4"	.012

the site and region in which the landscape is located. Wood chips look natural in areas where woodlands are common. Wood chips look out of place in an arid region. For the same reason, volcanic rock appears at home in a rocky area or where volcanoes are found, not in a prairie or woodland area.

Since some mulches can change soil pH, they need to be used with caution. Crushed limestone or marble raises the pH of soil over time. This can be a particular problem if the soil pH is already high. Pine needles have the opposite effect. They are acid and lower soil pH.

APPLYING MULCHES

Before spreading mulch over the soil, many landscapers install landscape fabric (discussed in chapter 10). The landscape fabric is helpful in reducing weed growth. Some landscapers apply the mulch directly over the soil. In each case, the mulch should be applied to a depth of 3 to 4 inches.

14-24. Spread mulch 3 to 4 inches deep.

Table 14-3. Mulches and Their Characteristics

Name	Positive	Negative	Uses
Cocoabean hulls	■ attractive dark brown color ■ absorb solar heat and warm the soil	■ develop mold when wet ■ light—may blow away	■ planting beds
Crushed corn-cobs	■ good weed inhibitor ■ retains soil moisture	■ reduces nitrogen level in soil ■ difficult for water to penetrate	■ vegetable garden ■ annual and peren-nial flower beds
Decorative wood chips	■ long lasting ■ available in various sizes	■ may be expensive ■ not a good source of organic matter	■ planting beds
Grass clippings	■ readily available ■ source of nutrients for the soil	■ form a mat ■ get moldy when wet ■ rot when spread thick	■ vegetable gardens
Gravel chips, crushed stone	■ permanent covering ■ dark colors absorb solar heat and warm the soil	■ does not supress weeds ■ expensive ■ heavy	■ highlight land-scape features
Leaves	■ add essential nutrients to the soil ■ readily available	■ some types pack flat ■ can become soggy	■ perennial beds ■ vegetable gardens
Peanut hulls	■ light weight ■ decompose quickly adding organic matter to the soil	■ may develop mold when wet	■ good mulch for tomato plants ■ annual and peren-nial flower beds
Pine needles	■ light weight ■ weed free ■ easy to handle ■ absorb little moisture	■ unattractive to worms ■ coarse in appearance	■ good mulch for broadleaf evergreens
River gravel	■ permanent cover ■ absorb solar heat and warm the soil ■ attractive appearance ■ available in different sizes	■ expensive ■ does not suppress weeds ■ heavy	■ highlight land-scape features ■ planting beds
Shredded bark	■ long lasting ■ allows moisture to penetrate	■ can be stringy and difficult to handle	■ planting beds

REVIEWING

MAIN IDEAS

Healthy plants are better able to defend themselves against disease and insect pests than plants weakened for one reason or another. Healthy plants also are more attractive and add value to the landscape appearance. Most woody landscape plants, if well established, require little care. Most plant care practices should be directed to newly planted plants and to plants under stress.

In determining care for woody plants, it helps to have an understanding of woody plant biology. The need for water and fertilizer is influenced by plant life cycles and the weather. In spring, when the leaves are developing and, in the fall, when roots are developing, plants have their lowest levels of energy reserves. Those plants under stress at these periods benefit from watering and fertilizer applications. Watering is also important at other times when drought conditions prevail.

Watering is one of three common treatments given to woody landscape plants to ensure good health. Before watering, determine if the soil is dry. If water is needed, soak the soil thoroughly. Soakings are recommended every two to three weeks during drought conditions. Watering methods include sprinkling, soaker hoses, watering bags, microirrigation systems, soil watering/feeding needles, and simply letting water trickle out of the end of a hose.

Fertilizer applications can give a plant a boost by providing nutrients. If needed, fertilize woody plants in the spring as the leaves unfold or in the fall when the plant goes dormant. Methods of fertilizing woody plants include dry fertilizer placed in the root zone, soluble fertilizer injected into the root zone, dry fertilizer broadcast over the ground, soluble fertilizer sprayed onto foliage, and solid fertilizer capsules placed in the trunk of a tree.

Mulching is a third practice beneficial to woody landscape plants. Mulches reduce water loss, prevent weed growth, keep soil temperatures uniform, improve soil tilth, and contribute to an attractive landscape setting. Organic mulches originating from living material and inorganic mulches with origins from nonliving material are used. When selecting a mulch, choose one that appears native to the area in which the house is located.

QUESTIONS

Answer the following questions using correct spelling and complete sentences.

1. Why is it important to maintain healthy landscape plants?
2. How does the biology of woody plant materials influence plant care?

3. What role does stress play in plant health?

4. When are the energy reserves the lowest in the life cycles of woody plants?

5. What factors affect watering practices?

6. What methods are used to water woody landscape plants?

7. When is fertilizer beneficial to woody plants?

8. What are the major methods of fertilizing woody plants?

9. Why are mulches beneficial to plants?

10. How should mulches be applied?

CHAPTER SELF-CHECK

Match the term with the correct definition. Write the letter by the term in the blank provided.

a. wilting
b. desiccation
c. soaker hose
d. microirrigation

e. chlorosis
f. respiration
g. soluble fertilizer

h. organic mulch
i. soil watering needle
j. mulching

_____ 1. A yellowing of the leaves caused by the absence of chlorophyll

_____ 2. The drooping of a plant due to a lack of firmness in the plant tissues

_____ 3. Originate from plant material

_____ 4. The chemical process in which cells convert sugars into energy

_____ 5. Made of rubber, oozes water

_____ 6. Water loss from tissues resulting in tissue death

_____ 7. The practice of spreading a material over the surface of the soil

_____ 8. Supply water directly to the root zone of the plants

_____ 9. Emitters and tubing deliver the prescribed amount of water to each plant

_____ 10. Dissolve readily in water before use

EXPLORING

1. Volunteer to care for the woody plants in your yard, a relative's yard, or a neighbor's yard. Apply the knowledge you learned in this chapter to plants in the landscape.

2. Walk around your neighborhood. Do any of the landscape plants you see show signs of stress? Based on what you have learned, would water or fertilizer applications help to relieve the stress?

15

Pruning Woody Landscape Plants

A large limb splits from the tree and smashes a brand new car in the driveway. The vigorous growth of shrubs that have grown over a paved walk force people to walk on the grass. One spring, white flowers appear on a pink flowering dogwood. These occurrences have happened. They are also undesirable. Each of these situations could have been avoided with proper pruning.

Pruning is a major landscape maintenance activity. Landscapers must be well trained in approved techniques in order to prune woody landscape plants properly. The why, what, when, and how of pruning woody landscape plants is the subject of this chapter.

15-1. Pruning can play a major role in the health and beauty of a plant.

OBJECTIVES

1. Explain the reasons for pruning woody landscape plants

2. Identify tools used in pruning woody landscape plants

3. Describe how to properly prune trees

4. Explain how woody landscape plants heal their wounds

5. Describe various pruning practices used with shrubs

6. Identify specialized careers related to pruning woody landscape plants

T E R M S

arboriculture
arborist
branch ridge bark
callus
candle stage
chain saw
collar
compartmentalization
dead zone
hand pruner
heading back
hedge shear
leader
loppers
pruning
pruning saw
rejuvenation pruning
renewal pruning
rootstock
scaffold branch
scion
shearing
sucker
U-shaped crotch
urban forester
V-shaped crotch
watersprout

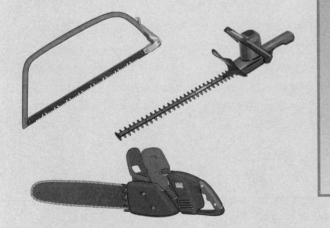

PRUNING . . . WHY?

Maintenance of woody ornamental plants in the landscape involves pruning. ***Pruning*** is the term used for the selective removal or reduction of certain plant parts. Pruning practices range from the removal of huge tree limbs to pinching off growing tips. Proper pruning contributes to maintaining the desired appearance of ornamental plants. Improper pruning techniques can produce unsightly plants. It can also cause injury to the plant.

It helps to first identify and understand the reasons for pruning. There are multiple reasons for pruning woody plants. Some of those include:

15-2. Damage to this Silver Maple, *Acer saccharinum*, caused by a weak framework of branches could have been avoided with proper pruning.

- Developing a strong framework of branches that resist breakage and provide an attractive appearance
- Restricting the size of the plant, often necessary when plant materials are selected without regard to the plants' mature size
- Repairing damaged limbs
- Improving flowering of trees and shrubs
- Removing diseased or insect infested limbs, thereby reducing spread of the pest
- Directing growth
- Maintaining desired cultivars
- Opening the crown to allow light and wind to pass
- Maintaining safe conditions for humans
- Improve quality of fruit on fruiting trees, shrubs, and vines

15-3. Pruning of this Littleleaf Linden, *Tilia cordata*, would make pedestrian traffic easier and safer.

WHAT TO PRUNE

Before any cuts are made, ask, why am I pruning this plant? Then, be sure your cuts contribute to the pruning goals you have established. Always consider the results of the cuts before the cuts are made. View the structure of the plant from a distance before any cuts are made. Between cuts, step away from the plant to see if the desired habit of the plant is being maintained.

Different types of woody landscape plants respond to different methods of pruning. However, some rules apply to all materials:

1. Make cuts that cause the least amount of damage to the plant.

2. Begin pruning practices when the plant is young.

3. In most cases, prune after the plant has flowered.

4. Use sharp tools suitable for the job safely.

PRUNING TREES

The best time to start pruning trees is when they are young. A strong, well-balanced branching structure can be developed at a young stage of growth. Well-balanced trees have a single, strong leader. A *leader* is a central branch that dominates over other branches on the tree. It leads the growth of the tree. Sometimes, trees develop co-leaders. These are not

15-5. The limbs on this American Sycamore, *Platanus occidentalis*, have U-shaped crotches and thus, are very strong.

15-4. This Littleleaf Linden, *Tilia cordata*, has a strong leader.

attractive and they usually result in weak V-shaped crotches. Select and remove one of the co-leaders.

Secondary branches or **scaffold branches** grow laterally from the trunk. The greatest weakness of a tree's branching structure occurs at the point of attachment of scaffold branches. Branches that exhibit a 45- to 90-degree angle of attachment, or a **U-shaped crotch**, are structurally strong. Where the angle of attachment is sharp and a **V-shaped crotch** develops, the joint is weak. This is because the bark is crushed between the branches as the tree grows and expands. The branches do not fuse. Trees with V-shaped crotches are prone to split from the

15-6. Co-leaders on this Sugar Maple, *Acer saccharum*, have formed a weak V-shaped union. Disease has entered the tree at the union.

15-7. A limb that once formed a V-shaped crotch on this American Elm, *Ulmus americana*, split from the tree.

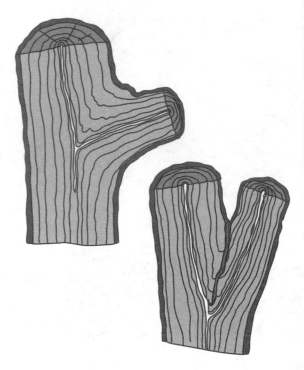

15-8. A comparison of U-shaped (left) and V-shaped (right) crotches.

15-9. Watersprouts are fast-growing vertical shoots that sprout from branches.

force of wind or the weight of ice and snow. Prune limbs that show V-shaped crotches while the tree is young.

Remove watersprouts that detract from the appearance of the tree. ***Watersprouts*** are soft, green shoots that typically grow vertically from existing branches. They seldom flower. Watersprouts often occur following severe pruning. A common result of watersprout growth is crossing branches.

Study the branching structure to determine if branches are crossing one another. Crossing branches are unattractive. More important, the friction of limbs rubbing on one another may open wounds. These wounds allow entry of disease and insect pests. Regular removal

15-10. Suckers are fast-growing shoots originating at the base of a plant. Shown is an American Linden, *Tilia americana*.

of branches growing back toward the center of the tree eliminates most crossing branches. It is best to look for these when the tree is young. On trees where the crossing branches have grown large, remove the less important of the two branches.

Suckers are soft, green shoots that develop at the base of the tree. Watersprouts and suckers offer no ornamental value and if allowed to grow they create an unsightly appearance. Removal of suckers is particularly important when a cultivar is being grown. Cultivars are propagated by grafting. The grafting process involves the union of a *scion*, or top growth, to a *rootstock*, or root system. The rootstock of the plant does not have the same qualities as the scion. If suckers from the rootstock are allowed to grow, they will interfere with the desired ornamental effect of the scion. Some plants that exhibit this problem are flowering crabapples and flowering dogwoods.

Look for and remove dead or diseased wood from the tree. The same recommendation goes for broken

15-11. This photograph shows a graft union. Suckers from the rootstock should be removed if they sprout.

branches. Dead wood left in the tree prevents the tree from healing. Dead wood and broken branches can also be safety hazards to those underneath. Cutting out diseased wood removes a source of disease that could spread to other limbs or other trees.

Pruning Newly Transplanted Trees

Transplanting places new trees under tremendous stress. This is due to a loss of a great majority of the roots in the digging process. Some trees never recover and die. The key to survival is the tree's ability to develop a new root system. Energy is required to regenerate new roots. The energy is in the form of sugar produced in the leaves of a tree. Some energy is also stored in the branches of a tree as starch. When needed, it is converted back to sugar for the production of roots. Severe pruning of the crown at the time of planting adds to the stress. Removing limbs means the loss of energy-producing leaves and stored starches. Since the root development hinges on the production of sugars, it is best to remove as little of the crown as possible at the time of planting.

15-12. Limit pruning to dead wood, diseased wood, and co-leaders when a tree is first planted.

Removal of over 15 percent of the crown at the time of transplanting slows tree growth for several years. Concentrate on removing only the limbs that call for the most urgent attention. Co-dominant leaders, dead wood, diseased wood, and V-shaped crotches should be removed or corrected at the time of transplanting. This assures that as many leaves as possible are left on the tree to produce energy.

Two to four years after planting, prune the tree again. During this second pruning, remove crossing branches, limbs that have died back, and some of the lower branches. Avoid removing all the lower branches. Removal of the lower branches over a longer period contributes to the development of a strong, healthy trunk. Choose to keep branches that will develop with U-shaped crotches.

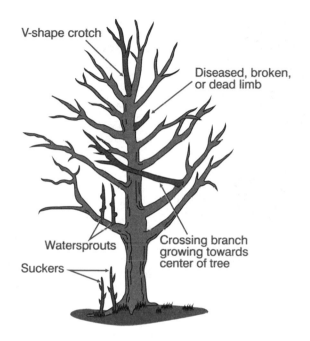

V-shape crotch

Diseased, broken, or dead limb

Watersprouts

Suckers

Crossing branch growing towards center of tree

15-13. Prune obvious faults from the tree.

Prune the tree again five to seven years after planting. The amount to prune at this time is minimal. Remove the remainder of the unwanted lower limbs. Also, remove dead wood, crossing branches, suckers, and watersprouts.

Closing of Wounds

Trees can close their wounds. It is not the way our wounds heal, such as when we skin a knee. Rather, trees produce chemicals that inhibit decay caused by fungi and bacteria. The wound is sealed by these chemicals. This formation of a chemical barrier is called ***compartmentalization***.

15-14. Decay has been compartmentalized in this American Sycamore, *Platanus occidentalis*.

The concept of compartmentalization is fairly simple. When a tree is injured, all the wood present at the time of the injury could become subject to decay. Wood produced after the injury is walled off from infection by the tree's defensive chemicals. The new wood is protected from decay by the chemical barrier. A common sight is a hollow tree. The wood present at the time of an injury decayed. Wood formed after the injury is disease free and supports the tree.

Chemical barriers are present at the base of every branch. At the base of every branch there is a branch bark ridge and a collar. The ***branch bark ridge*** is a raised line of bark that forms on the upper side of where the branch joins the trunk. The ***collar*** is swollen trunk tissue surrounding the base of the branch. These structures contain chemicals that inhibit the spread of decay in the trunk. In nature, decay that has entered a branch spreads until it reaches the chemical zone at the base of the branch. The branch eventually falls off the tree. Then, the tree forms a ***callus***, or protective growth of tissue, over the wound. Removal of the branch bark ridge and the collar, during pruning, destroys the tissues that defend the tree from infection and decay.

15-15. Callus tissue forms over these old wounds.

The physical closure of the wound with callus protects the tree from disease and insect infestation. As the callus grows, it slowly covers the wound. The rate of this growth depends on the tree species, the energy reserves of the tree, and the wound itself. The threat of disease and insect infestation is reduced with the closure of the wound. Knowledge of how trees close a wound can be applied to pruning practices. Remove limbs in a way that will help the tree mend itself.

Removing Large Limbs

Safety is the number one consideration in pruning large limbs. The weight of large limbs ranges from hundreds to thousands of pounds. That same weight, which can injure the person pruning the branch, can also damage the tree if not removed properly. Improper removal of large limbs often strips bark from the tree.

15-16. An improperly pruned limb has stripped bark from the tree.

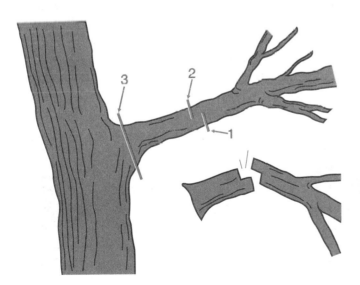

15-17. Use three cuts to remove most limbs.

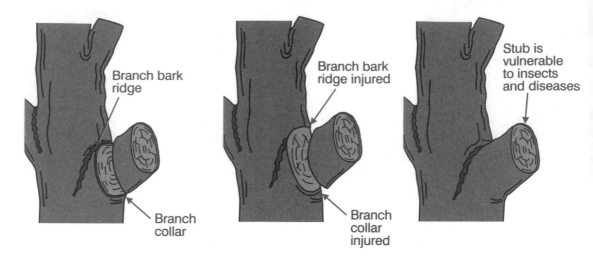

Branch bark
ridge

Branch
collar

Branch bark
ridge injured

Branch
collar
injured

Stub is
vulnerable
to insects
and diseases

15-18. A proper cut, a flush cut, and a stub cut.

To avoid stripping of bark, remove the bulk of the limb before making the final cut. First, make an undercut about one-third of the way through the limb, 1 foot away from the trunk. Second, cut the upper side of the limb about 1 inch from the undercut. If this upper cut is closer to the tree than the undercut, the branch will swing toward the tree before it drops. If the upper cut is outside the undercut, the branch drops straight down. The third and final cut involves the removal of the remaining stub. It is advisable to make an undercut before the final removal if the stub is large.

In making the final cut, the landscaper is left with three choices. The final cut can be flush with the trunk, thus removing the collar and branch bark ridge. It can be made to leave a stub vulnerable to diseases and insects. Or the proper cut can be made. The proper cut is one made as close to the collar and branch bark ridge as possible without causing damage to those tissues.

15-19. The proper cut keeps the branch bark ridge and collar intact. Note the wound is not sealed.

After the final cut is made, leave the wound exposed. For many years, the popular belief was the wound should be sealed with tar, asphalt pruning paint, or shellac. They are never needed. Sealers actually promote decay by keeping moist conditions favorable for the bacteria and fungi.

15-20. Topping of trees is both unsightly and unhealthy.

When pruning trees, never remove more than one-third of the crown. The loss of the leaves and energy stored in the limbs places stress on the plant. Also, never top a tree. Topping, or dehorning, is very unattractive. It places the tree under stress, and it opens wounds that are not easily healed.

When to Prune Trees

Late winter and early spring are the best times to prune most deciduous trees. There are some advantages to pruning trees when they are dormant. It is much easier to see the branching structure of a tree when the leaves are absent. The limbs are much lighter without the leaves. Also, cuts made in late winter or early spring have a full growing season in which to heal. A disadvantage is it is more difficult to identify dead or diseased branches when the tree is dormant.

Some trees respond best to pruning when the plant is actively growing. Maples, birches, elms, and dogwoods ooze sap from wounds if they are pruned in late winter or early spring. Although the sap is unsightly, it

15-21. Late winter or early spring is the best time to prune most trees.

15-22. Arborists are often called upon to remove large trees.

causes no damage to the tree. Prune these plants in midsummer when the sap is not flowing. The time of year when ornamental trees flower is another factor to consider before pruning. Trees that flower in the spring formed their flower buds the previous fall. Pruning in late winter or early spring removes the flower buds with the limbs. Therefore, it is best to prune a tree, such as a Flowering Dogwood, *Cornus florida*, after it has finished flowering in the spring so the flowers can be fully appreciated.

Tree Specialists

Removal of large limbs or entire trees requires care not only from a safety standpoint, but for the health of the tree. Professional tree care specialists, **arborists**, are the best qualified to tackle difficult pruning jobs. Arborists are trained in the culture of trees, **arboriculture**. Training in arboriculture includes plant identification, identification and diagnosis of tree diseases and pests, prescription of treatments, and safe removal of trees and tree limbs. A related profession is that of a forester. The type of forester who works with ornamental trees in city settings is an **urban forester**. The demand for urban foresters has increased as city populations have grown and inhabitants call for city greening.

PRUNING DECIDUOUS SHRUBS

Proper pruning of shrubs in the landscape assures many years of pleasure. Pruning helps keep shrubs vigorous and ornamental. Keep a few general rules in mind when pruning deciduous shrubs. In most cases, prune shrubs after they have flowered. Learn the shrub's natural habit of growth, its mature size, when it flowers, and on which year's growth flower buds are formed. Also, start pruning practices while the plant is young to develop a strong framework of branches. Several pruning techniques are used to prune deciduous shrubs. They are renewal pruning, rejuvenation, heading back, and shearing.

15-23. Urban foresters are shown pruning dead wood and directing tree growth away from utility lines.

Renewal Pruning

Renewal pruning is defined as the selective removal of older plant stems. By removing the older stems, new growth is encouraged, the plant size is maintained, and flowering is promoted. Cut the stems at ground level. Always choose which stems are to be cut carefully. This will help to ensure the natural shape of the plant is maintained. Annual spring pruning continues a steady production of new shoots. Some shrubs that respond well to renewal pruning are:

Lilac (*Syringa* species)

Lemoine Deutzia (*Deutzia x lemoinei*)

Mockorange (*Philadelphus* species)

Weigela (*Weigela* species)

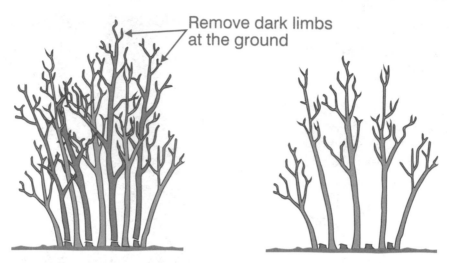

15-24. Renewal pruning is the selective removal of older plant stems.

Forsythias (*Forsythia* species)
Arrowwood Viburnum (*Viburnum dentatum*)
St. Johnswort (*Hypericum* species)
Redosier Dogwood (*Cornus stolonifera*)

Rejuvenation Pruning

Rejuvenation pruning is a method of pruning deciduous shrubs that involves the complete removal of all the stems to 4 to 6 inch stubs. The best time to prune a shrub in this manner is in late winter or early spring.

15-25. Rejuvenation pruning involves the complete removal of all the stems to 4 to 6 inch stubs.

15-26. This Dwarf Winged Euonymus, *Euonymus alatus* **'Compactus', is sprouting after rejuvenation pruning.**

Energy stored in the root system produces new stems in the spring. Shrubs that respond well to rejuvenation pruning include:

Anthony Waterer Spirea (*Spirea x bumaldi* 'Anthony Waterer')
Glossy Abelia (*Abelia x grandiflora*)
Honeysucklc (*Lonicera* species)
Beautybush (*Kolkwitzia* amabilis)
Privet (*Ligustrum* species)
Slender Deutzia (*Deutzia gracilis*)

Heading Back

Heading back involves the shortening of individual stems. Reasons for heading back are to remove dead or diseased wood and to restrict the size

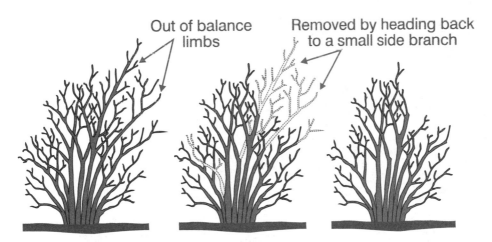

15-27. Heading back involves cuts made back to the parent stem rather than to the ground.

of the stem. Cuts are made back to the parent stem rather than to the ground, as is the practice with renewal pruning.

Shearing

The practice of shearing shrubs should be reserved for clipped hedges and formal gardens. **Shearing** effectively reduces the total leaf surface a

15-28. Shear hedges to be wider at the base than at the top to allow light to reach all the leaves.

15-29. This yew (*Taxus x media* 'Hicksii') hedge is sheared wider at the base to maintain leaf growth to the ground.

plant has to produce energy. As a result, the plant is placed under stress. From an ornamental standpoint, individual shrubs pruned tightly into geometric shapes draw the attention of the viewer. In the public area, the unnatural shapes divert attention from the house.

If a hedge is desired, shear the shrubs to be wider at the base than at the top. This allows light to reach all the leaves. Hedges pruned wider or the same width at the top as the bottom tend to have open growth at the bottom. This is because thick leaf growth occurs only when sufficient light is provided. It is also advisable to allow the hedge to grow slightly each year to maintain a good coverage of new leaves. A few plants that make good hedges are privet (*Ligustrum* species), honeysuckle (*Lonicera* species), spirea (*Spirea* species), and Alpine currant (*Ribes alpinum*).

PRUNING EVERGREENS

Different evergreens respond to different pruning methods. When to prune evergreens also varies with the species.

15-30. Prune the leader and lateral shoots of firs in early summer to produce dense growth. Shown is Fraser Fir, *Abies fraseri*.

- **Arborvitae**—These evergreens are easily maintained by heading back limbs with hand-held pruners. Prune arborvitae in the spring. Avoid severe pruning that exposes the dead zone. The **dead zone** is the region in the center of the plant that, when exposed to light, seldom produces new shoots.
- **Firs**—Annual pruning in early summer, to shorten the leader and lateral shoots, promotes dense growth. Severe pruning of shoots back to three-year-old wood is tolerated.
- **Junipers**—It is best to prune junipers using the heading back method in spring. Be careful not to cut into the dead zone of the plant as junipers do not produce new growth on old wood. It is important to start a pruning program while the plants are young to avoid overgrown situations that cannot be corrected.

Cut here

Before

After

15-31. Prune junipers using the heading back method in spring.

15-32. This juniper was pruned to expose the dead zone. It will not produce dense green growth again.

■ **Pines**—Prune pines when they are in the ***candle stage*** of growth. New growth on pines resembles candles. Cut the terminal candles leaving 8 to 12 inch stubs. Prune lateral candles to be 2 to 4 inches shorter than the terminal candles. Pines do not respond well to heavy pruning into old wood.

■ **Spruce**—Light pruning in early summer is best. Cut leaders leaving at least three buds on the remaining stub. Lateral shoots must be 1 to 2 inches shorter than the leader.

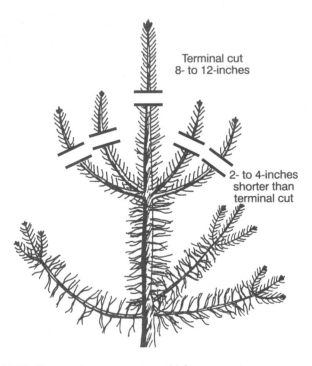

Terminal cut
8- to 12-inches

2- to 4-inches
shorter than
terminal cut

15-33. Prune pines to create a thick, compact appearance.

■ **Yews**—Yews respond very well to pruning. This characteristic makes yews a popular choice for clipped hedges. Prune yews in spring and again in early summer. The technique most often used is heading back. Yews also tolerate severe pruning, even when up to 50 percent of the plant is removed.

15-34. Yews respond very well to pruning.

BROADLEAF EVERGREENS

Broadleaf evergreens, such as rhododendron (*Rhododendron* species), holly (*Ilex* species), boxwood (*Buxus* species), and Japanese skimmia (*Skimmia japonica*), require very little pruning. Light heading back is recommended to maintain dense plants. Prune rhododendrons after they have flowered. Remove faded flowers and pinch back new growth. Boxwood, holly, and skimmia are used as clipped hedges. They tolerate shearing.

15-35. Remove faded flowers and pinch back new growth on rhododendrons to maintain dense growth.

PRUNING TOOLS

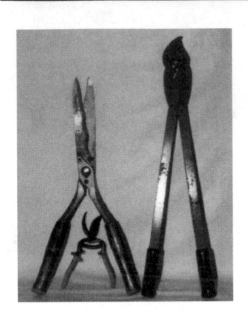

15-36. Scissors-style hand pruner (lower left), hedge shear (upper left), and a loppers (right).

There are a number of tools used for pruning purposes. For small branches, **hand pruners** or **loppers** are sufficient. There are two styles of hand pruners and loppers. The scissors style is the recommended style as they slice the stem. The anvil design is less effective as it crushes the stem as it cuts. Larger limbs may require the use of a pruning saw or a chain saw. **Pruning saws** have large teeth with wider spacing than carpenter's saws. The large teeth ease the cutting effort and speed the cut. **Chain saws** are gas powered or electric and have a continuous cutting chain. They are extremely dangerous if used improperly. Pole saws and pole pruners are specialty tools with long handles that allow the person to reach high limbs from the ground. **Hedge shears** may be hand operated, electric, or gas powered clippers used to trim hedges and shape shrubs in formal gardens.

15-37. A pruning saw.

15-38. An electric-powered hedge shear.

Keep safety in mind when selecting and using pruning tools. Select tools that are sharp. Sharp tools are easier to use, safer, and leave a smooth cut. Determine the cut to be made. Then, pick the tool that will do the job with the least amount of effort. For instance, a hand pruner is appropriate for removing small branches, but is a poor selection for the removal of a 2 inch limb. When using power tools, wear goggles to protect your eyes. Hard hats and ear plugs are additional safety precautions to employ when operating a chain saw.

15-39. Keep safety in mind when using a chain saw.

15-40. This person is using a pole pruner to trim a tree. (Courtesy, Illinois Landscape Contractors Association)

Pruning tree branches with a chain saw requires careful thought and constant attention. Determine which branches need to be removed and follow these guidelines:

- Study each branch before cutting.
- Accelerate the saw before you start cutting.
- Move your feet only when the chain completely stops turning.
- Do not cut with the upper tip of the guide bar.
- If the saw blade becomes pinched, shut the saw off before removing it.

It is recommended that individuals receive training from a well-qualified instructor on the safe use of chain saws before putting those skills to practice.

REVIEWING

MAIN IDEAS

Pruning is the selective removal or reduction of certain plant parts. It is a practice used in landscape maintenance of woody plants. Proper pruning promotes healthy and attractive growth. There are many reasons to prune landscape plants. Pruning is done to develop a strong framework of branches, restrict growth, direct growth, repair damage, remove disease, improve flowering, and provide a safe landscape.

Begin pruning trees while they are young to develop a strong branching structure. Identify certain faults when pruning trees. Establish a strong leader if more than one is evident. Prune diseased or dead wood. Remove crossing branches, watersprouts, and suckers. Consider the removal of limbs with V-shaped crotches as they are weak and prone to splitting. U-shaped crotches are much stronger. Perform a limited amount of pruning on newly transplanted trees. New trees need as many leaves as possible to produce food that will help the tree become established. Most trees can receive minor pruning throughout the year, but the best time is late winter or early spring.

Deciduous shrubs are pruned several ways. One method, known as renewal pruning, involves the removal of the older stems at ground level. Renewal pruning encourages new growth, maintains the plant size, and promotes flowering. Rejuvenation pruning is a method in which all the stems are cut to 4 to 6 inch stubs. New shoots develop the following growing season. A third method is heading back. Heading back is the reduction of stems back to the parent stem. A fourth alternative is shearing. Shearing is used for formal hedges. Different shrub species respond differently to the different pruning methods.

Evergreen woody plants usually do not require a great deal of pruning. It is important to know that different evergreens respond to different pruning methods. The best time of the year to prune evergreens also varies with the species. Broadleaf evergreens also require little pruning. Heading back is the most common method of pruning broadleaf evergreens.

Select the proper tool for the pruning job. The selection of tools includes hand pruners, loppers, hand saws, chain saws, pole pruners, pole saws, and hedge shears. Choose the tool that requires the least amount of effort, yet makes a clean cut. Sharp tools are safer, easier to use, and leave a smoother cut than dull tools.

QUESTIONS

Answer the following questions using correct spelling and complete sentences.

1. Why are woody landscape plants pruned?
2. What are some general rules that apply to all materials pruned?
3. How do watersprouts, suckers, and crossing branches differ?
4. What faults should be addressed first when pruning trees?
5. What special attention do newly transplanted trees require? Why?
6. How are large limbs removed safely?
7. How does a tree defend itself from decay and heal its wounds?
8. When is the best time to prune deciduous trees? Why?
9. What are the major methods of pruning deciduous shrubs? Explain each.
10. What tools are used for pruning woody landscape plants?

CHAPTER SELF-CHECK

Match the term with the correct definition. Write the letter by the term in the blank provided.

a. compartmentalization   e. collar   h. watersprout

b. rejuvenation   f. sucker   i. arboriculture

c. dead zone   g. leader   j. heading back

d. V-shape crotch

_____ 1. Swollen trunk tissue surrounding the base of the branch

_____ 2. Soft, green shoots that develop at the base of the tree

_____ 3. A central branch that dominates over other branches on the tree

_____ 4. The culture of trees

_____ 5. Involves the shortening of individual stems

_____ 6. Soft, green shoots that grow vertically from existing branches

_____ 7. A weak attachment of the branch to the trunk due to the sharp angle

_____ 8. The region in the center of an evergreen plant that when exposed to light seldom produces new shoots

_____ 9. A wound sealed off from decay by a chemical barrier

_____ 10. Method of pruning deciduous shrubs involving the complete removal of all stems to 4 to 6 inch stubs

EXPLORING

1. Take a walk in the neighborhood. Look for woody landscape plants that have been pruned. Decide for yourself based on what you learned in this chapter if proper pruning was practiced. Are you surprised with what you found? Did you see plants in need of pruning?

2. Visit a local arborist or urban forester. Find out what they like about their job. What are some challenges they have experienced while pruning trees?

3. Volunteer to prune the plants in your yard, in a neighbor's yard, or for a relative. Identify the plants to be pruned and determine the best time and method of pruning.

16

Establishing and Maintaining Turfgrass Areas

Beautiful, green turfgrass is appealing and useful in many ways. People enjoy lawns, playing fields, parks, and other places with turf. Turf is an integral part of the landscape.

Having good turf is more than throwing out a few grass seeds. Turf requires the same care as other plants. The soil must be tested and fertilized; the seedbed must be prepared, properly planted, and watered; pests must be controlled; and the turf maintained.

Southern and northern turfgrasses need many of the same general practices. The manner in which plants grow is the same. The differences are in the species used and the cultural practices in growing each. People also have different objectives for turfgrass in different locations.

16-1. Well-kept turf is important to the overall beauty of the landscape.

OBJECTIVES

1. Distinguish between warm and cool season turfgrasses

2. Describe how to establish turf

3. Name the factors necessary for good seed germination

4. Explain vegetative propagation of turf

5. Describe the best time of year to fertilize turf

6. Explain good mowing practices

7. List common turf management practices

T E R M S

cool humid region

cool season turfgrass

herbicide

plains region

plug

sod

sprigs

thatch

transition zone

turf

turfgrass

turfgrass blend

turfgrass mixtures

warm arid and semi-arid regions

warm humid region

warm season turfgrass

TURFGRASS USE IN THE UNITED STATES

People like the beauty of lawns, athletic fields, parks, golf courses, and other places where turf is grown. Turf is an integral part of the landscape in the United States. Good turf requires more than throwing out a few grass seeds and hoping for the establishment of a green lawn. Often, good turf management practices are put into effect at the wrong time of the year. This chapter provides a good foundation in proper turfgrass culture techniques.

16-2. Turf on playing fields must have good quality.

TURF FUNCTIONS

Turf is the plants in a ground cover and the soil in which the roots grow. *Turfgrass* is a collection of grass plants that form a ground cover. Quality turfgrass requires regular maintenance practices. Grass has three different uses in the landscape—ornamental or beauty, utility, and sports. Turf quality is related to the common visual factors of density, texture, uniformity, and color. All grass lawns and athletic fields must look good.

People enjoy seeing a large green lawn around a home, business, or park. A well-maintained yard can increase the property value of a house. Turfgrass planted along roads can stabilize the soil and reduce erosion. Turfgrass also has a cooling effect in hot weather and can clean air by removing toxic emissions. Athletes like the good surface turf provides. It can reduce player injuries.

CLIMATE AND TURFGRASS LIFE CYCLE

Turfgrasses are often placed in two groups—southern and northern. These groups are based on the ability of a species to grow and serve a useful purpose in a specific climate. The *cool season turfgrasses* grow best in a temperature range of 60 to 75°F. The *warm season turfgrasses* grow best in the range of 80 to 95°F and are dormant in weather below 32°F. The life cycles of grasses are related to the season in which the grasses grow.

Seeded annual turfgrasses complete a life cycle in one growing season. This includes the vegetative, reproductive, and senescence (death) stages. The life cycle of perennial grasses includes vegetative, reproductive, and dormancy stages. Mowing helps keep turfgrasses in the vegetative stage, rather than following a natural schedule into reproduction.

If cool season turfgrasses go into summer dormancy, they may not survive. Irrigation and syringing (misting for surface cooling) help minimize summer dormancy. Warm season turfgrasses have winter dormancy; unless, they are found in tropical climates where they remain green all year. The growth of cool season turfgrasses is limited by heat and drought. Warm season turfgrass growth is limited by cold weather.

Transition Zone

A *transition zone* is an area between major climate zones. The transition zone in the east is a zone separating temperate and subtropical zones in the eastern United States. This zone goes east and west at 37° north latitude and is 200 miles wide. Bluegrass and fescue meet the limits of their southern exposure in the lower eastern transition zone.

The climate in the eastern transition zone favors growth of some warm and some cool season turfgrasses, but is not really optimum for either. However, several warm season and cool season turfgrasses can be grown in this transition zone. Zoysia is the most cold tolerant of the warm season turfgrasses. Bermuda grass can be grown in this transition zone with some winterkill. Tall fescue and ryegrass are the best suited and most popular for the eastern transition zone.

Another transition zone is east of the Rocky Mountains. The zone includes areas in Oklahoma, Kansas, Nebraska, North Dakota, and South Dakota. The climate is semi-arid and wheatgrasses are grown in the northern areas. Buffalograss and gramagrasses are grown throughout most the Great Plains.

TURFGRASS REGIONS

Climate, soil conditions, and length of growing seasons differ greatly through the country. These ecological differences help divide the country into four major turfgrass regions. The kinds of grass grown and the management practices must be changed in each of these regions.

Cool Humid Region is suited to cool season grasses, such as bluegrass, ryegrass, fescue, or bentgrass. The soils are generally acid and some irrigation may be needed to supplement natural rainfall. Planting seed is the common way of starting new lawns in the cool humid region.

Warm Humid Region is suited to warm season grasses, such as Bermuda grass, zoysia, or St. Augustine grass. These soils are generally strongly acidic and may be relatively infertile. Establish warm season turf by vegetative techniques, not seed. Sodding, plugging, and sprigging are used to install new lawns in the warm humid region of the United States.

Plains Region is a dry part of the United States that has buffalo grass growing naturally. Cool season turf will only grow in this region with adequate irrigation. Buffalo grass is usually established by seed in this region.

Warm Arid and Semi-Arid Regions will only support the warm season turf with irrigation to supplement the very low natural rainfall. Soils in this region are usually alkaline and low in fertility. Lawns are established by sodding, plugging, and sprigging in the warm arid and semi-arid regions.

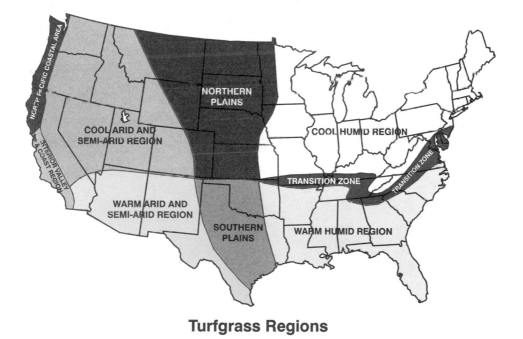

Turfgrass Regions

16-3. Turfgrass regions in the United States.

ESTABLISHING TURF

There are several commonly used methods of establishing turf-grasses—seeding, sodding, plugging, and sprigging. Establishment by seeding is the most common method in the cool humid region, and it is usually the least expensive of these methods. In the South, lawns are usually established by sodding, plugging, or sprigging of warm season turf species.

Table 16-1. Turfgrass Propagation Methods, Mowing Heights, and Recommended Type of Mower

Species	Propagation	Mowing Height		Type of Mower
		Inches	Centimeters	
Warm Season Turfgrasses				
Bahiagrass	Seed	2–4	5.0–10.2	Rotary
Bermuda grass				
Common	Seed	0.5–1.5	1.3–2.8	Reel or Rotary
Improved	Vegetative	0.25–1	0.6–2.5	Reel
Carpetgrass	Seed & Vegetative	1–2	2.5–5.0	Rotary
Centipedegrass	Seed & Vegetative	1–2	2.5–5.0	Reel or Rotary
St. Augustinegrass	Vegetative	1.5–3.0	3.8–7.6	Rotary
Warm/Cool Season Turfgrasses				
Zoysia				
Japanese lawngrass	Vegetative	0.5–2.0	1.3–5.0	Reel
Manilagrass	Vegetative	0.5–2.0	1.3–5.0	Reel
Cool Season Turfgrasses				
Blue gramagrass	Seed	2.0–2.5	5.0–6.4	Rotary
Buffalograss	Seed & Vegetative	2.0–3.0	5.0–6.4	Rotary
Bentgrass				
Colonial	Seed	0.5–1.0	1.3–2.5	Reel
Creeping	Seed (Veg. for a few)	0.2–0.5	0.5–1.3	Reel
Bluegrass				
Kentucky	Seed	2.5–3.0	6.4–7.6	Reel or Rotary
Rough	Seed	2.5–3.0	6.4–7.6	Reel or Rotary
Fine fescue	Seed	3.0–3.5	6.4–8.9	Reel or Rotary
Perennial ryegrass	Seed	2.5–3.0	6.4–7.6	Reel or Rotary

TURFGRASS ESTABLISHMENT BY SEED

The advantages of seeding a lawn are desired species or cultivars can be used, the plants develop in the environment in which they must ultimately survive, and establishment usually costs less than sodding or plugging. When establishing a lawn from seed, the following factors are necessary for good seed germination and growth: (1) live seed, (2) adequate moisture, (3) sufficient soil warmth, and (4) adequate soil aeration. Early spring (March and April) or late summer (August and September) provides the ideal weather conditions for good grass seed germination in the cool humid region. Warm season grasses should be established in early summer or just prior to their peak period of growth. It is important that adequate irrigation be available during the summer's heat.

Planting Site Preparation

Proper preparation of the planting site can reduce many drainage, aeration, pH, and fertility problems that may not become evident until after the lawn is established. It is much more difficult to correct these problems after the turf is established. Proper site preparation steps include: (1) control weeds at the planting site, (2) rough grade the site and remove debris, including rocks and wood, (3) conduct a soil test, (4) apply soil amendments as necessary, (5) thoroughly mix the amendments into the soil to a depth of 6 inches, (6) fine or finish grade the site.

Eliminating weeds, especially perennial grassy weeds, will reduce competition with developing turfgrasses. Herbicides are used to eliminate weeds prior to lawn establishment. After the weeds have been eliminated, rough grade the area to facilitate surface drainage. Generally, a 1 to 2 percent slope away from buildings is adequate. This is a drop of 1 to 2 feet for every 100 feet of run. Remove all debris, such as tree roots, stones, and other materials, brought to the surface by rough grading.

If topsoil is needed at the planting site, it should be incorporated into the existing soil during rough grading. Performing a soil test will provide a means to determine if soils can support turf growth and if amendments are necessary. Finish grade the site.

16-4. Preparing a seedbed.

16-5. The desert regions in the Southwest present additional problems in seedbed preparation and turfgrass selection. This shows established turf next to desert sand in California.

Blends and Mixtures

In selecting a turfgrass, choose cultivars that have shown resistance to diseases. Turfgrass may be of one cultivar or a blend. A *turfgrass blend* is a combination of different cultivars of the same species. Blends should have cultivars that are similar in appearance and competitive ability. At least one cultivar should be well adapted to the planting site. Blends usually have at least three cultivars. *Turfgrass mixtures* are combinations of two or more different species.

Planting

The seed label provides valuable information about the grass seed. Different turfgrasses have different seeding rates. They vary according to the size and weight of the turfgrass seed. When selecting seed, look for a high purity and germination percentage, fresh seed produced the previous year, and as low as possible weed content.

After choosing the turfgrass seed and determining the seeding rate, be sure to distribute it uniformly over the planting area. Avoid excessive seedling rates that can produce crowded, weak plants and increase seedling disease invasion. Use a broadcast or drop spreader. It is advisable to apply half the seed in one direction and the other half in a different direction to uniformly cover the entire area.

After the seed is in place, there are two additional steps that are crucial to successful turfgrass establishment. The first is making sure there is good seed-to-soil contact. This can be accomplished by using a rake to lightly mix the seed into the upper ¼" of soil. After raking, follow with

Table 16-2. Size and Seeding Rates

Species	Seeds per Pound	lbs./1,000 sq. ft.
Kentucky bluegrass	1,000,000 to 2,200,000	2–3
Red fescue	350,000 to 600,000	3–5
Perennial ryegrass	250,000	2–3
Tall fescue	170,000 to 220,000	7–9
Creeping bentgrass	5,000,000 to 7,000,000	1–2

16-6. A truckload of sod being delivered to the landscape site.

16-7. Pallets of dormant Bermuda grass.

a light rolling to produce a firm seedbed. A light rolling can be accomplished by using an empty water-ballast roller. Rolling not only increases seed-to-soil contact, but firms the seedbed and slows the drying of the soil. The seedbed area should be mulched to prevent or slow drying. A thin layer of clean straw is commonly used. Don't apply too heavily. The soil beneath the straw should be able to be seen. Usually one bale (35 to 50 lb.) per 1,000 sq. ft. is adequate. The straw is not removed after the seed germinates. Grass seedlings will grow up through the light straw layer and gradually cover it as the straw decomposes. Raking off the straw would injure the young grass plants. New mulches have been developed including paper materials and mesh for hillsides.

The second activity crucial to seed establishment is to make sure adequate water is available throughout the germination process. At the time of planting, water frequently and lightly, wetting the upper ½" of soil. Continue irrigation during the germination period. Water less frequently but more thoroughly and deeply as the turfgrass plants mature. Too much activity on a newly seeded lawn can interfere with seed germination also. The amount of activity on a newly seeded lawn should be limited as much as possible for two to three weeks.

First Mowing

The new lawn will be ready to mow when the turfgrass plants are higher than the height at which they will normally be maintained. For example, if the lawn is be cut regularly at 2½ inches, then mow for the first time when it is 3 inches tall. The general rule is to never remove more than 1/3 of the turfgrass leaf blade at any one time. Avoid mowing when the grass is wet. A sharp mower blade is important too. A dull

16-8. A low-compaction crawler unrolling large rolls of sod onto a burlap mat over prepared soil.

mower blade rips and shreds the grass instead of cutting it. This can also make the turfgrass plants more susceptible to diseases and other problems.

VEGETATIVE PROPAGATION

Sodding can provide the homeowner with an "instant" lawn. *Sod* is the surface layer of mature turf. It includes the grass plants and a thin layer of soil. Sod is harvested in rolls, squares, or strips. This is a common method of lawn establishment for warm season turfgrass. Use sod containing a mixture of grass varieties that will adapt to the climatic area. While speed of establishment is usually the reason for sodding, erosion control is also a valid reason to sod a lawn. The sod is cut from the turf farm field with a sod cutter, which removes a thin layer of soil with the grass plants. The pieces of sod are usually 18 inches wide, 6 feet long, and 5/8 of an inch thick. After cutting the sod, it is rolled up or stacked. Each roll usually contains one square yard of sod. High quality sod is dense, uniform, and free of weeds and disease. It should be transported to the landscape site and installed as soon as possible (within 24 hours).The steps in site preparation for sodding are the same as in seeding a new lawn area.

After tilling, level and roll the soil to provide a good base for the sod. Just before laying the sod, dampen the prepared planting area. Position the first piece of sod along a straight edge, such as a walk or building foundation. Lay rolls in a parallel manner, staggering the ends. Lay squares of sod in a staggered, checker board manner. Install sod that contains suitable grass varieties for the area to be covered, that is, shade-tolerant grasses for shaded locations, drought-tolerant grasses for steep slopes, etc. Too often, sod is selected and installed with little regard for the kinds of grass plants present in the sod or the environmental conditions of the site.

The best time of year for laying sod is early fall in the cool humid region.

16-9. Newly laid dormant Bermuda grass sod.

The normal cycle of new root formation begins during that season. However, sod can be laid in almost any season of the year when the soil is not frozen. Plant sod in the spring or summer in the warmer regions of the United States. Adequate irrigation should be available for the grass plants to become established in their new location.

Plugs of turf are mainly used to establish sub-tropical turfgrasses. A *plug* is a small 2- to 4-inch square

16-10. Hand sprigging a lawn with Bermuda grass.

or circular piece of sod that is 2 inches thick. Plugs are marketed by the tray and on pallets. They are used to establish turf without making a solid cover over the entire area. Plant the plugs 6 to 8 inches apart on a prepared seedbed. After planting, firm the soil around each plug and keep the area moist for two to three weeks. The plugs will grow and cover the entire area in one season. Zoysia grass is usually established using plugs in the late spring or summer, when zoysia is actively growing.

Sprigs can also be used to establish a lawn. *Sprigs* are pieces of turfgrass rhizomes or stolons with roots attached. They consist of at least three or four nodes (joints). Make shallow furrows 2 to 3 inches deep and 10 to 18 inches apart in the planting area. Bermudagrass is normally established with sprigs planted either by hand or with a machine. After sprigging, lightly cover the sprigs with top soil by raking or harrowing. Lightly firm the soil by rolling or tamping and provide adequate moisture for two to three weeks after planting every mid-day.

FERTILIZING ESTABLISHED TURF

Turfgrass growing in the cooler regions needs fertilizer applied four times a year (early spring, late spring, early fall, and late fall). Fescue and bluegrass growing in the eastern transition zone needs three applications (February, September, and November) at 1 pound of nitrogen per 1,000 sq. ft. Turfgrasses will start growing two to three weeks earlier in the spring, depending on the latitude, if fertilizer is applied in March or early April. Not only does early fertilization speed spring green-up but it also helps the cool season grasses heal injuries.

Fertilization during late spring will provide the turfgrass the nutrients necessary to survive the hot summer growing season. An early fall fertili-

16-11. Rotary spreader for rapid application of fertilizer to small or medium-sized turf areas.

zation will stimulate the production of new tillers and rhizomes for the following year. This fertilization will also help maintain a vigorous, green turf until late fall or early winter. Fertilizing at this time can also improve early spring green-up of the grass.

FERTILIZER COMPOSITION

Maintenance fertilizers should be high in nitrogen, but also have moderate amounts of phosphate and potash. To avoid over stimulation, immediately after fertilization, use a slow-release fertilizer. Slow-release fertilizers provide a sustained flow of nutrients to the grass. The exact analysis of the mixed fertilizer is not crucial. It may have a guaranteed analysis of 23-3-7, 32-4-8, or some similar content producing equal results if properly used.

16-12. The numbers on the fertilizer bag indicate the nutrient content.

16% nitrogen (N)– If it is a 100 pound bag, it contains 16 pounds of nitrogen.

4% phosphoric acid (as P_2O_5)– If it is a 100 pound bag, it contains 4 pounds

8% potash (as K_2O)– If it is a 100 pound bag, it contains 8 pounds of potash.

FERTILIZER

16 - 4 - 8

FERTILIZER RATE

The amount of fertilizer should be adjusted to the natural fertility of the soil, the length of the growing season, and the amount of foot traffic. Turfgrass growing on infertile or sandy soil needs extra fertilizer. The longer the growing season, the more fertilizer needed.

The rate or amount of nitrogen fertilizer that should be applied at one application is about 1 pound per 1,000 square feet. A common problem for a landscaper is determining how much fertilizer is needed to give the right amount of nitrogen to a specified area. A fairly simple equation is helpful and is explained through the following example:

Equation:

$$\frac{\text{pounds nitrogen to apply per 1,000 square feet}}{\text{percent nitrogen in the fertilizer}} \times 100 = \frac{\text{pounds of fertilizer to apply}}{\text{per 1,000 square feet}}$$

Sample problem:

The landscaper has been asked to provide a proposal for maintaining 16,000 square feet of turfgrass for a homeowner. Their selection of fertilizers has an analysis of 32-4-8. How much fertilizer needs to be spread on the lawn to provide the desired 1 pound nitrogen per 1,000 square feet?

$$\frac{\text{1 pound nitrogen to apply per 1,000 square feet}}{\text{32 percent nitrogen in the fertilizer}} \times 100 = \frac{\text{3.125 pounds of 32}-4-8\text{ fertilizer to}}{\text{to apply per 1,000 square feet}}$$

16 multiplied by 3.125 equals 50 pounds of 32-4-8 fertilizer to apply to the 16,000 square foot of lawn.

SETTING THE FERTILIZER SPREADER

All fertilizers must be spread uniformly over the turfgrass surface since fertilizers do not move laterally in the soil. Failure to provide uniform distribution will produce a very irregular response of the grass. The strips or spots missed will get no benefit from the fertilizer. Uniform spreading is also desirable to avoid over stimulation of grass in some areas.

Fertilizers should not burn the turfgrass if applied correctly. Adjust the fertilizer spreader to apply the desired amount in a given area. There are two major types of fertilizer spreaders. The drop or gravity spreader will provide a very accurate application of fertilizer. However, the application process will be very slow because the spreader only covers a 24- to 36-inch wide strip. The rotary spreader will cover a 6 to 12 foot wide strip and give a uniform application. These spreaders can quickly fertilize large turf areas.

MOWING

16-13. A walk-behind mower used by lawn maintenance firms.

There are four major types of mowers in common use today—rotary, reel, flail, and sickle. Rotary mowers are the most popular with landscape maintenance firms and homeowners. Reel mowers provide a high quality cut. The flail mower provides a good cut with improved safety for both operators and other people around the mower. It is often used for cutting coarse or tall grass along highways or in parks. The sickle type mower provides a low quality cut and is mainly used on very low maintenance areas, such as roadsides.

A rotary mower has one or more blades that are parallel to the ground attached to a shaft. The mowing height is adjusted by raising or lowering the wheels. A rotary mower may have a bag for collecting grass clippings or may mulch the clippings. Self-propelled walk-behind mowers in sizes from 21 to 61 inches wide are popular with landscape maintenance firms. A reel mower has a set of spiral blades rotating on a horizontal bar. The mowing height is adjusted by setting the height of the front roller. A reel mower is best used for closely mowed turf.

HEIGHT OF CUT

Table 16-1 provides recommended mowing heights for the various species of warm and cool season turfgrasses. Mowers for cool season grasses should be set to cut 2½ to 3 inches in height. Warm season grasses typically require 1 to 2 inch settings. Allowing the grass to grow taller induces a stemmy erect habit of growth, rather than the desired dense prostrate growth habit. The frequency of mowing should be such as to keep grass from exceeding 3½ inches in height. In periods of rapid growth, mowing may be needed twice a week; at other times, once a week may be sufficient. In cooler periods and in dry seasons, frequency of mowing may be only once in two or three weeks.

Continue mowing turf areas in the fall as long as they continue growing. Disease development will increase in the fall if turf is allowed to grow to tall.

REMOVAL OF CLIPPINGS

When the amount of grass clippings produced by mowing do not readily sift down into the turf, it is best to remove them. Excessive clippings are not only unsightly, but their continued presence on top of the grass is an invitation to turf diseases. Diseases prefer the high-humidity conditions found under this mat of clippings. If clippings are heavy enough to require removal, this should be done promptly, before fungus diseases have an opportunity to develop. The clip-

16-14. Proper mowing height is important when maintaining turfgrass areas.

pings that sift down through the grass to the soil are helpful. These clippings add to soil's fertility. Grass clippings decompose rapidly, return about 25 percent of the nitrogen to the lawn, and do not contribute to thatch build up.

16-15. This lawn tractor is equipped with an optional power bagger to remove clippings.

OTHER MAINTENANCE PRACTICES

16-16. A well-designed automatic sprinkler system is designed to give complete coverage.

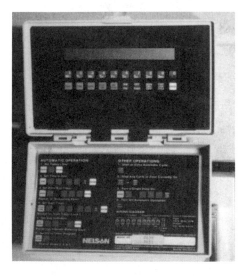

16-17. Home lawn irrigation controller.

WATERING TURFGRASS

In regions receiving less than 40 inches of annual rainfall, irrigation is essential for good turf maintenance. In humid regions, irrigation is desirable during periods of prolonged drought. A rain gauge should be installed to keep track of precipitation. The gauge should be set on a post in the open, and read after every rain. By keeping a record of rainfall, it is easy to assess the need for watering. After 7 to 10 days without rain, turfgrass plants start to wilt.

Water should be added only when needed. Lightly sprinkling turf in hot weather will benefit weeds more than the desirable turfgrasses. As a rule, water to wet each area to a depth of about 6 inches, moving the sprinkler from area to area as the watering system permits. Generally, 1 inch of water will soak the soil to a depth of 6–8 inches.

The time of day for watering is not important except that it should be completed early enough so the grass leaves are dry by nightfall. When grass goes into the night with wet leaves, the situation is ideal for development of leaf diseases. The claims that watering in the sun will scald grass leaves are not valid. Any such scalding is probably caused by water-logging of the soil and the resulting death of roots where drainage is inadequate.

THATCH CONTROL

Thatch describes the accumulation of excess grass stems and roots in the turf. In the past, turf experts believed that bagging grass clippings would prevent thatch buildups. However, grass clippings do not contribute to thatch buildups. Excess grass growth creates the conditions for thatch to accumulate. Over fertilization of turf can create thatch accumulation. Therefore, reduce fertilizer rates to prevent thatch problems.

Controlling thatch requires physical removal of the excess plant growth and adopting maintenance practices to prevent additional thatch buildups. Power rakes or thatching machines can physically remove thatch from the lawn. All the thatch must be removed from the lawn surface after thatching with a power rake.

A core aerifying machine removes small plugs of soil from the turf. Air penetrating into the thatch layer through these holes will allow soil microbes to destroy the thatch. This technique prevents thatch accumulation. Chemical thatch removers on the market today have limited value in controlling thatch problems.

AERIFYING TURFGRASS SOIL

Aerifying turf can provide temporary improvement of compacted soil conditions and reduce thatch accumulation. An aerifier machine drives hollow tubes called tines into the soil and removes a ½-inch diameter plug of soil. The tines on the aerifier are usually spaced 6 to 8 inches apart. The more holes, the better the aerification. Use machines that have closely spaced tines or go over the turf area several times.

The best type of aerifier is one that removes a soil core to depths of 2 to 3 inches. After aerification, the soil cores left at the surface can be broken up and spread over the surface by dragging with a flexible steel mat. This treatment, when needed, is most effective if done before applying fertilizer or lime. These holes allow the deep penetration of fertilizers and lime into the soil.

16-18. Using a core aerator can reduce thatch accumulation while improving soil aeration.

ROLLING TURF

Rollers are used after seeding and sodding to establish good contact of the seed or sod to the soil. In regions where winter freezing and thawing of the soil occur, the turf may appear rough in spring. There is a belief that spring rolling is necessary for a smooth turf. Use a light water-filled roller to "replant" the grass plants. Repeated rolling when the soil is wet and soggy, particularly with a heavy roller, causes undesirable compaction of heavy-textured soils. Since grass roots will penetrate only into soil layers that are well aerated, spring rolling may restrict the new roots to the uppermost layers of soil.

The freezing and thawing of heavy soils are effective natural means of producing a well-aerated soil, and unwise rolling in spring may nullify this natural aerifying process. The objective in sound turf maintenance should be to roll sparingly, if at all. Take full advantage of soil freezing to produce a soil structure favorable to grass roots. When absolutely necessary, a roller just heavy enough to press the crowns of the grass plants into the soil and smooth the soil surface may be used.

REMOVAL OF LEAVES

Under deciduous trees in autumn, leaves should be removed periodically to prevent them from covering the turf and cutting off light. It is also essential for newly seeded or renovated areas in order to allow development of the grass seedlings. Care in removing leaves is important to avoid injury to the grass plants. Leaf removal improves the overall appearance of the landscape.

16-19. Leaves should be removed to keep them from covering the grass and cutting off light.

CONTROLLING WEEDS IN TURF

A good weed control strategy consists of exploiting opportunities in the following ways. (1) Natural competition makes conditions more favorable for the desired grasses and less favorable for weed growth. (2) Always plant weed-free grass seed mixtures and prevent weed seed production in the turf. (3) Attack weeds with herbicides at growth stages when the weeds are most vulnerable.

From this general plan, it should be obvious the use of herbicides, without taking care of other factors, is not an adequate method of weed control. An abundance of weeds in a turf area is evidence that conditions are not satisfactory for good turfgrass growth.

Nature controls certain types of vegetation by providing stiff competition from the desired plants, crowding out undesirable plants. A healthy turf, composed of well-adapted grasses and properly managed, will make such a dense cover that weeds will have difficulty in gaining a foothold.

16-20. An abundance of weeds in a turf area is evidence that conditions are not satisfactory for good turfgrass growth.

MOWING PRACTICES AND WEED CONTROL

Adjust mowing practices to prevent weeds from producing seed. This combined with timely use of herbicides constitutes good weed control practice. Mowing home lawns too short is one reason for weedy turf.

Most home lawns will have fewer weeds if the height of cut is raised to 2½ to 3 inches instead of the usual 1½ or 2 inches. Taller grass can better compete with weeds for water and nutrients. Mowing the grass tall should be the rule, not the exception for turfgrass.

16-21. A rotary riding mower for lawns and parks.

HERBICIDES

Herbicides are chemicals that kill or prevent weed growth. The kinds of weeds controlled, how to use it, and any special precautions will be on the label. Herbicides are powerful compounds and may cause damage to desirable turf if improperly used. Always read the manufacturer's label and accompanying printed instructions.

16-25. Chemical methods can be used on turfgrass to control winter weeds. This shows henbit in a dormant Bermuda grass lawn before (top) and two weeks after spraying with a herbicide (bottom).

Treat turfgrass areas with herbicides when soil moisture is adequate and weeds are actively growing. The weeds are most vulnerable under these conditions. An exception to this general rule is the use of preemergent herbicides, such as for crabgrass control, to prevent the germination of weed seeds. Apply preemergent herbicides before the crabgrass seeds germinate.

The technician should take appropriate care that sprays do not drift onto other vegetation, such as flowers, shrubs, trees, and vegetables. Read the precautions on the herbicide package and protect susceptible plants.

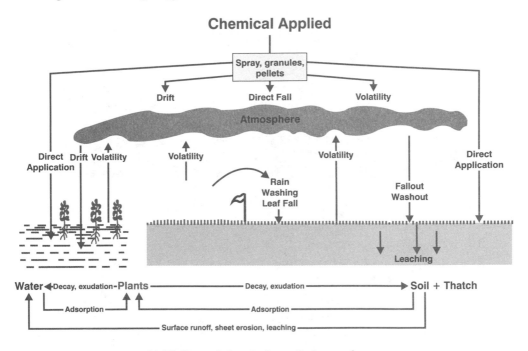

16-23. Fate of chemicals applied to turfgrass.

Seedling grasses are far more sensitive to herbicides than mature turf plants. It is important to apply herbicides well before any reseeding of grass, so the herbicide may be dissipated before planting grass seed.

Today, many herbicides are mixed with turf fertilizers to make application easy. Herbicides mixed with fertilizers may need to be applied to moist leaves for the herbicide to adhere to the weed leaf. Read and follow label directions.

After treatment, weed control may take from 3 to 10 days to complete. Do not retreat for 14 days if weed control is not complete. Over treatment is dangerous and may damage desirable turf.

16-24. Spraying pesticides on turfgrass.

The pesticide manufacturers have calculated the most effective rates of application and the correct time of year to apply the herbicide. Follow precautions to protect the environment. It is a violation of federal law to use a pesticide in a way not suggested on the label. Read the entire label before using the pesticide and apply according to label directions.

CONTROLLING DISEASE IN TURFGRASS

Adopting sound management practices is a major step in controlling disease in turfgrass. Although there are many turfgrass diseases, only a few are likely to cause serious problems.

The selection of grasses suited to the climatic region is important. Principles of soil management and proper use of fertilizers help the grass plants to develop resistance to disease and increase their ability to recover when invaded by an organism. Turfgrass mixtures are helpful because different species have different susceptibility to a specific pathogen. Avoiding close cutting, removing clippings, and avoiding excess moisture are all practices that help prevent disease from occurring in turf.

Many diseases in turf are caused by different species of fungi. They are controlled by applications of fungicides. General information on plant diseases is covered in Chapter 17. A turf management expert should be consulted if a disease is suspected.

16-25. Some important turf diseases include Pink snow mold (top left), Leaf spot (top center), Dollar spot (top right), Powdery mildew (bottom left), Brown patch (bottom center), and Pythium blight (bottom right).

REVIEWING

MAIN IDEAS

Kentucky bluegrass and ryegrass are the most popular lawn grasses in the northern part of the United States. Bermuda and zoysia grass are the popular lawn grasses in the southern part of the country. Tall fescue and ryegrass are the most popular in the east transition zone. Red fescue, perennial ryegrass, and tall fescue cultivars are also planted for special conditions, such as shade or low maintenance practices.

Quality turfgrass needs regular fertilizer applications. Slow-release types of fertilizer provide several months of sustained nutrient feeding. Always apply fertilizer according to the manufacturer's recommendations. Either a drop or rotary fertilizer spreader can be used to apply the granular fertilizer to the lawn. Do not overlap the spreader pattern when applying fertilizer.

When natural rain fall does not supply adequate water for good grass growth, artificial irrigation must be used to keep the grass vigorous. Thatch must also be controlled to have a quality lawn. Power rakes or thatchers can remove part of the accumulated thatch from a lawn. Aerification removes small plugs of soil and will improve water and fertilizer penetration into the root zone. Both power thatching and aerifying should be done when the grass is actively growing, not when under stress.

In the North, new home lawns are usually established by seed. Sod, plugs, and sprigs are commonly used in the South. Follow the steps given for proper soil preparation before seeding or sodding the new lawn. Mow Kentucky bluegrass with the mower set at 2½ to 3 inches high. This will allow the grass to compete with lawn weeds. Never remove more than 1/3 of the grass leaf blade at one mowing.

Unwanted lawn weeds can be controlled by applying the correct herbicide at the proper time. Spray lawns with insecticides to control insects that eat turfgrass. Always read and follow all instructions on the pesticide label.

QUESTIONS

Answer the following questions using correct spelling and complete sentences.

1. Name the popular grasses grown in the Warm Humid Region.
2. Name the popular grasses grown in the Cool Humid Region.
3. What is a transition zone?

4. What is sprigging?

5. How many pounds of fertilizer should be applied per 1,000 square feet of turf?

6. Why aerify turfgrass?

7. What is thatch and how can it be prevented?

8. What are the three times it may be necessary to roll turf?

CHAPTER SELF-CHECK

Match the term with the correct definition. Place the correct letter in the blank provided.

a. herbicide   d. plug   g. mulching mower
b. sod   e. fertilizer   h. aerifying
c. thatch   f. fungicide   i. turfgrass

_____ 1. Extra grass plant growth caused by over fertilization

_____ 2. Improve water penetration into the soil by punching holes in the turf

_____ 3. The grass plants and a thin layer of soil

_____ 4. Small pieces of turf

_____ 5. Chemical that kill or prevent weed growth in the home lawn

_____ 6. Mowers that cut and recut grass clipping before dropping them into the lawn

_____ 7. Plant food applied to the lawn to improve turf growth

_____ 8. A collection of grass plants that form a ground cover

_____ 9. Chemical that controls fungi that causes disease in turf

EXPLORING

1. Select a golf course in your community and scout the course observing all features and playing areas. Try to identify the different kinds of turfgrass growing in each area.

2. Prepare a seedbed following the procedures discussed in this chapter.

3. Collect and identify 10 lawn weeds growing in your home lawn or school lawn.

4. Visit a golf course and talk with the superintendent about job skills necessary for employment.

17

Controlling Pests in the Landscape

Pests in the landscape impact the health of the plants and their appearance. Plant pests can be controlled by biological, mechanical, and chemical ways. An understanding of integrated pest management strategies is important for the future of our environment. Certification by a state agency will be required in order to purchase and apply chemicals. Safety procedures must be followed when controlling pests in the landscape.

How can pest damage be reduced on plants? What precautions must be followed when applying chemicals to control pests? Can pests be controlled without using chemicals? What is IPM and why should this technique be considered? What type of personal safety protection should one wear when applying pesticides? The answers to these questions are important when controlling pests in the landscape.

17-1. Chemicals must be carefully used to prevent injury to people, domestic animals, and the environment. (Courtesy, Jasper S. Lee)

OBJECTIVES

1. Identify five major categories of pests

2. Describe complete and incomplete metamorphosis of insects

3. Explain the difference between selective and nonselective herbicides

4. Discuss alternate pest control techniques

5. Describe safety precautions necessary when handling and/or applying chemicals

6. Explain Integrated Pest Management (IPM)

TERMS

aesthetic injury level
algae
bacteria
biological pest control
contact herbicide
cultural pest control
exoskeleton
fungi
fungicide
herbicide
host plant
insect
insecticide
integrated pest management (IPM)
larvae
mechanical pest control
moss
nematicide
nematode
nonselective herbicide
nymph
parasite
pathogen
pheromone
pest
pesticide
plant disease
postemergent
preemergent
selective herbicide
systematic herbicide
viruses
weed

PESTICIDE	PEST CONTROLLED
Insecticide	Insects
Miticide	Mites
Acaricide	Ticks and Spiders
Molluscicide	Snails and Slugs
Fungicide	Fungi
Avicide	Birds
Rodenticide	Rodents
Nematicide	Nematodes
Bactericide	Bacteria
Herbicide	Weeds
Piscicide	Fishes
Predacide	Predatory Animals

INSECTS AND RELATED PESTS

Ornamental plants are subject to damage by pests. Healthy plants can be attacked by insects and die. A *pest* is anything that causes injury or loss to a plant. Most pests are living organisms, either plant or animal. Pests damage plants by making them less productive, by affecting reproduction, or by destroying them. Fortunately, most pests can be controlled and losses reduced or eliminated. Pests can be put into five major categories insects, diseases, weeds, nematodes, and rodents or other animals.

A **host plant** is one that provides a pest with food. Conditions must be right for pests to damage plants. The pest must be present to cause damage to the plant. Some plants are more likely to be damaged by pests than others. Many plants have a natural resistance to plant pests. Various pest management practices can be used to affect the environment and lessen or eliminate damage by pests.

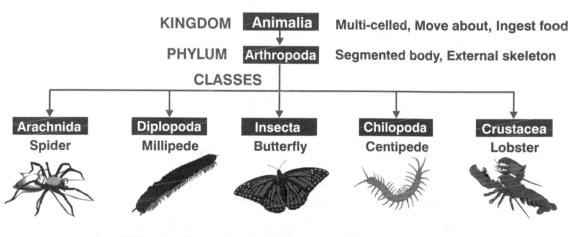

17-2. Scientific classification of insects and insect-related pests.

True *insects* are animals with three distinct body sections (head, thorax, and abdomen), three pairs of legs, and one or two pairs of wings. Bugs with more than three pairs of legs are in the group called insect-related. Spiders and mites have four pairs of legs and two body sections. Hundred-legged bugs, called centipedes, have one pair of legs for each body section. Millipedes, commonly called thousand-legged bugs, have two pairs of legs per body section. Sowbugs and pillbugs have seven pairs of legs. Snails and slugs belong to the crustacea group of animals.

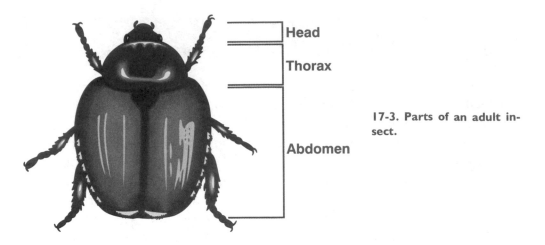

17-3. Parts of an adult insect.

There are more than 800,000 identified insect and insect-related animal species in the world. Less than 1,000 are pests of plants and people. Many different species are pests of ornamental plants and turf. In this chapter, the term insect will cover both true insects and insect-related organisms.

The insect body is cylindrical and segmented. It is made up of an external skeleton, called an *exoskeleton*, internal muscles, and organs. Insects breathe through pores on their sides called spiracles.

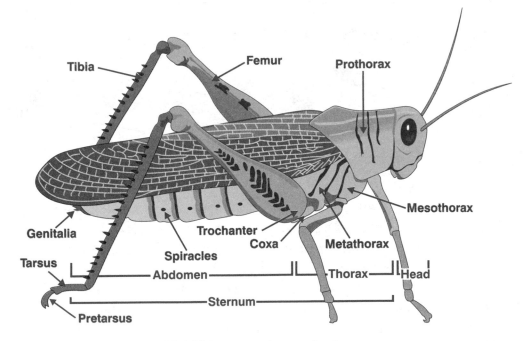

17-4. Major external parts of an insect.

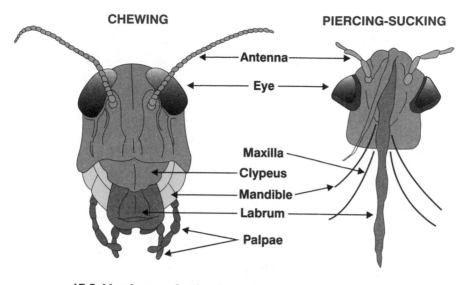

17-5. Mouthparts of a chewing and a piercing-sucking insect.

Insects are also divided by the kind of mouth parts, either chewing or sucking. Grubs, beetles, and caterpillars use chewing mouth parts to eat leaf, stem, and root structures. Aphids, scales, and leafhoppers insert an elongated beak (labrum) into the plant cell and suck out the cell contents.

LIFE CYCLE

Insects can be divided into two major groups related to their stage of development or metamorphosis. Insects with life cycles that undergo four distinct stages (egg, larvae, pupae, and adult) belong to the complete metamorphosis group. Moths, butterflies, and beetles all belong to this group. The insect egg develops into the *larvae,* which does not look any thing like the adult insect. Insects in the larvae stage cause the most damage to plants. A caterpillar is the larvae stage of a butterfly and moth. After feeding on plant tissue, the caterpillar goes into a resting stage called the pupae (cocoon stage). The adult butterfly emerges from the pupae stage and lays eggs to complete the life cycle.

Many other insects belong to a second group and go through incomplete metamorphosis. Insects in this group start as an egg but progress through a series of nymph stages. The *nymph* looks just like the adult insect but is much smaller. The nymph sheds its external skeleton four or five times. The stage between each shedding is called an instar. The nymph increases

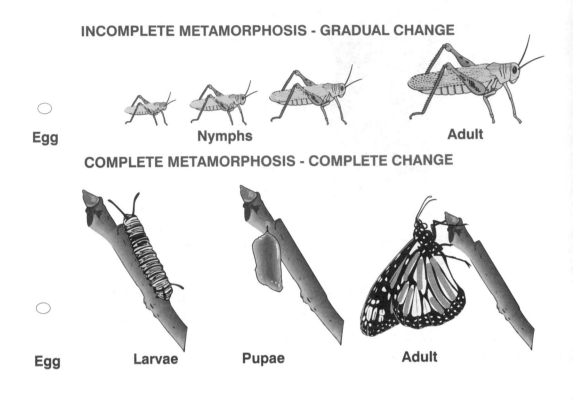

INCOMPLETE METAMORPHOSIS - GRADUAL CHANGE

Egg   Nymphs   Adult

COMPLETE METAMORPHOSIS - COMPLETE CHANGE

Egg   Larvae   Pupae   Adult

17-6. The life cycle of most insects is through complete or incomplete metamorphosis.

in size between each instar stage. Aphids, mole crickets, and chinch bugs are in this incomplete metamorphosis group.

Insects reproduce and go through several life cycles or generations each year. Aphids and red spiders can have ten complete generations each year. However, the periodic cicadas will take 13 to 18 years to complete one generation.

DAMAGE AND DETECTION

Some insects are beneficial, some are harmful, and others are simply a nuisance. Beneficial insects help plants grow. Beneficial insects improve the soil, help pollinate flowers, or destroy other harmful insects. Examples

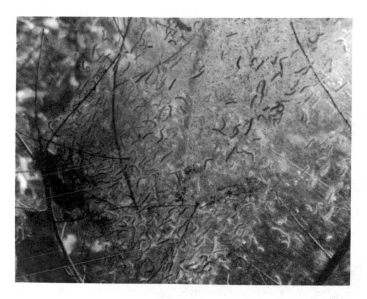

17-7. Tent caterpillar nest on a flowering crab apple tree.

of beneficial insects that destroy insect pests include the lady beetle, the praying mantis, and the common green lacewing. Honey bees cross pollinate plants, by transferring pollen from one flower to another flower, while collecting nectar.

Many insects feed on plant tissue during the larvae and adult stage. The larvae stage of the Japanese beetle (grub) feeds on plant roots; while the adult stage (beetle) feeds on plant leaves. Insect feeding can reduce the quality and vigor of the host plant. Burrowing, nesting, and mound-building insects can indirectly damage plants. However, ants improve soil aeration and tilth.

Many ornamental and turf insects are nocturnal (night) feeders. Watch bird feeding patterns to help detect insects. Birds feeding in a lawn at dusk or sun-up indicate an infestation of lawn insects. Use traps to detect

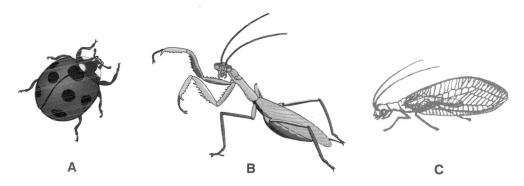

17-8. Some beneficial insects, (A) lady beetle, (B) praying mantis, (C) common green lacewing, attack and kill harmful insects.

17-9. Sticky pest traps are used to monitor insect populations.

and identify insects before starting control measures. Cut both ends from a coffee can and set the coffee can "tube" into a turf area suspected of harboring chinch buds or mole crickets. Fill the can with soapy water; wait 10 minutes; then, count the insects floating on the surface of the water. Treat the turf if more than three insects are found floating in the soapy water.

Cut and remove a sample of sod—1 inch thick × 1 square foot. Count the number of white grubs in the sample. Treat the lawn area when more than nine grubs are found in the sample. Several different beetle "traps" are sold and used to detect Japanese beetle populations. Place small, yellow, sticky 3 × 5 cards in a greenhouse to detect insect types and populations.

NEMATODES

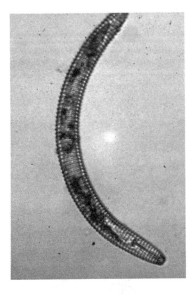

17-10. This threadlike worm is a nematode, greatly enlarged with a microscope. They invade the roots of plants and reduce the host plant's vigor. (Courtesy, Frank Killebrew, Plant Pathologist, Mississippi State University)

Nematodes are very small threadlike animals. These microscopic organisms live in the soil and damage plant roots. Nematodes vary in size from 1/75 to 1/10 of an inch long. There are approximately 500,000 species of nematodes in the world, including 2,200 species that cause damage to plants. More than 20,000 nematodes can be found in 1 pint of soil. Nematodes feed by penetrating root cells with a hollow stylet mouth structure and inject enzymes into plant cells. These enzymes digest the cell contents. Fungi and bacteria can enter the root tissue through the wounds left from the nematode.

Diagnosis of nematodes should not be made solely on observed symptoms on the host plant. Accurate diagnosis requires laboratory testing. Send a soil sample to a soil testing laboratory.

The laboratory will count the number of nematodes in 100 cc of soil. Treatment is recommended when 10 sting, 80 root-knot, or 100 stubby-root nematodes are found in the soil sample. Professional pesticide applicators using potent nematicide can control these soil-born organisms.

WEED PESTS

Unwanted plants can destroy the beauty of a well-landscaped yard and garden. Weeds detract from the overall appearance of the landscape. They can look different from desirable plants and compete for light, water, nutrients, and space. Weeds can reduce the vigor of landscape plants and turf.

CLASSIFICATION AND LIFE CYCLE

A *weed* is a plant growing out of place or an unwanted plant. Weeds may be classified as grassy (monocots), broadleaf (dicot), other (sedges or rushes), or moss and al-

17-11. A weed is a plant growing where it is not wanted or a plant out of place.

gae. The life cycle of the weed plant is very important in selecting a control measure. The life cycle includes germination of seeds, growth of plants, flowering, production of seeds, and finally death.

Summer annual weeds germinate in the spring, grow during the summer, produce flowers and seeds in the fall, and die at the first frost. Winter annual weeds germinate in the fall, grow that fall and winter, flower and produce seeds the next spring, and die in early summer. Perennial weed seeds can germinate spring, summer, or fall. These weeds grow for many years flowering and producing more seeds each year. The leaves and stems of many perennial weeds die in the fall but, new plants come from the strong healthy roots that survive the cold winter temperatures. Accurate identification is the first step in any weed control program.

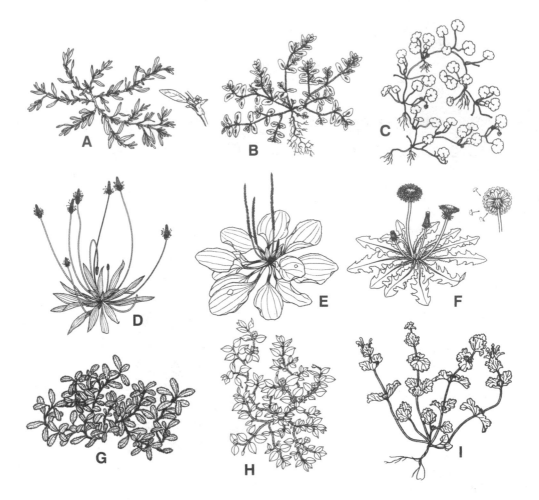

17-12. Common broadleaf lawn and garden weeds: (A) knotweed, (B) spotted spurge, (C) pennywort, (D) buckhorn, (E) broadleaf plantain, (F) dandelion, (G) mouse-ear chickweed, (H) common chickweed, and (I) henbit. (Courtesy, Amchem Products, Inc.)

MOSS AND ALGAE

Moss is a tangled green mat composed of thread-like growth that covers the soil surface. Shady areas with acidic, compact, poorly drained soil, provide an excellent environment for moss growth and development. Control is achieved by maintaining vigorous-growing desirable plants and adjusting the above factors.

Algae are a group of small, primitive, filamentous, green plants that manufacture their own food. They form a thick, slimy, greenish scum on bare soil in poorly drained wet areas of the lawn. This scum can dry and

17-13. Moss growing may indicate this soil has a low pH.

form a tough black crust that prevents water penetration into the soil creating isolated dry spots in the turf. Provide good surface and subsurface drainage, avoid overwatering, aerify compact areas, and increase light penetration to reduce algae growth.

DISEASE

Plant diseases are abnormal conditions that interfere with the normal appearance, growth, and structure of a plant. Each disease has characteristic symptoms or signs. Some diseases attack the entire plant, while others attack leaves or roots. Plant diseases can be divided into two major groups called infectious and noninfectious diseases.

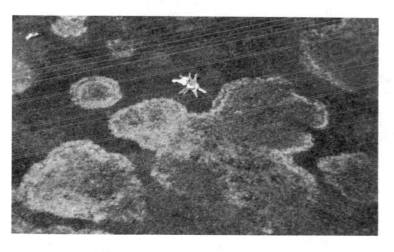

17-14. Pink snow mold turfgrass disease. The car keys are used for size comparison.

INFECTIOUS DISEASES

Parasites or pathogens cause infectious plant diseases. A *parasite* is usually a multi-celled organism that lives in or on other organisms. A *pathogen* is a biological agent or virus that can cause a disease. These organisms cannot manufacture their own food. They use the host plant tissue as a food source and disrupt its normal life. A microscope is often needed to see these organisms. Laboratory study is used to make accurate identification. For a disease to occur, a susceptible host, pathogen, and favorable environmental conditions must all be present. Plant pathogens are contagious and can be spread between plants usually by insects.

Diseases may be identified by the kind of damage done to the host plant. Symptoms of plant disease include: (1) rotting plant parts, particularly fruit; (2) yellow leaves called chlorotic; (3) wilting of plant leaves; (4) twisted leaves and/or stems; (5) buds, flowers, or fruits not developing or falling off; and (6) dead plants or plant parts called necrosis.

NONINFECTIOUS DISEASES

Noninfectious diseases are caused by elements in the plant's environment that are not right for good plant growth. Since plants vary in needs, their tolerance of poor environmental conditions varies. Some plants can live with a condition that will kill other plants.

Noninfectious diseases include the following: (1) weather, such as very cold or hot temperatures; (2) nutrient deficiencies, such as not enough potassium in the soil; (3) physical damage to plant parts, such as improper cultivation; (4) chemical injuries, such as incorrect applications of herbicides or insecticides; and (5) pollution injuries, such as smoke from car exhaust. Tissue analysis and soil testing may be needed to help identify these environmental diseases.

MAJOR ORGANISMS THAT CAUSE DISEASES

FUNGI

Fungi are small, one-celled, filamentous, spore-bearing organisms having no chlorophyll that grow on or in a plant. Fungi cause more plant diseases than all the other parasites. "Fungus" is the singular form and "fungi" is the plural word form. Parasitic fungi can cause many different plant diseases, such as mildew, rusts, wilts, and smuts.

Fungi are spread by wind, water, insects, and man from plant to plant. Aphids, feeding on a diseased plant leaf, can spread the fungus organisms to healthy leaves. Pruning a diseased shrub can spread the pathogen to a healthy shrub if the pruning shears are not disinfected after pruning each shrub.

BACTERIA

Bacteria are small, one-celled organisms that have a primitive nucleus. Some bacteria are beneficial while others cause plant diseases. Bacteria often get into plants through cuts or breaks in the bark or epidermis. Some also enter through flowers and natural openings in the stem and leaves. Fireblight, common on flowering crab apples, is carried by honey bees from tree to tree during their nectar gathering flights. Blight, leaf spots, wilt, scab, and wetwood are other diseases caused by bacteria.

VIRUSES

Viruses are small infectious particles made of a core of nucleic acid surrounded by a protein sheath. The small size (approximately one-millionth of an inch) of a virus makes it visible only with an electron microscope. Viruses are obligate parasites; they reproduce only in living cells of the host. The most common plant attacked by the virus and the general symptoms are combined to name plant virus diseases. Examples

17-15. Leaf spots caused by a mosaic virus disease.

include cucumber mosaic, aster yellows, and tomato ring spot. However, they can attack other plants besides the specific plants named.

RODENTS AND OTHER ANIMALS

Small and large animals can also damage plants. Animals can eat the stems, fruits, and leaves of ornamental plants. Birds, skunks, and raccoons disrupt the turf surface looking for grub-type insects. Mice, rabbits, and deer destroy the bark of many valuable trees and shrubs. Moles destroy the roots of turfgrass by digging tunnels in search of earthworms.

17-16. Some animal pests dig tunnels in the soil, which can damage the plant roots.

CONTROLLING PESTS

Many pest problems can be prevented. Good management practices will help to reduce other pest problems. The method selected must be right for the plant and the pest. Federal and state laws regulate the control practices that can be used.

There are four major ways of controlling plant pests: (1) cultural practices, (2) biological methods, (3) mechanical methods, and (4) chemical methods. Genetic engineering is a new technique that utilizes biotechnology to make plants resistant to specific pests. It eliminates the need for control by eliminating the pest.

CULTURAL PEST CONTROL

Cultural pest control is the use of management techniques to control pests. The techniques include proper plant management programs, sanitation, and using resistant varieties. Good management programs improve the overall growth and development of the desirable plants in the landscape. Grow better plants by correctly mowing, irrigating, fertilizing, pruning, aerifying, and mulching. Environmental plant damage may be caused by chemical burns, animals, vandalism, summer drought, winter desiccation, ice, air pollution, or salt. Plant managers can develop corrective measures to eliminate the above cultural problems.

Insect traps containing chemical sex attractants, called *pheromones,* can lure insects into a trap for proper disposal. Pheromones are substances secreted by insects or artificially developed in the laboratory. Plant breeding programs have developed many cultivars of turfgrass that have a natural immunity to common insects and diseases. Today, new cultivars of flowers, trees, and shrubs, with a natural resistance to insects and diseases and a natural tolerance to conditions that lead to noninfectious diseases are available.

17-17. Insect traps contain pheromones that attract specific insects.

BIOLOGICAL PEST CONTROL

Biological pest control uses living organisms that are predators to control plant pests. Biological control of insects includes nematodes feeding on mole crickets or bacterium that kill insects. Many beneficial insects feed on insect pests that damage ornamental plants.

The lady beetles are notorious for their roles in controlling aphids on fruit trees. Predatory mites have been used to control other mites on

17-18. Lady beetle feeding on aphids is an example of biological pest control. (Courtesy, Agricultural Research Service USDA)

flowering crab apple trees. Many gardeners like to have a few toads and turtles around to eat insects. Caution: Insecticides should not be used on plants to control insects if predator insects are present. The insecticide will kill the beneficial insects.

The bacterium *Bacillus thuringinensis* can kill a variety of caterpillar and grubs that attack turf and other ornamental plants. It will take from several weeks to years for the biological organisms to build up sufficient populations to control plant pests. However, once this population is established, the natural forces should control the pests for many years.

Several major insect pests have been controlled by altering their reproductive process. Since some insects mate only once, a female that mates with a sterile (no sperm) male lays eggs that will not hatch. The male insects are raised in laboratories and sterilized. The sterile males are then released in an area with an insect pest problem. Research is underway to develop other new ways of using plants and animals to control plant pests.

MECHANICAL PEST CONTROL

Mechanical pest control includes using tools or equipment for control. The pests are destroyed or removed from the host plants. The following are examples of mechanical methods:

- Rototilling—Rototilling destroys some pests, particularly weeds in large landscape beds. However, hand pulling of a few weeds in small beds may

17-19. Pine needle mulch used to control weeds in this flower bed.

be the best control technique. Some insects are also turned up to the soil surface by tilling where birds can feed on them.

- Mowing—Mowing cuts off weed flowers and seeds. Not only does it partially destroy the weed, but it also destroys places where other insect and disease pests can hide.

- Mulching—Covering the ground with a layer of plastic, bark mulch, or other material prevents weed growth. Mulching is used in the landscape beds that contain many ornamental plants.

- Picking— Remove insects from plants by picking them off. A few bag worms on evergreen trees can be removed by individual picking. Cut the branches of the tree to remove the tent caterpillar nests.

CHEMICAL PEST CONTROL

A *pesticide* is a chemical used to control pests. The term pesticide means a pest killer. Cide in Latin means to kill. Pesticides can be divided into the following major groups: *insecticides* kill insects, *fungicides* kill fungi, *herbicides* kill weeds, and *nematicides* kill nematodes.

Pesticides are complex compounds developed and tested in a laboratory. Pesticide use must be approved by various government agencies, such as the Environmental Protection Agency (EPA). Pesticides can be hazardous to humans; handle with care. Pesticides can be mixed with water, fertilizer, or other compounds to help apply them on the host plant. Wetting agents help disperse and spread the pesticide on waxy leaf surfaces.

Insecticides

Chemicals that control insects are known as insecticides. Some substances used are very poisonous. The active ingredient in the insecticide does the killing. By law, the labels on containers must describe the amount and kind of active ingredient.

Insecticides can be manufactured in several different formulations or forms—wettable powders, solutions, and granules. Each formulation is designed to work under certain condi-

17-20. Handle all insecticides with care.

tions. Mix wettable powders and solutions with water and apply this liquid to plants. Apply dry pesticides, called granules, to the soil surface.

INSECTICIDES CLASSIFICATION

- Stomach poisons—Stomach poisons are eaten by the insects. The insecticide must be on the plant leaf when the pest eats the leaf. Stomach poisons work best on chewing insects, such as caterpillars, armyworms, and bagworms.

- Contact poisons—These poisons are absorbed through the insect's exoskeleton. To work, the insecticide must come in contact with the insect. Apply after insects are damaging the plant. Use contact poisons for controlling sucking insects, such as aphids and scale insects.

- Systemic poisons—Systemic poisons are inside the plant tissue. Apply granules containing the systemic poison to the soil around the host plant. The roots will absorb the poison and translocate through the plant.

- Fumigants—Fumigants are insecticides in a gas form. The poison enters the insect's body through the respiratory system. Plow or rototill the soil and cover with a plastic sheet. The nematicide fumigant is injected into the soil after covering. Methyl bromide and chloropicrin (tear gas chemicals) are commonly used for fumigation. They will kill insects, nematodes, fungi, and weed seeds.

Take care in handling and applying insecticides. They are dangerous! Humans should wear protective clothing and masks. Always wash skin and clothes after using insecticides. Read all insecticide labels before using.

17-21. The soil under the plastic has been fumigated to kill insects and disease organisms prior to planting new turf.

An insect control program should include the following steps:

- identify and monitor insect population
- determine the potential for damage/economic threshold
- assess environmental hazards
- decide on an integrated control measure
- use control measures
- evaluate results

Nematicides

Chemicals used to control nematodes are known as nematicides. Since the nematodes are in the soil, treatments must penetrate into the soil. Most nematicides are granular in form. Water the soil and wash the pesticides down where the nematodes live.

Herbicides

Herbicide chemicals control weeds in the landscape. Herb is the Latin word for plant. Thus, herbicides are really plant killers. Herbicides applied

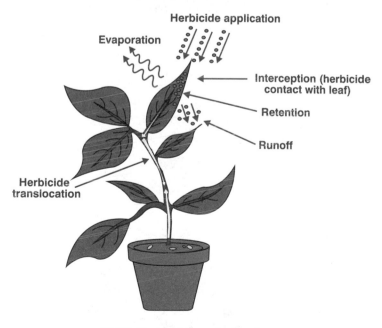

17-22. Herbicide uptake by plants.

to the soil before weed seeds germinate are called *preemergent* (pre=before). They prevent weed seeds from germinating. Apply *postemergent* (post = after) herbicides to the leaves of the weed after they have germinated. This group of herbicides will destroy actively growing weeds.

Selective herbicides are chemicals used to kill only certain plant species. They are effective in controlling broadleaf weeds in a lawn without damaging the desirable turfgrass. *Nonselective herbicides* will kill all vegetation without regard to species. *Contact herbicides* kill only the portions of the plants that they contact. *Systemic herbicides* are absorbed into a plant's vascular and root system, destroying the entire plant.

17-23. Apply granular preemergent herbicides to prevent weed seed germination.

The performance of herbicides depends upon temperature, rainfall, humidity, maturity of the weeds, soil characteristics, and the chemical concentration. Higher temperatures elevate metabolic rates in plants, thus speeding up the injurious effects of the herbicide. High humidity also increases herbicide uptake and action. Young plants are more susceptible to herbicide injury than old plants.

Chemicals to Control Plant Diseases

Many kinds of chemicals are used to control plant diseases. The kind used depends on the disease problem. Accurate diagnosis of the disease is important. Apply protective chemicals before the disease attacks the plant. Curative chemicals are applied to plants after they have the disease.

Fungicides control plant diseases caused by fungi. The best fungicides are systemic in action. Fungicides move into the vascular system of a plant and reach all parts. Fungi are killed all over the plant. Fungicides that kill by contact must be sprayed directly on the growing fungi. Bactericides control plant diseases caused by bacteria. Spray the systemic bactericides on the plant leaves to prevent and/or cure diseases. For viral diseases, remove the infected plants from the landscape to prevent the further spread of the disease.

Wet, shady landscape sites promote the growth of moss and algae. Prevent their growth by improving soil drainage and pruning trees and shrubs to increase light penetration to the affected surface. Control existing moss and algae by mixing 2 ounces of copper sulfate in 5 gallons of water. Use a sprinkling can to apply this mixture to the moss or algae infected area.

SAFETY PRACTICES IN PEST CONTROL

Many of the methods used to control pests are dangerous. They can injure people and other animals. They can pollute the environment and contaminate water and food. Government laws have been passed to regulate the use of pesticides. Also, pesticides are approved for specific pests and host plant application.

APPLYING PESTICIDES SAFELY

Understanding the proper use of pesticides is imperative to their effectiveness and to the safety of people. When applying pesticides, the user should wear the proper protective clothing and equipment the pesticide label recommends. The application equipment should be checked for leaking hoses or connections and plugged or dripping nozzles. All people, pets, or livestock should be cleared from the area before application. Pesticides should be applied only on days with no breezes to minimize drift, preferably in the morning.

Some safety guidelines when applying pesticides include:

- Use only approved pesticides—Government regulations allow the use of certain pesticides and prohibit the use of others. Follow the law!
- Read the label before application—Review specific warnings and precautions and other instructions before you begin.
- Use the pesticide with the lowest toxicity—Toxicity refers to how poisonous the pesticide is.
- Use the right equipment—The same sprayer should not be used for insecticides and herbicides since a residue can be left in the tank or other parts.

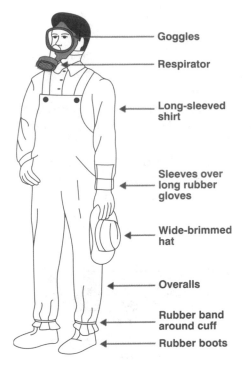

- Goggles
- Respirator
- Long-sleeved shirt
- Sleeves over long rubber gloves
- Wide-brimmed hat
- Overalls
- Rubber band around cuff
- Rubber boots

17-24. Wear protective clothing and equipment when applying pesticides.

- Mix according to the directions on the pesticide label—If mixing is required, use the recommended proportions, measure carefully, and mix thoroughly in a well-ventilated area.

- Apply evenly—The pesticide should be sprayed uniformly with a minimum of overlap.

- Avoid vapor damage—Vaporization is the evaporation of an active ingredient during or after application and can occur when it is windy or when the temperature following application will reach 85°F.

- Clean up—Thoroughly clean all equipment inside and out following the pesticide label instructions; including any excess pesticide mixed which cannot be used.

- Store properly—Pesticides should be stored in their original containers and be protected from temperature extremes.

- Know the correct emergency measures—Read the statement of practical treatment before you begin. It is a good idea to have emergency telephone numbers handy.

STORING PESTICIDES SAFELY

Proper storage of pesticides is important. Some reasons include protecting human health, preserving the environment, and maintaining chemical effectiveness. One should buy only the amount of pesticide that is needed for a particular job or for the current growing season. Smaller containers may be more expensive. However, they may be the best buy because they eliminate waste and the need for storage space.

If you need to store pesticides, always read the pesticide label for specific storage requirements. The chemical and the container must be maintained in good condition and disposed of properly.

When designing or designating a pesticide storage area, there are several considerations. The area should be easy to lock, well-ventilated, properly lighted, dry, and protected from extreme heat and freezing. The area should allow enough space so that the various types of chemicals can be separated. It should be enclosed in such a manner that leaks or spills can be easily contained and easily cleaned up. Storage areas must be designed so that there is no danger of chemicals being washed into local water supplies.

Use approved management techniques for storing pesticides safely. Some techniques include:

- Locate your storage area where clean-up materials, such as absorbents and water, are close at hand.
- Keep pesticides in their original containers with pesticide labels in place.
- Never store pesticides near food, medicine, or cleaning supplies.
- Do not store flammable materials with pesticides.
- Organize the materials so they are accessible and visible.
- Mark each container with the date of purchase.
- Routinely check containers for damage or leaks.
- Dispose of unwanted or outdated materials and containers according to the pesticide label recommendations.

INTEGRATED PEST MANAGEMENT (IPM)

Integrated pest management (IPM) uses cultural, biological, mechanical, and chemical techniques to control pests with the least disruption to the environment. Integrated pest management is an ecologically based pest control strategy that relies heavily on natural enemies and weather to control pest populations. Research has shown that no single control measure works consistently over a long period. One reason is pests can develop a resistance to the pesticide. The goal of IPM is to keep pest populations below the *aesthetic injury level*. At this point, visible plant damage justifies using pest control techniques.

17-25. Growers strive to hold plant losses and pest populations at or below the aesthetic injury level.

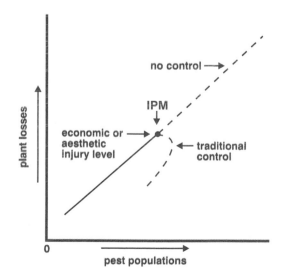

INTEGRATED PEST MANAGEMENT

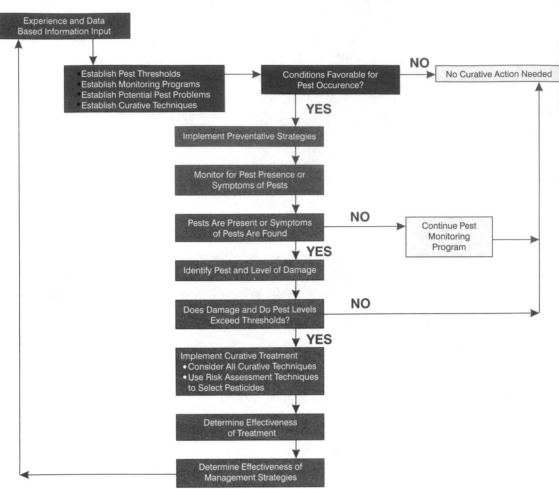

17-26. Integrated pest management (IPM) decision flowchart.

BASIC ELEMENTS OF AN IPM PROGRAM

- Knowledge and information needed to devise the system and make sound decisions

- Program for monitoring the ecosystem elements

- Pest densities at which control methods are put into action

- Techniques used to manipulate pest populations

- Agents and materials

REVIEWING

MAIN IDEAS

The presence of pests in our environment impacts the quality and growth of ornamental plants. Five major groups of pests are: (1) insects and insect-related, (2) weeds, (3) diseases, (4) nematodes, (5) rodents and other animals.

A pest is anything that causes injury or loss to a plant. A host plant provides a pest with food. Insects feeding on a host plant can reduce the quality and vigor of the host plant. Weeds compete with ornamental plants for light, water, nutrients, and space. Plant diseases interfere with the normal appearance, growth, and structure of a plant.

Many pests are not harmful to the plants, but some can destroy entire communities of plants. Pests that attack plants can be found growing actively above and below the soil. Understanding the life cycle of each pest can help improve control strategies and techniques. An integrated pest management (IPM) approach uses a combination of measures to control pests and involves biological, cultural, mechanical, and chemical control techniques.

Always follow safety procedures when using pesticides. Read the pesticide label twice before applying any pesticides. People should protect themselves and the environment from damage.

QUESTIONS

Answer the following questions using correct spelling and complete sentences.

1. Define integrated pest management (IPM).

2. What is a weed?

3. Name three beneficial insects.

4. What is the difference between preemergent and postemergent herbicides?

5. Describe incomplete metamorphosis.

6. What are important safety practices to follow when using pesticides?

7. What are the five major categories of pests?

8. What is included in cultural pest control techniques?

9. What is the meaning of the term "aesthetic injury level"?

10. Describe the difference between a selective and nonselective herbicide.

11. What is a plant disease?

12. Define the term "pesticide."

CHAPTER SELF-CHECK

Match the term with the correct definition. Place the letter in the blank provided.

a. host   d. preemergence   f. nematode
b. larvae   e. incomplete metamorphosis   g. pathogenic
c. pesticide

_____ 1. Very small worm-like organisms that invade the roots of ornamental plants

_____ 2. The stage of insect life that causes the most damage to plants

_____ 3. Chemicals that will control most pests on ornamental plants

_____ 4. Cause infectious plant diseases

_____ 5. A plant that has insect or disease damage

_____ 6. Herbicide applied before weed seeds germinate

_____ 7. The nymph stage belongs to this insect life cycle.

EXPLORING

1. Collect and identify ten weeds from your home lawn and landscape planting beds.

2. Collect and identify ten insects. Try to find at least two beneficial insects.

3. Make an inventory of all the pesticides at your home or school. List the pest controlled, active ingredient, and toxicity level for each pesticide.

4. Look at trees and shrubs at school and try to determine if any have disease problems. Are the problems caused by infectious or noninfectious diseases?

18

Calculating Landscape Maintenance Costs

One of the most common landscape maintenance activities is the mowing of a turfgrass area. If you were in the maintenance business, how would you determine what to charge for mowing the area? Would you charge the same amount for every job? Would you base your price on what your competitors charge? What would you charge for related maintenance activities?

Pricing maintenance work can be challenging. It can be particularly challenging for those people who love the horticulture work but have not been educated in the business aspects of the industry. This chapter will focus on how you might determine the cost for maintenance work performed.

18-1. Mowing turfgrass is one of the most common landscape maintenance activities.

OBJECTIVES

1. Identify the skills to be mastered by a landscape maintenance technician

2. Explain the need to calculate landscape maintenance costs

3. Describe how to estimate landscape maintenance costs

4. Define terms used in estimating landscape maintenance costs

TERMS

computer spreadsheet
contingency costs
cost summation
estimate sheet
landscape maintenance
landscape maintenance
    technician
overhead costs
profit

MAINTENANCE TECHNICIANS

Landscape maintenance is the continued efforts to preserve the existing landscape. Maintenance practices begin once the landscape has been installed. Landscape maintenance practices involve a wide range of activities. The **landscape maintenance technician**, the person trained in and given charge of maintaining a landscape, must be proficient in numerous maintenance skills.

Landscape maintenance technicians can learn numerous maintenance skills a variety of ways. Many begin their horticulture education at the high school level, and continue at a community college or a four year university. Others begin at a community college or on the job. Education is essential for the technician due to the technical nature of the skills in which he or she must be proficient. Some states have certification exams to obtain a license to perform landscape maintenance jobs.

18-2. A landscape maintenance technician must be proficient in numerous maintenance skills.

DETERMINING MAINTENANCE COSTS

Determining the cost of maintaining landscapes really begins with an understanding of the types of jobs conducted in the maintenance end of the landscape industry. Some of the most common jobs or technical skills to be mastered by landscape maintenance technicians follow.

LANDSCAPE MAINTENANCE SKILLS

Safety — Safety should be the number one priority for landscape maintenance technicians. An understanding of the proper use of tools and safety procedures can greatly reduce the risk of injury on-the-job. Training in first aid is highly recommended. First aid training should include CPR, treatment for burns, proper care of cuts, frostbite, heat cramps, heat exhaustion, heat stroke, chemical injury, and impaled objects.

Reading a plan — Plan reading is one of the most important aspects of determining maintenance costs. The technician should be able to interpret the designer's intent in order to maintain the desired landscape. Also, linear and area measurements can be obtained from the plan and used to calculate maintenance costs.

Identifying and caring for plants — Landscape maintenance technicians need expertise in plant identification and care. Being able to correctly identify landscape plants allows the technician to administer proper care. It is also beneficial for the technician to understand specific cultural requirements of plants.

Grading and establishing turfgrass — Turfgrass is the most common ground cover used in landscapes. It often needs to be repaired or replaced due to damage or disease. Landscape maintenance technicians should be able to level and grade an area and plant sod, plugs, or seed. Specific skills related to turfgrass are discussed in Chapter 16.

Identifying irrigation components — Irrigation systems have become common in landscape settings. Landscape maintenance technicians should have knowledge in the identification and function of the various irrigation system components. Such knowledge is useful in the maintenance and repair of those systems.

Programming irrigation controller — Irrigation controllers are the key to automated irrigation systems. They allow precise watering timetables and water management. Understanding how to install and program controllers is essential when working with automated irrigation systems.

Repairing lateral lines and head adjustments — Lateral lines make up an essential part of irrigation systems. Lateral lines often require repair, cleaning, and testing. A technician should be knowledgeable in these skills. An understanding of how to repair and adjust sprinkler heads that distribute the water is also valuable.

Trucks and trailers — Landscape maintenance technicians should have a thorough understanding of safety, maintenance, and operation of trucks and trailers. Mastery of skills required by state licensing agencies is critical.

Transplanting woody plants — On occasion woody landscape plants need to be transplanted to the landscape to replace existing plants or to alter the landscape appearance. Knowledge of planting procedures and care for the newly planted plants discussed in Chapter 10 is important for landscape maintenance technicians.

Pruning techniques — A critical aspect of maintaining existing landscapes is the pruning of woody plants. Reasons for pruning and pruning techniques discussed in Chapter 15 should be understood by landscape maintenance technicians.

Mowing turfgrass — An important facet of maintaining the landscape is the management of the turfgrass areas. Landscape maintenance technicians should be well versed in the safe use and maintenance of both walk behind and riding mowers. Skills pertaining to turf management and care are discussed in Chapter 16.

Aerating turfgrass — Aerators relieve soil compaction in turf areas. Landscape maintenance technicians should be able to operate and maintain these pieces of equipment.

Edging and trimming — Edging and trimming of turf areas provide a clean appearance to the landscape. Landscape maintenance technicians should be able to operate and maintain these pieces of equipment.

Using pesticides safely — It is critical that landscape maintenance technicians receive extensive training in the safe use and handling of pesticides. An important skill is the ability to mix and apply pesticides in accordance to the instructions on the label. Safe practices are explained in Chapter 17.

Fertilizing — Landscape plants may benefit from the application of fertilizers. Landscape maintenance technicians should be able to choose fertilizers for specific uses and calculate the exact amounts to be applied. Details on fertilizing landscape plants are covered in Chapters 14 and 16.

ESTIMATING COSTS

One of the first things to understand about costing landscape maintenance projects is nearly every company has a different method of reaching a final cost estimate. There is no standard used by the industry. However, from a business standpoint it is essential that landscapers determine a method to accurately price their services. Prices should provide a profit so the business stays viable. They should also be competitive to ensure a regular flow of customers. Finally, the work should be of high quality to maintain customer loyalty.

As with the pricing of landscape installation, an estimate sheet is a useful tool in calculating landscape maintenance costs. An *estimate sheet* is a form for calculating prices. It helps if the same form is used for each project. On the estimate sheet, identify the jobs to be completed, determine the size of the job, and estimate how many hours it will take workers to complete the project. Also, calculate the cost of labor and materials used to complete the job. The estimate sheet is for the landscaper only. Figures presented to the customer are placed on a proposal sheet or a contract.

Add overhead costs, contingency costs, and profit to the cost of labor and materials to obtain a grand total for the services to be provided. One procedure for establishing landscape maintenance costs is as follows:

1. List in detail the anticipated cost for both labor and materials. Use the actual wages the employees will be paid and the cost of the materials purchased.

2. The job cost is the cost of labor and materials required to complete a specific task or job. The same job could be completed a number of times during the year. An example is mowing the lawn. The job cost is multiplied by the number of times the job is performed annually to get a total annual cost.

3. *Overhead costs* are the general costs in running a business. Examples include mortgage or lease payments, legal fees, utilities, insurance, office expenses, trucks, trailers, and maintenance of equipment. To obtain the overhead costs multiply the total for labor and materials by 20 percent.

4. A *contingency cost* should be figured into all jobs. This cost accounts for theft of materials on the work site, mechanical break-

Table 18-1. An Example Landscape Maintenance Estimate Sheet

LANDSCAPE MAINTENANCE ESTIMATE SHEET

JOB NAME				DATE		
JOB LOCATION						
JOB DESCRIPTION						

Description	Number of times done annually	Hours per visit	Labor cost ($7.00/hour)	Material costs	Job cost	Total annual cost
Mowing and trimming 10,000 sq. ft.	30	2	$14.00	0	$14.00	$420.00
Edging	3	2	$14.00	0	$14.00	$42.00
Fertilize turfgrass	3	1	$7.00	$50.00	$57.00	$171.00
Broadleaf weed control	2	1	$7.00	$20.00	$27.00	$54.00
Aerate turfgrass	1	2	$14.00	0	$14.00	$14.00
Prune woody plants	3	2	$14.00	0	$14.00	$42.00
Fall clean up	1	4	$56.00	0	$56.00	$56.00
Subtotal annual costs (labor + materials)						$799.00
			Overhead costs (subtotal annual costs × 20%)			$159.80
			Contingency costs (subtotal annual costs + overhead × 10%)			$95.88
			Cost summation (subtotal annual costs + overhead + contingency)			$1,054.68
			Profit (cost summation × 20%)			$210.94
			TOTAL (cost summation + profit)			$1,265.62

downs, rain outs, etc. The contingency charge may vary from job to job. An accepted charge is to multiply the overhead plus labor and materials by 10 percent.

5. Add the labor, materials, overhead, and contingency charges to obtain a *cost summation.*

6. *Profit* is the amount of money the landscaper receives after deducting all costs of the project. The mark up for profit is included on the estimate sheet. A fair mark up for profit is 20 percent. Multiply the cost summation by 20 percent to determine the profit.

7. Total cost for the project is the addition of the summation costs and the profit.

When pricing landscape maintenance work, be aware that every job will be different from the others. Some properties are more difficult to maintain than others. For example, some properties might be hilly, while others are flat. Some lots may have numerous trees that take time to mow around. Pricing should reflect the difficulty of the job. Experience in the business will help in preparing accurate estimates for jobs with different degrees of difficulty.

Using Computer Spreadsheets

Computer spreadsheet software is a useful tool that can be used to calculate landscape maintenance costs, prepare estimates, and keep records.

18-3. An example of a computer spreadsheet used to calculate landscape maintenance costs.

A ***computer spreadsheet*** is an all-purpose computer program that is used for almost any task involving the organization of numbers based on columns and rows. Once the spreadsheet has been set up properly, it can be used over and over as a template with all of the calculations stored as formulas in place. A knowledge of how to enter formulas and formats for the particular software program being used is essential in setting it up properly. Some current computer spreadsheet programs include Excel, Lotus, and Paradox.

REVIEWING

MAIN IDEAS

Landscape maintenance involves the work of landscape maintenance technicians. To do maintenance work properly, the landscape maintenance technician must be versatile in many tasks. Skills considered necessary for these technicians include safety; reading a plan; knowledge in identification and care of landscape plants; grading and establishing turfgrass; identifying, programming, and repairing irrigation systems; and operating trucks and trailers. Other skills to master are transplanting woody plants, pruning landscape plants, mowing turfgrass, aerating turfgrass, trimming and edging, using pesticides safely, and fertilizing landscape plants.

The landscaper should determine his or her cost of services to be performed. This is done before presenting the customer with a proposal or contract. An estimate sheet is very helpful in calculating costs. On the estimate sheet the landscaper can determine his or her costs for labor and materials. Overhead costs, contingency costs, and profit can then be calculated based on the labor and materials. Computer spreadsheet software is a useful tool in calculating landscape maintenance prices.

QUESTIONS

Answer the following questions using correct spelling and complete sentences.

1. What are some skills a landscape maintenance technician should have mastered?
2. What type of education is required of a landscape maintenance technician?
3. How is an estimate sheet used in calculating costs?

4. What are the costs to be calculated in order to reach the total cost? Explain each.

5. What are some factors that might cause one landscape project to be priced differently than another?

CHAPTER SELF-CHECK

Match the term with the correct definition. Write the letter by the term in the blank provided.

a. contingency costs

b. profit

c. landscape maintenance technician

d. overhead costs

e. cost summation

f. estimate sheet

_____ 1. The amount of money the landscaper receives after deducting all costs of the project.

_____ 2. This cost accounts for theft of materials on the work site, mechanical breakdowns, rain outs, etc., and should be figured into all jobs.

_____ 3. Person given charge of maintaining a landscape who is proficient in numerous maintenance skills.

_____ 4. General costs in running a business including: mortgage or lease payments, legal fees, utilities, insurance, office expenses, trucks, trailers, and maintenance of equipment.

_____ 5. The addition of the labor, materials, overhead, and contingency costs.

_____ 6. A form used for calculating prices.

EXPLORING

1. Visit a local landscape company that performs landscape maintenance services, and perform an informal interview. Ask them how they got into the business. Ask them for recommendations on how to calculate prices.

2. Contact your local, state, and national professional landscape associations. Request information on the education needed to become a qualified landscape maintenance technician. Ask whether there is a landscape maintenance skills certification exam in your state.

Appendixes

Appendix A — Mathematical Conversion Chart

Equivalents	To Convert From:	To:	Multiply By:
1 sq. ft. = 144 sq. in.	sq. ft.	sq. in.	144
	sq. in.	sq. ft.	.006944
1 sq. yd. = 9 sq. ft.	sq. yd.	sq. ft.	9
	sq. ft.	sq. yd.	.111111
1 acre = 43,560 sq. ft.	acres	sq. ft.	43,560
	sq. ft.	acres	.0000229
1 cu. yd. = 27 cu. ft.	cu. yds.	cu. ft.	27
	cu. ft.	cu. yds.	.037037
1 cu. yd. gravel = 1½ tons	cu. yds.	tons	1.5
	tons	cu. yds.	.666666
1 ton = 2,000 lbs.	tons	lbs.	2,000
	lbs.	tons	.0005
1 lb. = 16 oz. = 1 pint	lbs. or pints	oz.	16
	oz.	lbs. or pints	.0625
1 pt. = 2 cups	pts.	cups	2
	cups	prints	.5
1 qt. = 2 pints	qts.	pints	2
	pints	qts.	.5
1 gal. = 4 qts.	gal.	qts.	4
	qts.	gal.	.25

Appendix B — Plant Materials List

ANNUAL FLOWERS

Common Name	Botanical Name	Height	Spacing	Exposure	Color	Use
Ageratum	*Ageratum houstonianum*	6–20"	9–12"	○	B,P,W	G/E/CF
Alyssum, Sweet	*Lobularia maritima*	2–4"	5–10"	○ or ●	W,P,V	E/GC
Aster	*Callistephus chinensis*	12–24"	10–12"	○	W,Y,Pr	B/CF
Baby's Breath	*Gypsophila elegans*	12–18"	12"	○	P,W	B/Br/CF
Balsam	*Impatiens balsamina*	12–28"	8–12"	●	P,R,W,M	B/Br
Begonia	*Begonia semperflorens*	6–10"	8–12"	●	P,R,W	B/C
Candytuft	*Iberis* sp.	6–12"	8–12"	○	W,Lc	E/B/G/GC
Carnation	*Dianthus* sp.	12–24"	12–18"	○	R,Y,W	B/E/CF
Celosia (Cockscomb)	*Celosia argentea*	6–36"	8–12"	○	R,Y,O	B/Br/CF
Coleus	*Coleus blumei*	12–24"	12"	●	R,Y,P	E/B/C
Cornflower	*Centaurea cyanus*	12–36"	12–18"	○ or ◗	B,P,W,R	B/G/CF
Cosmos	*Cosmos bipinnatus*	24–48"	12–18"	○	R,Y,O,P,W	CF/Br
Dahlia	*Dahlia* sp.	12–40"	12–24"	○	R,Y,P,M	B/E/CF
Dianthus				(See Pink)		

(Continued)

KEY

Use

A – Accent	G – Garden
B – Bed	GC – Ground Cover
Bg – Bedding	H – Hedge
Bk – Background	P – Potpourri
Br – Border	Ps – Poisonous
C – Container	S – Seeds
CF – Cut Flower	Sc – Screen
DS – Dried Seed	Sh – Shade
E – Edging	Sp – Specimen
F – Foundation	VS – Vine Screen

Texture

C – Coarse	MC – Medium Coarse
F – Fine	MF – Medium Fine
M – Medium	

Color

B – Blue	P – Pink
B-G – Blue Green	Pr – Purple
Bk-G – Black Green	R – Red
C – Crimson	Rs – Rose
G – Emerald Green	R-G – Red Green
Gr – Green	S – Silver
Gy – Gray	Sc – Scarlet
Gy-G – Gray Green	V – Violet
L – Lavender	W – White
Lc – Lilac	Y – Yellow
M – Multi	Y-G – Yellow Green
O – Orange	

Exposure

○ – Sun ● – Shade ◗ – Partial Shade

Appendix B (Continued)

ANNUAL FLOWERS (Continued)

Common Name	Botanical Name	Height	Spacing	Exposure	Color	Use
Dusty Miller	*Cineraria maritima*	8–24"	8–12"	○	Gy	B/Br
Forget-me-not	*Myosotis sp.*	6–12"	6–8"	○ or ●	P,B	E/B/CF
Four-o'clock	*Mirabilis jalapa*	20–36"	12–18"	○	R,Y,W	Br
Gaillardia	*Gaillardia pulchella*	12–30"	9–12"	○	R with Y	Br/CF
Geranium	*Pelargonium x hortorum*	6–30"	12–15"	○	P,R,W	Bg/C
Globe Amaranth	*Gomphrena globosa*	6–24"	6–12"	○	W,P,R,O	Br/B/CF
Hollyhock	*Alcea rosea*	18–72"	12–18"	○ or ◗	R,P,Y,W,L	Sc/Br
Impatiens	*I. walleriana*	6–15"	8–12"	●	R,P,W,M	B/C
Lantana	*Lantana sp.*	12–36"	2–15"	○	R,Y,B	B/C
Larkspur	*Delphinium sp.*	18–48"	12–18"	○	B,P,W,R	Sc/Br/CF
Lobelia	*Lobelia sp.*	3–6"	4–6"	◗	B,P,W	B/C
Lupine	*Lupinus sp.*	12–36"	8–12"	○	P,Y,W,M	B/CF
Marigold	*Tagetes sp.*	6–30"	6–12"	○	R,Y,P	B/E
Nasturtium	*Tropaeolum sp.*	12–15"	9–12"	○	M	B/E
Pansy	*Viola sp.*	6–8"	6–8"	○ or ◗	M	E/B/C/CF
Petunia	*Petunia x hybrida*	8–24"	12–15"	○	B,P,R,W	B/C
Phlox	*Phlox drummondi*	6–15"	6–15"	○	M	B/E
Pink	*Dianthus chinensis*	8–15"	6–12"	○	P,R,W,M	B/E
Poppy	*Papaver sp.*	18–36"	6-12"	○	R,Y,W	Br/B/CF
Rose Moss	*Portulaca grandiflora*	4–6"	6–12"	○	P,R,W,Y,Sc	B/E/G
Rudbeckia	*Rudbeckia sp.*	18–24"	18"	○	Y	B/Br
Salvia (Scarlet Sage)	*Salvia splendens*	10–36"	8-12"	○	R,W,Pr	B/Br
Snapdragon	*Antirrhinum majus*	10–36"	10–12"	○	M	B/Br/CF
Strawflower	*Helichrysum sp.*	12–36"	12–18"	○	R,Gr,W,Y,Pr	Br/CF
Sunflower, Common	*Helianthus sp.*	2–10'	2–4'	○	Y,O	Sc/B/S
Sweet Pea	*Lathyrus odoratus*	20–30"	8–12"	○	M	VS/B/Br
Verbena	*Verbena x hybrida*	9–18"	8–12"	○	R,W,P,B	B
Vinca (Periwinkle)	*Vinca rosea*	10–18"	8–12"	○	P,W,Cr	B
Zinnia	*Zinnia sp.*	6–48"	8–15"	○	M	B/Br/CF

(Continued)

Appendix B (Continued)

BIENNIAL FLOWERS

Common Name	Botanical Name	Zone	Height	Spacing	Exposure	Color	Use
Canterbury Bells	*Campanula medium*	4	3–4'	18–24"	○ or ◗	Y,W,B,P	CF/Br
Daisy, English	*Bellis perennis*	4	4–8"	10–12"	○	R,W,B,P	E/G
Forget-me-not, Alpine	*Myosotis sylvatica*	3	8–24"	12–18"	●	B	B/Br
Foxglove	*Digitalis purpurea*	4	2–4'	18–24"	○ or ◗	P,Y,W,Pr	B/Br/Po
Hollyhock, Old Fashion	*Alcea rosea*	3	4–8'	12–18"	○	R,Y,P,W	Br
Honesty (Money Plant)	*Lunaria annua*	4	3'	18–24"	◗	B,W	G/DS
Pansy	*Viola cornuta*	4	6–8"	10–12"	○ or ◗	M	E/B/Br
Sweet William	*Dianthus barbatus*	4	12–20"	12–18"	○	R,W,P	E/Br/CF

PERENNIAL FLOWERS

Common Name	Botanical Name	Zone	Height	Spacing	Exposure	Color	Use
Alyssum (Basket-of-Gold)	*Aurinia saxatilis*	4	12–15"	24"	○	Y	G/E/CF
Anchusa (Alkanet)	*Anchusa azurea*	3	1–4'	24"	◗	B	Br/CF
Anthemis	*Anthemis tinctoria*	4	30–36"	18–24"	○	Y,W	Br
Artemisia (Silver Mound)	*Artemisia schmidtiana*	3	8–12"	10–15"	○	Gy-Gr	B/E/Br
Aster, Hardy	*Aster sp.*	4	12–60"	36"	○	W	B/G/CF
Astilbe (False Spirea)	*Astilbe x arendsii*	4	15–40"	18–24"	●	R,W,P,Sc	Br
Baby's Breath	*Gypsophila paniculata*	4	2–3'	48"	●	W,P	Br/CF
Balloon Flower	*Platycodon grandiflorus*	3	20"	12–18"	○ or ◗	W,B,P	Br
Baptisia (False Indigo)	*Baptisia australis*	3	4–5'	3'	○ or ◗	W,Y,B	Br/GC
Bellflower	*Campanula sp.*	3	8–20"	12–24"	○ or ◗	B,W	Br/E
Bleeding Heart	*Dicentra spectabilis*	4	2–3'	1–3'	○ or ◗	W,P	G
Blue Fescue (Festuca)	*Festuca ovina*	4	8–12"	12–18"	○ or ◗	S-B	B/E/GC
Carnation	*Dianthus caryophyllus*	3	18–24"	12–15"	○	P,R,W,Y	B/Br/CF
Chinese Lantern	*Physalis alkekengi*	4	24"	36"	○	O	Br/Sp
Chrysanthemum	*Chrysanthemum sp.*	5	8–36"	12–30"	○	M	B/Br/E/CF
Columbine	*Aquilegia sp.*	3	30–36"	12–18"	○ or ◗	M	B/CF
Daisy, Painted	*Chrysanthemum coccineum*	4	12–24"	12–18"	○	M	Br/CF
Daisy, Shasta	*Chrysanthemum maximum*	4	15–36"	18–30"	○	W	B/CF

(Continued)

Appendix B (Continued)

PERENNIAL FLOWERS (Continued)

Common Name	Botanical Name	Zone	Height	Spacing	Exposure	Color	Use
Daylily	*Hemerocallis* sp.	4	12–48"	24–36"	○ or ◗	P,R	B/G
Delphinium	*Delphinium* sp.	4	48–60"	24"	○	B,W,Pr	B/CF
Dianthus (Pink)	*Dianthus* sp.	3	3–24"	12"	○	P	Br/E/CF
Gaillardia (Blanket Flower)	*G. x grandiflora*	3	12–30"	24"	○	Y,Sc	Br/CF
Globeflower	*Trollius europaeus*	3	30"	8–10"	●	Y,O	B/CF
Globe Thistle	*Echinops exaltatus*	4	4'	24–36"	○	B	Br/CF
Hibiscus	*Hibiscus* sp.	5	3–8'	24"	○	R,W,P,Rs	Br/B/G
Iberis (Candytuft)	*Iberis sempervirens*	4	8–12"	12–18"	○	W	G/E/GC
Lavender	*Lavandula angustifolia*	5	12–36"	12–18"	○	Pr	Br/G/P
Liatris (Gayfeather)	*Liatris* sp.	3	18–72"	18"	○ or ◗	Rs, Pr	Br/CF
Lobelia (Cardinal Flower)	*Lobelia cardinalis*	6	24–30"	24"	◗	Sc	Br/B
Lupine	*Lupinus* sp.	4	3–5'	3'	○	R,P,W,O,Y	Br/CF
Lychnis (Maltese Cross)	*Lychnis* sp.	3	1–3'	18"	○ or ◗	R	Br
Peony	*Paeonia* sp.	3	18–36"	24–36"	○ or ◗	P,R,W	B/Br/CF
Phlox, Moss	*Phlox subulata*	3	4–5"	8"	○	R,P,W,B	Br
Phlox, Summer	*Phlox paniculata*	4	36"	18–24"	○	R,P,W,B	Br/CF
Poppy, Iceland	*Papaver nudicaule*	2	12–18"	24"	○	R,P,W	Br/CF
Poppy, Oriental	*Papaver orientale*	3	24–36"	24"	○	R,P,W,O	G/Br/CF
Potentilla (Cinquefoil)	*Potentilla* sp.	4	24–36"	24–36"	○	W,Y,O,P	B/Br
Primrose	*Primula* sp.	3	6–12"	10–12"	◗ or ●	R,P,W,Y,B	G/Br
Primrose, Evening	*Oenothera* sp.	3	12–18"	8"	○ or ◗	Y	G/Br
Red-hot Poker Plant (Torch Lily)	*Kniphofia* sp.	5	3–5'	18"	○	R,W,Y	Br/Sp
Rudbeckia (Coneflower)	*Rudbeckia* sp.	4	2–4'	24–30"	○	R,P,W	B/Br/CF
Salvia (Sage)	*Salvia* sp.	4	3–4'	18–24"	○	R	Br
Snow-in-Summer	*Cerastium tomentosum*	2	6–9"	24–36"	○	W	G/GC
Speedwell	*Veronica* sp.	3	6–36"	18"	○	Pr	Br/G/CF
Thrift	*Armeria maritima*	3	18–24"	12"	○	P	E/Br/CF
Virginia Bluebells	*Mertensia virginica*	4	12–24"	12–18"	◗ or ●	B	Br
Yarrow	*Achillea* sp.	3	6–36"	36"	○	R,Y,W,P	Br/CF

(Continued)

Appendix B (Continued)

GROUND COVERS—Herbaceous Perennials

Common Name	Botanical Name	Zone	Height	Width	Exposure	Texture	Color
Ajuga (Bugle Flower)	*Ajuga reptans*	4–8	4–6"	6–12"	◗	C	R-G
Crown Vetch	*Coronilla varia*	3	1–2'	18–24"	○	M	B-G
Lily-of-the-Valley	*Convallaria majalis*	2	6–12"	6–8"	●	MC	B-G
Phlox, Creeping	*Phlox subulata*	2	2–6"	8–12"	○	F	G
Plantain Lily, Fragrant	*Hosta plantaginea*	3	18–24"	2–3'	◗ or ●	C	B-G
Sedum, Red Creeping	*Sedum spurium*	3	6–8"	12–18"	○	F	G
Spurge, Japanese	*Pachysandra terminalis*	4	6–8"	10–16"	○ or ●	M	Y-G
Thyme, Creeping	*Thymus serpyllum*	1–3	1–4"	12–18"	○	F	G

GROUND COVERS—Evergreens

Common Name	Botanical Name	Zone	Height	Width	Exposure	Texture	Color
Barren-strawberry	*Waldsteinia ternata*	4	6–12"	12"	○ or ●	MC	G
Bearberry	*Arctostaphylos uva-ursi*	2–6	8–12"	spreads	○ or ◗	F	G
Bearberry, Cotoneaster	*Cotoneaster dammeri*	5–8	12–18"	3–6'	○ or ◗	F	G
Candytuft	*Iberis sempervirens*	4–8	6–12"	18–24"	○ or ◗	F	G
Ivy, Baltic	*Hedera helix 'Baltica'*	4–9	6–8"	8–12"	◗ or ●	M	Bk-G
Euonymus, Purple Wintercreeper	*Euonymus fortunei 'Coloratus'*	5	6"	12–24"	○ or ●	M	G
Juniper	*(See Narrowleaf Evergreens)*						
Lilyturf, Creeping	*Liriope spicata*	5	8–12"	12–18"	○ or ●	F	G
Mahonia, Creeping	*Mahonia repens*	5	10"	18–24"	○ or ◗	M–C	G
Pachistima, Canby	*Pachistima canbyi*	5	12"	12–24"	◗ or ●	MF	G
Periwinkle, Common (Myrtle)	*Vinca minor*	3	3–6"	9–18"	◗ or ●	MF	G
Spring Heath	*Erica carnea*	5	6–12"	24–36"	●	F	G
St. Johnswort, Aaronsbeard	*Hypericum calycinum*	5–8	12–18"	spreads	○ or ◗	MF	G

(Continued)

Appendix B (Continued)

VINES

Common Name	Botanical Name	Zone	Height	Width	Exposure	Texture	Color
Akebia, Fiveleaf	*Akebia quinata*	4–8	20–40'	spreads	○ or ●	MF	B-G
Bittersweet, American	*Celastrus scandens*	3–8	20'	spreads	○	M	G
Clematis, Hybrid	*Clematis x hybrida*	3–8	6–18'	4–10'	◑	M	B-G
Fig, Climbing	*Ficus pumila*	8–6	climbs	spreads	◑ or ●	MF	G
Honeysuckle, Trumpet	*Lonicera sempervirens*	4–8	10–20'	spreads	○ or ◑	M	B-G
Ivy, Boston	*Parthenocissus tricuspidata*	4–8	25–35'	spreads	○ or ●	MC	G
Ivy, English	*Hedera helix*	4–9	climbs	spreads	◑ or ●	M	Bk-G
Moneywort	*Lysimachia nummularia*	4	climbs	spreads	○ or ●	M	G
Morning-glory	*Ipomoea purpurea*	4	5–10'	spreads	○	M	G
Silvervine	*Polygonum aubertii*	4	25–30'	30–35'	○ or ●	M	G
Trumpet Vine	*Campsis radicans*	4–9	25–35'	6–8'	○ or ◑	M	G
Virginia Creeper	*Parthenocissus quinquefolia*	3–9	25–50'	spreads	○ or ●	M	G
Wisteria, Japanese	*Wisteria floribunda*	5	25–30'	spreads	○ or ◑	M	G

BULBS/TUBERS

Common Name	Botanical Name	Hardiness/ Zone	Flower Time	Plant Time	Planting Depth	Spacing	Height
Allium	*Allium* sp.	hardy/4	late spring	fall	4–8"	3–6"	4'
Amaryllis	*Amaryllis* sp.	tender/5	summer	spring	top to ground level	12"	2–3'
Anemone	*Anemone blanda*	†/5	very early spring	spring	4"	12"	8"
Begonia, Tuberous	*Begonia x tuberhybrida*	tender	summer	late spring	top to ground level	6–8"	7–14"
Caladium	*Caladium* sp.	tender	summer	late spring	1–4"	10–18"	15–20"
Calla Lily	*Zantedeschia* sp.	tender/9	summer	late spring	3"	12–15"	7–14"
Canna	*Canna* sp.	tender/7	summer	spring	3–4"	1–2'	24–36"
Crocus, Spring	*Crocus* sp.	hardy/4	very early spring	fall	4"	2"	2–6"
Daffodil	*Narcissus* sp.	hardy/4	mid-spring	fall	8"	6–8"	7–12"

(Continued)

†Tender in northern zones and hardy in southern zones.

Appendix B (Continued)

BULBS/TUBERS (Continued)

Common Name	Botanical Name	Hardiness/ Zone	Flower Time	Plant Time	Planting Depth	Spacing	Height
Daffodil, Fall	*Stembergia* sp.	†/7	late summer	mid-summer	5"	3"	1'
Dahlia	*Dahlia* sp.	tender/8	summer	spring	4"	24–48"	40–48"
Eranthis	*Eranthis* sp.	hardy/4	spring	late summer	4½"	3–4"	3"
Gladiolus	*Gladiolus* sp.	tender/8	summer	spring	6"	4–6"	28–48"
Hyacinth	*Hyacinthus* sp.	hardy/4	mid-spring	fall	8"	6–8"	7–12"
Hyacinth, Grape	*Muscari* sp.	hardy/4	mid-spring	fall	4"	2–4"	1–4"
Hyacinth, Summer	*Caltonia* sp.	tender	summer	spring	4–6"	6–8"	1–6"
Iris, Bulb	*Iris reticulata*	hardy/4	summer	spring/fall	4"	12"	4–6"
Lily	*Lilium* sp.	hardy/3	summer	spring/fall	2–8"	12–18"	2–4'
Oxalis (Wood Sorrel)	*Oxalis* sp.	†/6	summer	fall	3"	6"	—
Ranunculus	*Ranunculus* sp.	†/3	summer	late spring	2"	12"	7–18"
Tulip	*Tulipa* sp.	hardy/4	mid–late spring	fall	8"	6–8"	7–20"

NARROWLEAF EVERGREEN SHRUBS

Common Name	Botanical Name	Zone	Height	Width	Exposure	Use	Texture	Color
False Cypress	*Chamaecyparis* sp.							
Dwarf Hinoki	*C. obtusa* 'Nana'	4–8	3'	3–4'	○ or ◖	Sp/G/F	M	Bk-G
Threadleaf	*C. pisifera* 'Filifera Nana'	4	6–8'	6–8'	○	Sp/G	M	Bk-G
Juniper	*Juniperus* sp.							
Andorra	*J. horizontalis* 'Plumosa'	3	2'	8–10'	○	GC	F	B-G
Blue Pacific	*J. conferta* 'Blue Pacific'	5–9	1'	6–9'	○	GC	M	B-G
Blue Rug	*J. horizontalis* 'Wiltonii'	3	3–6"	6–8'	○	GC	MF	B-G
Blue Star	*J. squamata* 'Blue Star'	4–7	2–3'	4–5'	○	Sp/GC/B	M	Gy-G,B-G
Creeping	*J. horizontalis*	3	6–18"	4–8'	○	B/GC	F	B-G
Compact Pfitzer	*J. chinensis* 'Pfitzeriana Compacta'	4	5–6'	5–6'	○	F/G	MF	G-G
Dwarf Common	*J. communis* 'Depressa'	3	2–4'	6–8'	○ or ◖	G/F	F	B-G
Japanese Garden	*J. procumbens*	5	18–24"	6–8'	○	G/F	F	B-G
Sargent	*J. chinensis* 'Sargentii'	4	12–18'	8'	○ or ◖	GC	F	B-G

(Continued)

Appendix B (Continued)

NARROWLEAF EVERGREEN SHRUBS (Continued)

Common Name	Botanical Name	Zone	Height	Width	Exposure	Use	Texture	Color
Pine	*Pinus* sp.							
Dwarf White	*P. strobus 'Nana'*	3	4–6'	4–5'	○ or ◗	G/Sp	MF	B-G
Mugo	*P. mugo var. mugo*	2–7	4–8'	12–20	○ or ◗	G/F	M	G,Bk-G
Spruce	*Picea* sp.							
Bird's Nest	*P. abies 'Nidiformis'*	2	1–2'	3–5'	○	Sp	M	G
Compact Colorado	*P. pungens 'Compacta'*	2	8–10'	10–12'	○	F/Sp	M–C	Gy-G,B-G
Dwarf Alberta	*P. glauca 'Conica'*	2	3'	2'	○ or ◗	G/F	M	G
Dwarf Globe Blue	*P. pungens 'Glauca Globosa'*	2	2–3'	3–4'	○	Sp	M–C	Gy-G,B-G
Dwarf Norway	*P. abies 'Pumila'*	3	3–4'	4'	○ or ◗	Sp	M	G
Yew	*Taxus* sp.							
Dense	*T. x media densiformis*	4	4–6'	4–6'	○ or ●	F/G	M	Bk-G
Hicks	*T. x media 'Hicksii'*	5	4–6'	4–6'	○	F/G/H	M	Bk-G
Japanese	*T. cuspidata var. nana*	4	5–6'	5–6'	○ or ●	F/H/Sp	M	Bk-G
Spreading English	*T. baccata 'Repandens'*	6	2–3'	3–4'	○ or ◗	F/GC	M	Bk-G
Tauton Anglojap	*T. x media 'Tauton'*	4	6–10'	8–10'	○ or ●	F/G	M	Bk-G

BROADLEAF EVERGREEN SHRUBS

Common Name	Botanical Name	Zone	Height	Width	Exposure	Use	Texture	Color
Aucuba, Japanese	*Aucuba japonica*	7–10	6–10'	7–9'	●	F/H	M	Bk-G
Barberry, Wintergreen	*Berberis julianae*	5–6	6–10'	4–6'	○	Sp/H	MF	G
Boxwood	*Buxus* sp.							
Common	*B. sempervirens*	6	15–20'	12–18'	○ or ◗	F/H	MF	Bk-G
Littleleaf	*B microphylla*	5	3–4'	3–4'	○ or ◗	F/H/Br	MF	G
Camellia	*Camellia* sp.							
Japanese	*C. japonica*	7–9	10–15'	6–10'	◗	Sp	M–MC	G
Sasanqua	*C. susanqua*	7	6–10'	5–8'	○ or ●	F/Br/Sp	M–MC	G
Daphne, Rose	*Daphne cneorum*	4–7	6–12"	2'	◗ or ●	G	MF	Gy-G
Euonymus, Bigleaf	*Euonymus* sp.							
Japanese	*E. japonica*	7–9	10–15'	4–6'	○ or ●	F/Br/Sp	M	Bk-G
Wintercreeper	*E. fortunei var. 'Vegetus'*	5–8	4–5'	4–5'	○ or ●	C/F/H	MF	G
Fatsia, Japanese	*Fatsia japonica*	7	6–10'	6–10'	●	G	C	G

(Continued)

Appendix B (Continued)

BROADLEAF EVERGREEN SHRUBS (Continued)

Common Name	Botanical Name	Zone	Height	Width	Exposure	Use	Texture	Color
Firethorn	*Pyracantha sp.*							
Formosa	*P. koidzumi*	8–10	8–12'	8–12'	○ or ◗	Br/Sp	M	G
Scarlet	*P. coccinea*	6–9	6–16'	6–16'	○ or ◗	Br/Sp	M	G
Gardenia, Cape Jasmine	*Gardenia jasminoides*	8–10	4–6'	4–6'	○ or ●	Br/Sp	M	G
Holly	*Ilex sp.*							
Chinese	*I. cornuta*	7–9	8–10'	8–12'	○ or ●	F/H/Sp	M–MC	G
Dwarf Burford	*I. cornuta 'Dwarf Burford'*	7–9	5–6'	5–6'	○ or ●	F/Sp	M–MC	G
Winterberry	*I. verticillata*	3–9	6–10'	6–10'	○ or ◗	Br	M	G
Laurel, Mountain	*Kalmia latifolia*	4–9	7–15'	7–15'	◗ or ●	F/G	M	G
Leucothoe, Drooping	*Leucothoe fontanesiana*	5–8	3–6'	3–6'	◗ or ●	F/Br	M	G
Nandina	*Nandina sp.*							
Dwarf Heavenly Bamboo	*N. domestica 'Nana'*	6–9	2–4'	2–4'	○ or ●	Br	M	B-G
Heavenly Bamboo	*N. domestica*	6–9	6–8'	4–5'	○ or ◗	F/Br	M	B-G
Oleander	*Nerium oleander*	8	8–10'	6–8'	○ or ◗	Br/Sc/Sp/Po	M	G
Oregongrapeholly	*Mahonia aquifolium*	4–8	3–6'	3–6'	◗ or ●	F/Br/Sp	M	G
Pieris, Japanese	*Pieris japonica*	5–8	9–10'	6–8'	◗ or ●	F/Sp	M	R-G,Bk-G
Privet	*Ligustrum sp.*							
Howard	*L. japonicum 'Howard'*	7–10	6–12'	6–8'	○ or ●	F/Br	M	Y-G
Japanese	*L. japonicum*	7–10	6–12'	6–8'	○ or ●	F/Sc/Sp	M	G
Rhododendron	*Rhododendron sp.*							
Carolina	*R. carolinianum*	5–8	3–6'	3–6'	○ or ◗	F/B/Br/Sp	M	G
Catawba	*R. catawbiense*	4–8	6–10'	5–8'	◗ or ●	F/B/Br/Sp	MC–C	G
Korean	*R. mucronulatum*	4–7	4–8'	4–8'	●	F/B/Br/Sp	MF	G
P.J.M.	*R. P.J.M.*	4	3–6'	3–6'	○ or ◗	A/Sp/G/B	M	G
Wilson	*R. x laetivirens*	4	2–4'	4–6'	○ or ◗	F/B/Br/Sp	MF	G
Skimmia Japanese	*Skimmia japonica*	7–8	3–4'	3–4'	○ or ◗	F/H/G	M	G
Viburnum	*Viburnum sp.*							
Japanese	*V. japonicum*	8–9	10–15'	10–15'	○	F/Sp/Sc	M	G
Laurustinus	*V. tinus*	9–10	6–12'	6–12'	○ or ◗	F/Br/Sc	M	G
Leatherleaf	*V. rhytidophyllum*	5–8	10–15'	10–15'	● or ◗	F/Br	C	G
Wayfaringt ree	*V. lantana*	4–8	10–15'	10–15'	○ or ◗	H/Sc/Br	M	G

(Continued)

Appendix B (Continued)

BROADLEAF EVERGREEN SHRUBS (Continued)

Common Name	Botanical Name	Zone	Height	Width	Exposure	Use	Texture	Color
Yucca	*Yucca* sp.							
Adam's Needle	*Y. filamentosa*	4	3'	3–4'	○	A	C	G
Spanish Dagger	*Y. gloriosa*	6	6–8'	3–4'	○	A	C	G
Spanish Bayonet	*Y. aloifolia*	7	8–12'	5–6'	○ or ◗	A	C	G

DECIDUOUS SHRUBS

Common Name	Botanical Name	Zone	Height	Spread	Exposure	Use	Texture	Color
Abelia, Glossy	*Abelia x grandiflora*	6	3–6'	3–6'	○ or ◗	A/Br/F	MF	Bk-G
Azalea	*Rhododendron* sp.							
Exbury Hybrids	*R. x exbury*	5–7	8–12'	5–8'	◗	Sp/G/Br	M	G
Flame (Yellow)	*R. calendulaceum*	5	4–8'	4–8'	○ or ◗	Br/Sp	M	G
Glenn Dale	*R. x 'Glenn Dale'*	6	4–5'	4–5'	◗	F/B/E	M	G
Karens	*R. kaempferi var. karens*	6	3–4'	3–5'	◗	F/B/E	M	G
Kurume Hybrids	*R. x obtusum*	6	4–6'	3–6'	◗	F/B/Br/G	M	G
Mollis Hybrids	*R. x kosterianum*	5–6	3–6'	3–5'	○ or ●	F/B/Br/G	M	G
Royal	*R. schlippenbachi*	4–7	6–8'	6–8'	○ or ◗	B/F/A	M	G
Barberry	*Berberis* sp.							
Crimson Pygmy	*B. thunbergii 'Crimson Pygmy'*	4	2'	2'	○	A/Br	MF	R-G
Japanese	*B. thunbergii*	4	5–7'	4–7'	○ or ◗	H/Br/Sp	MF	G
Mentor	*B. x mentorensis*	5	5–6'	4–5'	○ or ◗	H/A/Sp/G	M	G
Blueberry, Highbush	*Vaccinium corymbosum*	4	6–12'	8–12'	○ or ◗	Sp/H	M	B-G
Buckeye, Bottlebrush	*Aesculus pariflora*	5	8–12'	8–15'	○ or ◗	Sp/Br	C	G
Chokeberry	*Aronia* sp.							
Black	*A. melanocarpa*	5	3–5'	3 ⊦'	○ or ◗	Br	M	G
Red	*A. x arbutifolia*	5	6–10'	3–5'	○ or ◗	Br	M	G
Cotoneaster	*Cotoneaster* sp.							
Cranberry	*C. apiculatus*	5	2–3'	5–8'	○ or ◗	GC/T	F	G
Creeping	*C. adpressus*	5	1'	4–6'	○ or ◗	G	F	G
Many-Flowered	*C. divaricatus*	4 0	5–6'	6–8'	○ or ◗	H/Br/Sp	F	G
Rockspray	*C. horizontalis*	4	2–3'	5–8'	○ or ◗	GC/B/G	F	G
Spreading	*C. multiflorus*	3–7	8–12'	12–15'	○ or ◗	Sp	MF	Gy-G
Daphne, Fragrant	*Daphne odora*	7–9	3'	3'	○ or ◗	Sp	MF	G
Deutzia	*Deutzia* sp.							
Showy	*D. x magnifica*	5	6–10'	6–10'	○ or ◗	Sp/Bk	MF	G
Slender	*D. gracilis*	4–8	2–4'	3–4'	○ or ◗	B/G/Sp	MF	G

(Continued)

Appendix B (Continued)

DECIDUOUS SHRUBS (Continued)

Common Name	Botanical Name	Zone	Height	Spread	Exposure	Use	Texture	Color
Dogwood	*Cornus* sp.							
Redosier	*C. sericea*	2–8	7–10'	10'	◯ or ◗	H/Sc/Br	M	G
Tatarian	*C. alba*	2–7	8–10'	5–10'	◯ or ◗	H/Sc/Br	M	G
Elaeagnus	*Elaeagnus* sp.							
Autumn Olive	*E. umbellata*	2–7	18'	18'	◯	H/Sc	MF	Gy-G
Silver	*E. multiflora*	5–7	6–10'	6–10'	◯	H/Sc/Sp	MF	Gy-G
Euonymus	*Euonymus* sp.							
Dwarf Winged	*E. alatus* 'Compactus'	3	6–8'	5–6'	◯ or ●	H/B/Br	M	G
Winged	*E. alatus*	4–8	15–20'	15–20'	◯ or ◗	H/Sc/Sp	M	G
(Burning Bush)								
Forsythia	*Forsythia* sp.							
Border	*F. x intermedia*	5	8–10'	8–10'	◯ or ◗	H/Br/Sp	M	Y-G
Bronx	*F. viridissima* 'Bronx'	5	2'	2–4'	◯ or ◗	B/A	M	G
Fothergilla	*Fothergilla* sp.							
Dwarf	*F. gardenii*	4–8	2–3'	3–4'	◯ or ◗	Sp/F/G/Br	MC	G
Large	*F. major*	4–8	6–9'	6–8'	◗	G/Br	M	G
Hibiscus	*Hibiscus syriacus*	6	8–12'	6–10'	◯ or ◗	H/Br/Sp	M	G
(Rose-of-Sharon)								
Honeysuckle	*Lonicera* sp.							
Amur	*L. maacki*	2–8	12–15'	12–15'	◯ or ◗	H/Sc/Sp	MC	Y-G
Clavey's Dwarf	*L. x xylosteoides* 'Clavey's Dwarf'	4–6	6'	4–6'	◯ or ◗	H	M	Gy-G
Morrow	*L. morrowi*	4–6	6–10'	8–10'	◯ or ◗	H/Sc/Sp	M	B-G
Tatarian	*L. tatarica*	3–8	9–12'	10–12"	◯ or ◗	Sp/H	M	B-G
Winter Fragrant	*L. fragrantissima*	4–8	6–10'	6–10'	◯ or ◗	H/Sc/Sp	M	B-G
Hydrangea	*Hydrangea* sp.							
Hills-of-Snow	*H. arborescens* 'Grandiflora'	4	4–8'	5–8'	◯ or ◗	F/H/Br	C	G
Oak-Leaf	*H. quercifolia*	5	4–6'	3–5'	◗ or ●	Sp/Br	C	Gy-G
Peegee	*H. paniculata* 'Grandiflora'	3–8	10–15'	6–10'	◯ or ◗	Sp	C	G
Lilac	*Syringa* sp.							
Common	*S. vulgaris*	3	8–20'	4–10'	◯	Sp/H/Sc	M	G
Late	*S. villosa*	2–7	6–10'	4–10'	◯	Sp	M	G
Mockorange	*Philadelphus* sp.							
Minnesota Snowflake	*P. virginalis* 'Minnesota Snowflake'	4	8'	4–6'	◯ or ◗	A/Br	M	G
Natchez	*P. x* 'Natchez'	5	8–10'	8–10'	◯ or ◗	G/Br	M–MC	G

(Continued)

Appendix B (Continued)

DECIDUOUS SHRUBS (Continued)

Common Name	Botanical Name	Zone	Height	Spread	Exposure	Use	Texture	Color
Prunus	*Prunus* sp.							
Dwarf Flowering Almond	*P. glandulosa*	4–8	4–5'	3–4'	○	Sp/A/Br	M	Y-G
Nanking Cherry	*P. tomentosa*	3	8–10'	10–15'	○	Br/Sp	M	G
Quince	*Chaenomeles* sp.							
Flowering	*C. speciosa*	5	6–10'	8–10'	○	Sp/Br	M	R-G
Japanese	*C. japonica*	4	3–4'	4'	○	Br/F	MF	G
Spirea	*Spiraea* sp.							
Anthony Waterer	*S. bumalda* 'Anthony Waterer'	5	3–4'	3–4'	○ or ◗	Sp	MF	R-G
Bridal-Wreath	*S. prunifolia*	5	5–8'	6–8'	○ or ◗	H/Sp/Br	MF	B-G
Snowmound	*S. nipponica* 'Snowmound'	4	3–6'	3–4'	○ or ◗	Sp/Br	MF	B-G
Vanhoutte	*S. x vanhouttei*	4	6–8'	8–10'	○ or ◗	Br/Sp	M	B-G
St. Johnswort, Shrubby	*Hypericum prolifium*	3–8	1–4'	1–4'	○ or ◗	Br/G	MF	B-G
Sumac, Fragrant	*Rhus aromatica*	3	2–6'	5–8'	○	F/GC	M	R-G
Sweetshrub, Common	*Calycanthus floridus*	4–9	6–9'	6–12'	○ or ●	Br/G	M	G
Viburnum	*Viburnum* sp.							
American Cranberrybush	*V. trilobum*	2	8–12'	8–12'	◑ or ◗	Br/Sc	M	G
Arrowwood	*V. dentatum*	2–8	15'	15'	○ or ◗	Sp/Br	M	G
Compact American Cranberrybush	*V. trilobum* 'Compactum'	2	5–6'	5'	◑ or ◗	H/Sc/G/Br	M	G
Doublefile	*V. plicatum* var. *tomentosum*	5–8	8–10'	9–12'	○ or ◗	A/Sp	M	G
Dwarf European Cranberrybush	*V. opulus* 'Nanum'	3	2'	2'	○ or ◗	A/Sp/G	M	G
European Cranberrybush	*V. opulus*	3–8	8–12'	10–15'	○ or ◗	Br/Sc/G	M	G
Fragrant Snowball	*V. x carlcephalum*	5	6–9'	6–8'	◑ or ◗	Sp/Br	M	G
Koreanspice	*V. carlesii*	5	4–8'	5–8'	○ or ◗	B/Br	M	G
Linden	*V. dilatatum*	5–7	7–10'	5–7'	○ or ●	Sp/Br/Sc	M	G
Weigela	*Weigela florida*	5	6–10'	9–12'	○ or ◗	Sp/Br	C	G
Witchhazel, Vernal	*Hamamelis vernalis*	5	6–10'	6–10'	○ or ◗	Sp/Br	M	G

(Continued)

Appendix B (Continued)

FLOWERING TREES

Common Name	Botanical Name	Zone	Height	Spread	Exposure	Use	Texture	Color
Apricot, Japanese	*Prunus mume*	6–9	15–20'	15–20'	○ or ◗	Sp/Sh/Br	M	G
Cherry	*Prunus sp.*							
Dwarf Japanese	*P. serrulata 'Shogetsu'*	5–6	10–18'	10–18'	○	A/Br	M	G
Weeping	*P. subhirtella pendula*	5–6	20–30'	15–25'	○	Sp	F	G
Crabapple	*Malus sp.*							
Carmine	*M. x atrosanquinea*	4	15–20'	15–20'	○	Sp/Br	M	G
Japanese	*M. floribunda*	4	15–25'	30'	○	Sp	F	G
Crapemyrtle	*Lagerstroemia indica*	7–9	15–25'	15–25'	○	Sp	M–MF	G
Dogwood	*Cornus sp.*							
Cherokee Chief	*C. florida 'Cherokee Chief'*	5	20–30'	20–30'	○ or ●	Sp	M	G
Pagoda	*C. alternifolia*	3–7	15–25'	20–35'	◗	Br	M	G
Pink	*C. florida var. rubra*	5	20–30'	20–30'	○ or ●	Sp	M	G
White	*C. florida*	5	20–30'	20–30'	○ or ●	Sp	M	G
Goldenchain Tree	*Laburnum x watereri*	5–7	10–15'	9–12'	○ or ◗	A	MF	G
Hawthorn	*Crataegus sp.*							
Green	*C. viridis*	4	20–30'	20–30'	○ or ◗	Sp/Sc	M–F	G
Washington	*C. phaenopyrum*	4	30'	20–25'	○	Br	M–F	G
Magnolia	*Magnolia sp.*							
Big Leaf	*M. macrophylla*	5–8	30–40'	30–40'	○ or ◗	Sp	C	G
Lily	*M. liliiflora*	5–8	10–12'	8–12'	○ or ◗	F/Br/A	M–C	G
Saucer	*M. x soulangiana*	4–9	20–30'	20–30'	○ or ◗	Sp	MC	G
Star	*M. stellata*	4–8	15–20'	10–15'	○	Sp	M	G
Mimosa (Silk Tree)	*Albizia julibrissin*	5–7	25–35'	18–25'	○	Sp	F	Y–G
Pear, Bradford Callery	*Pyrus calleryana 'Bradford'*	5	30–40'	20–35'	○	Sp/Br	MF	G
Plum, Purple Leaf	*Prunus cerasifera 'Newport'*	5	15–30'	15–30'	○	A/Sp/Br	M	G
Redbud, Eastern	*Cercis canadensis*	5	20–25'	15–30'	○ or ●	Sp	MC	B–G
Serviceberry, Downy	*Amelanchier arborea*	4–9	15–25	15–20'	○ or ●	G/Br	MF	G

(Continued)

Appendix B (Continued)

DECIDUOUS TREES

Common Name	Botanical Name	Zone	Height	Spread	Exposure	Use	Texture	Color
Beech, European	*Fagus sylvatica*	5	60–80'	50–70'	○ or ●	Sp/Sh	M	G
Baldcypress	*Taxodium distichum*	5	50–70'	20–30'	○ or ◗	Sp/Br	F	G
Birch	*Betula* sp.							
Paper	*B. papyrifera*	3	50–60'	30'	○	Sp/A	MF	G
River	*B. nigra*	4	40–70'	30–60'	○ or ◗	Sp	MF	G
White	*B. pendula*	3	40–50'	20 30'	○ or ◗	Sp	MF	G
Black Gum	*Nyssa sylvatica*	5–6	30–50'	20–30'	○ or ●	Sp	MF	G
Buckeye, Ohio	*Aesculus glabra*	4	20–40'	30–40'	○ or ◗	Sp/Sh	MC	G
Corktree, Amur	*Phellodendron amurense*	4	30–45'	30–40'	○	Sp/Sh	M	G
Elm, Chinese	*Ulmus parvifolia*	5	40–50'	30'	○	Sp/Sh	F	G
Ginkgo	*Ginkgo biloba*	5	40–60'	40'	○	Sp/Br	M	G
Goldenraintree, Panicled	*Koelreutaria paniculata*	5	30'	20'	○	Sp	M	G
Hackberry, Common	*Celtis occidentalus*	3	50–70'	50'	○	Sh	M	G
Honeylocust, Common Thornless	*Gleditsia triacanthos* var. *inermis*	5	75'	40–50'	○	Sp	F	G
Japanese Pagoda Tree	*Sophora japonica*	5	45–70'	30'	○	Sp	MF	B-G
Linden	*Tilia* sp.							
American	*T. americana*	3	60–80'	30–50'	○	Sp/Sh	C	G
Littleleaf	*T. cordata*	3	50–70'	40'	○	Sp/Sh	M	G
Londonplane Tree	*Plantanus x acerifolia*	4–8	70–100'	65–80'	○	Sh	MC	G
Maple	*Acer* sp.							
Japanese	*A. palmatum*	5–6	15–20'	15–20'	○ or ◗	Sp	F–MF	G
Norway	*A. platanoides*	3–4	40–50'	30–50'	○	Sh	MC	Bk-G
Red	*A. rubrum*	3–6	40–60'	30–40'	○ or ●	Sp/Sh	M	G
Silver	*A. saccharinum*	3	50–70'	35–50'	○	Sh*	M	G
Sugar	*A. sacchurum*	3	60–120'	50–80'	○ or ◗	Sp/Sh	M	G

(Continued)

*fast-growing, softwood

Appendix B (Continued)

DECIDUOUS TREES (Continued)

Common Name	Botanical Name	Zone	Height	Spread	Exposure	Use	Texture	Color
Oak	*Quercus sp.*							
Northern Red	*Q. rubra*	3–8	70–90'	60–75'	○	Sp/Sh	M	G
Pin	*Q. palustris*	4–8	60–70'	25–40'	○	Sp/Sh	M	G
Southern Red	*Q. falcata*	7–9	50–60'	50–60'	○ or ◗	Sh	M	G
White	*Q. alba*	3–9	50–80'	50–80'	○	Sh	MC	G
Poplar, Lombardy	*Populus nigra 'Italica'*	3–9	90'	10–15'	○	Sc**	MC	G
Sourwood	*Oxydendrum arboreum*	5–9	25–30'	20'	○ or ◗	Sp	M	G
Sweetgum	*Liquidambar styraciflua*	4	60–90'	40'	○	Sp/Sh	M	G
Tulip Tree	*Liriodendron tulipifera*	4	60–90'	30–40'	○ or ◗	Sp/Sh	M	Y-G
Willow	*Salix sp.*							
Corkscrew	*S. matsudana 'Tortuosa'*	4	20–40'	20–30'	○ or ◗	Sp	F	G
Weeping	*S. babylonica*	6–8	30–40'	30–40'	○ or ◗	Sp	F	G

EVERGREEN TREES

Common Name	Botanical Name	Zone	Height	Exposure	Use	Texture	Color
Arborvitae	*Thuja*						
American	*T. occidentalis*	4	40–60'	○	Sc/H	MF	G
Oriental	*T. orientalis*	6	18–25'	○	Sc/H	MF	Y-G
Techny	*T. occidentalis cv. techny*	2	8–10'	○ or ◗	Sc/H	MF	G
Cedar, Eastern Red	*Juniperus virginiana*	3	30–40'	○	Sc/H	F	B-G (spring), R-G (summer)
Cryptomeria, Japanese Cedar	*Cryptomeria japonica*	5	50–60'	○	Sp	M	G,B-G
Cypress, Arizona	*Cupressus arizonica*	6	25–40'	○	Sp/Sc	F	G–GG
Douglasfir	*Pseudotsuga menziesii*	4	50–90'	○ or ◗	Sp/Sc	M	B-G,Bk-G

(Continued)

**short-lived

Appendix B (Continued)

EVERGREEN TREES

Common Name	Botanical Name	Zone	Height	Exposure	Use	Texture	Color
Fir	*Abies* sp.						
Balsam	*A. balsamea*	4	45–75'	○	Sp/G/Br	M	G
White	*A. concolor*	4	30–45'	○	Sp/G/Br	M–C	B-G,Gy-G
Holly	*Ilex* sp.						
American	*I. opaca*	6	20–40'	○ or ◗	F/H/Br	MC	Dark Y-G
Buford	*I. cornuta* 'Bufordii'	6	10–20'	○ or ●	F/H/Br	M	Bk-G
Hume	*I. x attenuata* 'Hume #2'	6	20–25'	○ or ●	F/H/Br	M	Bk-G
Yaupon	*I. vomitoria*	7	10–15'	○ or ●	F/Sp	MF	Bk-G
Laurel, Cherry	*Prunus caroliniana*	7	15–25'	○ or ◗	Sp/H	M	Bk-G
Magnolia, Southern	*Magnolia grandiflora*	7–9	60–80'	○ or ◗	Sc/H/Sh	MC	G
Pine	*Pinus* sp.						
Austrian	*P. nigra*	5	60–90'	○	Sp/Sc/Br	MC	Bk-G
Eastern White	*P. strobus*	3	60–80'	○ or ◗	Sp/H/Sc/Br	MF	B-G
Pitch	*P. rigida*	5	40–50'	○ or ◗	Sc/Br	M	Y-G,Bk-G
Scotch	*P. sylvestris*	2	30–40'	○	Sp/Sc/F	M	B-G
Spruce	*Picea* sp.						
Blue Colorado	*P. pungens f. glauca*	3	70–90'	○ or ◗	Sp/G	M–C	B-G
Colorado	*P. pungens*	3	70–90'	○ or ◗	Sp	M–C	Gy-G,B-G
Norway	*P. abies*	2–7	40–60'	○ or ◗	Sp/Sc	M	G,Bk-G
Weeping White	*P. glauca* 'Pendula'	2	40–50'	○ or ◗	Sp	M	G
White	*P. glauca*	2	30–50'	○ or ◗	Sp	M	G

Appendix C — Landscape Design Examples

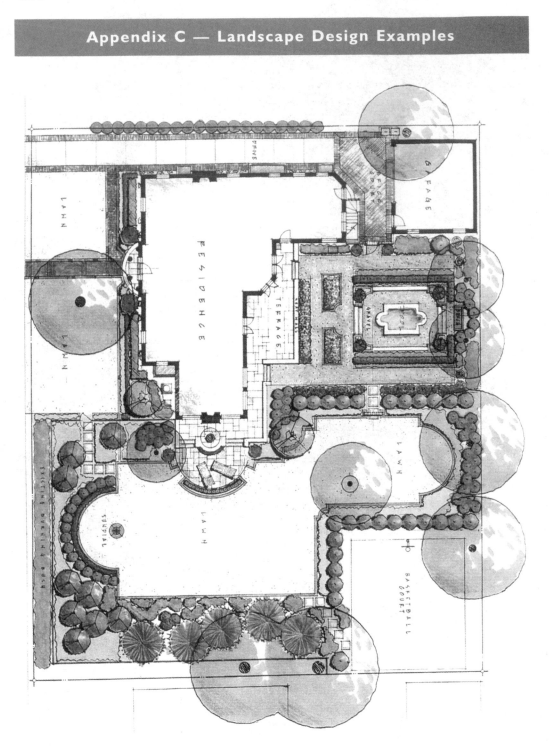

Color design courtesy of Matthew Haber, ASLA, Western DuPage Landscaping, Inc.

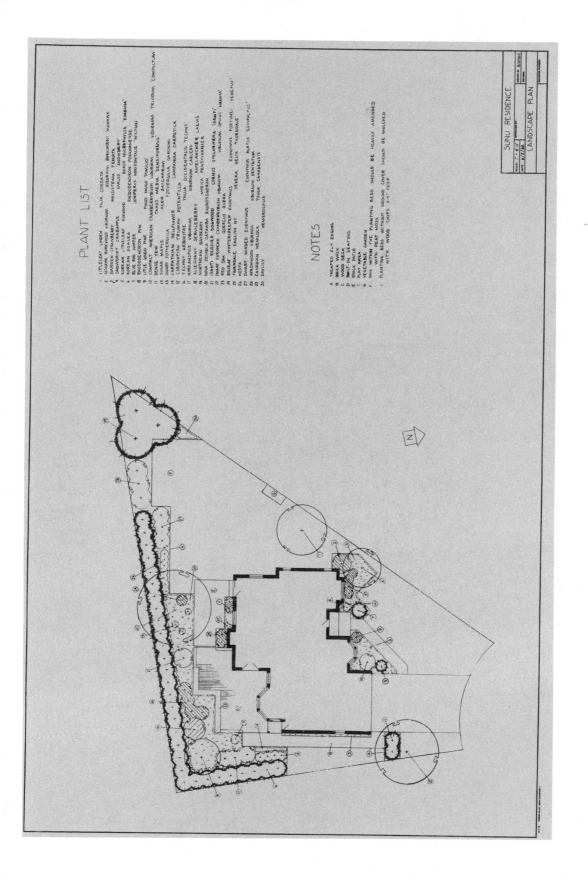

PLANT LIST

1. LITTLELEAF LINDEN — TILIA CORDATA
2. MOHAWK BURKWOOD VIBURNUM — VIBURNUM BURKWOODII 'MOHAWK'
3. DARTS/STRAWBERRY — WALDSTEINIA TERNATA
4. SNOWDRIFT CRABAPPLE — MALUS 'SNOWDRIFT'
5. KOREAN LITTLELEAF BOXWOOD — BUXUS MICROPHYLLA 'KOREANA'
6. KOREAN AZALEA — RHODODENDRON POUKHANENSE
7. BLUE RUG JUNIPER — JUNIPERUS HORIZONTALIS 'WILTONI'
8. RHODODENDRON PJM
9. LITTLE MUGO PINE — PINUS MUGO 'PUMILIO'
10. COMPACT AMERICAN CRANBERRYBUSH VIBURNUM — VIBURNUM TRILOBUM 'COMPACTUM'
11. DENSE YEW — TAXUS MEDIA 'DENSIFORMIS'
12. SUGAR MAPLE — ACER SACCHARUM
13. DWARF FOTHERGILLA — FOTHERGILLA GARDENI
14. CARPATHIAN BELLFLOWER — CAMPANULA CARPATICA
15. CORONATION TRIUMPH POTENTILLA
16. TECHNY ARBORVITAE — THUJA OCCIDENTALIS 'TECHNY'
17. KOREANSPICE VIBURNUM — VIBURNUM CARLESII
18. ALLEGHANY SERVICEBERRY — AMELANCHIER LAEVIS
19. NORTHERN BAYBERRY — MYRICA PENSYLVANICA
20. NOVA ZEMBLA CATAWBA RHODODENDRON
21. ISANTI REDOSIER DOGWOOD — CORNUS STOLONIFERA 'ISANTI'
22. DWARF EUROPEAN CRANBERRYBUSH VIBURNUM — VIBURNUM OPULUS 'NANUM'
23. RED OAK — QUERCUS RUBRA
24. BIGLEAF WINTERCREEPER EUONYMUS — EUONYMUS FORTUNEI VEGETUS
25. THORNDALE ENGLISH IVY — HEDERA HELIX 'THORNDALE'
26. HOSTA
27. DWARF WINGED EUONYMUS — EUONYMUS ALATUS 'COMPACTUS'
28. ARROWWOOD VIBURNUM — VIBURNUM DENTATUM
29. CANADIAN HEMLOCK — TSUGA CANADENSIS
30. DAYLILY — HEMEROCALLIS

NOTES

A. TREATED 2x4 EDGING
B. BRICK WALK
C. WOOD DECK
D. BUILT-IN SEATING
E. BRICK PATIO
F. VEGETABLE GARDEN
G. PLAY AREA
F. SOIL WITHIN THE PLANTING BEDS SHOULD BE HEAVILY AMENDED WITH PEAT MOSS
i. PLANTING BEDS WITHOUT GROUND COVER SHOULD BE MULCHED WITH WOOD CHIPS 3-4" DEEP

N

SUNU RESIDENCE
LANDSCAPE PLAN
SCALE 1" = 6'0"
DATE 6/1/88

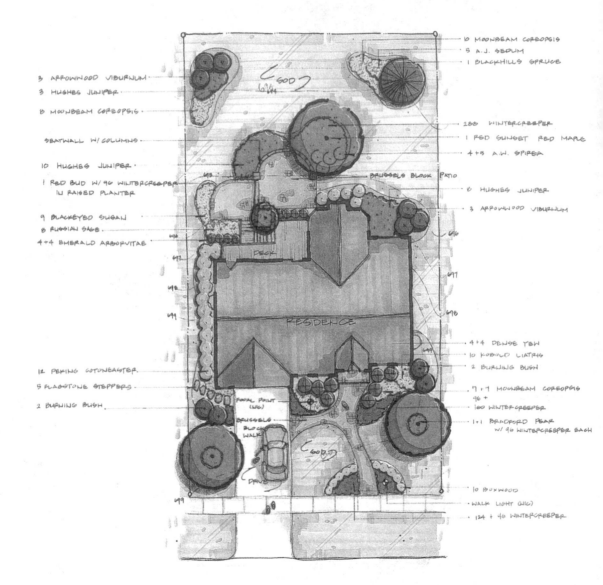

3 ARROWWOOD VIBURNUM
3 HUGHES JUNIPER
8 MOONBEAM COREOPSIS

SEATWALL W/COLUMNS

10 HUGHES JUNIPER
1 RED BUD W/96 WINTERCREEPER
IN RAISED PLANTER

9 BLACKEYED SUSAN
8 RUSSIAN SAGE
4+4 EMERALD ARBORVITAE

12 PEKING COTONEASTER
5 FLAGSTONE STEPPERS
2 BURNING BUSH

10 MOONBEAM COREOPSIS
5 A.J. SEDUM
1 BLACKHILLS SPRUCE

288 WINTERCREEPER
1 RED SUNSET RED MAPLE
4+3 A.W. SPIREA

8 HUGHES JUNIPER
3 ARROWWOOD VIBURNUM

4+4 DENSE YEW
10 KOBOLD LIATRIS
2 BURNING BUSH

7+7 MOONBEAM COREOPSIS
96 +
100 WINTERCREEPER

1+1 BRADFORD PEAR
W/96 WINTERCREEPER EACH

10 BOXWOOD
WALK LIGHT (N6)
124 + 96 WINTERCREEPER

RESIDENCE
DECK
BRUSSELS BLOCK PATIO
FOCAL POINT (N6)
BRUSSELS BLOCK WALK
DRIVE

Color design courtesy of Matthew Haber, ASLA, Western DuPage Landscaping, Inc.

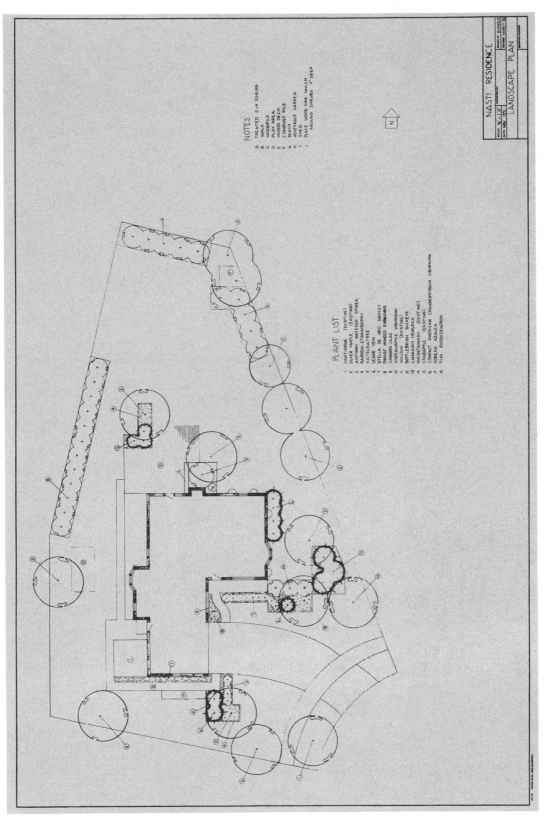

NOTES

A TREATED 2×4 EDGING
B WALK
C WOODPILE
D PLAY AREA
E WOOD DECK
F COMPOST PILE
G BENCH
H VEGETABLE GARDEN
I SHED
J PLACE WOOD CHIP MULCH
AROUND SHRUBS 4" DEEP

N

PLANT LIST

1 HAWTHORNE (EXISTING)
2 SILVER MAPLE (EXISTING)
3 ANTHONY WATERER SPIREA
4 BARREN-STRAWBERRY
5 KATSURATREE
6 DENSE YEW
7 STELLA DE ORO DAYLILY
8 DWARF WINGED EUONYMUS
9 COMMON LILAC
10 KOREANSPICE VIBURNUM
11 WILLOW (EXISTING)
12 BOTTLEBRUSH BUCKEYE
13 CANADIAN HEMLOCK
14 MOUNTAINASH (EXISTING)
15 CRABAPLE (EXISTING)
16 COMPACT AMERICAN CRANBERRYBUSH VIBURNUM
17 KOREAN AZALEA
18 PJM RHODODENDRON

NASTI RESIDENCE

LANDSCAPE PLAN

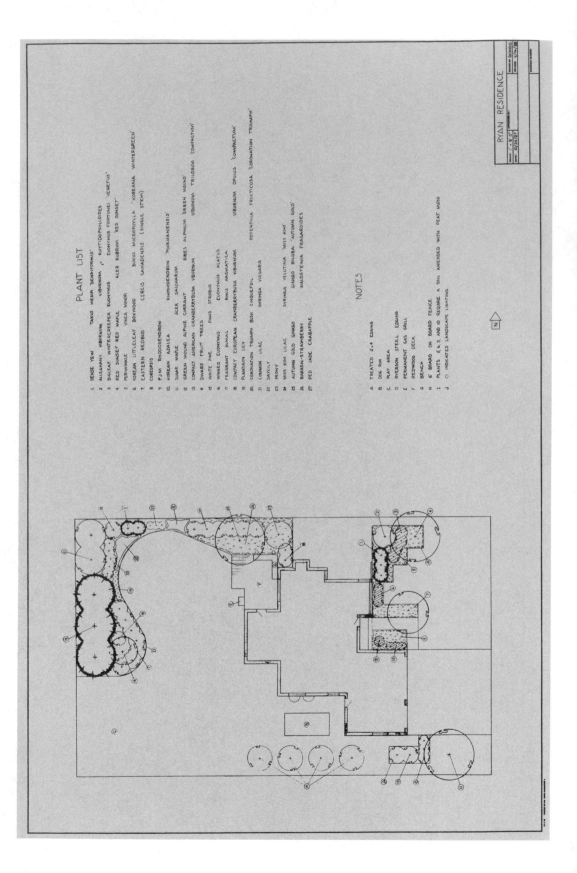

PLANT LIST

1. DENSE YEW   TAXUS MEDIA DENSIFORMIS'
2. ALLEGHANY VIBURNUM   VIBURNUM r RHYTIDOPHYLLOIDES
3. BIGLEAF WINTERCREEPER EUONYMUS EUONYMUS FORTUNEI 'VEGETUS'
4. RED SUNSET RED MAPLE ACER RUBRUM 'RED SUNSET'
5. PERIWINKLE   VINCA MINOR
6. KOREAN LITTLELEAF BOXWOOD   BUXUS MACROPHYLLA 'KOREANA WINTERGREEN'
7. EASTERN REDBUD   CERCIS CANADENSIS (SINGLE STEM)
8. COREOPSIS
9. PJM RHODODENDRON   RHODODENDRON 'PUKHANENSIS'
10. KOREAN AZALEA
11. SUGAR MAPLE   ACER SACCHARUM
12. GREEN MOUND ALPINE CURRANT   RIBES ALPINUM 'GREEN MOUND'
13. COMPACT AMERICAN CRANBERRYBUSH VIBURNUM   VIBURNUM TRILOBUM 'COMPACTUM'
14. DWARF FRUIT TREES
15. WHITE PINE   PINUS STROBUS
16. WINGED EUONYMUS   EUONYMUS ALATUS
17. FRAGRANT SUMAC   RHUS AROMATICA
18. COMPACT EUROPEAN CRANBERRYBUSH VIBURNUM   VIBURNUM OPULUS 'COMPACTUM'
19. PLANTAIN LILY
20. CORONATION TRIUMPH BUSH CINQUEFOIL   POTENTILLA FRUCTICOSA 'CORONATION TRIUMPH'
21. COMMON LILAC   SYRINGA VULGARIS
22. DAYLILY
23. PEONY
24. MISS KIM LILAC   SYRINGA VELUTINA 'MISS KIM'
25. AUTUMN GOLD GINKGO   GINKGO BILOBA 'AUTUMN GOLD'
26. BARREN-STRAWBERRY   WALDSTEINIA FRAGARIOIDES
27. RED JADE CRABAPPLE

NOTES

A. TREATED 2×4 EDGING
B. DOG RUN
C. PLAY AREA
D. RYERSON STEEL EDGING
E. PERMANENT GAS GRILL
F. REDWOOD DECK
G. BENCH
H. 6' BOARD ON BOARD FENCE
I. PLANTS 5, 4, 3, AND 10 REQUIRE A SOIL AMENDED WITH PEAT MOSS
J. ○ INDICATES LANDSCAPE LIGHTING

N

RYAN RESIDENCE

SCALE 1' = 8' 0"   DATE 10/24/87

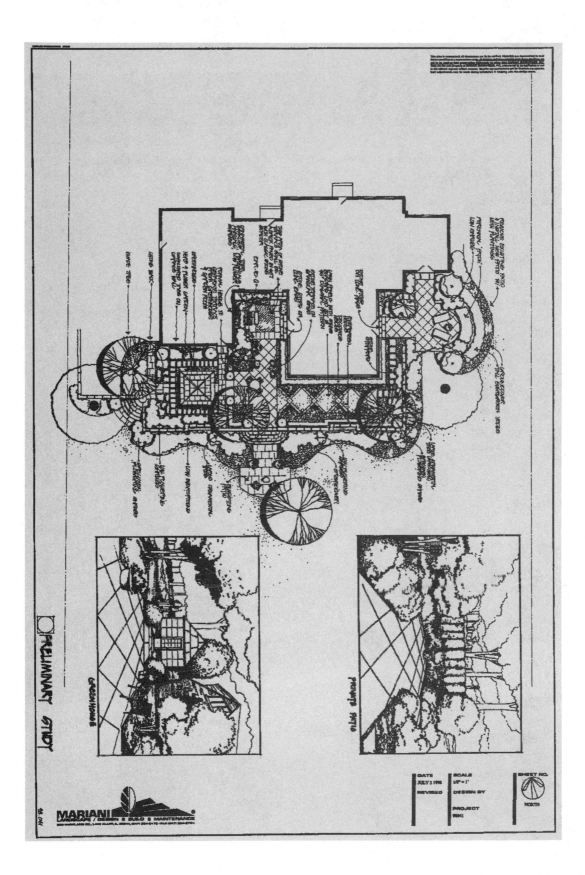

Appendix D — Professional Landscape and Nursery Associations

Alabama Nurserymen's Association

Linda H. Van Dyke

Executive Secretary

369 S. College Street

P.O. Box 9

Auburn, AL 36831-0009

Phone: 334-821-5148

Fax: 334-821-9111

alnurasso@auburn.campus.mci.net

Alaska Horticulture Association

Cathy Wright

c/o Alaska Plant Material Center

HC02 Box 7440

Palmer, AK 99645

Phone: 907-745-4469

American Association of Nurserymen

Robert J. Dolibois

Executive Vice President

1250 I Street NW, Suite 500

Washington, DC 20005-3994

Phone: 202-789-2900

Fax: 202-789-1893

American Horticultural Society

P.O. Box 0105

Mount Vernon, VA 22121-0105

Phone: 703-768-5700

American Society of Landscape Architects

David Bohardt

4401 Connecticut Avenue, NW 5th Floor

Washington, DC 20008-2369

Phone: 202-686-2752

Arizona Nursery Association

Cheryl Goar

Executive Director

1430 West Broadway Road, Suite A-125

Tempe, AZ 85282-1127

Phone: 602-966-1610

Fax: 602-966-0923

Arkansas Nurserymen's Association

Anne H. Borg

Executive Director

P.O. Box 21715

Little Rock, AR 72221-1715

Phone 501-225-0029

Fax: 501-218-0134

Associated Landscape Contractors of America

Debra H Atkins

Executive Director

12200 Sunrise Valley Drive, #150

Reston, VA 22091

Phone: 703-620-6363

Fax: 703-620-6365

Atlantic Provinces Nursery Trades Association

Tanya Morrison

130 Bluewater Road, Terra Nova

Landscape

Bedford, NS B4B 1G7

CANADA

Phone: 902-835-7387

Fax: 902-835-5498

British Columbia Nursery Trades Association

Jane Stock Executive Director

5830 176 A Street, Suite 101

Surrey, BC V3S 4E3

CANADA

Phone: 604-574-7772

Fax: 604-574-7773

California Association of Nurserymen

Elain Thompson
Executive Director
4620 Northgate Boulevard, Suite 155
Sacramento, CA 95834-1124
Phone: 916-567-0200
Fax: 916-567-0505
can@earthlink.net
www.can-online.org

Canadian Nursery Trades Association

Chris Andrews
Executive Director
7856 Fifth Line South
RR4, Station Main
Milton ONT L9T 2X8
CANADA
Phone: 905-875-1399
Fax: 905-875-1840
cntalc@spectranet.ca

Colorado Nursery Association

Kerstin Karloev
Executive Director
5290 East Yale Circle, Suite 204
Denver, CO 80222-6933
Phone: 303-758-6672
Fax: 303-758-6805

Connecticut Nurserymen's Association

Larry L. Carville
Executive Director
P.O. Box 117
Vernon, CT 06066-0117
Phone: 860-872-2095
Fax: 860-872-6596

Council of Tree & Landscape Appraisers

Ashby Ruden
1250 I Street, NW Suite 500
Washington, DC 20005
Phone: 202-789-2421

Delaware Association of Nurserymen

Marianne McGloin
Executive Director
952 Monroe Terrace
Dover, DE 19904-4120
Phone: 302-677-1895
Fax: 302-677-1895

Federation Interdisciplinaire de L'Horticulture Ornementale du Quebec

Jacques Coté
Directeur general
Envirotron, Cite Universitaire
Sainte-Foy QUE G1K 7P4
CANADA
Phone: 418-659-3561
Fax: 418-651-7439

Florida Nurserymen & Growers Association

Sherry Loudermilk
Executive Director
Highway 5 North
P.O. Box 369
Epworth, GA 30541-0369
Phone: 706-492-4664
Fax: 706-492-4668
ggia@mail.tds.net

The Garden Council

Rob Williams
500 North Michigan Avenue, #1400
Chicago, IL 60611
Phone: 312-661-1700

Hawaii Association of Nurserymen

Karen Bento
1085 South Beretania Street, #203
Honolulu, HI 96814-1601
Phone: 808-545-1533
Fax: 808-545-5026

Idaho Nursery Association

Ann Bates
Executive Director
1615 North Woodruff
Idaho Falls, ID 83401-2208
Phone: 208-522-7307
Fax: 208-529-0832
inagrow@srv.net

Illinois Landscape Contractors Association

Patricia Cassady
Executive Director
2200 South Main Street, Suite 304
Lombard, IL 60148-5366
Phone: 630-932-8443
Fax: 630-932-8939

Illinois Nurserymen's Association

Randy Vogel, CAE
Executive Director
1717 South Fifth Street
Springfield, IL 62703-3116
Phone: 217-525-6222
Fax: 217-525-6257

Indiana Association of Nurserymen

Kathy Edwards
Executive Secretary
401 Suinnyside Lane
New Albany, IN 47150
Phone: 812-949-7482
Fax: 812-949-7483

International Society of Arboriculture

William P. Kruidenier
6 Dunlap Court
P.O. Box GG
Savoy, IL 61874
Phone: 217-355-9411

Iowa Nursery and Landscape Association

Marge LePorte
Executive Director
7261 NW 21st Street
Ankeny, IA 50021-9644
Phone: 515-289-1790
Fax: 515-289-2650

Kansas Association of Nurserymen

Mary Odgers
Executive Secretary
411 Poplar
Wamego, KS 66547-1446
Phone: 913-456-2066

Kentucky Nursery and Landscape Association

Lee Squires
Executive Director
701 Baxter Avenue
P.O. Box 4037
Louisville, IY 40204-0037
Phone: 502-429-6171
Fax: 502-429-6205

Landscape Alberta Nursery Trades Association

Nigel Bowles
Executive Director
10215 176th Street
Edmonton, ALB T5S 1M1
CANADA
Phone: 403-489-1991
Fax: 403-444-2152
lanta@planet.com.net

Landscape Manitoba Nursery Trades Association

Evelyn Mackenzie-Reid
Executive Secretary
808 Muriel Street
Winnipeg, MANT R2Y 0Y3
CANADA
Phone: 204-889-5981
Fax: 204-888-0944

Landscape Ontario Hort Trades Association

Tony Di Giovanni
Executive Director
7856 5th Line South RR 4, Station Main
Milton, ONT L9T 2X8
CANADA
Phone: 905-875-1805
Fax: 905-875-3942

Louisiana Association of Nurserymen

Allen D. Owings
Executive Director
c/o Louisiana Cooperative Extension
   Service
P.O. Box 25100
Baton Rouge, LA 70894-5100
Phone: 504-388-2222
Fax: 504-388-1068
aowings@agctr.lsu.edu
www.lan.org

Maine Landscape & Nursery Association

Edith Ellis
Executive Secretary
Route 2, Box 1584
Turner, ME 04282-9658
Phone: 207-225-3998
Fax: 207-225-3998

Maryland Nurserymen's Association

Carville M. Akehurst
Executive Secretary
P.O. Box 18989
Baltimore, MD 21206
Phone: 410-254-3302
Fax: 410-882-0535

Massachusetts Nursery & Landscape Association

Rena M. Sumner
Executive Director
P.O. Box 387
Conway, MA 01341-0387
Phone: 413-369-4731
Fax: 413-369-4962
r10sum@aol.com
www.mnla.com

Michigan Nursery & Landscape Association

Richard P. Seely
President
2149 Commons Parkway
Okemox, MI 48864
Phone: 517-381-0437
Fax: 517-381-0638
rseely@mnla.org
www.mnla.org

Minnesota Nursery & Landscape Association

Bob Fitch
Executive Director
2151 Hamline Avenue North, Suite 109
P.O. Box 130307
St. Paul, MN 55113-0003
Phone: 612-633-4987
Fax: 612-633-4986

Mississippi Nurserymen's Association

David Tatum
246 Dorman Hall
P.O. Box 5385
Mississippi State, MS 39752-5385
Phone: 601-325-1682
Fax: 601-325-8379
dtatum@aac.msstate.edu

Missouri Landscape and Nursery Association

Sarah Woody Bibens
Executive Director
23750 State Route V
Clarksdale, MO 64430-9011
Phone: 816-369-3115
Fax: 816-369-3000
western@smartnet.net
www.plants.org/

Montana Association of Nurserymen

Robin L. Childers
Executive Director
P.O. Box 4553
Missoula, MT 59806-4553
Phone: 406-721-7334
Fax: 406-721-7016
man@montana.com

Nebraska Nursery and Landscape Association

Sarah Woody Bibens
Executive Director
23750 State Route V
Clarksdale, MO 64430-9011
Phone: 816-369-3115
Fax: 816-369-3000
western@smartnet.net

Nevada Landscape Association

Robyn Finch
Executive Secretary
P.O. Box 7431
Reno, NV 89510-7431
Phone: 702-828-1104
Fax: 702-828-0871

New England Nursery Association

M. Virginia Wood
Executive Director
8D Pleasant Street
South Natick, MA 01760
Phone: 508-653-3112
Fax: 508-653-4112
NEnsyAssn@aol.com
www.plants.org/nena

New Hampshire Plant Growers Association

Chris Robarge
56 Leavitt Road
Hampton, NH 03842-3938
Phone: 603-862-1074

New Jersey Nursery & Landscape Association

S. Howard Davis
Executive Director
605 Farnsworth Avenue
Bordentown, NJ 08505-2028
Phone: 609-291-7070
Fax: 609-291-1121
njnla@ix.netcom.com
www.plantamerica.com

New Mexico Association of Nursery Industries

Norm Lownds
Executive Director
Box 30003, Department 3Q
Las Cruces, NM 88003-8003
Phone: 505-646-1902
Fax: 505-646-6041

New York State Nursery/Landscape Association

Heather Nemier
Executive Director
2115 Downer Street Road
P.O. Box 657
Baldwinsville, NY 13027-0657
Phone: 315-635-5008
Fax: 315-635-4874
nysnla@aol.com
www.plants.org/associations/

North Carolina Association of Nurserymen

William A. Wilder, Jr.
Executive Director
7419 Highway 64 East, Suite 112
P.O. Box 400
Knightdale, NC 27545-0400
Phone: 919-266-3322
Fax: 919-266-2137

North Dakota Nursery & Greenhouse Association

Neal Holland
Immediate Past President
107 West Central Avenue
Minot AFB, ND 58704-1115
Phone: 701-727-5290

Ohio Nursery & Landscape Association

William Stalter
Executive Director
72 Dorchester Square
Westerville, OH 43081-3350
Phone: 614-899-1195
Fax: 800-860-1713
74577.1455@compuserver.com
www.onla.org

Oklahoma State Nurserymen's Association

Carroll Emberton
Executive Director
400 North Portland Street
Oklahoma City, OK 73107-6110
Phone: 405-942-5276
Fax: 405-945-3382

Oregon Association of Nurserymen

Clayton Hannon
Executive Director
2780 SE Harrison, Suite 102
Milwaukie, OR 97222-7574
Phone: 503-653-8733
Fax: 503-653-1528
clayton-hannon@oan.org

Pennsylvania Landscape and Nursery Association

Patricia Norman
Acting Executive Director
1924 North Second Street
Harrisburg, PA 17102-2209
Phone: 717-238-1673
Fax: 717-238-1675
plna@plna.com
www.plna.com

Professional Grounds Maintenance Society

John Gillan
120 Cockeysville Road, Suite 104
Hunt Valley, MD 21031
Phone: 410-584-9754

Rhode Island Nurserymen's Association

Kenneth A. Lagerquist
Executive Secretary
64 Bittersweet Drive
Seekonk, MA 02771-1103
Phone: 508-761-9280
Fax: 508-761-9260
76062.150@compuserve.com
www.uri.edu/research/sustland/rina.html

Saskatchewan Nursery Trades Association

Tim Van Duyvendyk
685 Reid Road
Saskatoon, SASK S7N 3J4
CANADA
Phone: 306-249-1222
Fax: 306-249-0151

South Carolina Nursery Association

Donna Shealy
Executive Secretary
2541 Glenwood
Columbia, SC 29204-2605
Phone: 803-787-1299
Fax: 803-787-6818

South Dakota Nursery and Landscape Association

Julie Hoffmann
Executive Director
East River Nursery
RR 5 Box 392A
Huron, SD 57350-8842
Phone: 605-352-4414

Southern Nurserymen's Association

Danny Summers
EVP
1000 Johnson Ferry Road, Suite E130
Marietta, GA 30068-2100
Phone: 770-973-9026
Fax: 770-973-9097
mail.sna.org
www.sna.org

Tennessee Nurserymen's Association

Neva Evans
Executive Secretary
115 Lyon Stree
P.O. Box 57
McMinnville, TN 37111-0057
Phone: 615-473-3951
Fax: 615-473-5883

Texas Association of Nurserymen

Eddy D. Edmondson
President
7730 South IH-35
Austin, TX 78745
Phone: 512-280-5182
Fax: 512-280-3012
goodwood@cutemet.net

Utah Nursery & Landscape Association

Stephen A. Linde
Executive Director
8372 Mesa Drive
P.O. Box 636
Sandy, UT 84091-0636
Phone: 801-565-8880
Fax: 801-565-8881

Vermont Association of Professional Horticulturists

Jane Wilkening
Executive Director
P.O. Box 64878
Burlington, VT 05406-4878
Phone: 802-865-5072
Fax: 802-865-5073

Virginia Nurserymen's Association

Jeffrey B. Miller
Executive Director
383 Coal Hollow Road
Christiansburg, VA 24073-6721
Phone: 540-382-0943
Fax: 540-382-2716
vna@swva.net
www.plant.org/assoc/vna/

Washington State Nursery & Landscape Association

Steve McGonigal
Executive Director
P.O. Box 670
Summer, WA 98390
Phone: 206-863-4482
Fax: 206-863-6732
wsnia@nwrain.com

West Virginia Nurserymen's Association

Shari Beckett
965 National Road
Wheeling, WV 26003-6440
Phone: 304-233-4140
Fax: 304-233-3628

Western Association of Nurserymen

Sarah Woody Bibens
Executive Director
23750 State Route V
Clarksdale, MO 64430-9011
Phone: 816-369-3115
Fax: 816-369-3000
western@smartnet.net

Wisconsin Nursery Association

Joe Phillips
9910 West Layton
Greenfield, WI 53228-3347
Phone: 414-529-4705
Fax: 414-529-4722

Glossary

Accelerator—a chemical to speed the hardening process.

Acidity—a pH below 7.0.

Aesthetic injury level—the point where visible plant damage in the landscape justifies using pest control techniques.

Aesthetic value—a benefit of the landscape which is sensitive to art and beauty.

Algae—a group of small, primitive, filamentous, green plants that manufacture their own food and are found under very wet conditions.

Alkaline—a pH over 7.0.

Ames lettering instrument—a tool used to draw eight parallel guidelines for lettering.

Annual—a herbaceous plant that germinates from seed, grows to maturity, flowers, and produces seed in one growing season.

Anti-transpirant—seals the stomata and helps prevent leaf scorch or leaf burn.

Arboriculture—the culture of trees.

Arborist—professional tree care specialist.

Architect's scale—a measuring instrument used for scale measurements of 1/16", 1/8", and 1/4".

Area measurements—those made of the surface.

Backflow prevention device—a safety device that eliminates the movement of irrigation water back into its source, a potable water system, which could become contaminated.

Bacteria—small, one-celled organisms that have a primitive nucleus.

Balance—implied equilibrium.

Balled and burlapped (B&B)—a harvesting technique where a plant is dug keeping a ball of soil around the root system and covering it with burlap to hold the soil and roots together.

Baluster—a vertical piece of wood between the top and bottom rails in a deck.

Bare root (BR)—a harvesting technique where a plant is dug without taking soil from the field.

Base plan—a drawing of the house on the lot.

Bay—the distance between two posts.

Beam—a large board that connects the posts and provides the support for the joists in deck construction.

Bedding plant—a flower already growing in a container and ready to begin blooming, rather than grown from seed.

Bed edging—the area where the landscape bed joins the lawn area.

Bed pattern—a border that outlines where plants are planted.

Berm—a mound of soil.

Bid—a fixed price placed on the work to be done.

Biological pest control—using living organisms that are predators to control pests.

Branch bark ridge—a raised line of bark that forms on the upper side of where the branch joins the trunk.

Broadcasting—involves the wide distribution of material on the surface of the soil.

Broom finish—the process of dragging a broom over concrete before it hardens to create a rough, nonskid surface.

Callus—protective growth of tissue; an undifferentiated mass of cells.

Candle stage—new growth on pines which resembles candles.

Capillary water—water held between the soil particles against the force of gravity.

Cement—a mixture of lime, clay, iron, and silica.

Chain saw—a gas powered or electric saw with a continuous loop cutting chain.

Chlorosis—yellowing of plant leaves caused by the absence of chlorophyll.

Circle template—an instrument used as a guide to draw circles and curves.

Cleat—a short board attached to posts for beams to rest on.

Closing—last step of the sales process in which an agreement between the customer and the salesperson is reached.

Collar—swollen trunk tissue surrounding the base of a tree branch.

Color—has greatest visual impact of all the design qualities; subdivided into warm and cool colors.

Communication—individuals participate in exchanging information.

Compartmentalization—the formation of a chemical barrier by a tree to seal a wound.

Complete metamorphosis—four distinct changes in an insect life cycle (egg, larvae, Pupae, and adult).

Computer assisted design (CAD)—refers to the use of computer hardware and software to produce drawings.

Computer spreadsheet—an all-purpose computer program used for almost any task involving the organization of numbers based on columns and rows.

Contact herbicide—a chemical that kills only the portions of the plants that it contacts.

Container grown—a cultural method where plants are grown in containers filled with a special soil mix.

Container nursery—grows nursery crops to marketable size in containers.

Contingency costs—the unforeseen expenses associated with a project, such as theft of materials at the work site, mechanical breakdowns, or rainouts.

Contour lines—represent the vertical rise of fall of the land.

Cool humid region—a turfgrass region suited to cool season grasses, such as bluegrass, ryegrass, fescue, or bentgrass.

Cool season turfgrass—a grass that grows best in a temperature range of 60 to 75°F.

Corner planting—plants placed at the corners of the house.

Cost summation—the total expenses for a job, including labor, materials, overhead, and contingencies.

Covenant—an agreement made between two or more parties to do or keep from doing a specific thing.

Cubic yard—a volume measurement 3 feet wide, 3 feet long, and 3 feet high.

Cultivar—a plant with a distinguishing characteristic from other plants in the species but does not transfer that characteristic to its offspring through sexual reproduction.

Cultural pest control—the use of management techniques to control pests.

Cure—get hard.

Cut—describes removing or excavating soil from an area.

Dead zone—the region in the center of a plant that, when exposed to light, seldom produces new shoots.

Deciduous—those plants that lose their leaves in the fall.

Deck—wooden surface area raised above the ground level.

Deck boards—those that cover joists and provide the flooring surface of a deck.

Desiccation—water loss from tissues resulting in tissue death.

Doorway planting—plants located on either side of the entry door.

Drawing paper—white vellum or tracing paper.

Drought tolerance—refers to the ability of a plant to live and grow with low amounts of moisture.

Dry fertilizer—nutrients packaged in dry form, commonly granular.

Eased—shape of boards whose edges have been rounded.

Ecosystem—a confined community; all the parts of a particular environment, such as all the contents of a lily pond.

Elevation view—a view of a house from the front.

Emphasis—dominance of some elements of the design over others.

Enclosure—the wall of the outdoor living room; the term used to describe both fences and walls in the landscape.

Engineer's scale—a measuring instrument used for scale measurements divided by tenths.

Erasure shield—a thin metal plate used to protect lines while erasing.

Estimate—an approximate price for the work to be done.

Estimate sheet—a form for calculating prices.

Evergreen—a plant that keep its leaves year round.

Exoskeleton—external skeleton.

Exposed aggregate—the gravel used to make concrete exposed by washing away some of the cement just before the concrete hardens in the finishing process.

Family inventory survey—a form on which the customer provides information on factors that affect the landscape project.

Fence—an enclosure having posts, rails, and in-fill.

Fertilizer capsule—a solid form of fertilizer implanted in a tree trunk after drilling a hole just under the bark.

Fertilizer spike—hardened form of dry fertilizer in the shape of a stake which is driven into the soil.

Field nursery—grows nursery crops to marketable size in fields.

Fill—describes the addition of soil to an area.

Filtration system—pool filters and pump to remove impurities and keep the water clean and clear.

Final grade—leveling the soil to a smooth appearance by breaking the soil clumps into marble-sized particles, which makes this surface suitable for planting and seeding.

Float—a tool used to initially smooth the surface of liquid concrete after screeding.

Flower bed—a planting bed that only contains flowers.

Flower border—flowers planted in front of shrubs in the planting bed with the shrubs providing the back drop.

Focal point—point of emphasis of a well-designed landscape.

Form—a frame or mold that holds liquid concrete to shape until it has set; the three-dimensional shape of the plant.

Formal design—the exact same plants on each side of a view.

Foundation plant—shrubs placed around the foundation of a house.

French curve—an instrument used as a guide to draw irregular curves.

Frost line—the maximum depth that the ground will freeze in winter.

Fungi—small, one-celled, filamentous, spore-bearing organisms having no chlorophyll that grow on or in a plant.

Fungicide—a chemical used to control fungi.

Garden accessory—an item in the landscape that attracts attention and provides interest, such as a sculpture, pool, or lawn ornament.

Gate—a moveable barrier in a fence.

Gate post—the post to which a gate is attached.

Genus—a closely related group of plants comprised of one or more species.

Geotextile—woven strips of plastic landscape fabric that allow the movement of air, water, and fertilizer into the soil.

Goose egg plan—a small sketch of the house and lot with rough ovals or circles to represent activities, such as lawn games, play area, patio or deck, vegetable garden, plantings, shed, screen, water garden, service area, or public area.

Grade—slope of the land.

Grading—the moving of soil and the reshaping of the land.

Gravitational water—water that drains down through the soil through the pore spaces because of gravity.

Ground cover—a woody or herbaceous plant that forms a mat less than 1 foot high covering the ground.

Ground fault circuit interrupter (GFCI)—a safety device designed to protect people using electricity in areas that may be wet or have water.

Group planting—one consisting of several different species of shrubs and trees.

Guying—supporting a tree by driving three equally-spaced stakes around the tree trunk and attaching a wire or cable from each stake to the tree trunk. The wire between stake and the trunk is split in the middle with a turnbuckle.

Hand pruner—a hand-held scissor or anvil style hand pruning tool.

Hardiness—refers to the ability of a plant to withstand cold temperatures.

Hardpan—densely, compacted layer of soil.

Hardscape—physical features, such as fences, terraces, retaining walls, patios, walks, drives, irrigation systems, or pools

Hardscaping—describes installing nonplant landscape features, such as fences, patios, walks, pools, or walls.

Hardware—describes the computer equipment.

Hardy plant—one that is less sensitive to temperature extremes.

Heading back—involves the shortening of individual plant stems.

Hedge—a group of all one type of shrub that defines space, ties other landscape elements together, and may screen views; may be clipped or unclipped.

Hedge shear—a hand operated, electric, or gas powered scissor-type cutter used to trim hedges and shape shrubs in a formal garden.

Herbaceous plant—a non-woody plant that dies back to the ground each year.

Herbicide—a chemical used to kill or prevent weed growth.

High interest planting—a planting designed to capture the attention of the viewer and to provide interest to the garden.

High-voltage—conventional 120 volt electricity.

Host plant—one that provides a pest with food.

Hygroscopic water—water that forms a thin film around individual soil particles.

Incomplete metamorphosis—the gradual change in an insect's life cycle from the egg through the nymph to the adult.

Infill—the material fastened to the rails of a fence that ensure security and privacy.

Infiltration—the process of the water soaking into the soil.

Informal design—different plants and different sized plants on each side of a view, but the visual weights of these plants balance one another.

Inorganic mulch—one that was never living, such as volcanic rock or river gravel.

Insect—an animal with three distinct body parts; head, thorax, and abdomen.

Insecticide—a chemical used to control insects.

Instar—the shedding of the external skeleton in the life cycle of insects with incomplete metamorphosis.

Integrated pest management (IPM)—using cultural, biological, mechanical, and chemical techniques to control pests with the least disruption to the environment.

Irrigation controller—a device which regulates and controls a sprinkler system.

J.U.L.I.E.—Joint Utility Location and Information Exchange finds and marks all underground utilities at the construction site.

Joist—a board run at a 90-degree angle to beams that flooring (deck boards) is attached to.

Landscape architect—a person trained in engineering, graphic arts, and architectural technology to design landscapes ranging from small gardens to entire cities.

Landscape construction—the segment of landscaping that involves the installation of materials identified in the landscape design.

Landscape contractor—the person hired to install the landscape.

Landscape design—the practice of creating a plan to make the best use of available outdoor space in the most attractive way.

Landscape designer—a person trained in the art of design and the science of growing horticultural plants whose work is primarily residential landscape designs.

Landscape fabric—a plastic sheet placed in the landscape bed to reduce weed competition.

Landscape maintenance—the care and upkeep of the landscape materials after installation.

Landscape maintenance technician—a person who has been trained in landscape maintenance skills.

Landscape supervisor—the person responsible for the crew.

Landscaping—focuses on the beautification of outdoor terrain and, to some extent, interior settings.

Larvae—the worm-like stage of an insect with complete metamorphosis.

Leaching—gravitational water moving through the soil carrying with it dissolved minerals, chemicals, and salts.

Leader—a central branch that dominates over other branches on a tree.

Line—the outline of plants, plant parts, and physical features.

Linear measurements—those made of a line.

Line post—a post between corner and/or gate posts.

Lopper—a larger, hand operated scissor style pruning tool.

Low-voltage—stepped-down 24 volt electricity.

Macroclimate—concerns the temperature, precipitation, humidity, and wind over large areas or regions.

Main post—a post located at a corner or gate.

Mechanical pest control—using tools or equipment for pest control.

Microclimate—the temperature, precipitation, humidity, and wind on the landscape site.

Microirrigation—a closed irrigation system characterized by low operating pressure and small orifice size.

Mirror lighting—a technique using reflected light on water.

Mortarless block wall system—a block wall system that uses precast concrete blocks stacked on top of one another without mortar to hold them together.

Moss—tangled green mats composed of a branched, thread-like growth over the soil surface usually found in highly acidic, excessively shaded, improperly watered, or low fertility compacted conditions.

Mulch—material used around plants to reduce water loss, prevent weed growth, keep soil temperatures uniform, or prevent erosion.

Mulching—the practice of spreading a material over the surface of the soil.

Native plant—a plant growing naturally, not introduced by people.

Nematicide—a chemical used to control nematodes.

Nematode—an appendageless, nonsegmented worm-like invertebrate with a body cavity and complete digestive tract, including mouth, alimentary canal, and anus.

Night-landscaping—describes the use of ornamental lighting to enhance the landscape after dark.

Nonselective herbicide—a chemical that kills all vegetation without regard to species.

Nurseries—grow many different varieties of trees, shrubs, and bedding plants.

Nutrient—chemical substance that supports the life processes.

Nymph—the stage of the life cycle of an insect with incomplete metamorphosis that looks similar to the adult, only differing in appearance by size and color.

Opening—the first meeting of the salesperson and the customer.

Ordinance—a governmental regulation or statute.

Organic mulch—one that originated from plant material, such as wood chips, shredded wood bark, or pine needles.

Ornamental grass—an annual or perennial grass plant valued for its texture and color in the landscape.

Ornamental horticulture—uses plants and other materials for decorative purposes.

Ornamental plant—a plant planted by people for its attractive characteristics.

Ornamental tree—a smaller tree having high visual interest.

Outdoor living area—includes all of the property to the rear of the house except the service area.

Overhead costs—general costs in running a business.

Parasite—usually a multi-celled organism that lives in or on other organisms.

Path lighting—walk lights to improve the safety of pedestrians while providing an interesting lighting effect in the landscape.

Pathogen—a biological agent or virus that can cause disease.

Patio—permanent hard surface, such as brick, concrete, or flagstone, that is level with the ground.

Paver blocks—specially made units constructed from molded and compressed concrete or molded clay into many types, styles, colors, and sizes.

Paving—covering the soil with a hard surface material to prevent soil erosion and compaction from traffic.

Percolation—the downward movement of water through the soil.

Perennial—a plant that has a life cycle of more than two growing seasons.

Permeable—a quality soil that allows water movement by infiltration and percolation.

Pesticide—a chemical used to control pests.

Pest—anything that causes injury or loss to a plant.

pH scale—a 14-point scale used to explain acidity or alkalinity.

Pheromone—a chemical insect sex attractant.

Photocell—a light sensitive switch.

Pilaster—a rectangular support or pier projecting partially from a wall.

Plains region—a turfgrass region that is dry and where buffalo grass grows naturally.

Planimeter/digitizer—a computer device to accurately and quickly calculate linear feet, area, and volume.

Plant disease—any abnormal conditions in plants that interfere with its normal appearance, growth, structure, or function.

Planting bed—describes the area in the landscape where shrubs and flowers are planted.

Planting plan—a drawing developed by the landscape designer which shows the exact location for plant materials, includes a plant materials list, and hardscape features. Contours and spot elevations may also be included.

Plant nomenclature—the common and botanical names of plants.

Plan view—a view of the house and lot from above looking down.

Plate compactor—a mechanical plate vibrator used to compact base materials and pavers.

Plat of survey—a legal document indicating exact locations of physical structures on a piece of property and the exact dimensions of the property.

Plug—a small block or square of turf including soil that is used to vegetatively propagate warm season turfgrasses, such as zoysia.

Polyethylene (PE)—a tough, black waxy plastic material derived by combining hydrogen and carbon that is commonly used to make flexible pipe which is used in landscape irrigation and drainage.

Polyvinyl chloride (PVC)—a tough, rigid plastic material made by combining coke, lime, and salt that is commonly used to make rigid pipe.

Pop-up rotating sprinkler—one that has a pair of nozzles that raise and revolve to distribute water over the area of coverage.

Pore spaces—holes in the soil between soil particles.

Portfolio—design work and photos of previous landscape projects.

Postemergence—after plant emergence.

Postemergent—(see postemergence)

Preemergence—before plant emergence but after planting.

Preemergent—(see preemergence)

Preformed pool—a ready-made pond of plastic or fiberglass material.

Preparation—first step in the sales process that involves a number of factors before the sale is actually conducted.

Presentation—the sales step where the designer introduces the service or product that meets the customer's needs identified earlier in the sales process.

Private area—includes all the property to the rear of the house except the service area; also known as the outdoor living area.

Probing—a practice of thoroughly investigating a customer's wants, needs, and problems.

Profit—the amount of money left over after deducting all expenses.

Pruning—selective removal or reduction of certain plant parts.

Pruning saw—a hand saw with widely spaced large teeth used to remove tree branches.

Public area—the portion of the property that is in full view of the public.

Pupae—the transformation stage in the life cycle of an insect with complete metamorphosis.

Rejuvenation pruning—complete removal of all stems to 4 to 6 inch stubs.

Renewal pruning—the selective removal of older plant stems.

Repetition—repeating forms, textures, and colors of the plants throughout the design.

Respiration—the chemical process in which cells convert sugars into energy.

Retaining wall—an enclosure constructed to retain or hold soil in place.

Retarder—a chemical to slow the hardening process.

Riser—the elevating vertical part of a step.

Rootstock—the root system used in the grafting process.

Root zone—the area in which plant roots are growing.

Rough grade—establishing the approximate grade and slope of the terrain, but the soil is usually coarse and not suitable for planting.

Sale—the exchange of goods or services at a price mutually agreed upon by the parties involved.

Scaffold branch—one that grows laterally from a tree trunk.

Scale—the proportion of one object to another.

Scion—the top growth (stem) used in the grafting process.

Screeding—leveling the liquid concrete surface with a straight edge by moving the excess concrete from the high spots and filling in the low spots.

Screen—a solid mass of one type of shrub serving as a living wall that effectively blocks views.

Selective herbicide—a chemical used to kill only certain plant species.

Sequence—the uniformity of change from one item in the landscape to the next.

Service area—area to the rear or the side of the house set aside for strictly functional purposes.

Shade tree—a large tree with a spreading canopy which screens the sun.

Shadow lighting—shining a light through a plant and onto a wall or fence surface.

Shearing—the removal of a shrub's surface by clipping in order to achieve a desired shape.

Shrub—a multi-stem, woody plant that does not exceed 20 feet in height.

Shrub border—a mass of many shrubs on the border of the property which helps to create the outdoor living room, screens views, and serves as a backdrop for flower borders.

Silhouette lighting—placing a light behind a plant and shining it onto a vertical surface which serves to outline the plant.

Site analysis plan—an accurate sketch of the house and lot on which observations are recorded.

Soaker hose—oozes water providing a slow application.

Sod—the surface layer of turf, including the plants and a thin layer of soil.

Soft paving—covering the soil with loose aggregates.

Software—the programs (instructions) which make computer equipment function.

Soil—that part of the earth's crust in which the root system of a plant grows.

Soil amendments—materials added to the soil to improve drainage, moisture holding ability, and aeration.

Soil ball—the soil surrounding the root system of a plant.

Soil structure—the arrangement of soil aggregates in the soil.

Soil texture—the proportion of different sized particles in the soil described as sand, silt, and clay.

Soil water needle—a device that is used to supply water directly to the root zone of a plant.

Soluble fertilizer—dissolved, liquid form.

Species—plants that show characteristics that distinguish them from other groups in the genus.

Specifications—written descriptions of materials, work, and time schedules for a project.

Specimen plant—one displaying outstanding form, texture, and color.

Spotlighting—a technique to direct attention to a specific object in the landscape.

Sprayhead sprinkler—one that emits single or double fans of water in a fixed pattern.

Sprigs—pieces of grass stems (rhizomes and stolons) without soil used to vegetatively propagate warm season turfgrasses, such as Bermuda grass.

Sprinkler—provides moisture to a large area.

Stake the site—describes writing plant names on small wooden or plastic stakes that are driven into the ground to show the exact center of each planting hole.

Staking—supporting a tree by driving two or three long stakes next to the soil ball and attaching a wire between the stakes and the three trunk.

Station—a single electric switch in an irrigation controller that turns on or off a solenoid valve.

Stomata—pore openings in the epidermal layer of plant tissue where transpiration occurs.

Subsoil—lighter colored layer of soil below the topsoil.

Sucker—a soft, green shoot that develops at the base of a tree.

Sun calculator—a drawing that can be put under the tracing paper and centered on the area to be shaded to help locate trees in the landscape with the angles suggested to block the sun's rays for a particular time of day.

Sunscald—describes a condition in which bark blisters from the intense winter sunlight.

Systematic herbicide—a chemical absorbed into a plant vascular and root system, destroying the entire plant.

Tender plant—one more sensitive to temperature extremes.

Terrain—describes the rise and fall of the land.

Texture—the appearance of a plant in terms of coarseness or fineness, roughness or smoothness, heaviness or lightness, denseness or thinness.

Thatch—describes the accumulation of excess grass stems and roots in the turf.

Topography—a record of an area's terrain.

Topsoil—soil found near the surface.

Transition zone—an area between major climate zones.

Transpiration—the loss of water from the plant through the leaves in the form of water vapor.

Tread—the level part of the step on which the foot is placed.

Tree—a single-stem, woody, perennial plant reaching the height of 12 feet or more.

Trowel—a tool used to bring a thin film of cement to the top after concrete has initially set, making a very smooth surface.

Turf—the plants in a ground cover and the soil in which the roots grow.

Turfgrass—a collection of grass plants that form a ground cover.

Turfgrass blend—a combination of different cultivars of the same species.

Turfgrass mixture—a combination of two or more different species.

Up-lighting—a technique that places a lamp at ground level which shines up at the base of a tree.

Urban forester—a forester who works with ornamental trees in city settings.

U-shaped crotch—tree branches that exhibit a 45- to 90-degree angle of attachment.

Variety—contrast in the design by selecting some plants with different qualities from the mass of plants; plants within a species that show a significant difference from other plants in the species and inherit those characteristics through sexual reproduction.

Video imaging—a technique that uses computer technology to superimpose a landscape design over a photograph of the customer's undeveloped landscape.

Vine—a woody or herbaceous plant that requires some type of support which climbs on objects or creeps along the ground.

Viruses—infective living agents of microorganisms, some with characteristics of nonliving matter, that can multiply only in connection with living cells and are regarded both as living organisms and as complex proteins sometimes involving nucleic acid, enzymes, etc.

Volume measurements—those of size or amount in three-dimensions.

V-shaped crotch—tree branches that exhibit a sharp, less than 45-degree angle of attachment.

Wall—an upright structure serving to enclose, divide, support, or protect an area.

Warm arid and semi-arid regions—turfgrass regions that will only support warm season grasses with irrigation to supplement the low natural rainfall.

Warm humid region—a turfgrass region suited to warm season grasses, such as Bermuda grass, zoysia, or St. Augustine grass.

Warm season turfgrass—a grass that grows best in a temperature range of 80 to 95°F.

Water bag—a bag filled with water which has tiny holes in the bag to allow the water to slowly seep into the ground.

Water requirement—refers to the amount of water plants need to live and grow.

Watersprout—a soft, green shoot that typically grows vertically from existing tree branches.

Water zone—an area in a landscape based on the amount of water needed by the plants.

Weed—a plant growing out of place or any unwanted plant.

Weep hole—a hole made through a wall to release the built-up water pressure.

Wilting—the drooping of a plant due to a lack of firmness in the plant tissues.

Winter burn—describes a condition in which bark blisters from the intense winter sunlight.

Wrought iron—an iron that contains some slag and very little carbon.

Xeriscape—water conservation through creative, appropriate landscaping and water management.

Xeriscaping—using a landscape design that is water efficient.

Bibliography

Biondo, Ronald J., and Jasper S. Lee. *Introduction to Plant and Soil Science and Technology*. Danville, Illinois: Interstate Publishers, Inc., 1997.

Dirr, Michael A. *Manual of Woody Landscape Plants*. Illinois: Stipes Publishing Company, 1990.

Giles, Floyd. *Pruning and Care of Trees and Shrubs*. Urbana: Vocational Agriculture Service, University of Illinois, Publication U5040.

Giles, Floyd. *Landscape Construction Procedures, Techniques, and Design*. Illinois: Stipes Publishing Company, 1988.

Hall, Larry, Editor. "The Kindliest Cut of All." Wheeling, Illinois: Hendrickson, The Care of Trees. *Arbor Topics*, Volume XXV, Fall and Winter, 1992-93.

Nelson, William. R. *Landscaping Your Home*. University of Illinois Cooperative Extension Service Circular 1111.

Nelson, William R., *Planting Design: A Manual of Theory and Practice*. Illinois: Stipes Publishing Company, 1985.

Powell, Kim. *Pruning Trees, Flushcuts and Wound Dressings*. North Carolina Cooperative Extension Service, Leaflet Number: 602, October, 1992.

Rosenau, Jim. "Trees a New Wisdom," *The Practical Homeowner*, November/December 1992.

Schroeder, Charles B., Eddie Dean Seagle, Lorie M. Felton, John M. Ruter, William Terry Kelley, and Gerard Krewer. *Introduction to Horticulture*. Danville, Illinois: Interstate Publishers, Inc., 1997.

Schroeder, Charles B., and Howard B. Sprague. *Turf Management Handbook*. Danville, Illinois: Interstate Publishers, Inc., 1996.

Smiley, Tom, Bruce Fraedrich, and Don Booth. "Pruning Young Trees." *Grounds Maintenance Magazine*, January, 1995.

Smith, Sarah L. "All in Good Time, An Overview of Tree Biology" (Based on "A New Tree Biology Seminar" by Dr. Alex Shigo), *American Nurseryman Magazine*, December 15, 1989.

Wyman, Donald. *Wyman's Gardening Encyclopedia*. New York: Macmillan Publishing Company, Inc.,1978.

_____ *Conducting an Agricultural Sales Call*. Urbana: Vocational Agricultural Service, University of Illinois, 1990.

_____ "Interview with Robert S Hursthouse." R.S.Hursthouse & Associates, Inc., Naperville, Illinois, 1996.

_____ "Interview with John F. Mitten." Church Landscape, Lombard, Illinois, 1996.

_____ *Landscaping*. Reston, Virginia: Associated Landscape Contractors of America.

_____ *Selecting Plants & Trees*. Lisle, Illinois: The Morton Arboretum, 1991.

_____ *The Value of Landscaping*. Tacoma, Washington: Weyerhaeuser Nursery Products Division.

Index